Classical Antiquity in Video Games

Imagines – Classical Receptions in the Visual and Performing Arts

Series Editors: Filippo Carlà-Uhink and Martin Lindner

Other titles in this series:

A Homeric Catalogue of Shapes by Charlayn von Solms
Art Nouveau and the Classical Tradition by Richard Warren
Classical Antiquity in Heavy Metal Music edited by K. F. B. Fletcher and Osman Umurhan
The Ancient Mediterranean Sea in Modern Visual and Performing Arts edited by Rosario Rovira Guardiola

Classical Antiquity in Video Games

Playing with the Ancient World

Edited by Christian Rollinger

BLOOMSBURY ACADEMIC
LONDON · NEW YORK · OXFORD · NEW DELHI · SYDNEY

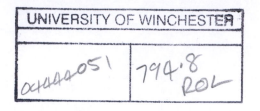
BLOOMSBURY ACADEMIC
Bloomsbury Publishing Plc
50 Bedford Square, London, WC1B 3DP, UK
1385 Broadway, New York, NY 10018, USA

BLOOMSBURY, BLOOMSBURY ACADEMIC and the Diana logo are trademarks of
Bloomsbury Publishing Plc

First published in Great Britain 2020

Cover design: Terry Woodley
Cover image © Apotheon (2015 © Alientrap Games Inc. All rights reserved)

A catalogue record for this book is available from the British Library.

A catalog record for this book is available from the Library of Congress.

ISBN: HB: 978-1-3500-6663-2
       ePDF: 978-1-3500-6664-9
       eBook: 978-1-3500-6665-6

Series: IMAGINES – Classical Receptions in the Visual and Performing Arts

Typeset by RefineCatch Limited, Bungay, Suffolk
Printed and bound in Great Britain

To find out more about our authors and books visit www.bloomsbury.com
and sign up for our newsletters.

Contents

List of Illustrations   vii

Notes on Contributors   ix

Preface   xiii

Prologue

    Playing with the Ancient World: An Introduction to Classical Antiquity
    in Video Games   *Christian Rollinger*   1

1   An Archaeology of Ancient Historical Video Games   *Christian Rollinger*   19

Part One   A Brave Old World: Re-Figurations of Ancient Cultures

2   *Ludus* (Not) Over: Video Games and the Popular Perception
    of Ancient Past Reshaping   *David Serrano Lozano*   47

3   Playing in a 'Real' Past: Classical Action Games and Authenticity
    Tristan French and Andrew Gardner   63

4   The Representation of Women in *Ryse: Son of Rome*   *Sian Beavers*   77

Part Two   A World at War: Martial Re-Presentations of the Ancient World

5   Battle Narratives from Ancient Historiography to *Total War:*
    Rome II   *Dominic Machado*   93

6   Digital Legionaries: Video Game Simulations of the Face of
    Battle in the Roman Republic   *Jeremiah McCall*   107

Part Three   Digital Epics: Role-Playing in the Ancient World

7   The Bethesda Style: The Open-World Role-Playing Game
    as Formulaic Epic   *Roger Travis*   127

8   Postcolonial Play in Ancient World Computer Role-Playing Games
    Ross Clare   141

9   Playing with an Ancient Veil: Commemorative Culture and
    the Staging of Ancient History within the Playful Experience
    of the MMORPG, *The Secret World*   *Nico Nolden*   157

Part Four   Building an Ancient World: Re-Imagining Antiquity

10   Choose Your Own Counterfactual: The Melian Dialogue as
     Text-Based Adventure   *Neville Morley*   179
11   Mortal Immortals: Deicide of Greek Gods in *Apotheon* and
     Its Role in the Greek Mythic Storyworld   *Maciej Paprocki*   193
12   The Complexities and Nuances of Portraying History in
     Age of Empires   *Alexander Flegler*   205
13   Simulating the Ancient World: Pitfalls and Opportunities of
     Using Game Engines for Archaeological and Historical Research
     Erika Holter, Una Ulrike Schäfer and Sebastian Schwesinger   217

Epilogue

14   *Quo Vadis* Historical Game Studies and Classical Receptions?
     Moving Two Fields Forward Together   *Adam Chapman*   233

Glossary of Video Game Terms   253
Bibliography   256
Mediography   286
Ludography   287
Index   291

Illustrations

Figures

1.1   *The Oregon Trail* screen announcement (1971/1974 © MECC)   20

1.2   A chariot race in *QVADRIGA* (2014 © Slitherine. All rights reserved)   28

1.3   Extract from *Hammurabi*'s BASIC code, indicating possible game endings (Ahl, 1973)   30

1.4   Opening screen of *Legionnaire* on an Atari 800 computer, depicting a wooded hill as battleground in ancient Gaul (1982 © Chris Crawford/Avalon Hill)   32

1.5   *Annals of Rome* gameplay on a Sinclair ZX Spectrum computer (1986 © Level 9 Computing/Personal Software Services)   34

1.6   *The Return of Heracles*, opening screen (1983 © Stuart Smith/Quality Software)   36

1.7   *The Return of Heracles*, gameplay on an Apple IIe computer (1983 © Stuart Smith/Quality Software)   36

3.1   Protagonist Bayek explores Alexandria in *Assassin's Creed: Origins* (2017 © Ubisoft. All rights reserved)   71

4.1   Boudica in *Ryse: Son of Rome* (*l.*, 2013 © Crytek GmbH. All rights reserved) and Keira Knightley as Guinevere in *King Arthur* (*r.*, 2004 © Buena Vista Pictures Distribution. All rights reserved. Photo: Jonathan Hession)   86

5.1   Meme-ing Augustus (*l.*, 'Rage FU'; *r.*, 'Y U NO')   96

5.2   Arminius' mask in *Total War: Rome II* (2013 © The Creative Assembly/SEGA. All rights reserved)   97

5.3   Nineteenth-century depictions of Arminius (*top*, Ernst von Bandel, *Hermannsdenkmal*, 1875 © Lippe; *bottom*, Johannes Gehrts, *Armin verabschiedet sich von Thusnelda*, 1884 © Lippisches Landesmuseum Detmold)   98

6.1   A bird's-eye view of the Roman and Carthaginian armies at the Battle of the Trebia in *Field of Glory 2* (2017 © Slitherine. All rights reserved)   112

6.2   A battlefield view in *Total War: Rome II* (2013 © The Creative Assembly/SEGA. All rights reserved)   113

8.1   Start-up screen from *Nethergate: Resurrection* (1998 © Spiderweb Software. All rights reserved)   144

9.1   Late Roman ruins in *The Secret World* (2012 © FunCom Oslo AS. All rights reserved)   163

9.2   Ancient Egyptian ruins with hieroglyphic friezes in *The Secret World* (2012 © FunCom Oslo AS. All rights reserved)   164

10.1   The first version of the 'Melian Dilemma' game in Varoufakis (1997: 89)   186
10.2   The opening of the Athenian version of *The Melian Game* (2018 ©
       Neville Morley)   187
10.3   Marked-up text of *The Melian Game* within Twine (2018 © Neville
       Morley)   188
11.1   Nikandreos (*l.*) encounters the Olympians' frustration in *Apotheon*
       (2015 © Alientrap Games Inc. All rights reserved)   197
11.2   Nikandreos (*r.*) battling Zeus (*l.*) (2015 © Alientrap Games Inc.
       All rights reserved)   199
12.1   Start of a game session in *Age of Empires: Definitive Edition*, with a
       'Town Centre', three 'Villagers' and unexplored area (2017 © Forgotten
       Empires/Microsoft)   207
12.2   Technology tree in *Age of Empires: Definitive Edition* – in every age,
       a new layer of technologies, units and buildings is unlocked (2017 ©
       Forgotten Empires/Microsoft)   211
12.3   The timeline in *Age of Empires: Definitive Edition* shows ups and
       downs during a session. Not every player's civilization is successful,
       and some are annihilated early on (2017 © Forgotten Empires/
       Microsoft)   212
13.1   (*Top*) Hill of the Pnyx today (Courtesy of the American School of
       Classical Studies at Athens: Agora Excavations). (*Bottom*) Model of
       the Pnyx Phase II in the game engine Unity3D (Courtesy of
       Analogue Storage Media II – Auralization of Archaeological
       Spaces, Humboldt-Universität zu Berlin. Created by Dirk Mariaschk
       and Una U. Schäfer)   218
13.2   (*Top*) Pnyx interface, (*bottom left*) listening point with floating ear,
       (*bottom right*) VR Annotator (Images courtesy of Analogue Storage
       Media II – Auralization of Archaeological Spaces, Humboldt-
       Universität zu Berlin. Created by Dirk Mariaschk and Una U. Schäfer)   223

Tables

1.1   Notable games set in the ancient world   27
3.1   *The Assassin's Creed* series   70

Contributors

Sian Beavers (@sianbeavers) studied for her PhD at the Open University, UK. Her academic background is in Classical Reception Studies, Game Studies and Educational Sciences. Her interdisciplinary thesis focuses on audience and player engagements with antiquity in popular culture, in particular digital games depicting ancient Rome. The research investigates the opportunities for informal learning that engagement with historical games may provide; players' associated off- and online learning activities in response to the represented historical content; and the relationships between different historical media forms in terms of the different types of historical understanding these popular engagements can elicit.

Adam Chapman (@woodlandstaar) teaches Game and Media Studies, Cultural Studies and Historiography and is Senior Lecturer in the Department of Education, Communication and Learning at the University of Gothenburg, Sweden. His research focuses on historical games, i.e. those games that in some way represent, or relate to, discourses about the past. He is the author of *Digital Games as History: How Videogames Represent the Past and Offer Access to Historical Practice* (2016), alongside a number of other publications on the topic of historical games. He is also the founder of the Historical Game Studies Network.

Ross Clare teaches Classics and Ancient History in the Department of Archaeology, Classics and Egyptology at the University of Liverpool, UK, and is currently the Co-ordinator for the Liverpool Schools Classics Project. He recently received his doctorate in Classics and Ancient History from the University of Liverpool, on completion of his thesis, applying transmediatic perspectives to the study of ancient Greece and Rome in video games. Ross works primarily with receptions of antiquity in popular culture, with a particular interest in video games, film, television and science fiction.

Alexander Flegler (@alexflegler) is an artist and game designer and has been working as Creative Director for Forgotten Empires and Microsoft on the *Age of Empires* and *Age of Mythology* franchises since 2014. He is currently studying History, Mathematics and Education at the Martin-Luther University Halle-Wittenberg, Germany.

Tristan French (@titanfrench) is a Public Archaeologist, having completed his MA at the Institute of Archaeology, University College London (UCL), UK, in 2016. His past work has included an analysis of video games as an alternative method of exploring the past, with particular focus on the wide reach of the games industry and the influence that the archaeological discipline has had on franchises such as *Assassin's Creed* and *Far Cry*.

Andrew Gardner (@andy_n_gardner) is Senior Lecturer in the Archaeology of the Roman Empire at the Institute of Archaeology, University College London, UK. His publications include *An Archaeology of Identity* (2007) and *Evolutionary and Interpretive Archaeologies* (edited with Ethan Cochrane, 2011). Andrew is currently working on a monograph on Roman Britain. His research interests are centred on the social dynamics of Roman imperialism and the nature of frontier cultures, but he is also active in work on public/political engagement with archaeology, including through computer and video games.

Erika Holter is a PhD candidate in Classical Archaeology at Humboldt-Universität zu Berlin, Germany, writing her dissertation on mosaic-floor ensembles in Roman houses. She holds a scholarship from the Interdisciplinary Laboratory, Image Knowledge Gestaltung, and is a researcher for the project, 'Analogue Storage Media II – Auralization of Archaeological Spaces'.

Dominic Machado (@dominicmachado1) teaches Classics and Ancient History and is Assistant Professor in the Department of Classics at the College of the Holy Cross in Worcester, MA. He studies the history and historiography of the Roman Republic, with a particular focus on the ability of non-elite groups to organize and act collectively. He is also interested in the reception of antiquity in modern media like TV, movies and video games, and the ways in which such receptions can be used pedagogically.

Jeremiah McCall (@gamingthepast) specializes in the political culture of the Republic and the mechanics of ancient battle. He has written four books on topics in these areas, including *The Cavalry of the Roman Republic* (2001) and, most recently, *Clan Fabius* (2018). Jeremiah has also researched and written at length on the intersection of history and video games, most notably in his book, *Gaming the Past* (2011). He maintains *Gamingthepast.net*, the leading website devoted to historical video games inside and outside the history classroom. He has taught History at Cincinnati Country Day School, in Ohio, USA, since 2002, and continues to explore effective uses of video games for teaching and learning history.

Neville Morley (@nevillemorley) is Professor of Classics and Ancient History at the University of Exeter, UK. He works on a wide range of topics, including ancient economic and social history and classical reception in modern social science. In recent years, he has focused on the reception and influence of Thucydides and how his work might still be relevant and useful today. His most recent book is *Classics: Why it Matters* (2018). He blogs regularly at *thesphinxblog.com*.

Nico Nolden (@niconolden) teaches Public History and has been a teaching and research assistant at the University of Hamburg, Germany, since 2014. His 2018 PhD thesis centred on the nexus of digital historical games and commemorative cultures. At the Department of Public History in Hamburg, he is responsible for work on history in and of digital games, and is currently building a diverse games collection for the department's GameLab. Nico has been writing about history and digital games on his research *blog keimling.niconolden.de* since 2009. He is a founding member of the Arbeitskreis Geschichtswissenschaft und digitale Spiele, a working group for historical sciences and digital games.

Maciej Paprocki (@maciejwpaprocki) is an affiliated fellow in the Distant Worlds Graduate School at the Ludwig-Maximilians-Universität in Munich, Germany. He is interested in ancient Greek gods as depicted in epic poetry: their powers, limitations, fears and wants. His previous research projects concerned culture studies and desert road archaeology. An avid gamer, he has worked as a historical consultant, helping to develop two video games set in antiquity: *Apotheon* (2015), and, currently, *Builders of Egypt*, a city-builder game set in ancient Egypt.

Christian Rollinger (@DrCRollinger) is Lecturer in Ancient History at the University of Trier, Germany. His research interests include the economic and cultural history of the late Roman Republic, late antique imperial ideology and ceremonial, seafaring in the ancient world, and Classical Reception Studies. He has previously published on Roman elite society and friendship, including a monograph on friendship in the Roman Republic, *Amicitia sanctissime colenda. Freundschaft und Soziale Netzwerke in der Späten Republik* (2014), and is currently working on a monograph on the imperial ceremonial of the late antique court. He is a founding member of the Arbeitskreis Geschichtswissenschaft und digitale Spiele, a working group for historical sciences and digital games.

Una Ulrike Schäfer studied Archaeology, Cultural History and Theory at the Humboldt-Universität zu Berlin, Germany. She is a research associate of the project, 'Analogue Storage Media II – Auralization of Archaeological Spaces', at the Interdisciplinary Laboratory, Image Knowledge Gestaltung, Germany, where she explores new research practices and methods regarding the integration of game engine and VR technology in academic research contexts in a hands-on approach.

Sebastian Schwesinger is a is PhD candidate in cultural history and theory at the Humboldt-Universität zu Berlin and coordinator of the project, 'Analogue Storage Media II – Auralization of Archaeological Spaces', at the Interdisciplinary Laboratory, Image Knowledge Gestaltung, Germany. He is writing a dissertation on, 'The Genealogy of Numeric Acoustic Simulations'. He has been organizing the public lecture series 'KlangDenken', in collaboration with the Sound Studies Lab since 2012.

David Serrano Lozano is a PhD student at the University of Santiago de Compostela, Spain. His research interests include Latin Epigraphy and Classical Reception in contemporary popular culture. David's publication on both areas include analysis on provincial constructions and Roman epigraphy in north-western Spain, as well as classical reception in cinema and video games. He is a member of the international independent project Fasti Congressuum, for the diffusion of academic activities about Antiquity.

Roger Travis (@rogertravis) is Associate Professor in the Departments of Literatures, Cultures and Languages and of Digital Media and Design in the University of

Connecticut, USA. He received his Bachelor's degree in Classics from Harvard College, and his PhD in Comparative Literature from the University of California, Berkeley. He is a founder of and contributor to the collaborative blog *Playthepast.org*, where he writes about the fundamental connection between ancient epic and digital games. He also works on developing and studying a form of game-based learning, practomimetic learning, in which learners play the curriculum as a role-playing game wrapped in an alternate-reality game.

Preface

Video games are everywhere.

In the summer of 2017, my wife and I were sitting in the shadow of what may conceivably have been an oak tree (I am not a botanist) growing at the edge of one of the many archaeological sites of the charming city of Arles in the south of France. Situated in the Rhône delta, Arles had been Arelate before, had been a Gallic *oppidum*, a Greek *emporion* and the Roman colony Iulia Paterna Arelate *Sextanorum*. It had briefly seen Constantine the Great residing there and, when Trier had become unsafe in the early fifth century, was to become the home of the Gallic prefecture. Foremost among the archaeological remains of the cities' storied history are the Roman theatre and amphitheatre, the former built at the end of the first century BCE, immediately after the establishment of the *colonia*. The arena was a later addition, constructed after an interval of roughly a century, not much before 100 CE. As I soliloquized on these basic facts, affecting an air of archaeological expertise that was wholly unjustified, my half-listening wife nodded knowingly and said that it made perfect sense. As she is herself an accomplished scholar and teacher and as I assumed that she had background information that eluded me, I asked what she meant. 'Well, remember when we used to play *Caesar*,' she replied, referring to an older city-building game we had both enjoyed, 'we always had to build theatres before we could build arenas'. *Caesar III* and *IV*, two entries in this particular video game series that we both had played, on and off, for years, were released in 1998 and 2004, respectively. As a special subgenre of economic simulations, they afforded players the opportunity to do what even Roman emperors had not been able to do: to build a new Rome in a single day. Even fifteen years later, the impressions and memories of that game lingered with me. Perhaps more surprisingly, they also lingered with my wife, a far less avid video game player than I had been.

Video games are everywhere and, just as movies, music and literature can, they are able to form lasting impressions and memories, mostly without their audience knowing it. 'Gamers', to use a now slightly problematic term, that is people who routinely spent dozens if not hundreds of hours mastering a single game, will remember how they spent their time, particularly in stand-out games of their formative years. They will remember special moments from among the countless hours spent in front of computer screens: forging a career as an apothecary in a seventeenth-century town; defending the liberal world order against the vaguely evil Brotherhood of Nod; executing the war-ending bombing run over the planet of Kilrah. While these memories, entertaining as they may be, rarely have any direct influence on players' lives or their views of the world, video games set in or depicting past societies and history are different. They are influential in forming conceptions and perspectives of the human past. Players' memories of avenging the Auditore family's murder by assassinating Cesare Borgia are intricately connected with the depiction of Renaissance Italy and the manner in which the machinations and intrigues of that time formed part of what has been called a (Hi)Story-Play-Space. Playing this kind of video game, in short, is conceivably a form of 'doing' or even 'living' history.

And video games are everywhere – and I mean *every*where. They are no longer limited to the home or the hardware boundaries of dedicated game consoles or home computers. Every time you enter a doctor's waiting room, public transport or, *horribile dictu*, a university lecturing theatre, you will find people taking out their phones to play a quick round of *Candy Crush*, one of the infinite variations of *Angry Birds*, or a mobile action-adventure. Games have also begun to enter the scholarly mainstream, not only in the realm of Game Studies but also in the historical disciplines, where the study of what is increasingly being called 'historical video games' has proliferated in the last decade. Books, articles and dissertations have been written on the subject of history in games; conferences dedicated to the subject have been organized. Classics and Ancient History are fashionably late to the party but catching up fast.

The aim of this book is to attempt to level the playing field with regard to the advances in studying historical video games for other historical periods by providing a collection of case studies illustrating the breadth of possible research and demonstrating the promise of engaging with the subject matter. It is not intended as either a theoretical or a practical introduction to the field. There are few discussions of questions of methodology or of reception theory as foundation for historical game studies. Though both are much needed, they cannot be provided in a collection of essays such as this, particularly as this field of research is not yet by any means unified or even completely coherent. Instead, this book means to provide an open-ended, multi-perspective view on an emerging research area. It aims to stimulate interest in historical video games within the disciplines of classics and ancient history by highlighting promising areas of research. This approach has been chosen despite obvious shortcomings. The focus on case studies means that it will be (on the whole) relatively undertheorized (though not on an individual chapter level), while the focus on classical antiquity means that case studies will primarily engage with video games set in the Graeco-Roman period of history (though, again, individual chapters will go beyond this limitation). It is not concerned with establishing historical video games as a historical form, though, as Adam Chapman's 2016 *Digital Games as History* has shown, this is a worthwhile pursuit. It is also limited in the sense that case studies are focused on classical receptions instead of the role that video game technology can play, for example in Digital Heritage or the completely new archaeological discipline pioneered by Andrew Reinhard in his 2018 book *Archaeogaming*. Nevertheless, it is hoped that readers will come away with a net benefit – and the impulse to pick up one or the other ancient game title (to say nothing of the two works just mentioned). Despite its inevitable shortcomings, this book will hopefully prove stimulating and the research contained within will hopefully inspire other gamer-historians to help turn their hobby into an exciting new field of classical reception.

It has come into existence through the kind invitation and occasional prodding of the series editors of IMAGINES, Filippo Carlà-Uhink and Martin Lindner, for which they have my heartfelt gratitude. I am also grateful for the tireless work of the editors and the staff at Bloomsbury, in particular Alice Wright and Lily Mac Mahon, who were instrumental in hammering this book into shape, as well as the anonymous referees, who provided valuable feedback and encouragement. I am also grateful to Jesse McGibney and Lee Vermeulen at Alientrap Games Inc. for generously allowing us to use artwork from their 2015 title *Apotheon* for the book cover, to Daniel Yamanian, who came up with the original idea for the book cover, and to Lisa Dünchem, who helped with the Bibliography.

The authors of the individual chapters will understand my saying that they jumped at the opportunity to participate in this project and know that I mean this in the most positive way imaginable. All of them have my deepest gratitude for their contributions and for agreeing to devote considerable time and effort towards this publication. I can only hope that they will be as happy with the result as I am.

On a more personal level, thanks are also due to the organizers and discussants of several guest lectures and seminars in Mainz, Koblenz, Chemnitz, Hannover, Augsburg, Potsdam and Barcelona, during which I have been able to workshop some of my own research on video games over the years. Supervisors and colleagues in the Department of History at the University of Trier, while occasionally expressing mild bewilderment at the subject matter, have allowed me to work on this project in an atmosphere of benevolent neglect and I thank them for it. Lastly, as ever, I thank F., for everything, always.

Thinking back to that day in the very early 1990s, on which a brand-new Nintendo NES game console was waiting under the Christmas tree, there was little indication then (or in the years since) that what must have seemed to my parents an unhealthy obsession with pixels and Italian plumbers, would one day play any part in an academic career. In so far as it is permissible as editor to dedicate a collective work, then, I would like to do so: to my parents, with indulgence for all the gaming consoles that they didn't get me and gratitude for the ones that they did.

C. R.
Near Ulm

Prologue
Playing with the Ancient World

An Introduction to Classical Antiquity in Video Games

Christian Rollinger

Video games[1] are neither a new nor even a recent development. They spluttered into existence in the late 1950s as the result of more or less idle experiments on North American university campuses.[2] William Higinbotham is generally credited with inventing the first 'true' video game in 1958: *Tennis for Two* consisted of an analogue computer that was programmed to calculate ballistic trajectories of a simulated 'tennis ball'.[3] A connected oscilloscope offered a visual interface and the game was played by means of a makeshift controller – the very first gamepad – which was used to propel the 'tennis balls' over the 'net'. The graphics were rudimentary (to say the least) and there were no sound effects, but the close relationship to the later hit arcade video game *Pong* is obvious. *Pong*, released by the then newly founded company Atari Inc. in November of 1972, was a significant hit and launched the video game era, with the so-called 'Golden Age' of mostly arcade video games, that saw cultural classics such as *Space Invaders* (1978), *Asteroids* (1979) and *Pac-Man* (1980), lasting from roughly the end of the 1970s until the crash of the video game industry in 1983.[4]

That crash of 1983 saw an almost total collapse of what in the late 1970s and early 1980s had already been a multibillion-dollar industry: Atari, the company that largely dominated the arcade market with a market share of around 80 per cent, had seen a rise in sales from $75 million in 1977 to $2.2 billion in 1980.[5] The total US video game market in 1982 was worth approximately $8.9 billion (or roughly $23 billion in 2018 terms, adjusted for inflation), according to industry figures.[6] By contrast, in 1984, sales had dropped by almost 30 per cent to $6.4 billion, market leader Atari had incurred total losses of $536 million ($1.36 billion in 2018 currency) and was forced to drop more than a third of its employees.[7] This is not the place to analyse the reasons for the market collapse, so suffice it to say that they included a general market saturation with huge numbers of largely indistinguishable arcade and home video systems (including the classic Atari VCS 2600) and the general economic situation of late 1970s and early 1980s. Tellingly, however, the crash also more or less coincided with the introduction of the Personal Computer (PC) by IBM in 1981 and the subsequent availability of relatively cheap multipurpose personal computers such as the IBM 5150 PC, the Sinclair ZX series or the Commodore for home use. The existence of affordable PCs (that could be used, among numerous other things, for gaming), together with the advent of a new generation of home video game consoles in the mid-80s (such as the Nintendo NES, available in the USA from 1985), launched a revolution in home gaming and revived a seemingly moribund industry. This renaissance of video games has held to the present day.

Since the Nintendo NES, which belonged to the 8-bit, third generation of consoles, hardware cycles have continued to improve on gameplay and graphics until the present-day (8th generation, for those keeping count) consoles such as the Playstation 4 and the Xbox One. As the computing power of consoles has advanced in lockstep (though with some delays) with the general development of microchip technology used in personal computers, PCs have also experienced a continuous phase of rapid and unbroken technological advance. This is exemplified in the famous observation in 1965 of Gordon Moore, co-founder of microchip giant Intel, that the number of components (transistors) of integrated circuits (microchips) – and thus their processing power – was likely to double every year (Moore's Law, as it became known, was later revised to a doubling every two years).[8] In contrast to older pixelated graphics, contemporary games rely on increasingly photorealistic rendering of characters and places, and often breathtaking visual effects that rival Hollywood blockbusters. The video game industry, likewise, has more than recovered in the intervening four decades and has now reached a total global worth of roughly $140 billion, according to industry reports such as the NEWZOO Global Games Market Report – far more than double the value of global film markets in 2017.[9]

However, despite the fact that video games in one form or another have now been in existence for more than half a century, they have only very recently become the subject of scholarly study. Since the 1990s, a distinctly new field of research established itself: Game Studies, a field that emerged 'within the interdisciplinary brew of Media Studies, and developed rapidly'.[10] Although the historical sciences have been slow to embrace video games as a form of historical reception or even of 'doing' history, video games have, from very early on, embraced history and the human past. In fact, as the example of 1971's *The Oregon Trail* shows, the appearance of historical video games can be traced back to the pioneering days of computer research and experimentation.

Historical game studies, the subgenre of the study of historical reception at the intersection of digital culture, public history, memorial studies and media studies, have been slower to form. Perhaps not strictly the first but, in any case, the most influential early study in this new discipline was William Uricchio's 'Simulation, History, and Computer Games' (2005). He forewent the detailed analysis of individual titles in favour of looking at historical games 'both on their own terms and as an entire historical form, beginning to examine the variations and patterns of this new mode of expression'.[11] Despite the fact that, since then, innumerable research articles, monographs and PhD dissertations have been written on the subject of the representation of history in video games, games have not yet been able to completely shed their stigma of 'unseriousness' or even 'childishness'. As Adam Chapman, Anna Foka and Jonathan Westin have recently pointed out in an introduction to a special issue of *Rehinking History*, it has been over sixty years since the English translation of Johan Huizinga's *Homo Ludens* appeared. Yet, despite this cultural historian's significant work on the importance of play across a host of different media, doubt still attaches to scholarly engagement with the medium of video games.[12] The 'defensive attitude' identified by these authors in papers related to the study of video games is very real. Scholars still tend to feel the impulse to defend their particular interest by citing apotropaic statistics pointing out the increasing economic relevance of the video game sector (as, indeed, I have done above). By quoting sales numbering in the tens of millions for some of the more well-known game series and referring to the increasing body of statistical work showing the depth of societal engagement with video games, scholars attempt to pre-empt criticism of their work on the ground of relevance.

While I tend to agree in principle with the statement that it is 'perhaps time that we move beyond this kind of simplistic measure of significance [...] and that the field of game studies has perhaps outgrown this defensive posture',[13] I feel that, in the disciplines of classics and ancient history particularly, this point has not yet been reached – is, in fact, still far from being reached.

Classical reception, history and video games

Those engaged in the study of video games as historians or classicists are still confronted with an old question: Why do they do it?[14] Are video games really, *really* deserving of serious study at all? They are. Even though the area of research (it can hardly be called a coherent field yet) known as 'classical reception' (not to be confused with the more established 'classical tradition') is still difficult to delineate with any precision, the study of ancient historical video games (i.e. of video games which are set in, or use to a significant degree themes or features from, ancient history and classical civilization) undoubtedly should be seen in the context of this heterogenic field. If 'classical reception' is the 'study of the afterlives of ancient Greece and Rome: from medieval romances to Renaissance architecture, nineteenth century art to modern cinema', as the introductory text to Durham University's Centre for Classical Reception claims, video games are a part of this afterlife.[15] Others would, however, rightly, argue that 'reception' is a different category than 'afterlives' or 'tradition'.

Reception theory, a concept pioneered mainly as an interpretative aid in literary studies (particularly in German studies as *Rezeptionsästhetik*) by scholars such as Hans Robert Jauss and Robert Charles Holub, argues that a single, definitive or objective meaning or interpretation of any work of art, as intended, for example, by the author of a novel or as defined by art critics or self-proclaimed experts, does not exist. Rather, as Charles Martindale has put it in a chapter hugely influential for the development of classical receptions, 'meaning [...] is always realized at the point of reception'.[16] Historiography – writing ancient history – in this view, is a form of classical reception. Thus, the reception and interpretation of any given 'text' – in the jargon of reception studies, all content that is 'received' is interpreted as a 'text' – is inevitably itself a creative act that is the result of a discourse between 'text', 'recipient' and his sociopolitical context. Classical reception is thus, in some ways, what Dunstan Lowe has called 'the postmodern view' of the classical tradition.[17] It does not offer (read: 'force') 'a canonical reading of the classical model to the detriment of its reception. Reception is about our dialogue with the classical past, whatever form that takes, and as a two-way conversation rather than as a monologue prioritizing one or the other'.[18] Put another way: it is 'what you make of it', and it has steadily expanded its horizons and now includes the study of, for example, TV shows, Hollywood blockbusters, advertisement and fan-fiction as well as classically 'high' culture.[19] It must also include video games, and although the (relatively few) individual scholars writing on the subject from the point of view of a classicist or ancient historian have fervently argued for this to be the case, it has not yet done so in anything approaching a systematic way.

The reasons for this are no doubt manifold and it is not my intention to polemicize the issue. However, one may be forgiven for thinking that there is a strong tendency among classicists to associate their field with a very specific version of 'high' culture, in turn inspired and sometimes dominated by the 'classics'. Because of this close association of their field of study with 'high culture' in general, classicists and ancient historians, perhaps more than representatives of other historical fields, frown on what might be considered (in the words of that foremost representative of English-language high culture) 'base, common and popular'.[20] It would also be pointless to deny both the existence and consequence of a considerable generational gap among those scholars interested in studying classical reception in general and in video games in particular, and those who are not. Nor should we ignore the importance of age structure in academia as a whole. For the most part, those early career scholars – the accepted German euphemism would be *Nachwuchswissenschaftler* – dabbling in historical video games have come of age in the nineties or early aughts and have thus grown up together with the medium or have been born into a world in which video games, computers, consoles and the internet were commonplace – the notorious 'digital natives'. The term was coined by Marc Prensky in a paper for *On the Horizon* (the antonym, incidentally, of a digital native is a 'digital immigrant', who may be identified by his behavioural traits, which include, 'printing out your email [or having your secretary print it out for you])'.[21] Their familiarity with both the technology and the development of the medium perhaps predisposes them to see them as a worthwhile subject of study, in a way that more senior scholars and academics do not. In fact, in one of the earliest articles by two classical scholars on the potential value of engaging with historical video games, this notion was explicitly stated by (one surmises) the more senior author: 'for those of us who grew up at a time when *Pong* (the first widely distributed video game, released in 1975 [*sic*]) was all the rage, the idea of taking video games seriously does not necessarily come naturally'.[22]

Existing scholarship

This reserve on the part even of classical reception scholars has led to a noteworthy discrepancy in scholarly output for video games set in the ancient world and other periods of history, respectively. While a steady stream of research articles and monographs have engaged with, for example, the depiction of the medieval and early modern period in video games or the special place that video games set in the Second World War have carved out in the collective cultural memory,[23] the total scholarly output on ancient history in video games is less than twenty articles or book chapters and a single monograph.[24] This is naturally not to say that seminal studies from scholars outside the disciplines of classics or ancient history dealing with the representation of history in video games do not apply to ancient history (they do). However, the fact that the chapters of this present volume collectively almost double the total amount of scholarly output in this field is more than telling and it demonstrates the hitherto resounding lack of interest. Given that not much work has been undertaken yet concerning ancient history and video games, it is difficult to trace a development of scholarly thought, except by comparing this work with the larger field of historical game studies, which provides a broader context.

Generally, then, the discussion and analysis of historical video games has largely focused on three distinct areas of research: first, the analysis of individual games and their representation and depiction of historical cultures and specific periods, with a special focus on questions regarding the historical 'accuracy' and/or 'authenticity' of these games; second, the study of the way in which historical processes and history itself is presented or 'simulated' in different games and across different genres; and third, the didactic potential of video games in classroom use and in public engagement.[25]

The first area of research has attracted the most interest. This is hardly surprising, given that it is essentially a continuation of a long-standing trend in classical reception studies of, for example, Hollywood movies or television series. Small-scale studies have shown, for instance, the way in which ancient architecture and ruins (even in games set in antiquity itself) are employed by game designers to immediately create a feeling of 'being' in an ancient world. Dunstan Lowe has called it a 'box-ticking approach', 'whereby certain highlights of the classical world (those firmly anchored in the popular imagination) must be present, regardless of chronological, geographical and other pragmatic constraints'.[26] For developers, then, ticking these boxes is essential for evoking a sense of 'pastness', as defined by David Lowenthal.[27]

One example of this is the ubiquity of the Colosseum: just as many films set in (modern-day) Rome feature a scene of the protagonist driving or being driven along the Via dei Fori Imperiali, with the Colosseum beautifully framing the background to signify that they are, in fact, in Rome, so, too, does the Flavian amphitheatre feature in many video games, even those not explicitly set in Rome itself. In the city-building simulation *Caesar*, for instance, the 'Colosseum' is a type of building that players can construct if they have enough money and a large enough population (as they have a pronounced positive effect on inhabitant morale and public safety, the experienced player is severely tempted to construct three or four at once); in *Civilization*, it is one of the 'World Wonders' which signify cultural advances.

Although recently case studies have also explored the aesthetics of ancient worlds in video games and of the gamescapes themselves, much of the research undertaken in this area is focused on the notoriously difficult question of historical 'authenticity' and 'realism' (or 'historical accuracy').[28] Both terms should not be confused; in the analysis of historical video games, 'authenticity' is a subjective value; what is perceived by players as 'authentic', is more a consequence of rarely explicated preconceptions and assumptions than of specific historical knowledge. It is a more or less diffuse feeling, whereas 'realism' – in the sense advanced by Adam Chapman in his categorization of historical video games as either 'realist' or 'conceptual' simulations[29] – is often the product of a game's accurate and detailed (and often visually resplendent) reproduction of ancient material culture, which 'anchors' players in a given setting. Both aspects of any given game's representation of history have to be balanced against each other. As Stephen Poole has memorably said, excessive realism can get in the way of authenticity: 'you don't want it [sc. the game] to be too real. The purpose of a video game is never to simulate real life, but to offer the gift of play.'[30]

Tobias Winnerling has coined the term of 'affective historicity' for the combination of a feeling of authenticity and a tendency to pay close attention to, for example, archaeological details.[31] In order to be fruitful enterprise, however, historical game studies must not limit themselves to pointing out obvious historical or antiquarian errors (of which there are a great many, although this is hardly specific to video games, as anyone who remembers the proud proclamation by Senator Falco in *Gladiator* that 'Rome was founded as a Republic, after all', should well know). It is, frankly, unhelpful to gleefully enumerate such mistakes or misconceptions in video games; what is interesting is the attempt to gain an appreciation of how game designers go about producing 'authenticity' – and why they feel the need to do so, at all. What trade-offs are made behind the scenes in order to ensure playability and, perhaps most importantly in an age where video games present large investments on the part of the developing studios, commercial success?

The second important area of research concerns not so much the representation of historical periods or cultures, but rather of history as a process. This research often (though not exclusively) focuses on (grand) strategy or '4X' games, which cast the player as ruler of a city-state, nation-state or world-empire. Such games claim (to a larger or lesser extent) to simulate *history*. Importantly, however, they do not. Instead, they are rather both the product and a simulation of historiographical narratives, meta-history, and the college curricula of North American and European universities of the last decades.

As Andrew Elliott and Matthew Kapell have pointed out in their very useful introduction to 2013's *Playing with the Past*, video games are akin to historiography, in that they are 'simulations' (or, in poststructuralist jargon, 'texts') based on preselected input; they are 'constructed', just as, in this view, history (as opposed to the 'past') is itself a construct. The quality of this text (in this case, a game's historical simulation) depends very much on what the input is, what 'facts' are available in the historic record, and what decisions and choices of 'facts' are made by the game designers. Video games, then, like history, are both 'a process of selection *and* assembly'. Since this assembly is not only the product of game designers' decisions but, according to reception theory, also of the engagement of players with the game, video games have the capacity 'to engage players actively in constructing meanings and understanding history as a process rather than a master narrative of Great Men and their actions or acknowledged Social Forces and their effect'.[32] Video games can thus be seen as part of 'public' history; 'public' in the sense that this sort of 'historying' (a term coined by Adam Chapman) is decidedly not history 'as an academic or exclusive field of study (what Rosenstone famously terms "History with a capital H") but as "the past", a more inclusive and inviting concept that [...] refers to its relationship to the present.[33] Building on this, Adam Chapman, in his 2016 study on *Digital Games as History*, views historical video games as 'systems for historying', that is a 'dialectical and dialogic' process of engaging with the past.[34] He thus interprets video games as a historical form, as means of meaning-making, not by Historians (with a capital H) but by what he terms 'developer-historians' and 'player-historians'.[35]

If we accept this view – and the jury still seems to be out on this – then the obvious problems of video games in 'simulating' the past and thus in 'historying' are amplified. If the historiographical and epistemological foundations of game designers' choices of historical 'facts' are flawed, then the resultant ludonarrative in historical video games can potentially reinforce outdated, traditional narratives of history. For instance, much criticism has (rightly) been aimed at the depiction of history in games such as the *Total War* or *Civilization* series, which, it is shown, tend to present history as a linear process that typically does not allow for the possibility of failure or regression. One aspect, in particular, has been the subject of scholarly scrutiny: the 'tech [technology] tree', is a frequently used device in simulation games that allows game designers to give the impression of progress, of states and civilizations actually advancing. They are a means of presenting technological, cultural and political achievements; however – and crucially for a medium that, regardless of genre, relies on predictable progress over different levels of achievement – these achievements are presented as following in a linear fashion and leading to ever greater perfection, thus reproducing a very specific (and teleological) view on the very principle of historical 'progress'. Alexander Flegler's chapter in this volume shows, this view of history is not necessarily (and not always) the result of errant opinions on the part of game designers not keeping up with historical research. In this case, a deeper appreciation of the constraints of game design and the commercial pressures of the industry could significantly advance our understanding of why historical processes are depicted in this fashion – and thus help us better deal with it, for instance in the classroom or lecturing theatre.

The use of video games as didactic tools in secondary and tertiary education is the final area of research that we shall briefly discuss. Again, the contributions by classicists and ancient historians to this field are, given the relatively few scholars engaging with the subject, scant, though by no means non-existent.[36] On the whole, the question of whether or not video games are suitable for classroom use has not been finally decided yet. It should also be noted that there is a remarkable discrepancy between national traditions that informs that judgement. Generally, anglophone scholars are more willing to see the virtues of using video games in that setting, both in the context of history lessons and beyond: 'Regardless of how one approaches the subject, there can be no doubt that video games are valuable not just because of their educational utility, but also because many students find them to be very engaging, much more engaging than a textbook or even a movie.'[37] The benefits of video games in terms of student engagement are frequently emphasized, although there are of course examples of scholars who remain sceptical, indeed decidedly so.[38] However, German didactics, for instance, have for the most part been exceedingly sceptical. The very fact that, in order to be palatable as a game, history and historical processes have to simplified to a sometimes alarming degree in their view militates against their use in a classroom setting.[39] As Angela Schwarz has emphasized, a large number of historical video games tend to reduce history to a mixture of sheer facts and dates, and violent conflict presented in excruciating detail. Didactically relevant aspects of history – multiperspectivity, analytical criticism, contextualization, the questioning of personal motives – are noticeably lacking.[40] In fact, the very mechanics of producing 'authenticity' (as discussed above), are problematic: the more convincing a video game looks, sounds, and feels, the greater the tendency to accept it as 'accurate'. The different judgements on this question are, perhaps, also a consequence of differing national school curricula. For instance, the hesitancy on the part of German teachers to employ tools that, by nature of their sensory impact and the fact that their employ implies their sanctioning on the part of the teacher, could reinforce traditional and outdated notions of history and 'how it really was', is closely connected with the declared aims of history as a school subject in Germany: that is to say, to foster critical and independent thinking and a feeling for source criticism. Although this is by no means meant to imply that other school systems do not emphasize these values, it is perhaps legitimate to think that recent German history especially influences the specific nature of teaching history in German schools and feeds the didactic reluctance to (over)simplify.

Lastly, in very recent years, a growing number of scholars have opened promising new research trends. They no longer see games only as an *object* of research, but also as a *tool* – and not only in a didactic context, but for research as well. Some of these projects are represented in this book: Neville Morley's chapter shows how treating the Thucydidean Melian Dialogue as a game can open up valuable perspective of counterfactual history. A research team in Berlin, under principal investigator Susanne Muth, use a video game engine to reconstruct ancient acoustic spaces such as the Athenian pnyx. The chapter by Erika Holter, Una Ulrike Schäfer and Sebastian Schwesinger in this volume discusses the project and its prospects. Similar projects, dealing with the auralization of Roman Republican political spaces or the Hagia Sophia, are currently being undertaken at the University of Stuttgart and at Stanford University.[41] A project led by Sandra Blakely at Emory University uses a custom-made video game as a research tool for exploring the maritime connectivity of the northern Aegean around the island of Samothrace in archaic Greece. *Sailing with the Gods* lets players assume the role of an Argonaut. The gamescape is a simulation of the northern Aegean, based on readings of the *Argonautica*, scientific data concerning winds, currents and weather systems, and archaeological data. Non-player characters are based on known epigraphical evidence, specifically on people and places mentioned in relation to *theoriai* and it is hoped that actions of players within this gamescape can be used to deduce the circumstance of Greek seafaring in the first half of the first millennium BCE.[42]

Resources

Given this proliferation of historical game studies as a whole (as opposed to within classical receptions) in recent years, it is worth pointing out a further peculiarity of this particular field. Perhaps fittingly, given the digital and 'popular' (that is, pop cultural) nature of the subject matter, much of current research is published across a plethora of media beyond the traditional scholarly output of articles, book chapters and monographs. Though recent years have also seen a marked increase in international conferences and workshops convened to study historical video games – including a session at the Leeds International Medieval Congress – with a concomitant rise in publications, articles, research reports, updates and hypotheses are also often presented in the form of blog posts, interviews and discussions and video sequences.

There are now a number of influential blogs in existence that are devoted to the study of video games and that are maintained by established scholars. Roger Travis' *Play the Past* (playthepast.org), for instance, is dedicated to, 'thoughtfully exploring and discussing the intersection of cultural heritage [. . .] and games/meaningful play', and features entries from acclaimed scholars. Similarly, Jeremiah McCall's site, *Gaming the Past* (gamingthepast.net), publishes contributions on 'theory, design, research, and use of historical games in and beyond history education'. In addition to these private initiatives, institutional and quasi-institutional blogs abound: *Interactive Pasts* (interactivepasts.com) is the blog of the Leiden University VALUE project on video games and archaeology; *gespielt* (gespielt.hypotheses.org) is the official internet presence of the scholarly working group *Arbeitskreis Geschichtswissenschaft und Digitale Spiele*, founded in 2016 to further the cause of historical game research in German academia. The *Archaeogaming* blog (archaeogaming.com) founded by Andrew Reinhard approaches digital games from the point of view of a digital archaeologist, not only interested in the representation of antiquity and archaeology *in* video games but also in undertaking digital archaeology *of* and *within* the games. The similarly titled *ArchaeoGames* (archaeogames.net), founded and run by Dom Schott, is something of an outlier, in that parts of its content are hidden behind a paywall, but provides regular new content at the intersection of classical archaeology, digital heritage and archaeogaming. In addition to these 'traditional' (in the fast-moving online world sense of the word) sites, the historical game studies community also makes use of social networks to communicate and exchange ideas. Most scholars engaging with video games (including many of this book's authors, whose Twitter handles are included in the 'Notes on Contributors' section) are in possession of active and heavily frequented Twitter accounts, and Facebook groups such as the *Historical Game Studies Network* or the *AKGWDS Geschichte & Digitale Spiele* are useful (and very welcoming) tools in this academic exchange.

Using these channels has become increasingly important in recent years for the simple purpose of accessing and keeping up with a mounting scholarly output that is (so far) still mostly absent from traditional publishing venues for classical scholarship. This new approach to communicating ideas and discussing video games and ancient history, however, has fostered a culture of open sharing of insights and ideas with numbers that would be difficult to achieve by scholarly articles and book chapters alone and social media (and blogs) frequently act as knowledge multipliers for scholars interested in ancient history and video games.

To illustrate this, we may take the recently released *Assassin's Creed: Odyssey* as an example. Its historically detailed and visually breathtaking depiction of classical Greece has rightly garnered rave reviews across gaming media. It has also attracted the attention of scholars. But, while no academic literature has been produced on the subject yet – which would, in any case, have been very difficult to do, given the timeframe – social media, blogs and online groups have been teeming with observations and insights. Being more informal publications whose authors, moreover, sometimes themselves have contacts in the gaming industry, they also have the advantage of better being able to attract input from people involved in game design and production.

A recent interview with Stéphanie-Anna Ruatta, an ancient historian and on-staff consultant with Ubisoft who was directly involved in creating the version of classical Greece seen in *Assassin's Creed: Odyssey*, on archaeogaming.com shows this.[43] While this short interview is by no means as informative as a full account in the form of, for example, a book chapter would be, it nevertheless provides us with insights into the development process that are important to consider.[44] Similarly, Twitter and blog posts are ideal venues for exchanging observations and details that would (perhaps) not merit the full-fledged engagement that is a necessary condition for a scholarly article but that is relevant, nonetheless. In a tweet from 23 November 2018, Mark Walters, an archaeologist now working with a Welsh aerial photography and photogrammetry company, pointed out that the Greek herms littering roads in the gamescape of *Odyssey* seem to be based on a particular extant piece in the Getty collection.[45] Kiwi Hellenist Peter Gainsford, on the other hand, has posted a lengthy entry on his blog (kiwihellenist. blogspot.com) featuring an analysis (including transcription) of sea shanties sung by the NPCs crewing the player's trireme in the same game. Far from being made-up songs, these are based on examples of actual ancient Greek poetry, which they adapt, including Alcaeus, Archilochus and the *Anacreontea*.[46] This blog post was then taken up by popular gaming website *Kontaku*, with the resulting piece[47] being read over 20,000 times – not a bad result for what was essentially a scholarly contribution to Classical Receptions.

For those familiar with both the video games themselves and the possibilities and advantages of social media, these resources can serve a vital function. In reverse, however, the nature of parts of the scholarly discourse about (ancient) history and video games can also be a hindrance to wider acceptance of the subject matter itself and for similar reasons as laid out in the earlier section on classical receptions' hesitancy to engage with a medium that has for a long time been deemed 'unserious'. #ClassicsTwitter by no means encompasses all ancient historians and classicists.

This book

In addition to these challenges, historical game research (by which I mean the study and analysis of historical video games) can also be hampered by the unfamiliarity of the subject to large parts of the academic audience.[48] In order to counter this and to make the present volume accessible to as wide an audience as possible – including those uninitiated in the intricacies and occasional jargon of the gaming world – the first chapter, 'An Archaeology of Ancient Historical Video Games', will serve as an extended introduction to the different modes of 'receiving', representing and 'playing' antiquity in the video game genre. It sketches out a history of the medium and offers a brief review of some notable examples of video game genres and specific examples to illustrate the salient characteristics of depicting the ancient world in a video game setting. A complete register of games and media quoted and referred to in individual chapters, as well as a glossary of the most salient examples of gamer jargon are also included in this volume.

The book brings together a number of classical scholars and historians from a diverse and vibrant new field of research. The common thread is their interest in the representation, remediation and refiguration of Antiquity in a comparatively young medium, although their methodological approaches and individual research areas may vary. In order to reflect the multi-facetedness of authors and approaches, the main part of this volume is divided into four parts, with specific overarching themes that are the core of the individual chapters.

Part One – A brave old world: Re-figurations of ancient cultures

The first part of the book titled, 'A Brave Old World: Re-Figurations of Ancient Cultures', focuses on the question of video game aesthetics, the notoriously fickle concept of 'authenticity' in depicting past societies in video games, and questions of gender representations.

Chapter 2, '*Ludus* (not) Over: Video Games and the Popular Perception of Ancient Past Reshaping' by David Serrano Lozano, is preoccupied with questions of intermediatic influences on the representation of antiquity in modern video games. He questions the ways in which the specific nature and the cultural impact of video games are contributing to modify and create new popular perceptions of antiquity, different from those already established by other media such as films or television. How are classical cultures, concepts and characters being redefined when the player presses the 'Start' button? Serrano Lozano posits that, generally speaking, twenty-first-century popular culture has seen a closer and more complex relationship between film and video games visual narratives, particularly after the release of Zack Snyder's *300*.

Tristan French and Andrew Gardner, in Chapter 3, 'Playing in a "Real" Past: Classical Action Games and Authenticity', engage with a very recent trend in the meeting space between classical archaeology and video games: archaeogaming.[49] Their chapter explores the different means by which authenticity is constructed and experienced in video games in balance with effective gameplay and storytelling. In *Ryse: Son of Rome* and *Assassin's Creed: Origins*, French and Gardner use two very well-known recent entries into the ancient historical video game catalogue as test cases in order to examine the different forms of authenticity that may be important to players, how authenticity is measured and judged, and how different gameplay formats – and genres – highlight different aspects of authentic experience.

In the final chapter of Part One, 'The Representation of Women in *Ryse: Son of Rome*', Sian Beavers analyses the representation of gender in the aforementioned game, contrasting and comparing individual female characters in *Ryse* with examples of the depiction of ancient females across other mass media. The representation of Iceni Queen Boudicca is used as a central example to highlight unique properties of video games affecting gender representation, aspects of remediation in depicting gender, and how video games reflect contemporary sensibilities of gender and identity more than the ancient context.

Part Two – A world at war: Martial re-presentations of the ancient world

Part Two, 'A World at War: Martial Re-Presentations of the Ancient World', is centred on one of the most popular elements of classical antiquity in video games, the depiction of violent conflict and empire-building, with the individual chapters providing in-depth analyses of video game 'faces of battle' and genre-conventions, battle-narratives and procedural aspects of battle simulations.

Dominic Machado's chapter, 'Battle Narratives from Ancient Historiography to *Total War: Rome II*', uses the antiquity-centred *Total War* games, arguably the most successful video games inspired by the classical world, to draw a connection that goes from ancient battle narratives to the cinematic cutscenes that introduces players to a set of famous 'scenario' battles (in the nineteenth-century tradition of 'Decisive Battles'). Focusing on the Battle of Teutoburg Forest, he shows how game designers use, adapt and modify ancient accounts of these conflicts in order to create a compelling narrative and ideal gaming experience for its players, in a situation of simultaneous abundance and absence of ancient evidence.

By contrast, Jeremiah McCall's chapter, 'Digital Legionaries: Video Game Simulations of the Face of Battle in the Roman Republic', compares two well-liked entries in the real-time strategy genre, *Fields of Glory 2* and, again, *Total War: Rome II* to explore the battle models, calculations and preconceived assumptions underlying the depiction of battles in video games. McCall argues for a stronger engagement with simulations of ancient battles, hypothesizing that, since games, unlike the fundamentally static text representations of battles, are dynamic interactive models of what was essentially a dynamic and interactive affair, using them in a critical and reflective fashion affords opportunities for better accessing and understanding them.

Part Three – Digital epics: Role-playing in the ancient world

The third part of the book, 'Digital Epics: Role-Playing in the Ancient World', grapples with the influence and presence of the ancient epic tradition in the RPG/MMORPG genre as well as the role that games of these particular genres play in perpetuating or undermining traditional notions of antiquity.

Roger Travis demonstrates that the digital role-playing games of Bethesda Softworks possess common features best analysed by means of an adapted version of oral formulaic theory. His chapter, 'The Bethesda Style: The Open-World Role-Playing Game as Formulaic Epic', shows that the superficial, though increasingly frequently drawn, comparison of role-playing game narratives to processes bardic r-composition has its roots in games like Bethesda's open-world RPGs, which embody a sort of new birth of thematic recomposition. A description of player performance in the Bethesda RPGs as a bardic practice allows him to study the differences between the composition of Homeric epic and the design and play of digital games, enabling a more complex discussion of identity formation through performance in the open-world RPG.

Ross Clare's chapter, 'Postcolonial Play in Ancient World Computer Role-Playing Games', investigates how antiquity is received and altered by the role-playing video game, and what effects the associated conventions of the RPG have on these representations of ancient worlds when they are fitted into this specific framework. Using two classic RPGs, *Nethergate* and *Titan Quest*, as test cases, Clare shows that the gamespaces presented in RPGs can be defined in a broad sense as 'colonial spaces'. He subsequently uses elements of postcolonial and classical reception theory to identify postcolonial practices in RGPs, thus demonstrating how different readings and meaning can be arrived at, depending on ad hoc cultural processes, ancient materials and genre conventions.

Nico Nolden's chapter, 'Playing with an Ancient Veil: Commemorative Culture and the Staging of Ancient History within the Playful Experience of the MMORPG, *The Secret World*', is situated at the crossroads of historical game studies, public history and memory culture. Writing about massively multiplayer online role-playing game *The Secret World*, Nolden demonstrates that such games, which provide players with a historical setting and allow them to form online communities, move in a context that is relevant to the culture of memory and public history. His chapter analyses the reconstruction of material culture, historical narratives, game mechanics and world systems in *The Secret World*, which combine to influence a historical performance of antiquity. Building on this, Nolden explores how the game's player communities are acting and communicating in and about this complex historical structure and proposes research methods necessary in order to trace their historical memory culture.

Part Four – Building an ancient world: Re-imagining antiquity

The last part of the book, 'Building an Ancient World: Re-Imagining Antiquity', shifts perspective from the player-historian to the historian-developer. Individual case studies provide a behind-the-scenes perspective of the creative processes and the developing decisions of historical video games and their role in public engagement with the ancient world.

In the first of four chapters, Neville Morley, 'Choose Your Own Counterfactual: The Melian Dialogue as Text-Based Adventure', shows the results of his having combined his interest in Thucydidean politics with a fascination for text-based adventures and counterfactual history. In *The Melian Game*, a web-based text adventure created by Morley with open-source tool Twine, the player can choose between the Athenian and Melian side of the conflict and 'relive' the famous Thucydidean dialogue. There is no fixed goal for either side; instead, determining what might constitute 'winning' is a core part of the exercise.

Maciej Paprocki, a scholar involved in the creative direction of 2016 indie hit *Apotheon*, then provides a detailed account of his role as mythology consultant and writer for Alientrap Games, in his chapter, 'Mortal Immortals: Deicide of Greek Gods in *Apotheon* and Its Role in the Greek Mythic Storyworld'. He especially focuses on the twin challenges that had to be overcome in order to make *Apotheon* appealing to a mass audience: divine character design and balancing the conflict between mortals and immortals in the game's backstory. His chapter not only recounts the decision process behind the game's creation but also provides a *raisonnement* for the narrative from the perspective of a mythology scholar and classical philologist.

In, 'The Complexities and Nuances of Portraying History in *Age of Empires*', Alexander Flegler, a rare figure in that he is a game developer and student of Ancient History, draws on the *Age of Empires* franchise to shed light on how different conceptions of history can shape the developing process of games. What are the challenges of turning historical sources and historiography into a compelling video game? Which aspects of ancient material culture are important to a game's visuals and why are other cultural aspects often discarded? Which concessions have to be made in the interest of 'playability'? His contribution thus illuminates how the representation of history can change its meaning through a complicated process of video game creation and the interactive nature of the game itself.

Chapter 13, by Erika Holter, Una Ulrike Schäfer and Sebastian Schwesinger, 'Simulating the Ancient World: Pitfalls and Opportunities of Using Game Engines for Archaeological and Historical Research', critically analyses the functionality of digital reconstructions of public life in Greco-Roman antiquity, in the context of research projects and the recent trend towards efforts in digital and virtual heritage. In a case study involving the Athenian Pnyx and Agora, the authors digitally recreate these spaces in order to simulate and analyse their aurality and to reflect on methodological problems that arise because of the gap between the intrinsic logic of game engines and their intended use, and research interests and expectations.

A final chapter, the Epilogue by Adam Chapman, '*Quo Vadis* Historical Game Studies and Classical Receptions? Moving Two Fields Forward Together', is meant to serve as an epilogue to this volume, providing a synthesis of previous scholarship in the wider area of historical game studies and this volume's contributions. It highlights some of the trends apparent in the representation of antiquity in digital games and explores these trends in relation to ideas that have emerged from historical game studies, outlining the ways in which historical game studies and classical receptions have the potential to function cooperatively to mutual benefit and simultaneously expand our understanding of the representation and uses of antiquity in games. While it is intended as a coda to the entire volume, readers more unfamiliar with the development of game studies and historical game studies could conceivably profit from reading it in conjunction with this introduction and the first chapter, so as to get a solid grounding in the subject matter of the following chapters.

A way forward

Having pointed out what this book does – or attempts to do – it is incumbent on the editor also to acknowledge what it does not – cannot – do. It is not a complete review of ancient history in video games (in fact, I would argue that the point at which a single book, even a research monograph, could conceivably and convincingly succeed in such an undertaking has now passed us by). Individual readers will inevitably find game titles that they consider to be more important or more relevant to the field (or which they enjoyed playing themselves) not treated in the following pages. Others will miss a unified theoretical and/or methodological perspective or a stronger focus on representation and gender issues. All of these points are valid and the lack of these elements constitute a weakness of the present volume – a weakness, however, that is mostly due to the fact that this field of studies is really still in its infancy. As a collection of essays written by a selection of authors who depended not only on the editor's own interests and predilections but also on their own (as well as their time, effort and willingness), this volume cannot aspire either to completeness or systematicity. It is – and must be – an ensemble of case studies highlighting individual titles, genres and facets of ancient historical video games.

It also cannot, in and by itself, engage with some of the most glaring methodological difficulties inherent in the study of video games, even if individual chapters do take up these problems. In his chapter on MMORPGs, for instance, Nolden argues that the very nature of video games and the act of playing them present a methodological challenge. Games are fundamentally interactive. Depending on the nature of the gamescape and the narrative emplotment of the specific game, instances of play are not reproducible. In contrast to the study of, for example, ancient historical movies, there is no time index to which we can jump to follow any given scholar's interpretation of a scene. Nolden's solution is to record his instances of play ('paths') and to make these available in digital form, although that, in itself, again presents a new series of methodological issues and raises questions about feasibility and future-proof storage.[50]

There is also a gaping lacuna in all the research undertaken in the realm of historical video games, one that is also not limited to the subsection of games devoted to ancient history. As of the time of writing, there is almost no empirical research of processes of historical receptions through video games. This may seem surprising at first glance. However, the kind of qualitative research necessary in order to study the actual people involved in the reception of history in video games does not come naturally to classicists, or, indeed, historians. It would ideally involve questionnaires and interviews conducted with dozens, if not hundreds of participants, all geared towards better understanding the thoughts and interpretations of, for want of a better term, 'lay people' when confronted with a mediated and interactive version of history. The almost complete lack of any kind of systematic (or even selective) empirical study of audience/player responses to and engagement with historical video games is probably the greatest desideratum and the most pressing issue in historical game studies. As Chapman emphasizes in his stimulating epilogue, 'the advantages offered by empirical work on production/reception are significant'.[51] But the consequences of the hitherto lack of such works are even more significant. A book-length study by Daniel Giere based on a Hannover PhD thesis was unfortunately published too late to be systematically included in the present overview but promises just such research (on audience receptions of *Assassin's Creed III*).[52] The promise of such work is borne out by the (very) few case studies undertaken on, for example, audience reactions to historical movies or television series, such as those published by Amanda Potter on *Xena: Warrior Princess, Charmed* and *Wonder Woman*.[53] It is also shown briefly in Nolden's discussion in this volume of the community of *The Secret World* players, whose discussions on the official online forums of this MMORPG title demonstrate the deep engagement of players not only with the game itself, but also with the historical aspects that infuse it.

The lack of empirical research is more than a simple unfulfilled wish, however: it is a clear methodological deficit. As was alluded to above, there is no consensus as to the applicability or potential benefits of employing video games in classrooms and lecturing theatres – in part, because there is no empirical research to prove or disprove its advantages. Beyond the field of didactics, historians, who are trained to interpret mostly written sources and thus tend to treat video games as (ergodic)[54] texts, can offer only their own personal readings of specifics game situations, processes or narratives, based on the video game equivalent of 'close reading'. As with, for example, Tacitean historiography, these interpretations are open to debate, as is demonstrated by the analyses of different video games in several of the chapters of the present volume. Meaning, to quote Charles Martindale again, is 'realized at the point of reception' and the interpretation of female NPCs from the point of view of feminist critical theory in Beaver's chapter may not convince all readers equally (as the infamous 'Gamergate' controversy amply demonstrated). Nor should we assume that every reader will share Dominic Machado's identification of Arminius as main protagonist – perhaps even as hero – in the cutscenes accompanying the depiction of the Teutoburg Forest battle in *Total War: Rome II*'s historical battle mode.

In the absence of concrete work done on player reactions and receptions, scholars are forced to fall back on published opinions and impressions, for instance in the guise of published reviews of individual games, as French and Gardner do in their analysis of the (critical) reception of *Ryse: Son of Rome*. All of these readings, interpretations and approaches are legitimate, to be sure, and can be convincing on their own terms. On the whole, however, we should be careful in assuming too freely what 'general' reactions on the part of 'most' players are. Moreover, strictly speaking, hypotheses about 'historying', historical 'meaning-making', student engagement or, simply, player opinions can only be based on studies of the actual players which are not yet available.[55] For the moment, and to a certain degree, we are thus hypothesizing in a void and readers should bear this in mind as they engage with the subsequent chapters.

Notes

1   Hereinafter and throughout this volume, the term 'video game' will be used to refer to the whole set of computer and console games.
2   For an equally informative and entertaining account of the rise of the video game industry, see, Herman (1994) and Kent (2001), although both are heavily focused on the early days of the medium.
3   There is some debate as to whether the *Cathode-Ray Amusement Device* created by Thomas T. Goldsmith Jr. and Estle Ray Mann in 1947 and patented in 1948 qualifies as a video or computer game. Its claim is weakened by the fact that no actual computer, analogue or otherwise, was used to display or control the game, which was 'run' purely on a cathode-ray tube (CRT) screen and operated by manipulating controls on the screen itself, which, in turn, modified the direction of the CRT beam spot. Cf. Donovan (2010: 1–9).

4 For this Golden Age, see Kent (2001: 123–78). Atari, one of the premier companies of that era, and, arguably, the one with the greatest cultural impact, is heavily featured in the accounts by Kent (ibid.) and Herman (1994); see also, Cohen (1984), as well as the documentary, *Atari: Game Over* (2014).

5 Kent (2001: 185).

6 Smith (2013).

7 Kent (2001: 239–40).

8 Moore (1965, 1975). In 2016, according to an article in *Nature*, as microchip production was nearing absolute physical limitations, the validity of Moore's Law was nearing its end; cf. Waldrop (2016).

9 NEWZOO (2018). Compare this with a total worth of about $100 billion in 2017 (ibid., 2017) and with a global box office revenue in 2017 of less than $50 billion (cf. statista, 2018).

10 Lowe (2009).

11 Chapman, Foka and Westin (2016: 358); cf. Uricchio (2005); and for earlier works, see, e.g., Squire (2004).

12 Huizinga (1955); cf. Chapman, Foka and Westin (2016).

13 Chapman, Foka and Westin (2016: 2).

14 For some examples of the breadth of contemporary classical reception studies, see, e.g., the chapters of the recent *Companion to Classical Receptions* (Hardwick and Stray, 2008a).

15 Durham Centre for Classical Reception.

16 Martindale (1993: 3). Cf. Jauss (1982, 1994) and Holub (1984).

17 Lowe (2009: 65).

18 Bakogianni (2016: 97–8).

19 Lowe (2009: 65).

20 For a recent critical discussion of elitism in Classics, see Morley (2018b); the quote is from Shakespeare's *Henry V*, Act 4, Scene 1.

21 Prensky (2001: quote at p. 2).

22 Christesen and Machado (2010: 107).

23 For the middle ages, see Heinze (2012); the early modern period, Kerschbaumer and Winnerling (2014a, as well as an English-language version, 2014b); and for the Second World War, Bender (2012).

24 Aguado-Cantrabana and Etxeberria Gallestegi (2016), André and Lécole-Solnychkine (2008, 2013a), Bembeneck (2013), Blakely (2018), Christesen and Machado (2010), Coert (2018), Furtwängler (2012), Gardner (2007, 2012), Ghita and Andrikopoulos (2009), Lowe (2009, 2012), McCall (2018b), Rollinger (2014, 2015, 2016) and Wottge (2011). The monograph is André (2016). Cf. also, Rollinger (2018). Chapters on ancient history and video games by Annalisa Quattrocchio, Jordi Rodríguez Danés, David Serrano Lozano and Fabian Schulz will be included in the publication associated with the IMAGINES Conference, 'The Fear and the Fury: Ancient Violence in Modern Imagination', held on 29 September–1 October 2016 in Turin, see, Torino Abstracts (2016).

25 For a very useful overview of scholarship on historical video games in general, i.e. not focused on the ancient world, see Schwarz (2015).

26 Lowe (2009: 76). For his analysis of the role of ruins in ancient historical video games, see ibid. (2012).

27 Lowenthal (2015: especially, 289–410). For the iconicity of certain artefacts and images associated with antiquity and their adaptation from other media, such as cinema, see David Serrano Lozano's chapter in this volume.

28 For gamescape analyses, see André (2016) and André and Lécole-Solnychkine (2008, 2013). The question of authenticity/accuracy is analysed in Gardner (2007), Ghita and Androkopoulos (2009), Lowe (2009), Rollinger (2015, 2016), Aguado-Cantabrana and Etxeberria Gallastegi (2016) and Coert (2018).

29 For which, cf. Chapman (2016: 59–89) and see the chapter by Rollinger in this volume.

30 Poole (2000: 77).

31 Winnerling (2014) and cf. Rollinger (2016) for a case study of an ancient video game.

32 Kapell and Elliott (2013a: 14).

33 Ibid., 3. Cf. Rosenstone (2006: 2) for the quote; Lowenthal (2015), in general, for conceptions of 'the past' and Lowenthal (1968: especially 105–72) on the difference between history and heritage.

34 Chapman (2016: 22).

35 Ibid., 15.

36 Wottge (2011) and McCall (2011).

37 Christesen and Machado (2010: 109).

38 Squire (2004, 2013) and McCall (2011). For a critical judgement, see De Groot (2008: 7–8), who contends that the 'underlying ludicness' of games has 'little innate value outside of the game structure'. Cf. also Ruggill and McAllister, who state that: 'Commercial games have not only become intellectually and pedagogically acceptable, but de rigueur in the mainstream classroom, effectively stripping the medium of much of its potential to undercut presumption [sic] and the *status quo*' (2013: 101).

39 Cf. Wolf (1996, 1998), Pöhlmann and Walter (1998) and Grosch (2002).

40 Schwarz (2015: 404).

41 Cf. the project homepages at: Universität Stuttgart (n.d., Peter Scholz); and Hagia Sophia (n.d., Bissera Pentcheva).

42 Cf. the project homepage, Samothracian Networks (n.d.); and see Blakely (2018).

43 See Reinhard (n.d.).

44 For a more critical accounting of the role of historical consultants (in Hollywood), see Coleman (2004).

45 Walters (2018).

46 Gainsford (2019).

47 Plunkett (2019).

48 For a concise introduction into historical game studies, see Chapman, Foka and Westin (2016).

49 For both the term and the underlying concept, see Reinhard (2018).

50 See Nolden's chapter in this volume, particularly the section entitled, 'A Historical Knowledge System for Ancient History'; and cf. Nolden (2018c: 487–501). See also, the 'Manifesto' of the *Arbeitskreis für Geschichte und Digitale Spiele* for proposals on how to deal with these issues (Arbeitskreis, 2016). The *Arbeitskreis* welcome further input from scholars.

51 See Chapman's chapter in this volume, pp. 233–51.

52 Giere (2019).

53 Potter (2013, 2018).

54 For video games as ergodic texts, see Aarseth (1997: 1, where it is written that: 'In ergodic literature, nontrivial effort is required to traverse the text'); cf. Mäyrä (2008: 8).

55 Schwarz (2016). For one example of a project focusing on 'audience/player learning practices and their engagements with, and responses to, classical content', see, for instance, the PhD project of Sian Beavers [2017].

An Archaeology of Ancient Historical Video Games

Christian Rollinger

In most accounts of the history *of* video games and of history *in* video games, the credit for creating the first historical video game (by which I mean a game with a specifically historical setting) goes to educators and computer aficionados Don Rawitsch, Bill Heinemann and Paul Dillenberger at Carleton College in Northfield, Minnesota. In 1971, they developed the first version of *The Oregon Trail*, though, as we shall see, *The Oregon Trail* was not, in fact, the first historical video game. To play, users of the first version of the game had to input text on a mainframe computer on the college campus; the player interacted with the software purely via manual text input and printouts; it was only the later (1978) versions and the commercial edition (1985) ported to Apple and Commodore systems that would introduce a rudimentary graphic interface. Players found themselves in the role of a wagon leader travelling from Missouri to Oregon in 1848. Their mission was to ensure the survival of their party in the face of natural obstacles such as rivers or mountain ranges, weather, sickness, thieves, Indian raids and bandits. Designed as an educational tool for teaching nineteenth-century US history, specifically the story of the American western expansion, the game was rather text-heavy and has been described as an ancestor of the modern serious game subgenre.[1] It was published by the Minnesota Educational Computing Consortium (MECC) and pioneered computer teaching by attempting to present a realistic experience of nineteenth-century settlers for the benefit of pupils and students.[2] The game itself, and especially some individual aspects of gameplay have acquired cult status among its modern fans, particularly the announcement that the player or members of their party have contracted or died of dysentery (an unnervingly frequent occurrence; see Fig. 1.1).

As early computers had limited to no graphic display options, the first historical games were ipso facto text-based and this significantly limited the options of both game developers and gamers. As we shall see, hardware developments are not inconsequential for the ways in which (ancient) history and culture is presented in video games. As computers slowly evolved from house-, then room-sized apparatuses into compact, desk-fitting machines, video games underwent a cultural sea change and began their transformation into a mass medium.

Fig. 1.1 *The Oregon Trail* screen announcement (1971/1974 © MECC).[3]

Hardware and genre

Games of the early 1970s were thus predominantly text-based adventures, with William Crowther's *Colossal Cave Adventure* (1975) being the first entry in a genre later known as 'adventure games' ('adventures'). Programmed for the PDP-10 minicomputer, *Colossal Cave Adventure* 'simulates' its gamescape – a term coined in 2006 by Shoshana Magnet to denote the virtual landscape of a video game[4] – not by depicting a bitmap-based graphic or rendering it in real-time, but rather by describing it in text form. The player, whose 'mission' is to explore a mysterious cave system, in turn, entered simple commands such as 'yes/no' or 'go south/north', which were parsed by the software and prompted in-game developments (such as the player falling into a pit and breaking his bones). The game was recognizably a computerized version of classic role-playing games of the 'pen-and-paper' genre (e.g. *Dungeons & Dragons*).[5]

During the 1970s, arcade games and home video game consoles became capable of displaying adequate bitmap or vector graphics and with the addition of graphical interfaces, video games changed immeasurably. Thanks to titles such as *Pong*, they ceased to be the exclusive domain of 1970s and 1980s college campus hacker culture. Coin-operated arcade games ('coin-ops') appeared in bars and amusement arcades and were the motor behind the first video game surge. Even with relatively simple, not to say archaic, vector graphics, they allowed for a completely new experience, for example in piloting spaceships and destroying *Asteroids* or, in a game rather glumly inspired by Cold War reality, attempting to intercept enemy nuclear missiles, for instance *Missile*

Command. As arcade consoles progressed technologically, graphics likewise improved, gaining both in colour and in complexity. The same, however, cannot be said for the games themselves, which, despite the addition of new genres such as fighting and racing games, as well as vertically or horizontally scrolling action games (jump-and-runs, for example *Donkey Kong*), remained tied to 'the purest, most elemental videogame pleasure': the 'heathen joy of destruction'.[6] While arcade games survived into the 1990s and, in one form or another, survive to this day, they, together with their home-based equivalents in early gaming consoles (perhaps the most famous of which was the second-generation Atari 2600 VCS, or video computer system, released in 1977), were inevitably supplanted by Personal Computers (PCs).

Personal computers, as well as third-generation consoles, changed gaming forever, by introducing first 8- and 16-bit, then VGA/SVGA, and, finally, the high-resolution, quasi-photorealistic graphics that are now de rigueur. The level of technological advancement in computer processing power naturally had a significant impact on the development of video games in general, an impact that went far beyond the superficial aspect of graphics quality. Although the impact of technological innovation is unfortunately often ignored in the analysis of historical video games, it was only through such innovation that historical video games found a market and a hitherto unsuspected mass appeal. The prime example of this is the advent of a seemingly inconspicuous instrument that, nevertheless, had a tremendous impact on gaming: the computer mouse.

The first computer mouse prototype was built as early as 1964 and mentioned in a 1965 report from the Stanford Research Institute in Menlo Park, California, but it was only popularized by the appearance of the Apple Macintosh 128K computer in 1984, which was sold with a Macintosh Mouse included.[7] The importance of the mouse for computer game development (and for the domestic and business applications of personal computers, in general) can hardly be overstated. As an integral part of graphical user interfaces (GUIs) since the mid-1980s, the mouse has facilitated easy-to-use computing and software. Transforming movements on a lateral physical plane into movements of a pointer on the computer screen, the mouse allows for extremely precise controlling which the control mechanisms even of contemporary gaming consoles lack to a certain degree. Consoles are typically used by means of a more or less elaborated handheld device, the gamepad or 'controller'. It typically consists of a set of multiple buttons and one to two direction controllers (either in the form of a digital cross or as an analogue control stick); both elements are to be used simultaneously to control, for example, player avatars or games. Although they have evolved in terms of complexity (and now include wireless connections and touchscreen elements), gamepads are thus little more than an elaborated version of the typical control elements of even the earliest arcade coin-ops. Video games played on PCs, although they can naturally also be played with a gamepad, are mostly controlled by a combination of keyboard and mouse commands.

The difference in hardware has deep ramifications: as gamepads are extremely efficient in controlling three-dimensional player movements, console games tend to either emulate older scrolling jump-and-run games (such as *Mario Bros.*), simulate control of vehicles such as racing cars, planes or helicopters, belong to the first-person shooter (FPS), where the player assumes the point of view of, for example, a soldier, or, lastly, show an external view of the player's avatar in a three-dimensional space (role-playing games or RPGs, action-adventures). Sports and fighting games are likewise best played with gamepad and are thus predominantly console games. On the other hand, as players can move or aim a mouse with a significantly larger degree of precision than a gamepad, PCs are also very popular platform for FPS games, as well as for RPGs and action-adventures. Games belonging to the strategy genres are played almost exclusively on PCs, as their controls can be quite complicated and necessitate keyboard shortcuts.

In recent days, industry reports show a strong growth in a relatively recent addition to the gaming world, i.e. mobile games, mostly played on touchscreen-based smartphones or tablets. These, unheard of a mere decade ago, now constitute around half of the total market, with consoles (25 per cent) and PCs (21 per cent) making up most of the remainder.[8] As touchscreen controls on the typically small(ish) screens of mobile phones and tablets are largely imprecise and depend on both the dexterity and physicality of users' hands, mobile game design for the main part follows the template laid down by consoles or belongs to a new, simplified category (casual games).

Genre and history

The peculiarities of the two main gaming hardware ecologies thus shape gamers' preferences as to the genres of games that they play on respective hardware. What does this mean, then, for the representation of history? As we shall see, questions of genre and genre conventions have a significant impact on the way that history is 'played'. Generally, video games can be divided into two categories: 'human-scale games' and 'God games'.[9] While the first typically cast the player as the main character of a game that involves a distinct narrative (from epic quests to more mundane tasks such as 'Win this race') and represents the diegetic perspective of an individual, in the latter, players assume the role of a quasi-omnipotent force, guiding the development of cities, economies or global empires. God games are thus process-oriented and often use different forms of maps as central controlling element of gameplay, which makes the use of a gamepad wildly inconvenient, while human-scale games give the point of view of a specific character and can thus be played equally well by keyboard/mouse or gamepad. Strategy games, likely the most important category of God games, are played almost exclusively on PCs. Likewise, as a combination of mouse and keyboard controls allows for a far higher degree of accuracy (particularly in 'aiming'), PCs are also very popular platform for FPS games.

While the dichotomy of human and God-scale games is an important criterion in analysing and interpreting video games, it tends to obfuscate the minutiae of individual genres belonging to both categories. Various other proposals have been made to identify categories. In his study of *Trigger Happy: The Inner Life of Video Games* (2000), Steven Poole listed a total of nine different genres: (first-person) shooters, racing games, vertically or horizontally scrolling platform games, beat'em-ups (i.e. fighting games), strategy games, sports and simulations, adventures and role-playing games

(RPGs), puzzles.[10] The differences between genres, in this view, are marked by their contents, by what the games are about. There is significant room for debate, though. Not everyone would agree, for instance, that adventure games and RPGs belong to the same genre at all; even less so in the case of sport games and simulations. However, in travelling too far down the road of detailed differentiations, we may arrive at the unhelpful number of 42 individual genres identified by Mark Wolf.[11]

For the purposes of convenience, the following differentiations in genre will be used in this chapter:

- *First-person shooters (FPS)* – are typically set in military contexts. The player assumes the role of a soldier, warrior, or insurgent, and gameplay involves navigating a three-dimensional space which is shown in first-person perspective. FPSs centre around violent confrontation and can be set in historical conflicts (the Second World War being the most popular) or in a generic present-day or future-war scenario. Significant examples include the *Call of Duty* and *Medal of Honor* series.

- *Action-Adventure games* – are perhaps the classic form of video games or, put differently, are a passepartout category for a number of different subgenres, rather than a unified game genre in itself. They encompass classical platformer (e.g. *Mario Bros.*), as well as first- and third-person action-adventure games. Both of the latter incorporate significant elements of the FPSs genre but add adventure elements such as problem-solving challenges, puzzles and a more or less complex plot (which FPSs typically eschew). The difference between first- and third-person action-adventures lies purely in the different perspective adopted, although third-person games tend to be less action-centric. While *Half-Life 2* and the *Far Cry* series are examples of a first-person action-adventure, *Tomb Raider* and the *God of War* series are examples of a third-person perspective in such games.

- *Role-playing games (RPGs)* – are not dissimilar to action-adventures. In RPGs, the player assumes the role of specific characters or creates these characters themselves. In contrast to action-adventures, character development, a greater narrative arc, and the immersion of both player and avatar in a fully developed world is much more heavily emphasized. As player decisions significantly alter the course of the game, RPGs lend themselves very well to replaying. Titles such as *Diablo*, *The Witcher* or *The Elder Scroll* series (the latter being the subject of Roger Travis' chapter in this volume) are stand-out titles. A subgenre, or, rather, a natural continuation of RPGs are MMORPGs.

- *Massively Multiplayer Online Role-Playing Games (MMORPGs)* – such as *World of Warcraft* or *The Secret World* (which is the subject of Nico Nolden's chapter here). These games follow the same basic rules as RPGs, with the significant difference that the gameworld is populated not by software-based non-player characters (NPCs), but by other players, sometimes numbering in the hundreds of thousands or millions (or, in the case of *World of Warcraft*, more than 100 million), hence the 'massively' multiplayer moniker.[12]

- *Sports and fighting games* – typically depict specific sports (e.g. [European] football), sportive events (e.g. Olympic Games) or fighting scenarios (various martial arts genres, which are often laced with fantastical elements) from a third-person perspective. Examples include the multimillion-dollar franchises of FIFA, the NFL or NHL.

- *Vehicle games* – are essentially racing games depicting a variety of vehicles ranging from Formula 1 to street cars to futuristic spaceships. A subgenre of the vehicle simulation that enjoyed great success in the late 1990s and early aughts was the military simulator, with player being put at the helm of military vehicles.
- *Strategy games* – give the player control over military units, nation-states or whole empires and are either round-based (i.e. players take turns making their moves in individual 'rounds') or occur in real-time (real-time strategy or RTS games). The objective of strategy games is usually militaristic in nature, as the player is expected to win battles and expand empire, thus often combining a strategic and tactical outlook in one game. Battles can be presented and fought out in three-dimensional perspective, but this is not always the case. Importantly, strategy games mostly feature a so-called 'strategic map', which can be either photorealistic or abstract. On this map, the player must control his faction's economy and military infrastructure, erect military buildings and fortifications, and move army units. The most well-known example of a strategy game franchise is the *Total War* series, which incorporates both tactical and strategic, as well as both round-based and real-time elements.
- *Economic simulations or city-building games* – games such as *SimCity*, the *Caesar* franchise or *Theme Park*. In titles of this genre, the player is tasked with building and running a socioeconomic collective, such as a city, a theme park or a railroad network, which all follow a distinct set of rules and presumptions.

None of these categories or typologies should be seen as absolute. They are a convenient way of categorizing games but should not mask the fact that there are a number of games that do not fit neatly because they incorporate elements from a number of genres. For instance, *EVE Online* is mostly understood as a subscription-based MMORPG that has been running since 2003. As of 2013, when the last official numbers were released, more than half a million subscriptions were active. What differentiates *EVE Online* from other MMORPGs, however, is its enormous scope and complexity: as a simulated sci-fi universe, the game contains roughly 7,800 star systems, an extremely intricate player-driven open economy, and, naturally, space battles on a truly epic scale. Instead of being 'simply' an MMORPG, *EVE Online* is also an economic simulation and a real-time strategy game that has, in many ways, transcended not only genre conventions but even reductionist notions of what a video game is. Its economy has been studied and written on by former Greek finance minister and political economist Yannis Varoufakis;[13] its wars and battles – the most notorious of which was the 'Bloodbath of B-R5RB', a two-day battle fought in January of 2014 and involving more than 7,500 active participant players – have occasioned the developing of in-game traditions of historiography and public history, which would themselves be interesting subjects of study.[14]

In fact, however, beyond the genre categories used by the gaming industry in market research and advertisement, the question of how to approach genres in video games (though by no means unstudied) has hitherto been relatively undertheorized. One noteworthy recent approach has been to categorize genres according to 'a game's criteria for success': Simon Egenfeldt-Nielsen, Jonas Heide Smith, and Susana Pajares Tosca thus differentiate between action games, involving 'fighting or some kind of physical drama', adventure games ('requiring deep thinking and great patience'), strategy games ('somewhere between action and adventure'), and process-oriented games, which, for them, fall somewhat outside the formal definition of 'games' ('think of populating and watching an aquarium as opposed to playing chess').[15] Arguing from the point of view of a historian interested in digitals games as historical practice, Adam Chapman has proposed a different categorization, with 'bookends' at either end of a spectrum being the 'realist' and the 'conceptual' simulation styles. The 'realist' style, according to Chapman, adheres to a quasi-Rankian ideal of claiming to show the past 'as it was', employing a high degree of 'visual specificity' and claiming 'historical accuracy' in its audiovisual representation. In order to be effective at this, 'realist' simulations are closely connected to the diegetic level of the avatar and thus have a narrow focus. At the other end of the spectrum, 'conceptual' simulations are much less 'literal' and often evince a degree of 'visual simplicity'; they are an abstract simulation of history on a macro scope that can deal with abstract 'concepts, theories and processes'; as such, they are as much 'a simulation of discourse about this past' as they are simulations of the past.[16] Individual titles can be arranged on a fluid scale between both extremes or even incorporate aspects of both, such as the *Total War* games, which feature a 'realist' style simulation on a tactical battle-level and a 'conceptual' simulation on the strategic, empire-governing level of play.[17]

Depending on the context and the heuristic interests, different genre categorizations can be used. In general, video games centred on or around a specific historical period or theme, perhaps somewhat surprisingly, exist in almost all genres and categories. Classic FPS titles (the very epitome of 'realist' simulations) have been set in historical conflicts such as the First World War (*Battlefield 1*) or Second World War (e.g. classic titles such as *Call of Duty* or *Brothers in Arms*, but also including the very first FPS, *Return to Castle Wolfenstein*) and have even been identified as contributing to a specific memorial culture relating to twentieth-century conflicts.[18] Action-adventure games (typically also belonging to the 'realist' end of the spectrum) such as the extremely popular *Assassin's Creed* franchise are set in the Crusader states of Outremer, Renaissance Italy, or during the French Revolution. While RPGs are more often set in a quasi-medieval fantasy setting (e.g. *The Witcher*), there have been noteworthy role-playing games and even MMORPGs that are firmly settled in historical periods, such as fifteenth-century Bohemia in the controversial *Kingdom Come: Deliverance* or ancient Rome in the now defunct (and grammatically questionable) *Roma Victor*.[19] As with FPS, strategy games and economic simulations/city-building games – classic examples of process-oriented games, or 'conceptual' simulations – often feature historical conflicts: the *Total War* series, for one, has seen entries set in antiquity, medieval Europe, feudal Japan and the Age of Imperialism (but also the fictional world of the *Warhammer Fantasy* universe), with economic simulations such as the *Anno* franchise similarly adapting a number of historical settings.

It is only relatively minor genres such as fighting or racing games that have seen almost no titles with a historical setting released (although they do exist, as we will see later). While it is difficult to be certain of statistical information relating to absolute numbers or percentages of video games that focus on the depiction of history, some indications seem relatively reliable. From 1982 to 2015, tens of thousands of video games were released, some of which have gained either cult status (such as the popular *Super Mario* or *Zelda* franchises) or notoriety (such as *CounterStrike* or the *Grand Theft Auto* series). According to recent statistical data (from the USA alone), the FPS (25.9 per cent of video game sales in 2017) and action-adventure (a combined 31 per cent of sales) genres remain the most popular, followed at some distance by sport and fighting games (17.6 per cent), RPGs (11.3 per cent), vehicle simulations (6.4 per cent), and strategy games (4.2 per cent).[20] These numbers, however, are not representative for historical video games, a subgenre that follows other rules. As there is no publicly available database for historical video games nor are game sales categorized in this fashion in statistical reports, it is difficult, if not impossible, to precisely quantify the importance of historical video games. However, German historian Angela Schwarz has compiled a private database of historical video games and calculates in a 2015 article that more than 2,300 gaming titles can be categorized as historical.[21] Additionally, more than a hundred new historical games have appeared each year since 2003.[22] Among these games, however, the genre disparity is striking: almost half (40 per cent) of all titles belong to the strategy genre. Other popular genres are action-adventure (12.7 per cent), economic simulations and city-building games (11.9 per cent), FPSs (9.3 per cent) and, somewhat surprisingly, vehicle simulations (11.9 per cent), although the latter category is mostly made up of historical military simulators such as, for example, *IL-2 Sturmovik* (in which the player is a pilot in the Soviet Air Forces during the Second World War), rather than racing games.[23]

Ancient history in video games

When looking at the chronological distribution of historical video games, titles set in the twentieth century amount to roughly 45 per cent of all games, with the Second World War alone making up for 26 per cent. Of all historical video games, 11 per cent are set in the ancient world, including ancient Egypt.[24] There is, as far as I know, no statistical information publicly available on the distribution of games set in Antiquity across different game genres (see Table 1.1). However, even a non-systematic look at recent titles shows a clear numerical superiority of strategy-based games and action-adventures, which includes the most prominent examples of ancient historical games (*Rome: Total War, Total War: Rome II, Assassin's Creed: Origins* and *Assassin's Creed: Odyssey*). Though numbering considerably fewer titles, the genre of economic simulations/city-building games was, for a time, also well represented, though it should be said that games of this genre have generally decreased in number in recent years. As David Serrano Lozano states in his discussion of early game genres involving representations of antiquity in this volume, the preference of game designers to use an ancient setting in these genres is 'the result of the intersection between video games' needs for narrative and interactive dynamics, and the search for semiotic, visual, and cultural references through which the creation of a new game project is mediated'.[25] Antiquity was thus a means to an end: 'because of the inherent possibilities and restrictions of early video game developers', the already mentioned box-ticking approach to antiquity was an efficient way to create a gamescape even with simple technological means.

Table 1.1 Notable games set in the ancient world.

Historical period	Name	Year	Genre	Platform
Antiquity (overall)	*Rome: Total War*	2004	RTS/TBS (4X)	PC
Antiquity (overall)	*Total War: Rome II*	2013	RTS/TBS (4X)	PC
Antiquity (overall)	*Age of Empires: Definitive Edition*	2018	RTS	PC
Antiquity (overall)	*Civilization I–VI*	1991–2016	RTS/TBS (4X)	PC
Greek Mythology	*Rise of the Argonauts*	2008	Action-adventure	PC/Xbox 360/PS3
Greek Mythology	*Odyssey: The Search for Ulysses*	2000	Action-adventure	PC
Greek Mythology	*Zeus: Master of Olympus*	2000	City-building	PC
Greek Mythology	*Age of Mythology*	2002	RTS	PC
Greek Mythology	*Apotheon*	2015	Action-adventure (scroller)	PC/PS4
Classical Greece	*Assassin's Creed: Odyssey*	2018	Action-adventure	PS4/Xbox One
Hellenistic Period	*Assassin's Creed: Origins*	2017	Action-adventure	PS4/Xbox One
Roman Republic	*Numantia*	2017	TBS	PC/Xbox One/PS4
Roman Empire	*Nethergate*	1998 (Remake, 2007)	Action-adventure	PC
Roman Empire	*Caesar I–IV*	1992–2004	City-building	PC
Roman Empire	*Imperium Romanum*	2008	City-building	PC
Roman Empire	*Grand Ages: Rome*	2009	City-building	PC
Roman Empire	*CivCity: Rome*	2006	City-building	PC
Roman Empire	*Ryse: Son of Rome*	2013	Action-adventure	PC/Xbox One
Roman Empire	*Spartan: Total Warrior*	2005	Action-adventure	PS 2/Xbox/Gamecube
Roman Empire	*Annals of Rome*	1986	TBS	PC
Roman Empire	*Field of Glory I–II*	2011/2018	TBS	PC
Roman Empire	*Europa Universalis: Rome*	2008	RTS (4X)	PC
Roman Empire	*Imperator: Rome*	2019	RTS (4X)	PC
Late Antiquity	*Total War: Attila*	2015	RTS/TBS (4X)	PC

But, in general, despite the possibility of breaking out beyond these genres provided by modern gaming technology, the genre focus still holds today. Occasionally, titles will transcend the recognizable emphasis of ancient historical games on the three main genres, but these are relatively rare. Ancient warfare, with its melee weapons and archery, does not lend itself naturally to the FPS genre, and vehicle simulations are likewise few and far between. The few exceptions to this rule show why: they are not commercially (or, less importantly, critically) successful. Titles like *Circus Maximus: Chariot Wars*, in a mixture of traditional racing games, action-heavy genre entries such as *Mario Kart*, and the famous *Ben-Hur* race sequence, have players control horse chariots with two-man driving teams across various racing grounds and generic roads of the Roman Empire. There is a significant action element, in that the second person of the driving team is tasked with fighting off their opponents with various weapons (both characters are controlled by a single player). The game was released for PlayStation 2 and the original Xbox in 2002 to little critical acclaim or, indeed, commercial success. A similar title, *Colosseum: Road to Freedom* (2005), casts the player in the role of a gladiator fighting for recognition and his own release; through three-dimensional action sequences in the guise of gladiatorial contests, the player can earn both cash prizes and experience points, thereby 'levelling up' and, eventually, being able to buy their own freedom.

More recent titles improve on the repetitive gameplay of these early-aughts games. In *QVADRIGA* (see Fig. 1.2), released in 2014, instead of assuming the role of the chariot driver himself, the player is instead cast as manager of a racing stable and has to recruit drivers, manage and train horses, and compete successfully in a number of contests. Individual races are shown in a stylized two-dimensional form from above. The player can interfere with the actual course of the race only by means of a simplified action menu (e.g., go faster, change lanes, etc.). The game is thus more a manager-centred economic simulation than a racing game.[26] Similarly, *Age of Gladiators* and *Age of Gladiators II* combine managerial gameplay – the player acts as a (middling) *lanista* and attempts to bring his stable of gladiators to fame and success – and rudimentary fighting action. Games such as these are only superficially connected to the ancient world; however, their 'antiquity' is purely aesthetic. With minor modifications, *QVADRIGA* and *Age of Gladiators* would work equally well as 'simulations' of NASCAR racing or professional boxing.[27]

Despite the lack of commercial success, these games have found a certain niche market, which is very probably connected to the advent of game distribution portals such as Steam or the iTunes App Store. Circumventing the traditional system of developer/publisher combinations for gaming titles, these portals allow individual

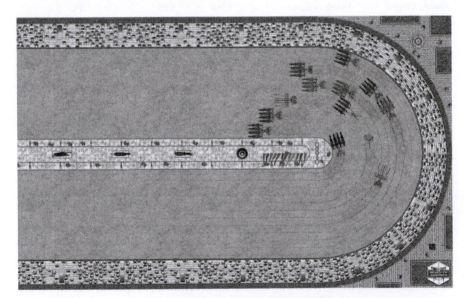

Fig. 1.2 A chariot race in *QVADRIGA* (2014 © Slitherine. All rights reserved).

developers or small independent studios to design and create games with minimal investment and to release and market them themselves. In this environment, niche titles can survive; as for the larger-game mass market, it seems that antiquity is destined to remain bound to its three 'original' genres, as player expectations have solidified. It is thus incumbent on us to engage more closely with these genres and a selection of 'ancient' titles.

Economic simulations and city-building games

The very first economic simulation in video game history was set in the most ancient of ancient worlds. A little-known – or, indeed, almost completely forgotten – program called *The Sumerian Game* was developed between 1963–7 by a team under Richard L. Wing, the head of the Board of Cooperative Educational Services of the Northern Westchester county in New York, originally as part of a project entitled on the 'Use of Technical Media for Simulating Environments to Provide Individualized Instruction'. The game itself – meaning its programming code – is unfortunately lost, but its history as well as an attempt at reconstructing gamescape and gameplay has recently been assembled in painstaking detective work by Tobias Winnerling.[28] It was played on a room-filling IBM 7090 mainframe (the same computer used by NASA for parts of the Mercury programme); player input and output occurred via an IBM 1050 terminal and printouts. Before starting the game, players were treated to an audio lecture introducing them to the historical period and the game setting: Sumer, around 3,500 BCE. As visual aids, a number of photographs were shown on a slide projector, depicting contemporary setting in Mesopotamia.[29] The player then assumed the role of Luduga I, priest-ruler of the Mesopotamian city of Lagash, and was presented with ancient dilemmas relating to agriculture (such as floods or fires) which he had to manage. In case of failure, the player was not yet confronted with the unsympathetic *Game Over* of later games. Instead, the final line of the printout rather charmingly read: 'Your population has decreased to zero. Do not go on. Call the teacher.'[30]

In 1968, a similar game was developed by Doug Dyment at the Digital Equipment Corporation (DEC). Entitled *The Sumer Game*, it was a simulation of personal and resource management programmed in the then recently invented FOCAL, a programming language for the DEC PDP-8 minicomputer. An expanded version of the game was released in BASIC language in 1973 by David H. Ahl as *Hammurabi* (published not on physical media but rather in the form of a printed version of the game code, to be typed in by players themselves).[31] According to the introduction by Ahl, in *Hammurabi*, 'you direct the administrator of Sumeria, Hammurabi, how to manage the city. The city initially has 1,000 acres, 100 people and 3,000 bushels of grain in storage.'[32] Depending on the player's skill, the outcomes could vary (Fig. 1.3) Success or failure was communicated by comparing the player with historical figures (e.g. 'A fantastic performance!!! Charlemagne, Disraeli, and Jefferson combined could not have done better!' or 'Your heavy-handed performance smacks of Nero and Ivan IV. The people [remaining] find you an unpleasant ruler, and, frankly, hate your guts!!'). In contrast both to *The Sumerian Game* and to *The Oregon Trail*, the BASIC version of *Hammurabi* was meant to be played on the then new microcomputers, that is personal computers with integrated microprocessor chips as

```
860 PRINT „IN YOUR 10-YEAR TERM OF OFFICE,";P1;"PERCENT OF THE"
862 PRINT "POPULATION STARVED PER YEAR ON THE AVERAGE, I.E. A TOTAL OF"
865 PRINT D1;"PEOPLE DIED!!": L=A/P
870 PRINT "YOU STARTED WITH 10 ACRES PER PERSON AND ENDED WITH"
875 PRINT L;"ACRES PER PERSON.": PRINT
880 IF P1>33 THEN 565
885 IF L<7 THEN 565
890 IF P1>10 THEN 940
892 IF L<9 THEN 940
895 IF IF P1>3 THEN 960
896 IF L<10 THEN 960
900 PRINT "A FANTASTIC PERFORMANCE!!! CHARLEMAGNE, DISRAELI, AND"
905 PRINT "JEFFERSON COMBINED COULD NOT HAVE DONE BETTER!":GOTO 990
940 PRINT "YOUR HEAVY-HANDED PERFORMANCE SMACKS OF NERO AND IVAN IV."
945 PRINT "THE PEOPLE (REMAINING) FIND YOU AN UNPLEASANT RULER, AND,"
950 PRINT "FRANKLY, HATE YOUR GUTS!!": GOTO 990
960 PRINT "YOUR PERFORMANCE COULD HAVE BEEN SOMEWHAT BETTER, BUT"
965 PRINT "REALLY WASN'T TOO BAD AT ALL. ";INT(P*.8*RND(1));"PEOPLE"
970 PRINT "DEARLY LIKE TO SEE YOU ASSASSINATED BUT WE ALL HAVE OUR"
975 PRINT "TRIVIAL PROBLEMS."
990 PRINT: FOR N=1 TO 10: PRINT CHR$(7);: NEXT N
995 PRINT "SO LONG FOR NOW.": PRINT
999 END
```

Fig. 1.3 Extract from *Hammurabi*'s BASIC code, indicating possible game endings
(Ahl, 1973).

the central part of their central processing unit (CPU). Microchips would soon replace
the cumbersome transistor-reliant minicomputers and mainframes, which, in turn, had
replaced earlier vacuum-tube mainframes.

Still, the gaming world had to wait until 1992 for the next economic simulation or,
as I should rather say, the very first city-building game set in the ancient world: *Caesar*.
The *Caesar* franchise, which saw four titles released between 1992 and 2004, took its
inspiration from one of the all-time classics of PC gaming: 1989's *SimCity*. Designed by
Will Wright of the iconic game studio Maxis Software, *SimCity* cast the player in the
role of mayor of a modern city that they had to build from scratch. It was a strictly
process-oriented game in the typology proposed by Egenfeldt-Nielsen, Smith and
Tosca, as there was no specific game objective other than the creation of a functioning
and prosperous city. An expansion pack released in 1991 and tantalizingly entitled
Ancient Cities offered the possibility of building 'historical' cities, although the
modifications done to the original were entirely cosmetic.

The *Caesar* franchise, developed and released by Sierra Entertainments, brazenly
copied *SimCity* and its cult-classic sequel *SimCity 2000* (1993). As with the *Ancient Cities*
expansion pack, the changes were only superficial: instead of police precincts, the player
had to build 'prefect bureaus' to ensure public safety; instead of industrial or commercial
zones, they had to provide 'markets'. Other aspects of the game remained even superficially
unchanged (except for the graphics): 'public schools' and 'hospitals', for instance, were
anachronistically still available to the player. In fact, as I have shown elsewhere, the
fundamental problem of the series was that it was a carbon copy of *SimCity* and the
theories of urban life and urban politics that lay at the foundation of that game – more a
simulation of 1980s Reaganomics than of ancient life.[33] Fundamental and distinctive
aspects of ancient city life were not incorporated or were ignored in favour of significant
landmarks of antiquity: slavery is nowhere present, but, naturally, the Colosseum is.[34]

Other games in the *Caesar* mould, such as *Pharao* (1999), *Cleopatra: Queen of the Nile* (2000), *Zeus: Master of Olympus* (2000) and *Poseidon: Master of Atlantis* (2001), released by the same studio, graphically adapted the game to different ancient civilizations, but regardless of whether they were set in ancient Rome or a fantastical version of Atlantis, the games played in an identical fashion. Nowhere, for instance, does the player in *Pharao* and *Cleopatra: Queen of the Nile* have to take the annual flooding of the great river – the basis of ancient Egypt's economy – into account, although the settlements they manage border the Nile and it would have been easy to incorporate the occasional flooding into the gameplay. Indeed, all of the games listed above are similar in that they confront players with intermittent challenges: barbarian invasion or fires, for instance.

After *Caesar IV*, (ancient) historical city-building games and economic simulations went out of fashion and the intervening years have seen few titles of this genre (e.g. *Grand Ages: Rome*). This will perhaps change soon, when one of the most interesting projects (from the perspective of the scholar of the ancient world) of recent years will come to fruition in 2019. *Builders of Egypt*, developed almost single-handedly by Polish programmer Jacek Turek, is nearing its Alpha-release phase and, according to the official press kit will be 'an economic type of city building [game] taking place in the valley of the Nile'.[35] The game, which has been developed with the input of Classicists and Egyptologists,[36] promises to be a modern adaptation of a classic game genre and will hopefully not only boast of impressive graphics but also of an intricate simulative model. In fact, as pioneering research of recent years has emphasized, there is not so vast a difference between the simulative processes used in video games and those used in academic research, such as in what is known in (digital) archaeology as agent-based modelling. According to Shawn Graham, one of the foremost digital archaeologists, 'an agent-based model is, in fact, just a special class of video game where the player, in point of fact, does not play. She sets it all up and then sits back to watch and see how that world reacts'.[37] As anybody who has ever played *SimCity 2000*, let the machine run the simulation overnight and then awakened to either a thriving megalopolis or an unrecognizable cesspit of crime and poverty knows, this is the very essence of city-building games, a genre that could conceivably be at the very crossroads of video games and digital humanities – a meeting point for which Andrew Reinhard has since elaborated the concept of 'Archaeogaming': 'Procedurally generated cities could give us a deeper insight into the life of ancient cities, if we can but frame our understandings in the code of the game'.[38]

'How many legions for you?'[39] Strategy games

As the work of, among others, Jeremiah McCall has shown, video games that centre on military conflict (i.e. strategy games) also have the potential to advance our understanding (if not our knowledge) of ancient battle, as well as to prove helpful in communicating this understanding.

The strategy game genre was tellingly invented in 1980 for the personal home computer. Arguably the first genre title (or, at least, the first commercially published one) was *Computer Bismarck* for TRS-80 and Apple II, a simulation of the famous German battleship's short-lived career. As is common for strategy games, the main game interface of this turn-based strategy game is a tactical map depicting the North Atlantic. The game is not now generally known, nor are the very first strategy games set in ancient Rome: *Legionnaire* (1982, see Fig. 1.4) and *Annals of Rome* (1986; see Fig. 1.5).

Both titles are among the earliest examples of two specific subgenres of strategy games that are set in the ancient world: turn-based (TBS) or real-time strategy (RTS) games, and the so-called '4X games'.

The most famous franchise of TBS games is perhaps *Panzer General*, released by studio behemoth Strategic Simulations (not coincidentally also the releasing studio of *Computer Bismarck*) from 1994 to 2000, that featured turn-based Second World War battles on hexagonal grids and became the inspiration for a large variety of imitations.[40] Though turn-based strategy titles have been supplanted by real-time strategy (RTS) games (in which both combat simulations and tactical decision occur in real-time) starting with 1992's popular *Dune II*, the genre has enjoyed steady popularity. As McCall's chapter in this volume shows, recent titles such as *Field of Glory 2* (2017) and *Numantia* (2017) are noteworthy for depicting extremely intricate and realistic combat models of ancient armies.[41] As is the case for TBS games, RTS games are also simulations of military conflict, typically as tactical battles. In contrast to the slower, more deliberate turn-based gameplay, RTS games see tactical battles play out 'live', with players having to react and adapt to battlefield conditions as these develop. The genre is commonly held to have originated with a classic video game, *Dune II*, released in 1992 by industry legend Westwood Studios. However, the RTS genre had its beginning much earlier, as early, in fact, as 1982, with the release of *Legionnaire* by Avalon Hill. The game was designed by creator Chris Crawford as an unofficial 'sequel' to *Eastern Front 1941*, which had been released a year earlier with similar (crude) graphics. The turn-based

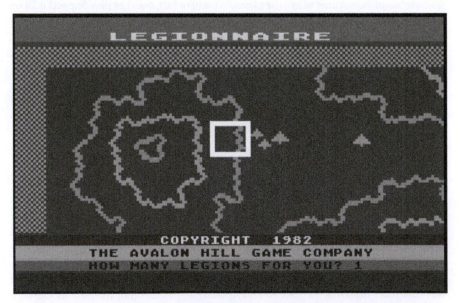

Fig. 1.4 Opening screen of *Legionnaire* on an Atari 800 computer, depicting a wooded hill as battleground in ancient Gaul (1982 © Chris Crawford/Avalon Hill).[42]

gameplay of that earlier title had been replaced, however, with a real-time AI opponent in battles set during Caesar's conquest of Gaul.

In contrast, the 1986 *Annals of Rome* (Fig. 1.5) belongs to the second-largest subdivision of the strategy genre: '4X games', wherein the 'X's stand for 'eXplore, eXpand, eXploit, and eXterminate'.[43] These games are among the most popular historical video games, as players guide the fates of empires or nation-states through history. Kevin Schut has succinctly summarised the appeal of this genre in a 2007 paper for *Games and Culture*: 'History textbooks claim that Julius Caesar conquered Gaul in a series of campaigns stretching from 58 BC to 51 BC. But when I did it, I used my general Quintus the Mighty, and I captured Alesia by 240 BC.'[44] While 4X strategy games are rarely what one would call 'easy' or 'casual', there are significant differences in complexity and, for want of a better word, 'realism'.[45] Titles such as *Total War: Rome II* or the famously intricate games of Paradox Entertainment (*Europa Universalis IV*, *Imperator: Rome*) place players at the helm of city-states, empires, or nation-states, others, such as the *Civilization* franchise take place on an even broader scale, with players influencing and changing world history on a monumental scale.[46]

Annals of Rome (Fig. 1.5) is somewhat different from other entries in the genre, in that world conquest is not the prime goal. Instead, players are asked to survive as long as possible and to keep the Roman Empire intact in the face of constant challenges and revolts. Despite its surprisingly complex game mechanics that emphasised economics and personnel management (i.e. recruiting and managing generals and senators), the game was not well received upon release.[47]

It has rightly been said that:

> most historical digital games [...] almost exclusively focus on politics, economics, and war. Strategy games that are historical simulators almost always have an economic component and frequently have a political dimension as well. [...] More blatant than the two themes of economics and politics, however, is the centrality of war [...]; war is the raison d'être.[48]

Although the author was talking about historical video games in general, his conclusion is no less valid (indeed, even more so) for historical games set in the ancient world in general. There are exceedingly few games about antiquity that, if not set in a military context per se, do not feature violence and conflict as an integral part of gameplay. The inherently agonistic principle of games – which are played against an opponent, be they software algorithms or another human player – thus comingle with a perceived notion of an ancient world steeped in violence and war. Perhaps this should not surprise us. The perception of ancient cultures as militarized or even militaristic, particularly in the case of Rome, has a long tradition in western culture: ancient generals such as Alexander or Julius Caesar have long been seen as the epitome of military success across a wide variety of media, from popular history literature, to documentaries, to Hollywood cinema and historical novels. Hence, ancient battles and generals also play an outsized role in the depiction of Antiquity in video games, the developers and publishers of which have long since recognized that the 'fights historical' are a strong sales draw.

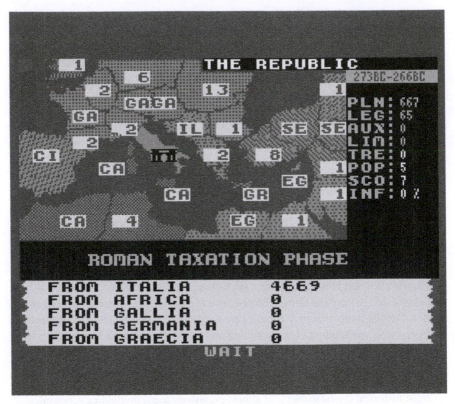

Fig. 1.5 *Annals of Rome* gameplay on a Sinclair ZX Spectrum computer (1986 © Level 9 Computing/Personal Software Services).[49]

Perhaps the quintessential strategy games set in the ancient world are *Rome: Total War* (2004), its sequel, *Total War: Rome II* (2013), and the various add-on, expansion packs and DLCs that have appeared since.[50] In these games, the player assumes responsibility for an ancient city-state or polity and must attempt to guide it through the centuries, increasing its military and economic might and ultimately conquering large swathes of the Mediterranean world. On the 'strategic' map of *Total War: Rome II*, which shows the Mediterranean as well as its neighbouring territories, a total of 117 polities are represented. They control a sum of 173 individual regions, each with its own principal settlement. By conquering a region, the player can access that regions economic and military resources, constructing relevant buildings and recruiting different military units (of which there are more than 500 different kinds in the game). War and conquest are the primary driving factors of the game. This is reflected in the infrastructure buildings that are available to the player: even those buildings that have no obvious military connections, such as temples, are nevertheless integrated into a holistic war economy. Fisheries provide food to the populace, which can then grow; an increase in population means an increase in available building projects, taxes and recruits. Building a temple to Mars provides the player's armies with moral bonuses. Once the player has recruited their troops, they must then move them across the strategic map to conquer opposing provinces in round-based play; when they encounter an enemy army, a tactical battle screen is triggered, the topography of which reflects the situation as it presents itself on the strategic map. Battles can either be fought, in which case the game switches to real-time tactical battle (for which, again, see Jeremiah McCall's chapter), or the result calculated.

While it is technically speaking possible to play the game without aggressively expanding, continued peace is virtually impossible as the player faction is sooner or later attacked by other expanding powers. The game incorporates a 'Diplomacy' mode that allows the player to enter into alliances or peace treaties with other factions; while this can sometimes be of help, it is not possible to achieve the game's objectives solely through diplomatic means. Thus, *Total War*, and 4X games in general, recycle notions of the necessity of hegemonic order and perpetuate canonized and standardized narratives of history.[51] These narratives can be succinctly summarized as an endless cycle of infamous Great White Men successfully generalling their way into history, 'from Marathon to Waterloo in order categorical', in the words of W. S. Gilbert and A. Sullivan. History in the (in this sense very appropriately titled) *Total War* series is reduced to war or, rather: to the level of the individual, decisive battle as both marker and motor of historical processes.[52]

Action-adventure games[53]

This is not the case with action-adventure games, which function differently in terms of gameplay. The action-adventure moniker itself is a hybrid creation, as, originally, purely adventure games in the definition of Egenfeldt-Nielsen, Smith and Tosca, 'are characterized by requiring deep thinking and great patience. These skills are employed to participate in, or uncover, narratives that are often based on detective story templates. Typically, the player is represented by an individual character involved in a plot of mystery of exploration, and faces puzzles of various kinds.'[54] According to Ernest Adams in *Fundamentals of Game Design*, the term 'adventure game' is itself historical: it is 'short for *Adventure*-type game, meaning a game similar to the one named *Adventure* (sometimes referred to as *Colossal Cave*)'.[55] While city-building and strategy games derive a significant part of their fascination for players from the possibility of 'out-building' and 'out-generalling' historical figures, action-adventures, as the quintessential mainstay of video games, are typically centred on a narrative that the players themselves are instrumental in uncovering.

This is true, in a limited way, even for the earliest action or action-adventure titles set in the ancient world, such as *The Return of Heracles* (1983) or *The Battle of Olympus* (1988).[56]

In the first, players take on the role of, among other ancient heroes, Hercules, whose 12 labours provide the narrative framework of an adventure game that is a mixture between basic graphics and classic text-based adventures (Fig. 1.6 and Fig. 1.7). Both the graphic interface and the gameplay itself are crude, though at the time of publication, the game was lauded in an idiosyncratic review written in metre: 'Lively and colourful,

Fig. 1.6 *The Return of Heracles*, opening screen (1983 © Stuart Smith/Quality Software).

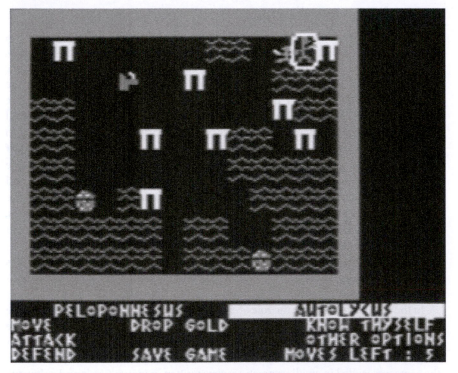

Fig. 1.7 *The Return of Heracles*, gameplay on an Apple IIe computer (1983 © Stuart Smith/Quality Software).

this game possesses a might / to be envied by others who try to share the same light. / The Return of Heracles is certainly no bust / and should be considered by gamers truly a must.'[57] Interestingly, other reviewers, while also lauding the 'colorful, fast-moving (!) joy-stick controlled graphic adventure', bemoaned the inaccuracies of the game's depiction of Greek mythology: 'Play it as a game, but don't think that it substitutes for actually reading the myths themselves.'[58]

If adventure games are, by their nature, perhaps less reliant on spectacular graphics than, for example, FPS titles, there is nevertheless a specific subset of adventure game, which is to say, action-adventures, that developed in tandem with technological innovations. Released five years after *The Return of Heracles*, *The Battle of Olympus* also takes place in a Greek mythological age: the player, in the role of Orpheus, must rescue his girlfriend Helene, who has been kidnapped by Hades. Though the game is optically similar to earlier 8-bit titles such as *Pandora's Palace* (1984) or *Kid Icarus* (1987), the similarities end there. While these early jump 'n' run games are reduced to the barest of backstories, *The Battle of Olympus* is a true precursor of modern action-adventures: the player is granted increasingly powerful skills by the gods of Olympus, who support him in his quest against the troublesome Hades. Side quests provide additional bonuses, thus allowing for gradual up-levelling.

As the genre developed throughout the 1980s and 1990s, from being purely text-based to including 2D bitmap graphics to the first three-dimensional action-adventures, such as *Alone in the Dark* (1992),[59] adventure games began to include more and more elements of action games. Perhaps the best illustration of this new hybrid genre of action-adventure games – and arguably the stand-out video game title of the 1990s – and the one most instrumental in establishing the popularity of the genre to this day, was *Tomb Raider* (1996), which introduced one of the most memorable characters in video game history to the public.[60] Lara Croft was a protagonist equipped with, among rather a lot else, a backstory and a personality that was to be further developed in no less than 18 game titles (as well as three movies and innumerable comics) released over more than two decades. As an intelligent, brave, and improbably resilient archaeologist – whose precise biography was subject to repeated change over the years – Lara Croft was both a puzzle-solver and a female action hero in a largely male-dominated decade. Her mission across all titles is an archetypical heroic quest, which, again according to game designer Ernest Adams, 'traditionally involves a movement from the familiar to the unfamiliar and from a time of low danger to a time of great danger'.[61] The quest is accomplished by solving puzzles (such as finding keys to locked doors, uncovering and interpreting clues, obtaining objects, collecting things, or navigating mazes) as well as by shooting people. Action-adventures such as *Tomb Raider* also typically feature sprawling gamescapes populated by large numbers of non-player-characters (NPCs), who both provide background atmosphere and essential plot points. Among the different video game genres, action-adventures perhaps most closely resemble Hollywood blockbusters: the avatars of such games are not merely hollow stand-ins for the players themselves. They are frequently characters with rich backstories and motivations, 'the hero of the story', true protagonists.[62]

Due to their similarity to movies, action-adventure games are well suited to portray narratives set in historical periods. In fact, some of the most critically acclaimed titles of the genre (or, indeed, of video games in general) are set in past societies: *Red Dead Redemption I–II* (2010–18), set in the American west of the late nineteenth century, and the *Assassin's Creed* franchise, whose individuals hail from periods as diverse as Classical Greece (*Assassin's Creed: Odyssey*, 2018), Hellenistic Egypt (*Assassin's Creed: Origins*, 2017), or Industrial Revolution London (*Assassin's Creed: Syndicate*, 2015). The *Assassin's Creed* franchise, in particular, has by now established itself as a dominant player on the global market, combining engaging gameplay, engrossing narratives, sympathetic characters and spectacular graphics. The two titles set in Antiquity are painstaking recreations of ancient settings, rich in atmosphere and surprisingly conscientious in detail. In both cases, players follow the typical action-adventure template: jarringly uprooted from their normal lives, the protagonists – which, for the first time, includes a female avatar in *Odyssey* – embark on a heroic quest to rid their world from the nefarious influence of a secret society (the Cult of Chaos in *Odyssey*, the forerunners of series-long antagonists, the Templars, in *Origins*). In doing so, players are given the opportunity to explore an enormous open-world ('sandbox') recreation of ancient Egypt and the Aegean, replete with reconstructions of ancient monuments, Easter eggs, and historical NPCs that act as guides, informers or antagonists. The *Assassin's Creed* franchise is well known for using historians and expert consultants to advise the developing team on background and archaeological detail and the result is an often surprisingly authentic image of ancient societies, even for the classical scholar.[63] It often depicts a very up-to-date scholarly consensus, though that is often intermingled with fantastical elements necessary in order to further a narrative that recounts the millennia-old story of a duel between opposing philosophies (Assassins vs. Templars), an advanced pre-human civilization (the Isu), and contemporary technology that allows the unlocking of 'genetic memory' (the Animus).

Thus, the very same game can veer quite abruptly from 'classical' adventure – although the two most recent *Assassin's Creed* titles have strayed into decidedly RPG territory – to science fiction, with scenes set in ancient worlds alternating with contemporary settings. In the 'ancient' setting, the depictions particularly of monuments and archaeological landmarks are recognizably influenced by state-of-the-art research. From the Pharos lighthouse in Alexandria (*Origins*) to the appropriately Periclean phase of the Athenian Acropolis (*Odyssey*), and from the myriad of NPCs speaking a hypothetical variant of ancient Egyptian based on Alan Gardiner's grammar (*Origins*) to the Greek statues and reliefs painted in a variety of vibrant colours (*Odyssey*), players versed in classical culture and ancient history can find much to be delighted about in these games. One can but wonder at the loving attention to detail in even the minutiae of the games, such as when attending a symposium at the home of Pericles in *Odyssey*. The guests include Herodotus, who functions as the player's guide throughout the game, Pericles' mistress Aspasia, Sophocles, Euripides, Aristophanes, Socrates, Thrasymachus, and Alcibiades. All are painted with a broad brush to reflect the most extreme aspects of the personalities associated with them: Aristophanes is the archetypical comic, disrespectful, but entertaining. Socrates and Thrasymachus are engaged in a philosophical discussion about the nature of statecraft. Alcibiades, the prime example of Athenian *jeunesse dorée*, pulls the player's avatar (regardless of their sex) into a tryst with a woman and, somewhat incongruously, a goat.

Antiquity, gamified

But the most interesting and fascinating aspect of *Origins* and *Odyssey* isn't the original and entertaining mixture of graphical opulence, ancient alien conspiracy theories, gripping narrative and the whimsical integration of historical personages and events. All these elements are typical of the *Assassin's Creed* franchise and are now more or less givens for action-adventure titles set in historical periods. What is special is the sheer scope of these games. The player is at complete liberty to either pursue the main narrative, a myriad of side-quests and individual missions, or to just go and explore a minutely reconstructed, living and breathing Greek world. In this, they are rather more similar to an RPG than to a run-of-the-mill action-adventure. The player's avatar levels-up with experience, can gather treasure and resources to craft new weapons and armour, with which to further explore a sandbox world of astonishing dimensions. They can do so on foot, on horse or at the helm of a small penteconter. They can explore Corinth, Thebes, the oracle of Delphi, the ruins of Akrotiri, Olympia, or the Asclepeion of Epidaurus. They can pursue the Minotaur in Knossos or play the pirate in the Aegean Sea. They can help people or oppress them, fight in the Peloponnesian War or become a soldier of fortune. The options are numerous and players actions can have consequences down the road.

In a pivotal scene in *Origins*, the player avatar, Bayek, enters the *soma*, the historical tomb of Alexander the Great in Alexandria to gaze, together with Cleopatra and Caesar, on the mummy of Alexander, enclosed in a crystal sarcophagus adorned with a Greek script that holds a clue to the further progress of the narrative. It is scenes such as this one that explain the fascination that games like *Assassin's Creed* exude for millions of players: they allow the person to participate in history, or even to (re)enact it.[64] It is this special blend of immersiveness, the open-ended, sandbox nature of the gamescape coupled with the impression of actually 'living' through history that make the *Assassin's Creed* titles such successes.

Beginning with *Origins*, Ubisoft has started to take advantage of the immersive nature of their games in different ways. With the release of the Discovery Tour, Ubisoft stripped its bestselling game of its core characteristic: narrative and fighting.[65] Instead, players are now free to roam the recreation of late-Hellenistic Egypt in peace, with 75 interactive tours added. These tours, created with the input of Egyptologists and classicists, are intended to teach players about the historical setting, its culture, language, social practices, architecture and history. As players have no objective, they are free to play the tourist, witnessing ancient practices of embalming, exploring the great pyramids of Gizeh or can return to the tomb of Alexander and learn what they can. The game mode provides pop-up dialogue, explanatory texts and background information, archaeological reconstructions, historical paintings or photographs. Mostly, however, players are free to glory in the visuals and sounds of ancient Egypt, turned into a digital, interactive museum. In effect, the game becomes a form of time travel, blurring the differences between history, games and heritage.

The 'history' of ancient history in video games is by no means at an end and this brief overview cannot cover each and every facet of the reception of ancient history in this particular medium. Nor does it mean to. There is much yet to be done in this area, many questions to ask and answers to find. How video games produce authenticity – and what exactly authenticity, as opposed to historical accuracy, *is* exactly, is an ongoing and lively discussion. Mutual influences between video games and other genres such as comics or movies are obvious in many instances but little-researched.[66] All this and much more is still to be examined. However, such analyses have to take into account not only the specific game at hand, the case study, but also the history of the genre itself, as well as the technological history of video games and the hardware it is played on. Genre definitions are also equally important, as they often come with very specific approaches to ancient history and historical processes in general. Not all genres are equal in terms of research possibilities. Economic simulations such as *Caesar* are well suited to study questions of accuracy vs. authenticity, but must also be studied with a view to the underlying assumptions coded in to the game's software. Strategy games, especially those of the 4X category, can be studied with regard to conceptions of history and technological and civilizational 'progress'. The Discovery mode of select action-adventure titles (such a mode has been announced for *Odyssey*, as well) can be used didactically, to introduce an audience to antiquity.[67] Other genres, including those that have been neglected in recent historical scholarship (and in this volume), may yield surprising results. Before *Apotheon*, if asked about particularly interesting examples of classical culture in video games, the side-scrolling jump-and-run genre would likely not have been anyone's first guess. The possibilities for further research are enticing. We have but started to scratch the surface.

Notes

1   Djaouti et al. (2011: 31–2).
2   The game can be played by modern audiences by way of online emulators such as the *PlayClassics* site (https://playclassic.games/game/play-the-oregon-trail-online/play (accessed 6 November 2018).
3   This video game classic has now been transformed into a popular culture meme: https://knowyourmeme.com/memes/you-have-died-of-dysentery (accessed 6 November 2018). For the concept of memes, see Shifman (2013b).
4   Magnet (2006).
5   Cf. Barton (2008). For text-based adventures, see also the chapter by Morley in this volume.
6   Poole (2000: 46).
7   Cf. English, Engelbart and Huddart (1965).
8   Mobile games: 41 per cent; and tablet games: 10 per cent. Cf. NEWZOO (2018). This is a significant increase from 2018, when mobile games only made up 27 per cent of the market (NEWZOO, 2017; the share of tablet games has remained steady).
9   See also the chapter by David Serrano Lozano in this volume and cf. Poole (2000: especially pp. 34 and 66–9), and particularly Schwingeler (2008: 103–46) for the importance of the adopted spatial perspective with regard to game genres.
10 Poole (2000: 35–58).
11 Wolf (2001: 113–34).
12 Sarkar (2014).
13 Varoufakis (2014).

14 As the relevant Wikipedia entry informs us, two alliances (the 'Clusterfuck Coalition' and 'Russian Alliances' vs the 'N3' and 'Pandemic Legion') fought a 21-hour battle, with significant economic fallout and over 11 trillion InterStellar Kredits (the in-game currency) being wiped out. The battle was part of a larger, ongoing conflict and, as many historical battles, was the result of minor happenstance. For an account of the events that led to the battle as well as for the real-life economic costs, see Moore (2014). As of August 2018, an even larger ongoing conflict is taking place (again, involving those apparently incorrigible troublemakers, the 'Pandemic Legion'); cf. Messner (2018).

15 Egenfeldt-Nielsen, Smith and Tosca (2008: 22–44, especially 43f.). Cf. Rauscher (2011: 28–38).

16 Chapman (2016: 56–89).

17 For the specifics of the 'realist' part of *Total War: Rome II* and the means by which audiovisual specificity and (claimed) accuracy is created, see Rollinger (2016).

18 Bender (2012).

19 For the controversy surrounding *Kingdom Come: Deliverance*, see Heinemann (2018).

20 According to the Statistics Portal 'statista', available at: https://www.statista.com/statistics/189592/breakdown-of-us-video-game-sales-2009-by-genre/ (accessed 6 November 2018).

21 Schwarz (2015: 439) and cf. ibid. (2012a) for earlier data. There is, as I said, no publicly available database of all historical video games, but for a significant sample, see the excellent French collection at: http://www.histogames.com (accessed 2 November 2018).

22 Schwarz (2012a: 11, fig. 1).

23 Ibid., 12, fig. 2.

24 Ibid., 14, fig. 3.

25 Cf. Serrano Lozano in this volume.

26 There exists a significant market for sports management games across platforms (though most titles have appeared for PC), with some franchises having existed since 1992. They often centre around beloved and lucrative sports (*Football Manager 2017*) or franchises MLB (*Out of the Park Baseball 18*), but also, idiosyncratically, more niche pursuits such as cycling (*Pro Cycling Manager 2017*).

27 See also Serrano Lozano in this volume.

28 Winnerling (2018). The *Sumerian Game* was not the only game developed as part of the project. Two further titles, *Sierra Leone Game* and *Free Enterprise Game*, were also created by 1967. For all three games, as well as a brief review of his practical findings on their use, see Moncreiff (1965) and Wing (1966, 1967).

29 39 of these slides, together with three teletype printouts of gameplay, are among the last physical remains of the game. They are archived as the *Sumerian Game* Collection of the Brian Sutton-Smith Library and Archives of Play (cf. Brian Sutton-Smith, 2016).

30 Winnerling (2018).

31 Ahl (1973). Modern-day audiences can play it by typing or copying the code into a BASIC emulator such as VintageBASIC, available at http://www.vintage-basic.net/index.html (accessed 6 November 2018).

32 Ahl (1973: 78).

33 Rollinger (2015).

34 There are occasional exceptions: in *Grand Ages: Rome* (2009), players have to take slavery into account and incorporate it into their economic models so as to successfully complete missions. For the import of the Colosseum in creating 'authenticity', see Lowe

(2009: 76), who sees its presence as part of a 'box-ticking approach' to antiquity, 'whereby certain highlights of the classical word (those firmly anchored in the popular imagination) must be present, regardless of chronological, geographical and other pragmatic constraints', to ensure that the players *know* they are in antiquity. Cf. also Rollinger (2016) with further references.

35 HAL Press Kit 2018, available online: http://www.hardancientlife.com/index.php/press-kit/147-hal-press-kit-eng (accessed 6 November 2018). The original name of the project was *Hard Ancient Life* (HAL) but this was changed in early 2019.

36 Cf. Rollinger (2018: 28–9).

37 Graham (2017a: at 05:25 timestamp); and cf. Graham (2017b).

38 Shawn Graham, private communication (7 March 2017). For various reasons, a contribution by Graham (entitled, 'We Built this City on Rock and Code: The Ancient City as Process') could not be included in this volume. The passage quoted above is from the abstract of this proposed chapter.

39 Opening screen message of *Legionnaire* (1982).

40 Strategic Simulations (also known as SSI) cornered the market for turn-based strategy games throughout the 1990s.

41 Turn-based strategy games also differ from RTS game, in that they can comfortably be played on gaming consoles, as the turn-based system put no time pressure on the player.

42 *Legionnaire* can be played by means of online emulators. This screenshot was taken from one instance of emulated play on an Atari 800 computer via: http://archive.org/details/a8b_Legionnaire_1982_Avalon_Hill_US_k_file (accessed 6 November 2018).

43 Cf. Ghita and Andrikopoulos (2009) for 4X games set in the ancient world. For definitions of strategy games, see Dor (2018).

44 Schut (2007: 213).

45 For the thorny issue of what is 'realistic' in 4X games (or 'simulations'), see, e.g., Köstlbauer (2013).

46 The *Civilization* franchise is among the most well-studied historical video games. Cf. Ford (2016) and Vrtačič (2014), with older literature.

47 Anon. (1987).

48 Schut (2007: 221).

49 *Annals of Rome* can be played by means of online emulators. This screenshot was taken from one instance of emulated play on a ZX Spectrum computer via: https://archive.org/details/zx_Annals_of_Rome_1986_PSS_a2 (accessed 4 May 2019).

50 They are also among the most frequent case studies for historians: cf. ibid., Lowe (2009), Ghita and Andrikopoulos (2009), Christesen and Machado (2010) and Coert (2018). See Gardner (2007) for a study of other strategy games set in the ancient world.

51 Reichert (2008: 192, and at p. 207: 'Sie recyceln hegemoniale Ordnungsvorstellungen politischer Macht und tradieren dabei kanonische sowie standardisierte Narrative der Geschichtsschreibung').

52 For the decisive battle paradigm, see, Harari (2007) and Loo (2009).

53 Though RPGs and their early predecessors, the MUDs ('multi-user dungeons'), could legitimately be classified as belonging to the adventure games genre, they are not included in this discussion, as there is no significant ancient world-based RPG.

54 Egenfeldt-Nielsen, Smith and Tosca (2008: 43).

55 Adams (2010: 546).

56 Playable at: https://archive.org/details/a2_Return_of_Heracles_1983_Stuart_Smith and https://emulatoronline.com/nes-games/the-battle-of-olympus/ (accessed 6 November 2018).
57 Lesser (1984: l and 49–52).
58 St. Andre (1984).
59 This title was also one of the originators of a significant subgenre, the survival horror action-adventure. Other titles include the *Resident Evil* and *Silent Hill* franchises.
60 For the storied history of *Tomb Raider*'s protagonist, Lara Croft, in academic discourse, see, e.g., Kennedy (2002) and MacCallum-Stewart (2014).
61 Adams (2010: 558).
62 Ibid., 547.
63 For Ubisoft's use of historical consultants, see Kamen (2014), Jenkin (2015, for *Assassin's Creed: Unity*), Sapieha (2017), Nielsen (2017, for *Origins*) and the recent short interview with Stéphanie-Anna Ruatta (for *Odyssey*) (http://archaeogaming. com/2019/04919/consulting-for-ubisoft-on-assassins-creed-odyssey (accessed 4 May 2019).
64 For gaming as historical re-enactment, see Rejack (2007).
65 Cf. the largely positive echo in popular media, MacDonald (2018) and Webster (2018).
66 For instance, the 'Spartan kick' is a powerful special move, available to players of *Assassin's Creed: Odyssey* that has to be unlocked by character progression. It is also obviously inspired by the famous 'This is Sparta!' scene in Zack Snyder's movie, *300*, which, in turn, is an almost frame-by-frame recreation of Frank Miller's eponymous graphic novel.
67 Porter (2018) and Crecente (2018).

Part One

A Brave Old World

Re-Figurations of Ancient Cultures

Ludus (Not) Over

Video Games and the Popular Perception of Ancient Past Reshaping

David Serrano Lozano

Cinema and video games were born as purely sensorial experiences and both developed to discover their own narrative possibilities and different tools of expression. However, video games developed in a world where cinema and, to a lesser extent, television, were the dominant channels for the creation of popular culture. Consequently, cinema and television posed an unavoidable reference for video games as a newly born audiovisual format.[1] Likewise, in the emerging field of classical reception, the strongest set of referential codes for popular classical reception up to the early aughts was the golden age of the *peplum* genre, the 1950s and 1960s.[2]

However, from the 1980s onwards, antiquity in video games was not directly employed as a historical referential frame, as was the case with movie adaptations. Responding to the ludic needs (mainly environmental and narrative) that were raised through the evolution of hardware, formats and genres, antiquity in video games would have been initially employed as a (pseudo)historical alibi as was the case with cinema,[3] which provided a convenient, pre-established context and a set of referential codes within which to set certain games. The progressive intertwining of antiquity and gaming preconfigured the mimetic, referential and re-enacting nature of classical reception in video games,[4] and consequently pre-configured the (current) state of the issue. The development of this internal evolution of video games constitutes the epistemological distinction between filmed and digitally played classical reception. Video games have obviously borrowed cinematic techniques throughout their evolution,[5] and certain clear and direct references can be identified in games before the twenty-first century.[6] However, the use of antiquity in video games was not developed as a reference to or heritage from *peplum*. This could explain why direct screen-to-video game adaptations were not found until well into the 1990s (e.g. Disney's *Hercules*, 1997; *Xena: Warrior Princess*, 1999). It could also be the reason why the genre canon of antiquity in gaming, i.e. the ludic space which the ancient world would occupy within games, was defined at an early stage. Throughout the existence of video games, antiquity has been displayed within a broad yet consistent range of genres:

- Real-time strategy (RTS), turn-based strategy (TBS) and 4X (eXplore, eXpand, eXploit, and eXterminate) games, based on aerial views or maps that recreate long-range campaigns (e.g. *Legionnaire*, 1982; *Annals of Rome*, 1986; *Legions of Death*, 1987) and/or specific battlefields (e.g. *Centurion: Defender of Rome*, 1990; *Warrior of Rome (Caesar no Yabou)*, 1991).[7]
- Economic simulations or city-building games on a global, regional and/or local scale, developing and expanding a city, a region or a polity (e.g. *Hammurabi*, 1978; *Populous: The Beginning*, 1998; *Caesar*, 1992).
- (Action)-adventure games, scrolling jump-and-runs, first-person shooters (FPS), role-playing games (RPGs) and massively multiplayer online role-playing games (MMORPGs), following the steps of a single, mostly male, main character, defined as a warrior, hero or simply player's avatar (*The Return of Heracles*, 1983; *Pandora's Palace*, 1984; *Kid Icarus*, 1986; *The Battle of Olympus*, 1988; *Myth: History in the Making*, 1989).

These three genres encompass the vast majority of depictions of the ancient world in video games since the very beginning of the medium itself.[8] This set of depictions could be interpreted as the intersection between video games' need for narrative and interactive dynamics, and the search for semiotic, visual, and cultural references to mediate the creation of a new game project. The use of antiquity as a reference within early titles was thus not likely undertaken for reasons of historical or cultural importance, but rather because of the inherent possibilities and restrictions of early video game developing. However, intentionally or not, they were starting to develop exercises of meaning-creation from the past (i.e. 'making' history)[9] through play,[10] as well as setting the foundations for new referential codes for contemporary popular perceptions of Antiquity. These foundations would not be effectively altered even after the first great milestone of classical reception in both video games and cinema: the year 2000. For cinema, this date represented the beginning of the twenty-first-century *peplum* following the release of *Gladiator*.[11] On the part of video games, it signified the arrival of the sixth generation of consoles, together with the revolution in 3D-rendering and graphic processors (GeForce, ATi Radeon or DirectX series). This technology would lead to a whole new world of possibilities in visual (*God of War*, 2005), spatial (*Grand Theft Auto III*, 2001) and narrative (*Metal Gear Solid 2: Sons of Liberty*, 2001) display.[12]

The twenty-first century's closer interchange between cinema and video games has led to the display of action sequences, photography or cinematically influenced semiotic elements, with visual cues such as Spartan warriors,[13] Maximus' gladiatorial helmet,[14] or referential catchphrases.[15] This intensified transmediatic relationship has also introduced an undeniable new stage in the popular reception of classical antiquity in video games. However, this should not be considered a holistic change. Popular game series such as *Imperium*, *God of War*, *Caesar* or *Rome: Total War*, though technologically more advanced, respond to the very same intrinsic relationship between ludic needs and (para)historical references as in video games from the 1980s and 1990s. The post-2000 period has implied a continuation and progress – not an alteration – of the nature of classical reception in video games.[16] After almost forty years, video games have developed their own way of creating meaning out of the representation of antiquity, and do not simply imitate movies,[17] despite their undeniably mutual relationship. This may suggest either a self-consistent subset within historical video games, a still early stage of an ongoing development,[18] or perhaps both.

The most remarkable change after the turn of the century, rather than the modification of the general scope of video games, may, in fact, be the development of a new subgenre. This centres on the use of antiquity as a 'cosmetic' layer of history in a set of gaming mechanics marked by simple and cyclic spatial action through a dynamic of competition and progression, for example in gladiatorial fights (*Colosseum: Road to Freedom*, 2005; *Gladiator Begins*, 2010; *Spartacus Legends*, 2013; *Age of Gladiators*, 2016) or chariot races (*Circus Maximus: Chariot Wars*, 2002; *Chariot Wars*, 2015; *Ben-Hur*, 2016). Player competence, progression and spatial action are generally essential elements in all video games, but titles set in the past usually include a framing narrative recreating a historical context and development.[19] Within this newer subgenre, however, there is hardly any (real or fictive) time progression. Player's ludonarrative[20] development through framing narrative fragments[21] is not truly defined by time (historical or individual), but by ascendant progression (upgrading, levels and greater difficulty). This use of history as a self-explanatory aesthetic background is rather exclusive to the reception of the ancient world, especially in upmarket video games, while prehistoric, medieval, modern or contemporary settings mostly count on a (real or fictive) time progression or context. This phenomenon can be linked to the vast and complex set of referential codes that have been (re)negotiated and (re)transmitted in successive exercises of classical reception ever since the Renaissance. Five centuries of metonymic, mimetic and representational interpretations in painting, architecture, opera, literature, cinema and TV (among other media) have made antiquity one of the most tokenistic historical contexts.[22] Manifold popular, academic and artistic receptions have,[23] over the years, resulted in a complex mosaic of 'virtual memory places',[24] which video games employ as semiotic codes of reference.[25]

Focus and scale: God vs human-scale games

In two seminal works, Robert Rosenstone (1995) and Marcus Junkelmann (2004) each proposed syntheses of the main features of *peplum* as a cinematographic genre, most of which can also be extended to twenty-first-century titles.[26] An analogous analysis for video games portraying antiquity should yield positive results, considering the internal consistency of this video game 'subgenre'. However, a primary consideration must first be noted, bearing in mind the dual semiotic and mechanical nature of video games.[27] While every film genre can potentially employ and refer to a common range of visual and narrative devices (montage, photography, performance, plot), differences among individual video game genres (RPG, FPS, action-adventure, economic simulation) are the result of not only narrative, but also of different ludic and interactive formats, mechanics, structures, and tools. Therefore, the channels and forms through which ancient historical meaning is expected to be aimed at (and received by) players are intrinsically dissimilar in terms of concepts, speech, scope, etc. In other words, there exist fundamental differences between genres that have no parallel among those of the cinematic. This suggests an initial differentiation into two main categories of analysis for classical (or historical) reception in video games:

- God games (including TBS, RTS, 4X, economic simulation and city-building games),[28] defined by the use of 'maps as organizing structures, as portals into the narrative, rather than merely as illustrations'.[29]
- Human-scale games (including FPS, (action)-adventure games, RPGs, MMORPGs and scrolling jump-and-runs), marked by the use of avatars as the main tool for ludonarrative development.

Though influenced by Uricchio's categories for historical games,[30] these subsets will not only be considered according to their display of historical contexts and processes, but also their dissimilar implications in terms of ludonarrative[31] and classical reception.[32] Classification criteria are based here on spatial and time displays, since these can be considered as a projection of historical and analytical concepts of *scale* and *focus*.

Scale, as the geographical and temporal extension and impact of historical processes under analysis, is usually tackled in two markedly different ways. In God games, the map/board is the entirety of the visual and interactive display of the gamescape,[33] and time is generally stretched along large units through the use of tools that alter the perception of its passing.[34] Human-scale games portray an individual perspective of the gamescape during gameplay (maps tend to be tools for orientation and transportation) and individual lifetimes generally frame the whole of gametime. It is true that historical meaning can be made from local- or individual-scale processes in God games, and human-scale ones can address (gaming) world-scale realities; however, these are not the prevailing displays of time and space in each category.

The video game equivalent of *focus*, as the referential point of attention from and through which historical meaning is developed, would be the player's point of view. A player's development of ludonarrative, their role as a second author in video game creation,[35] is to some extent analogous to a historian's labour placing a specific focus of attention within a historical discourse.[36] God games mostly place their *focus* on large-scale historical processes and abstract analytical concepts portrayed as framing controls (e.g. HUDs).[37] Meanwhile, human-scale games' *focus* employs the player's avatar as both the main source and the means for the creation of historical meaning, generally out of individual or small-collective processes. While in God games the development and impact of large-scale processes are continuously in the player's sight – and their individual or local layer must be interpreted – global-scale processes in human-scale games are usually to be interpreted according to a ludonarrative that is mostly fixed on an individual perspective.

It is on the basis of these analytic criteria that I intend to outline the main objective of this contribution. Far from aiming at a definitive conclusion, this study intends to show specific examples of the emerging and distinctive slants which video games are setting in the reception of the classical world. Being such determinant epistemological features, *focus* and *scale* must (among other components) be considered when analysing academic historical studies, and there is also an imperative to consider these two factors in the creation of historical meaning in video games. Consequently, the following sections are conceived as case examples that contribute to defining an answer to the question of how video games are affecting the redefinition of the perception/reception of the ancient world.

Classical reception in video games: A set of features

A middle ground between alien and familiar

Antiquity has a quite singular position in pop-cultural perception. It is generally understood as a great *totum*, a 'foreign country'[38] with which it is possible to feel some personal identification but is simultaneously dissimilar from present time. It thus represents a conceptual place between the familiar and the alien. Pre- or proto-history are also marked by a popular conceptualization as wholes, with scarce attention paid to chronological or geographical variances, while modern or contemporary ages tend to count on a greater level of accuracy and familiarity, placing them in closer relation to the present. The ancient world has developed a sort of middle-ground relationship with popular culture of the twentieth and twenty-first centuries through the reception and perception of its material culture.

Concerning its reception, this middle-ground condition has been built and strengthened with tools such as presentism,[39] projection or analogy. A history of self-identification with antiquity can be traced from the Middle Ages through to modern-day TV productions, via the European Enlightenment and/or national histories. Spectators have historically been provided with tools and tokens to perceive diverse ancient contexts, individuals or events as familiar tropes, defined by concepts, topics or mottos (which by no means imply historical accuracy).[40] Conversely, classical reception has simultaneously reinforced the (un)conscious idea of antiquity as a fascinating 'foreign country', a comprehensible but inevitably dissimilar context from the spectator's own reality. Furthermore, facets of antiquity such as sexuality, religion,[41] technology or food have been explored to stress the border between the habits and customs of ancient and contemporary societies (e.g. Pompeii's secret cabinet, the persecution of Christians in historical paintings or grotesques as a visual tool in recent cinema and TV titles).[42]

Regarding the perception of ancient material culture, the intermediate position between familiar and alien is the result of both historical distance and the specific channels of diffusion aimed at contemporary observers. Ancient material culture displays a particularly visual variety and a fascination for contemporary eyes:[43] temples, aqueducts, pyramids, panoplies or hieroglyphics are just a few examples of canonized visual references, either through their direct (museums, tourism) or indirect reception (documentaries, movies, books). Simultaneously, the recognition of these references as 'ancient' is inevitably connected with their perception as ruins, i.e. not as 'living', present parts of material life. Ancient material culture is mostly non-familiar (i.e. not intertwined with contemporary material culture), while a considerable amount of medieval (castles, churches), modern (palaces, fortresses) or contemporary (factories, homes) buildings belong to current urban configurations. This contributes to their perception as becoming more familiar the closer they are to the present time. The interweaving of past and present (alien becoming domestic) is very scarce in the case of ancient remains which, even when inserted into urban landscapes, are usually conceived of as *ruins*.[44]

The implicitly re-enacting immersion of video games[45] helps to diminish the alien component by bringing antiquity into a (virtually) functional, living, original-like state. Alien contexts, recognizable thanks to player's virtual memory places,[46] are thus brought closer to his or her daily familiarity: a real-life ruin becomes a building, musealia appear as working tools. However, despite this potential for familiarity, the middle-ground condition has been inherited and reshaped in played antiquity.[47] The means for displaying the alien in video game antiquity is predominantly based more on historical differentiations than on components such as science fiction or fantasy.[48] For developers, the ancient stands for an environmental and narrative context wherein the fictional and the real (alien and domestic) are mutually compatible, without disruptive perceptions. The *Assassin's Creed* saga has carried out this combination of alien (science fiction and supernatural) and familiar (projection from and towards the present) in several historical contexts. In fact, this combination of science fiction and supernatural elements with the ancient world is one of the distinctive hallmarks of the *Assassin's Creed* series. For the most part, there is little combination of the supernatural (in the widest sense) and historical periods after the Middle Ages in video games. Rather, there is a distinct tendency on the part of developers to construct prehistoric (or medieval-ish) framing contexts for games that are, at their core, non-historical or fantastical (e.g. *Far Cry Primal*, 2016; *The Witcher 3: Wild Hunt*, 2015; *The Elder Scrolls IV: Oblivion*, 2006). Nevertheless, antiquity clearly stands out in relation to this angle.

Alien or supernatural elements in ancient contexts are generally more pronounced in human-scale games (e.g. *Apotheon*, 2015). This is likely due to the inherent possibilities of genres such as action-adventure games for referring to mythological elements in combination with fantasy and the supernatural (*The Return of Heracles*, 1983; *Pandora's Palace*, 1984; *Mytheon*, 2011; *God of War*, 2005).[49] God games, for their part, tend to bring historical authenticity to the fore (e.g. *Annals of Rome*, 1986; *Cohort: Fighting for Rome*, 1991; *Rome: Total War*, 2004), despite the existence of certain exceptions such as *Zeus: Master of Olympus* (2000), *Poseidon: Master of Atlantis* (2001) or *Age of Mythology* (2002). The tools for developing familiarity in human-scale games are mostly based on human components (ideas, family, emotions) and visual authenticity (on which, see below). The latter, however, is combined in God games with the display of large-scale historical processes,[50] dynamics and structures on a presentistic (or anachronistic) base, as has been noted with *Civilization*,[51] *Total War*[52] or *Caesar*.[53] God games set markers of historical differences between the ancient and the contemporary more subtly, employing the same resources as with any other historical context. Such resources are based on the nature of their (usually) numerous framing tools: differences in cultural principles or technologies, together with perceivable contrasts in aesthetics through time compression, remind players of the (not only chronological) distance between that 'foreign country' and their own, though this factor is smaller regarding human-scale games.

Diffused iconicity

The average observer will probably have rather predictable visual associations with ancient characters and concepts such as Spartacus, Cleopatra, Mark Antony, gladiators or chariot racing. By no means is this a phenomenon exclusive to cinema, though it has been accelerated by the cinematic reception of antiquity. Movies have an extraordinary capacity for the creation of visual icons,[54] especially through their imaging of individual characters. Though video games also have an undeniably iconic capacity,[55] they function differently from cinema in this regard. Since this issue demands a much more complex treatment than the limits of this section allow, I will attempt to illustrate this transmediatic contrast in the reception of antiquity between cinema and video games through case studies.

As the only historical period whose cinematic portrayal can be identified as a sub-genre on its own with three different stages of production,[56] antiquity has come to develop a notable number of icons.[57] However, it would be rather more difficult to think of any iconic element linked to antiquity from video games, with perhaps the exception of the main character of the *God of War* series, Kratos. This character's distinguishing physical features and panoply[58] have made him a sufficiently recognizable and content-filled icon. Kratos' case is a particularly useful touchstone for analysing this contrast in iconicity through the role of individual characters.

Characters, constantly in the audience's sight while viewing as (mostly) external observers, are one of the main narrative tools in cinema. Their iconic potential is determined, to a great extent, precisely by this near constant attention and visuality. Video games are quite the opposite. God games, even those which display prominent characters, tend not to develop a particularly notable visuality for them. Even when depicted, they do not usually embody a particularly outstanding visual or performative presence, depriving them of iconic potential. In human-scale games, the *focus* comes from the player's (and thus the character's) point of view.[59] The visuality of protagonists is thus denied in first-person games during gameplay (although not during those moments outside the player's agency, such as cinematic cutscenes, menus, etc.), or limited to fixed points in third-person ones. These conditions are notably deleterious to video games characters' iconicity, so that for them to become visually striking, identifiable and meaningful icons, a considerable set of distinguishing physical features must be established. This is the case with Kratos. In addition, the *God of War* series' main character benefits from a wide range of camera movements designed around him as the central figure during gameplay sequences, bringing the game's spatial portrait a step closer to the cinematic.[60] Kratos is almost constantly in the player's sight, both during gameplay and cinematic cutscenes, displaying distinguishing physical characteristics and accessories. His presentation is thus rather similar to the iconic characters of *peplum*.

Concerning non-character icons, let us consider one of the pioneering *peplum* films, *Cabiria* (1914). This movie produced an enduring visual icon in the shape of the famous statue and temple of Moloch (both central figures in most of the movie posters), which established them as the cinematographic 'epitome of Carthage',[61] further influencing titles such as *Metropolis* (1927).[62] From such an early starting point, *pepla* have repeatedly shown their outstanding power to fix visual archetypes: *Ben-Hur*'s chariot races, Cleopatra's entrance into Rome, gladiatorial fights in the Colosseum. Video games have scarcely (if ever) developed such solid, non-character iconic elements. The main factor when trying to explain this difference would be the diverse ways in which each medium makes use of environments, sceneries and props. Non-character icons in *pepla* count on a central, magnified position in their respective narratives and/or on recurrent, highlighted exposition on screen, underlining their outstanding nature and confronting spectators with their visuality. The specific weight of the spatial element in historical video games[63] leads to a continuous use of movement and spatial action.[64] This is hardly compatible with focusing (i.e. fixing) attention on a specific sequence, set, or physical element for any extended gaming or cinematic time. An outstanding element is usually only briefly highlighted among a vast and complex range of lexia,[65] which can easily blur its potential specific weight, both in God games and human-scale ones. Even the most important lexia show difficulties in achieving a similar degree of attention as their cinematic counterpart could, at least without significant risk of interrupting the pace of the game.

Thus, in marked contrast to cinematic portrayals of the ancient world, the 'played antiquity' of historical video games struggles with the notable limitation of the medium for its ability to produce visual, archetypical icons as a semiotic tool of classical reception. The visual impact of video games on players is undeniable,[66] but the visual relationship between player and avatars, and the density of visual components, make it comparatively more difficult for a specific piece of lexia to stand out as a fully developed, meaningful icon. Most of the visual memory of lexia in video games is linked to its interactive role and dynamic of use. Video games visual semiotics thus produce a diffused iconicity, in contrast with the more static and archetypical icons of cinematic portrayals, which can successfully generate fixed images filled with content.

Visual semantics as prevailing authenticity tool

Authenticity is one of the key concepts developed in the historiography of historical games studies. Thanks to the development of additional analytical concepts such as *affective history*,[67] a consistent historiographical consensus has been developed on *authenticity* in video games. This is understood as the creation of historical content which, regardless of its factual accuracy, is perceived as credible and acceptable by the player.[68]

Numerous attempts have been made to analyse how *authenticity* is developed in video games – among them the chapter by Andrew Gardner and Tristan French in this volume – and many more are likely to follow.[69] Here, rather than an ontological analysis, I propose to undertake a comparison between the mechanisms of creating *authenticity* in cinema and video games.[70] Though affective history and *authenticity* have also been applied to classical reception analysis in cinema,[71] I posit the existence of a different proportion in the mechanisms of *authenticity* in video games, namely the specific weight of narrative and the aesthetics within them.

Characters and their narratives (principles, motivations, behaviours, outcomes) certainly stand out as *authenticity* tools in *peplum*.[72] Since historical authenticity is only accepted if it suits the audience's pre-established set of cultural codes and expectancies,[73] the factual exposition and 'realistic' behaviour of characters are essential, despite the undeniable importance of props. As an example, consider the contrast in the portrayal of Alexander the Great or Leonidas in largely biographical movies separated by roughly half a century: *Alexander the Great* (1956) and *Alexander* (2004), *The 300 Spartans* (1962) and *300* (2007).[74] The marked differences in the portrayal of these characters' principles and actions is a response to the (re)adaptation for two different kinds of audiences and are representative of cinema's struggle to 'meet genre- and audience-imposed expectations', following Winnerling's definition of affective historicity in video games.[75]

While character arcs and their narratives tend to be developed alongside the films' progression, video games are only able to rely on relatively few, short cinematic cut-scenes for this purpose.[76] The ludonarrative dynamics of gaming dictate that much of the character development in films must, in the case of video games, happen in other ways, such as player progression and mission accomplishment. Visuals and gaming aesthetics must thus bear an additional responsibility as historical authenticity tools.[77] In fact, historical authenticity in video games has been linked to a hypermediatic 'graphic opulence'.[78]

The transformation of the observer's engagement with antiquity – from being watched to being played – necessarily implies a redefinition by developers and a re-understanding by players on the basis of aesthetics as the predominant field of referential codes. This can be illustrated by comparing the incidence of fan-fiction and modding, the two main trans-media engagement strategies developed, respectively, after movies and video games.[79] Both fan-fiction and modding can be understood as an audience's attempt to expand and/or redefine a referential work, to provide it with elements and take it to narrative places considered to be more fulfilling for audience's expectations. In the case of modding, the expectation most often attempted to fulfil is that of historical authenticity. The main difference would be the divergent predominant interests between fan-fiction and modding. The former has a significant bias towards exploring narrative aspects (characters' relationships, 'shipping', alternative plotlines, narrative twists),[80] while the latter tends to focus on the alteration of visual lexia. Of course, there are further considerations concerning this bias, not least the legal and physical access to game code in order to run deep modifications on it; the greater technical difficulty of modifying interactive dynamics, stages and conditions in comparison with visual lexia. Nevertheless, a reasonably thorough analysis of specialized modding websites show a clear slant on the users' part.[81]

Among God games, a representative and widely-known example within the field of classical reception is *Rome: Total Realism* (2005–10), a complete mod pack developed by an assorted team including professional classicists and ancient historians.[82] Some of its modifications undeniably entail a reflection on historical processes and their ludic display, such as the recruitment of local historical units. However, interestingly, most of the mod's applied changes were applied to the user interface or aesthetic components such as 'skins' (i.e. the visual representations of individuals such as soldiers) or languages.[83] Likewise, modifications of interactive, processual and narrative dynamics from the original work tend to be a comparatively minor part (*Roma Universalis*, 2015;

the *Mount and Blade: Warband* mod *Rome Rise of an Empire*, 2015; *Civilization V Ancient Mediterranean Civilizations*, 2012), whereas the aesthetical component is clearly the most renegotiated.

Similarly, human-scale game mods are generally defined by a predominant pattern of aesthetical alteration, modifying certain elements or the entirety of its visual components (outfits, graphics, textures, particles, faces).[84] Fundamental narrative and ludic concepts or interactive dynamics are rarely altered. Correspondingly, downloadable contents (DLC) mainly address points of variation in specific kinds of aesthetical lexia (costumes, guns, tools, vehicles), or additional narrative content which fit into the reference work without effectively modifying it.

A recent and notable case of such a DLC is the new 'Discovery Tour Mode' of *Assassin's Creed: Origins* (2017). The original game, set in Ptolemaic Egypt of *c.* 49 BC, had already been praised for its 'painstaking' level of accuracy;[85] the Discovery Tour Mode, which dispensed with all narrative, missions, or ludic purpose, was marketed as a 'purely educational' tool.[86] Most of the praise for the game's historical accuracy is based on its aesthetical and spatial coordinates; neither the physically impossible manoeuvres that the player's avatar can perform, nor the ancient Egyptian mythological beings coming to life as enemies, are considered detrimental to that accuracy. To be clear, I do not intend this to be a criticism, but rather consider it entirely logical within the video games' mediatic logic. The predominant tools of authenticity creation (aesthetics, visuals, spaces) are remarkably effective, as they build a sense of 'realism' that is then able to weather additional (science-)fictional or fantastical layers. If the environmental, visual or spatial coordinates (in short, the aesthetics) – understood to be the main source of game authenticity – are compatible with player cultural codes, other possible disruptions are less likely to have an impact in this respect.[87]

Violence

Violence in video games has been a polemic issue for decades.[88] Far from tackling a controversial facet, this section seeks to deal with the defining nature of violence in video game's classical reception.[89] The display of violent action is a notably extended feature in most video games genres and contexts, but violent actions and lexia have had a predominant and recurrent presence since the first steps of digital ludic classical reception.[90] This is probably one of the most closely shared characteristics between *pepla* and video games. Although romantic, religious or social plotlines have traditionally featured in *peplum*, most of these productions have, to some extent, had a violent component to their stories, to the point of defining an object of study in itself.[91]

Video games not only inherited this aspect, but promoted it to be a predominant feature.[92] We can trace a decades-long history of video games showing the same patterns for certain depictions of violent actions.[93] This trajectory could have set the foundations for violence to become a necessary and sufficient condition for video games' portrayal of antiquity. It would be a rather complex (if not impossible) task to complete the main goals of a certain game involving the ancient past that intentionally omitted violence.[94] This recurring theme could have led to the development, conscious or not, of a defining feature beyond the boundaries of casuistry. As a player, one can perceive a certain association between a game's setting and its interactive dynamics. The absence of violence within an ancient environment thus eventually tends to evoke a digital recreation or virtual reality exploration, rather than a ludic experience suited to the 'authenticity' expected in such a medium.

A review of past titles shows that there is almost no place for a ludonarrative development beyond violent action. The most notable exceptions could be *Pompeii: The Legend of Vesuvius* and the *Egypt* saga (*1156 B.C.: Tomb of the Pharaoh*, 1997; *The Heliopolis Prophecy*, 2000; and *The Egyptian Prophecy*, 2004), together with Deck13's *Ankh* saga (*Ankh*, 2005; *Heart of Osiris*, 2006; and *Battle of the Gods*, 2007). All these titles are point-and-click adventures, the former being first-person time-travelling stories with a notable aspect of historical re-enactment, while the latter consists of third-person, three-dimensional adventures with cartoonish graphics, combining riddles with a distinctly humoristic side. These productions received mixed reviews and were (rightly) labelled as either family-friendly, educative or even childish games, placing them closer to 'serious games' in a non-explicit way. I believe this perception is related to their lack of violence, since portrayals of antiquity (especially accurate ones) based on purely naïve, non-violent action were not considered to be as appealing or entertaining as expected.[95]

Developers and players can seemingly hardly understand ancient settings for video games unless violent action is a/the centrepiece of ludonarrative progression, making violence an almost monopolistic presence within this subgenre. Despite the rich set of cultural codes as a result of classical reception history and the capacity of video games to appeal to player's familiarity, antiquity's conceptual place in popular culture seems not to be suitable for displaying other types of action. Complex reproductions of deeply studied, alternative aspects of antiquity such as explorations, large-scale trade or the Olympic Games have not been developed as narrative and interactive components. The only game that could be interpreted as an interesting alternative approach to ludonarrative in an ancient setting is *Rome: Pathway to Power* (released in 1992 as *Rome: AD 92* in Europe). This real-time, isometric adventure tells the story of Hector, a Pompeian slave escaping after the eruption of Vesuvius. Fleeing to Rome, Hector attempts to climb the social ladder by buying votes or sneakily obtaining social and political power. Though gladiatorial fights and battles are involved, in a marked contrast to the usual approach, they are subsumed as a means for the framing narrative's main objective. However, this single title was not followed by any sequels, nor did it establish a precedent for other titles to follow.

In terms of violent action, human-scale games usually entail a heroic narrative combined with individual fighting, while God games mostly feature warlike violence[96] through the display of battlefields (open field, sieges or skirmishes) and wars. City-building games (here classified as God games) focused on construction and development, usually include a warlike aspect, though not as a dominant dynamic.

Considering the two aforementioned aspects – the initial development of antiquity in video games independently from movies and the great capacity of video games for approaching alien and familiar perceptions – an overall interpretation can be proposed. In general terms, video games need a quick insertion and adaptation to gaming dynamics on the player's part. Antiquity offers a set of cultural codes of reference, easy and quick to apprehend by players, which provide a broadly logical conceptual environment to any degree of interactive dynamic (action-adventure, FPS, 4X). Similarly, violence could be providing a convenient bridge over the historical gap, namely between the alien and the familiar. Violence represents a simplifying and easily comprehensible dynamic through which complexities liable to make players lose their connection and acceptance implied in the perception of 'authenticity'. Violent action, in all of its forms, would thus be understood by developers as a guarantee to ensure the perception of any new title as not only appealing to potential consumers, but also (and equally, if not more, important) never inapprehensible. Let's not forget that the vast majority of video games are conceived, developed and played as commercial products far more than as historical texts.[97]

In conclusion, the general state of the question suggests that the reshaping of classical reception that video games entail makes violent action a dominant tool of ludonarrative meaning-making, (un)consciously shaping players' perception of antiquity as a naturally violent context. Consequently, video games would have redefined violence from its role as a narrative tool in cinema, turning it into an authenticity tool, creating an additional contrast with that of movies (concerning visual semantics, as mentioned above). Consequently, it would represent a rather notable challenge for video game developers to create a title in which concepts or dynamics of interaction would prevail over violence or visuals in order to build up an ancient world, especially one to be understood by players as a comprehensible model of our world, centuries ago. Perhaps not by chance, such a definition seems to be much closer to that of an academic paper.

Notes

1　Aarseth (2001) and King and Krzywinska (2002: 1–2).
2　Though technically referring to a specific film genre (Siclier, 1962) within the cinematic tradition of portraying antiquity (Solomon, 2001; Berti and García Morcillo, 2008), the term *peplum* will be herein metonymically employed for all movies displaying real or fictional ancient worlds.
3　Wyke (1997: 13).
4　Agnew (2007) and Chapman (2013b: 319, 323–4; and 2016: 198–230).
5　Lowe (2009: 68–74).
6　By way of example, *Hercules: Slayer of the Damned* (1988) and *Herc's Adventures* (1997) show a clear visual heritage from Ray Harryhausen's work in *Jason and the Argonauts* (1963).
7　Lowe (2009: 79).
8　For a brief history of these genres and ancient video games in general, see the chapter by Rollinger in this volume.
9　Rosenstone (2006: 594).
10　Schut (2007: 219) and Chapman (2013b: 313, 319; and 2016: 7–24).
11　Lowe (2009: 72) and Richards (2015).
12　Wolf (2012: 140).
13　Lowe (2009: 81).
14　Ibid., 73.

15 A recent example of this is the mission, 'Are you not entertained?', in *Assassin's Creed: Origins* (2017), which involves a notable gladiator from the city of Cyrene. The name of the mission is a clear reference to the famous line spoken by Russell Crowe's character, Maximus, in *Gladiator* (2000).
16 Lowe (2009: 65).
17 King and Krzywinska (2002: 6).
18 Lowe (2009: 81).
19 Chapman (2016: 121–2).
20 Ibid., 119–21.
21 Ibid., 121–2.
22 Lowe (2009: 85–6; and 2012: 78).
23 Ibid., 70.
24 Cf. Bender (2012: 94, 'virtuelle Erinnerungsorte').
25 Ibid., 81; and Rollinger (2015: 18; and 2016: 325).
26 Diak (2017).
27 Aarseth (2012: 19).
28 Friedman (1999: 142–3) and Schwingeler (2008: 120–4).
29 Ayers (1999: § 17).
30 Uricchio (2005: 329).
31 Chapman (2016: 128–31).
32 García Martín and Cadiñanos (2015: 346).
33 For the term 'gamescape', see, Magnet (2006).
34 On the use of time in (historical) video games, see, Juul (2004), Rughiniş and Matei (2015) and Chapman (2016: 90–9).
35 Gardner (2007: 271), Lowe (2009: 66) and Rollinger (2014: 88).
36 Chapman (2013b: 315).
37 Ibid. (2016: 122–3).
38 Lowenthal (2015).
39 Understood as the historical fallacy defined by David Fischer (1970: 135), in which 'the antecedent in a narrative series is falsified by being defined or interpreted in terms of the consequent'.
40 Lowe (2012: 56).
41 Ibid. (2009: 79 n.38).
42 The film *300* (2006) and the television series *Britannia* (2018) are two recent representative examples.
43 Lowe (2009: 89–90).
44 Perhaps the most outstanding example would be the ruins of the Colosseum. Isolated exceptions are Agrippa's Pantheon in Rome or the Hagia Sophia in Istanbul. These buildings have kept a continuously renewed, contemporary function and their insertion into daily activity brings them into the realm of the domestic. Significantly, they are rarely branded as *ruins*.
45 Rejack (2007) and Agnew (2007).
46 Lowe (2012: 59 and 63).
47 Gardner (2007: 270) and Lowe (2012: 53–4).
48 Gardner (2007: 260) pointed out this feature for the game *Praetorians*, but many more examples could be raised, such as *Serious Sam* (2001–17), *Kid Icarus* (1986) or *Assassin's Creed: Origins* (2017). See also Rollinger (2016: 325).
49 Lowe (2012: 78).
50 Uricchio (2005: 329).

51 Watrall (2002: 165) and Gardner (2007: 267–9).

52 Rollinger (2014: 90; and 2016) and Brown (2013).

53 Rollinger (2015: 28 and 30).

54 Understanding icons as dominant visual referents for the popular perception of a concept, idea, character, etc. For the case of cinema, see, Winkler (2009: 66–70).

55 Lowe (2012: 85) and Bender (2012: 94).

56 Systematically exposed in Richards (2008), these three periods correspond to the silent film stage up to the 1920s (Michelakis and Wyke, 2013), the sound film era from the 1930s including *peplum*'s golden age up to the middle 1960s and twenty-first-century new *peplum* wave (Diak, 2017).

57 E.g. Paul (2013: 240), Jancovich (2014: 62) and Royster (2003: 61–7).

58 Lowe (2009: 82).

59 Rollinger (2016: 327–8).

60 This technique, now increasingly common in sandboxes, can also be observed in other games not set in antiquity: e.g. the *Uncharted*, *Assassin's Creed*, *Tomb Raider*, *Halo* or *Red Dead Redemption* series. Interestingly, all of these are also examples, among many others, of games which have employed their respective main characters as referential icons, especially in their marketing products and particularly on the covers of games.

61 García Morcillo (2015: 141 and 151).

62 Seymour (2015: 34).

63 Chapman (2014; and 2016: 100–10).

64 Schut (2007: 229–30) and Jenkins (2002: 120–2).

65 Understanding lexia as 'combinable ludic representations of agents, objects, social structures, architecture, processes, actions and concepts' (Chapman, 2016: 123–5).

66 Lowe (2009: 77).

67 Agnew (2007) and Brown (2013).

68 Lowe (2009: 76), Hatlen (2013: 189–90), Winnerling (2014: 152, 159, 162–3) and Rollinger (2016: 313–16).

69 E.g. Hatlen (2013), Raupach (2014) and Winnerling (2014).

70 Bolter and Grusin (1999: 53–5) and Salvati and Bullinguer (2013: 154–8).

71 Rosenstone (1998).

72 Winkler (2004: 16–24).

73 Rollinger (2016: 319).

74 Concerning the figure of Alexander in cinema, see, Pomeroy (2008), Pierce (2004), Paul (2010), Shahabudin (2010), Chaniotis (2008), Wieber (2008), Petrovic (2008) and Berti and García Morcillo (2008). For the case of Leonidas, see, Lillo Redonet (2008), Beigel (2013), Lauwers, Dhont and Huybrecht (2013) and Blanshard and Shahabudin (2011).

75 Winnerling (2014: 151).

76 Howells (2002: 110–13).

77 Lowe (2012: 72–3), Winnerling (2014: 158–9 and 163) and Rollinger (2016: 330).

78 Cf. Rollinger (2014: 90, 'graphische Opulenz').

79 Although fan-fiction, i.e. textual narratives inspired by the original medium but produced by fans, has been created for video games, it cannot rival that inspired by cinema and/or TV in either quantity or impact. Fanfiction.net (https://www.fanfiction.net/game/ (accessed 24 June 2018) offers a wide and interesting range of video game-based fan-fiction. It is noteworthy that the most renegotiated games in this medium belong to those genres with a higher narrative weight (MMORPGs, graphic adventures, sandbox). One could posit that the significant number of video game fan forums available online limit the impact of fan-fiction in this realm, since they fulfil the

need for spaces to comment, (re)negotiate and, to some extent, also provide space for creative output. However, this would need further study which cannot be undertaken here.

80 Cf. Spierings (2007) for a stimulating analysis of *Xena: Warrior Princess* (1995–2001) from this perspective.

81 For such an analysis, I would especially recommend the *forum* and *requests* pages on such sites. To mention some well-known ones: https://www.nexusmods.com; https://gamemodding.com; https://www.moddb.com; https://www.worldofmods.com/ (all accessed 4 April 2019).

82 Ghita and Andrikopoulos (2009).

83 Ibid., 119–24.

84 A quick but illustrative check in this respect can be done by examining the brief descriptions of the manifold mods available at: https://www.moddb.com (accessed 24 June 2018).

85 Cf. Nielsen (2017). On the subject of the game's accuracy, see also, Murnanes (2018) as well as the analysis of professional Egyptologist Peter Der Manuelian for the popular YouTube channel, History Respawned (Manuelian, 2018).

86 As laid down in Ubisoft's official site: https://support.ubi.com/en-GB/Faqs/000031846/Discovery-Tour-Mode-of-Assassin-s-Creed-Origins-ACO (accessed 23 June 2018).

87 Rollinger (2015: 13, 17).

88 Goldstein (2005).

89 Serrano Lozano (forthcoming).

90 Lowe (2009: 80, 84).

91 McCall (2014b) and Aguado Cantabrana (forthcoming).

92 Gardner (2007: 265) and Lowe (2009: 81).

93 See titles such as *Legionnaire* (1982), *Field of Glory II: Rise of Rome* (2017), *The Battle of Olympus* (1988), *God of War* saga (2004–18), *Populous: The Beginning* (1998) or *0 A.D.: Empires Ascendant* (2017).

94 Such practice, defined as 'subversive gaming', has actually been explored concerning violence in the case of the *Grand Theft Auto* series: http://kotaku.com/one-players-quest-to-play-gta-online-without-violence-1644393866 (accessed 7 April 2019).

95 Blatantly exposed by Ray Ivey in the case of *Pompei* (Ivey, 2000). See also Gardner (2007: 266).

96 Schut (2007: 221).

97 As Al Bickham, Creative Assembly communications manager stated: 'Fun wins out over strict, dogmatic adherence to the history books' (Brown, 2013).

3

Playing in a 'Real' Past

Classical Action Games and Authenticity

Tristan French and Andrew Gardner

Archaeogaming and the developing agenda

A decade ago, when computer- and video gaming began to be a subject of scholarly research and writing within archaeology, history and related fields, it was commonly felt to be necessary for authors to begin with a lengthy justification of why games were worthy of investigation.[1] Comparison with the output of Hollywood, the growing and developing demographics of gamers and serious study in other fields, might all be used to make this argument in the early 'archaeogaming' literature.[2] This is no longer the case.[3] There is no need for any special pleading about the cultural relevance of gaming when the gamification of many aspects of twenty-first-century society is widely discussed.[4] Furthermore, while it is perhaps still a small, and divided, field, research into computer and video games in historical disciplines is well established and can now begin to chart a more adventurous agenda than the initial commentary on games as representations of popular pasts. This was, and remains, a worthwhile endeavour, but just as games themselves have become ever more sophisticated, so we, too, can start to pose more involved questions about the nature of the past and our relationship to it, which games help us to think through. That is to say, we can make games a means to broader intellectual ends, rather than have their critique be an end in itself. There are several ongoing research projects and groupings exploring these issues,[5] and one particular theme, the nature of past reality presented in games and how 'authenticity' comes to be of importance to players, is the focus of this chapter. This is a theme that is not confined to gaming – it might be as relevant to live re-enactment, heritage reconstruction or, indeed, the very nature of the archaeological imagination – but games have particular utility in helping us to develop our ideas about it.

This is precisely because of the uniquely interactive character of games, which is of course a major factor in their increasing popularity and central to much discussion in games studies. Here, this aspect is relevant in allowing us to encompass not only authenticity of representation, but also authenticity of experience, in our consideration of popular engagement with the past. As we will see in our two case studies, the former is an important theme, and not only to historical or archaeological commentators, but also to the wider gaming public, and to gaming journalists. It may be, though, that authenticity of representation – that is to say, accuracy of material features of a particular past context, and historical integrity with respect to depicted events – is significant because it helps to facilitate a further level of 'authenticity' – that of experiential immersion into a past which 'feels real'.[6] This, in turn, has interesting implications for the nature of cultural definitions of 'reality' in the twenty-first century.[7] Games are interesting in this regard because while they may be regarded as inherently inauthentic in relation to experience, in that the immersion of a gamer in a game is manifestly a different phenomenon to the life of an ancient Roman (or whatever), paradoxically they do at least require an active engagement with a perceived world in ways which no other media demands. This is, in fact, closer to the lived realities of the past than watching a film.[8] In addition, therefore, to the gamification of teaching,[9] historical research,[10] and public engagement agendas in archaeology and heritage[11] – among other developing applications – we can consider using games as tools to think with when addressing fundamental questions about our orientation to the past, in the classical or any other period. In our chapter, we will develop this argument via two case studies, both of action/adventure games. We have chosen this genre both because of its inherently more experiential ('human-scale') perspective, compared, for example, to strategy games ('God games') which take a 'god's eye-view', and because authenticity, particularly of representation, is much discussed in relation to recent titles. Indeed, our first case study, *Ryse: Son of Rome*, illustrates how the inclusion of fantastical story elements does not give a games developer a 'free pass' to ignore historical context, in the eyes of players and reviewers. Our second case study, the *Assassin's Creed* series, shows how greater investment in representational authenticity creates greater immersion and greater gameplaying satisfaction, and therefore greater experiential authenticity, such that successive iterations of the game are making more and more of this feature. This, in turn, shows that archaeologists, historians, and games developers can be allies in exploring playable pasts.

Fantastic pasts: *Ryse: Son of Rome*

When a game is set against a historical backdrop and the developers choose to diverge from the archaeological/historical record as it is widely understood, gamers and reviewers notice. Perhaps one of the most prominent examples of this is the historical action/adventure title, *Ryse: Son of Rome*. A launch title for Microsoft's Xbox One in November 2013, *Ryse: Son of Rome* was criticized for its historical (in)accuracy, as well as for its linear, level-based design (as opposed to the open-world model favoured by other games of the genre). Indeed, while these might seem to be separate points of critique, they may in fact reveal relationships between different forms of authenticity. The game is set during the reign of Emperor Nero, and the player takes control of a fictional Roman soldier, Marius Titus, on a quest for vengeance following the murder of his family. Whilst praised for its rendered environments and overall presentation, *Ryse: Son of Rome* was critically panned for its storytelling and obvious warping of a period of history that is very well documented.[12] The fictionalized lineages and confused mythologies, as well as limitations in the gaming experience, led to a backlash for the title, which sold very poorly within its first month of release (at approximately 30,000 units). As of July 2018, the game has sold just 1.47 million units,[13] which is not particularly noteworthy when compared to other releases of that year or other games within the genre – *Grand Theft Auto V*, for example, sold 26.75 million units worldwide and *Call of Duty: Ghosts* 12.71 million.[14] *Ryse: Son of Rome* highlights a key issue which has less to do with developers choosing to 'alter history' but more that these choices were noticed by gamers because they failed to enhance the game's story and had very little bearing upon the gameplay itself.[15] Indeed, beyond the deeper implications of the interrelation of different forms of authenticity here, we might draw some encouragement from the negative response of gamers to a title that failed to justify its fictionalization of a well-known historical period.

Distortion of historical figures and conflict of setting

Ryse: Son of Rome is set against the backdrop of an invasion of Rome by Celtic barbarians, during the reign of Nero. Starting *in medias res* during a siege carried out by the characters Boudica and Damocles, the protagonist Marius, and the emperor, take refuge within Nero's concealed vaults, whilst Marius recounts the actions that had led him to the point of the siege. One of the most jarring inaccuracies noticeable in this opening tutorial and cinematic of the game, is the fact that Nero is depicted as an aged emperor who has fathered two sons. As is well known to Roman historians, Nero fathered no children and also died at the age of 30, meaning that *Ryse: Son of Rome* seems to present some form of fictionalized timeline following the year 68 CE, after Nero's historical death.[16] As Nichols also points out, it is also very well known that while, during his reign, Nero did face an uprising from Boudica and the Iceni tribe, this rebellion was confined to Britain and quelled by Nero's general Paulinus. The British rebels had not attempted to reach mainland Europe, let alone Rome.

Nero is not the only historical figure to be portrayed in a wholly inaccurate way in *Ryse*. Queen Boudica is portrayed in the game as the daughter of a barbarian chieftain, King Oswald. Within the game, Boudica assumes command of her tribe, following her father's death at the hands of Nero's son Commodus during a ceremony of peace, eventually leading Boudica to storm Rome's centre with elephants and fully fledged siege equipment.[17] Whilst Boudica's depiction in *Ryse: Son of Rome* maintains some elements of her historical background, it is all too apparent that many liberties have been taken when adapting the warrior queen for the game. Historically, Boudica did assume control over her tribe, the Iceni. However, this was assumed from her husband, Prasutagus, following his death, and the subsequent treatment of the Iceni by the Roman state led to the revolt against Rome, although there are also a range of other long-term factors.[18] Not only have known details been ignored by the developing studio, Crytek, but the character's motivations for a rebellion against Rome have been altered to suit the title's fantastical story;[19] it seems that a recognizable character name was the only aspect of Boudica relevant to the developer.

The fact that the in-game 'Celtic' barbarians have access to a full arsenal of siege equipment, as well as war-mounted elephants and even gunpowder and explosives further illustrates the liberties taken by developers Crytek in order to suit *Ryse: Son of Rome*'s action-driven gameplay. Indeed, this points to a transmediatic overlap between gaming and cinematic representational tropes,[20] which enfolds one of the other Roman characters in the game. Nero's in-game son Commodus obviously stands out as a further fictionalization. Historically, of course, Commodus was the son of Emperor Marcus Aurelius, eventually becoming emperor himself. Nichols highlights the fact that the character of Commodus would be familiar to fans of the award-winning 2000 film *Gladiator*, as the film's central antagonist, and he suggests that this is the main reason for the character's inclusion in the game.[21] This would echo the way in which elements of 'Brand WW2' come to be transposed between movies like *Saving Private Ryan* and games like *Medal of Honor*.[22]

It is not just the game's protagonists that were highlighted in some of the critical reaction that *Ryse* received. The environment of the game has also been highlighted as containing various elements which are out-of-place within the relevant time period. Probably the most prominent example of this is the presence of both Hadrian's Wall and the Antonine Wall, constructed from the years 122 CE and 142 CE, respectively. Of course, while some of the game's critics recognized that there are bound to be inaccuracies in games set in historical time-periods, they have argued that a basic level of sympathy for the time period must be adhered to when presenting this material to the public.[23] Another spurious inclusion, highlighted by Nichols, is the construction of a giant wicker man, built in the game as the method of Commodus' execution by the Caledonian barbarian tribe. Whilst there is a brief (and probably derivative) reference to this in Caesar's account of Gaul, there is no corroborative evidence of any such practice, and this seems to be another cinematic reference-point, not least to the eponymous classic horror movie set in an isolated pagan community in modern times.

The depiction of the Northern British tribes themselves is another point of contention. Nichols[24] discusses the Caledonian tribes, who occupied what is now Scotland, and their depiction in the game as bone-wearing, club-wielding, brutish barbarians. Whilst it is known that Caledonia (or the region named so in the game) was not densely settled at the time of *Ryse*'s setting, it was far from the dense, dark woodland that is rendered in the game. Interestingly, Nichols suggests, perhaps charitably, that this might be based on Roman opinion about Caledonia at the time, as Roman writers were obviously working mainly with certain stereotypes about the lands and peoples of Britain.[25] The clothing worn by the Caledonians in *Ryse*, featuring goat/cow skull helms and armour of leather and bone, is also part of this, and again echoes cinematic conventions in films like *King Arthur* and *The Eagle*, now reiterated again in the Sky TV series *Britannia*. Overall, it is apparent that major liberties were taken with the historical setting of the game, from anachronistic siege equipment, to fictionalized character depictions and landscapes derived from deep-rooted stereotypes. Though extreme in this case, such inaccuracies are perhaps to be expected in an action/adventure game that treats a historical period as somewhat of a fantasy setting. What is interesting, however, is how these inaccuracies enfolded with poorly designed gameplay into a mixture that was not too popular with the gaming public.

Gameplay and player limitations

The action/adventure genre often deploys a 'sandbox' map.[26] Unlike more open-ended role-playing games (such as *Assassin's Creed: Origins*, see below), a sandbox map contains elements of open-world environments to encourage exploration and discovery of new locales, but also limits the area of play so that the player cannot veer too far from the tasks and missions at hand.[27] However, *Ryse's* gameplay could not be further from this model, with each game's stage following a very linear chain of operations, combined with a predictable, repetitive combat system.[28] During each stage of the game, players are presented with waves of enemies, which can only be reached by defeating previous waves, comparable to games developed by Capcom, such as *Bayonetta* and the acclaimed *Devil May Cry* series.

Despite being set during an intriguing historical period, Crytek chose to limit player exploration with *Ryse*, having the player reach wing-emblazoned overhead markers to complete objectives, rather than allowing the player the freedom to explore and develop an immersion in the time-period that might be turned to their advantage in later missions.[29] *Ryse* also utilized cinematics and quick-time events (interactive moments within cutscenes/cinematics), that can only be executed by specific button prompts, for much of its combat, and this has been highlighted by critics as damaging to the game itself by removing key elements of player involvement. Jenkins mentions this as a major drawback for the game, as well as noting the historical inaccuracies, and explains that the limitations to player engagement and interaction with the surrounding terrain/areas, including monuments such as the Colosseum,[30] lead to a system of 'player hand-holding', as they are constantly given instructions throughout the game. Walton expands on this, stating that whilst *Ryse* may have been marketed as having a larger scale environment in the lead-up to the game's release, it was soon evident from player and professional reviews that the final product presented gamers with a much narrower scope.[31]

While evaluating the precise balance between gameplay limitations and historical inaccuracy in accounting for the poor response to the game would require detailed audience research, which is not yet available, the way these two themes have been highlighted by different critics shows both some of the problems historical games can pose, but also ways forward. The heavily fictionalized historical interpretations are obviously likely to draw scorn from specialist critics, but they can also be detected by a wider audience of players, and Crytek's effort is conspicuous by its lack of more in-depth knowledge presented in other games of the historical fiction genre.[32] The limited representational authenticity is more significant, though, when linked to the lack of player involvement and influence in both the story and ultimate outcome of the game. As highlighted by Nichols, Hoggins, and Walton,[33] the narrow scope offered by *Ryse* presents players with iconic historical surroundings, but considerably curtails the parameters for exploring the regions of Rome and *Britannia* in-game. It is apparent that players are not able to deviate from a given path in the game, and whilst cinematics and quick-time battle animations may have showcased the graphical capabilities of the Xbox One, *Ryse* did not aim to depict both the chosen period of the game nor serve to engage players beyond a storytelling level.[34] Whilst games such as *Ryse* might be seen as justifying dismissive treatment of gaming by scholars, the responses to the game, and its poor sales compared to games like the *Assassin's Creed* series, starts to indicate that the public is alert to more nuanced forms of authenticity in other games, and that this is revealing of deeper trends. *Ryse's* problems are thus more effectively observed when compared to other titles of historical fiction and the action/adventure genre, which have succeeded where Crytek's model did not.

Modes of authenticity

As discussion of the nature and utility of games set in historical periods has developed, so authenticity has become an understandably key issue. Hitherto, traditional disciplinary boundaries have somewhat siloed the debate in history, archaeology, and classics, but – as this volume as a whole will demonstrate – there is much common ground in the concerns of scholars across these fields. As noted in the introduction, the initial focus on critique of authenticity of representation has developed in new directions, though the example of *Ryse* illustrates why this is still worthwhile. Some of the ways in which *Ryse* fits into a wider pattern of particular conventions of representational (in)authenticity have already been mentioned in the foregoing. Use of cinematic tropes, for example, is clear, and as Salvati and Bullinger have shown with games set in the Second World War,[35] this is a common feature of historical games. In itself, this raises some interesting questions about whether people are judging the authenticity of representation with respect to a 'real' past, that they have experienced from visiting actual places or museums, or academic sources, or a past mediated by the creators of other visual media.[36] Of course, in reality, there is no such thing as an unmediated past,[37] and this is precisely where we reach the limits of the representational mode of authenticity, on which more below.

Other conventional tools that games developers use to convey authenticity in representation, which are highlighted by Salvati and Bullinger, include 'technological fetishism', which typically applies most to weapons and military equipment in both action/adventure and strategy games.[38] Certain aspects of the material world are highlighted which are important in gameplay but which also have well-documented real-world referents. This, along with the documentary authority conveyed by real historical figures,[39] is an area that *Ryse* did not particularly succeed in, and which laid its developers open to criticism, as gamers do indeed notice problems in these areas. This is why modification of games by users ('modding') is often done to create more technically accurate graphics rather than fix more ambiguous issues, though the former are perhaps easier to address from a technical point of view.[40] Again, though, even with very well-documented periods, we soon run into the problem that representation of the past is always mediated and can never be perfect, and indeed that this was also true in the past itself. Past people had a patchy understanding of the world they lived in and its historical composition.[41] This realization actually takes us closer to the virtue of the unique quality of games: players do not just want to represent the past, but to relive it.

Authenticity of representation is thus an important part of the story when it comes to the successful creation, and enjoyable playing of, historical games, but it is only a part. The other major element is authenticity of experience, which depends on reasonably accurate material world-building but also has a lot to do with gameplay mechanics. *Ryse* failed on both counts, whereas games in the *Assassin's Creed* series, as we will shortly discuss, have succeeded in both areas, and, indeed, got better at it as the developers have realized what players want from the game. What this seems to constitute, for a lot of gamers, is an experience which transcends the passivity of watching a film or TV show set in a historical period – as accurate and/or entertaining as this might be – and moves closer to something like re-enactment,[42] but might actually be felt to be even more 'real' than the latter, because it takes place in a fully real 'past' world with fewer jarring abutments against contemporary life. As long as the game presents an environment that is 'real enough',[43] which means not only that it conveys a sense of historical accuracy but also that its gameplay mechanics, modelling of physics and so on are plausible to the player, then the gamer can be immersed in the environment to the exclusion of the outside world. Beyond this, Hong has argued that gamers are seeking in the digital past an escape to 'authentic' living – in the sense of being alive at a time, and doing the kinds of activities within that time, when something significant was at stake.[44] Thus, because life and death is at stake, to fight in a battle in the ancient world becomes a more 'real' experience than the humdrum safety (or everyday stresses) of much modern living. Games are thus in some ways part of new relationships between people and their pasts, but at the same time replicating much of the function of mythologies and ritual acts of previous cultures.[45] How they do this can be effectively demonstrated by the example of games from the *Assassin's Creed* series.

Realism and representation: *Assassin's Creed*

Who are we, who have been so blessed to share our stories like this? To speak across centuries?

Ezio Auditore de Firenze, *Assassin's Creed II*

The *Assassin's Creed* series, as a mainstream gaming title, has become a household name in the past decade. With the game reaching a clear milestone with its ninth canon release, it is useful to view the arc of the series' development. The inaugural title was released in 2007 by developer/publisher Ubisoft, to widespread critical acclaim. The popularity of the series has arguably climbed since, with each main title in the series exploring a different period of history (Table 3.1).

As of 2014, the franchise had sold over 73 million copies worldwide (which is thought to have increased to 100 million in 2016).[46] However, with global recognition comes a wider scope for criticism, with the historical accuracy and potential educational benefit of each release in the series being called into question on online message boards/forums and gaming blogs.[47] This is where the overarching storyline of the series comes into play, as each historical setting must slot into the grander narrative. Each game is focused on a (seemingly never-ending) conflict between two fictitious parties, the revolutionary order of Assassins and the reactionary faction of the Knights Templar, or their antecedents, as both chase after artefacts dubbed 'Pieces of Eden'.[48] Due to the game's fantastical setting in the modern world, with an in-game virtual-reality machine

Table 3.1 *The Assassin's Creed* series.

Game title and release year	Historical setting
Assassin's Creed (2007)	The Third Crusade, 1191 CE
Assassin's Creed II (2009)	Renaissance Italy (15th/16th century CE)
Assassin's Creed: Brotherhood (2010)	Renaissance Italy (16th century CE)
Assassin's Creed: Revelations (2011)	Constantinople, 1511 CE
Assassin's Creed III (2012)	American Revolutionary War, 1754–1783 CE
Assassin's Creed IV: Black Flag (2013)	Golden Age of Piracy, 1715 CE
Assassin's Creed: Unity (2014)	French Revolution, 1789 CE
Assassin's Creed: Syndicate (2015)	British Industrial Revolution, 1868 CE
Assassin's Creed: Origins (2017)	Ptolemaic Egypt, 49 BCE
Assassin's Creed: Odyssey (2018)	Ancient Greece, 431 BCE

called 'the Animus' enabling the reliving of ancestral memories by the player-controlled character, the developer Ubisoft have been able to explore a wide range of historical timeframes, and allow for playful creativity as well as both modes of authenticity.[49] As a mechanic that allows the player to move into different past horizons, the Animus enhances the sensation of exploration within the games and is an interesting and indirect way to bring an archaeological approach to the series.[50] The gameplay of the series, coupled with the continuous narrative between games, is of vital importance to consider when discussing the place of the series in the wider context of the relationship between archaeology and the virtual world.

Gameplay, exploration and customizability

Whilst the *Assassin's Creed* releases are set against a vibrant historical backdrop, the central facet of the gameplay is based around stealth and adaptive exploration. The mechanics revolve around the location of targets and their subsequent termination, allowing the player to choose the most effective method of doing so. Meyers highlights that this mechanic, whilst appearing simple, is central to the potential educational prospects that the *Assassin's Creed* series might hold. Although the foremost thought for most players is the elimination of the target, through the element of free choice and exploration, the games indirectly allow players to adapt to their historical surroundings, to recognize and utilize the architecture and major landmarks to their strategic advantage. This, in turn, can generate a subliminal form of learning about the historical setting of the game,[51] further contributing to the use of history as a key game element.[52]

It is here that we introduce the series' arguably most acclaimed and inventive entry so far (at the time of writing, *Assassin's Creed: Odyssey* was released in October 2018 and could not be included in this study), in 2017's *Assassin's Creed: Origins*, which is also directly relevant to the Classical context of this volume. Unlike previous releases in the franchise, which purely focused on reaching objectives and eliminating targets, *Origins* expands upon the explorative nature of the series, rewarding innovation over completion. Set in Egypt during the Ptolemaic period, *Origins* focuses on the beginnings of what would become the Assassin Order and the sparks of their battle against the

Fig. 3.1 Protagonist Bayek explores Alexandria in *Assassin's Creed: Origins* (2017
© Ubisoft. All rights reserved).

Knights Templar (here represented by their antecedent, the Order of the Ancients). As
a result, many of the series' previous tropes and signatures are gone, allowing Ubisoft
to manipulate the origin story framework to introduce new game mechanics. Perhaps
the most striking is the reinvention of the 'Eagle Vision' ability. In previous games,
players could select a button on their game controller or keyboard to initiate a vision
skill that would allow them to easily detect guards, enemies and targets, as well as
explore key points in their surroundings.[53] However, in *Origins*, this mechanic is
replaced by a pet Bonelli's eagle (called Senu) belonging to the main protagonist, Bayek
(Fig. 3.1). Not only is this bird of prey native to the Egyptian area, but it is utilized
almost like a modern-day scout drone, to carry out reconnaissance from the sky (quite
similar to the owl from fellow Ubisoft title, *Far Cry: Primal*). Senu is not only used for
spotting, attacking, and distracting enemies and targets, but also for tracking wild game
and pin-pointing map locations in order to secure resources for armour and weapon
upgrades.[54]

This leads on to another fresh element in *Origins'* reimagining of the series, in the
now customizable weapons and armour mechanic, introduced in this release. Players
can now carry multiple handheld weapons such as swords, pikes, bows, shields and the
Egyptian *khopesh* (curved blade), which can be purchased from merchants or looted
from guards and enemies.[55] These items can all be upgraded through completing side
quests and hunting tasks, or using resources gathered from the indigenous wildlife,
such as crocodiles and hyenas and hippopotami. Whilst this mechanic existed in its
infancy in *Assassin's Creed IV: Black Flag*, in the game's whaling missions, these were
used to unlock specific sets of clothing and armour, and it is only in *Origins* that we see
this depth of customizability for individual player elements.

This level of crafting and character-building draws in a role-playing element to the series' action/adventure moniker, similar to other titles in the genre such as the PlayStation 4 exclusive *Horizon Zero Dawn*, and Nintendo Switch launch title, *The Legend of Zelda: Breath of the Wild*. This new customizability allows players to become truly connected to the protagonist, their surroundings and in the case of *Assassin's Creed: Origins*, the time period in which the game is set. It is this level of connection that some have highlighted as being useful for educational purposes, as the player truly feels enveloped and attached to the environment which inhabits them.[56]

Archaeological sites and integration into gameplay

Considering each title's historical setting, it is to be expected that each *Assassin's Creed* entry will depict respectable renderings of key historical monuments. According to Nielsen,[57] developer Ubisoft's research team provides the skeletal framework of each game and its historical setting. This is especially evident in *Assassin's Creed IV: Black Flag* and *Assassin's Creed: Origins*. *Black Flag* presents players with an in-game rendering of the Mayan site of Tulum. In the game, Tulum is where the game's protagonist, Edward Kenway, is stranded with pirate captain Charles Vane. Following an in-depth exploration of the ruins, and the introduction of a series of puzzles centred on Mayan stelae,[58] the player discovers that Tulum functions as the spiritual home of the titular Assassins in the area, and also houses the game's chief artefact and goal. The aforementioned Mayan stelae puzzle side-quest is also fascinating, as the player utilizes actual architectural artefacts in order to complete mapping and puzzle-solving stages, giving the protagonist themselves an archaeological focus (not that we would go so far as to call the Assassin's Order an archaeological group, of course!). The inclusion of such a prominent archaeological site and its integration into the story is yet another example of *Assassin's Creed's* apparently seamless ability to merge representational authenticity with fictional gameplay.[59]

Origins, of course, expands on this greatly, as players are essentially given freedom to roam over the landscape of Ptolemaic Egypt and its many prominent sites. Arguably, the most spectacular locations featured in *Origins* are the Pyramids of Giza. As part of a key explorative side quest in which players are required to gather items from tombs, they can not only climb the Pyramids, but also explore their inner networks, these being depicted with reasonable accuracy.[60] This is due to Ubisoft not only utilizing their in-house historians, but also from working with external archaeologists, including Egyptologists Jean-Claude Golvin and Mark Lehner. Golvin in particular was apparently very involved in mapping key locations in the game, and provided drawings, schematics and maps, including of the Giza Plateau and its iconic monuments.[61] Not only is this a key example of crucial interactions between archaeologists and game developers, but it also shows the aspirations of some developers to provide players with as authentic a historical representation as possible. This, in turn, helps to generate an immersively authentic experience.

Franchise historian Maxime Durand and game director Ashraf Ismail both explained, in a recent interview, that the *Assassin's Creed* series, and *Origins* in particular, might not be the most accurate of historical portrayals among digital games, but that

Ubisoft and each subsequent development team aims for each entry to be as 'authentic' a player experience as possible.[62] This can be seen most clearly in Ubisoft's latest downloadable content (DLC) for *Origins*, the aptly named 'Discovery Mode'.[63] This newly developed game mode essentially transforms *Origins* into a fully playable virtual museum. The mode removes the story, combat and mission objectives, leaving the player to roam the landscape and view iconic monuments and archaeological sites at their own leisure. The DLC currently features 75 guided tours for players to experience, each peppered with checkpoints. Players can also utilize this mode in order to learn about practices such as mummification, or to explore the hidden rooms of the Great Library of Alexandria.[64] The value of this mode as an educational tool is deliberate and is being recognized widely. Ubisoft supplied secondary schools with early versions of Discovery Mode in order to collect feedback, which was overwhelmingly positive from younger students, allegedly helping them retain greater amounts of information about the time period.[65] Durand also states that this Discovery Mode is simply the start of a greater effort to use the *Assassin's Creed* games as an immersion tool, taking their value above simply enjoying the series' already intricate plotlines.[66]

The fact that Durand recognizes this is vital, as when a series as prominent as *Assassin's Creed* gains global recognition for its historical settings, it is also placed under more detailed scrutiny. An example of this is an article by Sawula.[67] Writing for the online blog 'Play the Past', Sawula is one of the few authors who has held *Assassin's Creed* up to critical standards,[68] utilizing the third (*Assassin's Creed III*) and fourth (*Assassin's Creed IV: Black Flag*) entries as prime examples. Durand's and Ismail's own statements, to the effect that they aim with each entry for an authentic experience which does not always equal complete historical accuracy,[69] do need to be borne in mind. However, writing of *Black Flag*, Sawula states that, '*Assassin's Creed* is not good history', highlighting as problematic the focus on a singular historical perspective, which developer Ubisoft appears to present as fact. In *Assassin's Creed IV*, the player controls fictional sailor-turned-pirate captain Edward Kenway, who chooses to rebel against the naval forces of Britain and Spain, depicting piracy and its Golden Age as a key bastion of freedom and liberty.[70] While it is clear that sailors and civilians alike turned to piracy for a variety of reasons, the game instead portrays pirates as a rather democratic force – again, a recognizable trope (cf. the STARZ television series *Black Sails*), but of questionable authenticity, at the intersection of both representational and experiential modes.

The central issue that Sawula highlights is that Ubisoft claim to be presenting 'true stories' against the backdrop of historical fiction. Combining this with the overarching narrative of the *Assassin's Creed* series, it is implied that the player is replaying events as they occurred, and that their presence has no true bearing on history in the grander scheme of the game's narrative.[71] Connecting this with the overarching framework of revolutionary good vs authoritarian evil, Sawula claims that each game confirms popular opinions of each era and that player's expectations are never challenged. However, we need to bear in mind Hussey's remark that the *Assassin's Creed* series are certainly not the first games to utilize historical and archaeological settings, but that they are arguably the most popular.[72] Why are they so successful? Harris highlights that whilst the series may at times function on a superficial level of engagement, it is still dangerous to dismiss them as 'just games', and class them as lower than historical literature/film/television.[73] Harris, Nielsen and Hussey all share a common view, that in representing and rendering our world and the human past, video games must be considered seriously, as the narrative driving force of the digital age.[74] Indeed, the developers of the *Assassin's Creed* series are perhaps among the first to take this role seriously and start to leverage it to do precisely what Sawula demands, and challenge expectations as the series moves on.

This balance between their striving for authenticity, and the critical questioning of accuracy, is also perhaps why Ubisoft have chosen time periods that are slightly more ambiguous and unfamiliar, to allow greater manipulative potential. Whilst the Ptolemaic Egyptian setting of *Origins* might include some of the more iconic monuments of world archaeology, the era itself was chosen for its relative lack of familiarity, which, in turn, allows the developers greater creative freedom.[75] However, this is not to say that Ubisoft have run roughshod over this ancient setting, as is displayed by their collaboration with leading experts in the field, as well as a solid grounding in factual research before enveloping this into the wider *Assassin's Creed* narrative.

Conclusion: The value of critical gaming

The two, contrasting, case studies that we have examined in this chapter highlight that different games help us to think through the interactions between authenticity of representation and of experience, and what these mean for the relationship between contemporary people, including archaeologists, and the past. These insights are helpful for archaeologists and historians in considering their own imaginative reconstructions of past worlds, and indeed their own practices,[76] of research as well as of teaching. Beyond the academy, there is room for optimism about the direction of travel which the *Assassin's Creed* series seems to point towards. A decade ago, when games studies in archaeology were taking off, it was easy to feel that it was a subfield destined not only for the scorn of many peers, but also for being completely ignored by the commercialized behemoth of the global games industry. Yet, the recent developments in the *Assassin's Creed* franchise show that there is a wide, and critical, public out there, to whom software companies want to direct increasingly 'authentic' (representationally and experientially) games. Those companies are therefore also increasingly interested in engaging with archaeologists and historians. That makes it all the more important that we nurture a sympathetic, but also, of course, critical, attitude to games more widely among the scholarly community. At the time of writing, *Assassin's Creed: Odyssey* was the next instalment in the series, and was released in October 2018. What that game brings to the debate, and how, or if, other major commercial games take up some of the challenges that the series has laid down, remains to be seen. There can be little doubt, however, that gaming will be a crucial narrative form in the twenty-first century, as much as new archaeological techniques or theoretical paradigms, and, therefore, they should be seen as the future of the past.

Notes

1 The authors would like to thank Christian Rollinger for his invitation to contribute to this volume, and for his helpful comments on the chapter, along with Adam Chapman. TF thanks Andrew Gardner, Gabriel Moshenska, Tim Schadla-Hall, Khalid Winter, Charlotte Frearson, Ben Hiam, Luke McGarey and the University College London (UCL) Institute of Archaeology. AG thanks my co-author and members of the Interactive Pasts network for fruitful discussions of issues addressed in this chapter. Portions of this work originally formed part of a dissertation by Tristan French entitled 'Playing through the Past: An Analysis of Video Games as a Method of Public Engagement with Archaeology', submitted as part of an MA in Public Archaeology at the UCL Institute of Archaeology in 2016.
2 For the term, see Reinhard (2018).
3 Cf. Chapman, Foka and Westin (2017).
4 E.g. McGonigal (2012).
5 E.g. the *Interactive Pasts* network, which originated in Leiden (http://interactivepasts.com).
6 Cf. Holtorf (2005: 135–44), Rollinger (2016) and Winnerling (2014).
7 Hong (2015).
8 Cf. Fogu (2009) and Uricchio (2005).
9 E.g. Graham (2014).
10 E.g. Spring (2015).
11 E.g. Gardner (2012).
12 Nichols (2014).
13 VGChartz (2018).
14 *Fiscal Times* (2013).
15 Nichols (2014).
16 Ibid.
17 Ibid.
18 Hingley and Unwin (2006).
19 Nichols (2014) and cf. Beavers, this volume.
20 Cf. Salvati and Bullinger (2013).
21 Nichols (2014).
22 Salvati and Bullinger (2013).
23 Nichols (2014) and cf. Lowe (2009).
24 Nichols (2014).
25 Ibid. and cf. Woolf (2011). For an analysis of similar tropes in the depiction of ancient Germans in video games, cf. Coert (2018).
26 Antunes (2013).
27 Ibid.
28 Hoggins (2013).
29 Ibid.
30 Jenkins (2013); and cf. Maiberg (2014) and Nichols (2014).
31 Walton (2013).
32 Stuart (2010).
33 Nichols (2014), Hoggins (2013) and Walton (2013).
34 Walton (2013).
35 Salvati and Bullinger (2013: 159–60).
36 Cf. Copplestone (2017).

37 Cf. Dow (2013).
38 Rollinger (2016) and Salvati and Bullinger (2013: 158–9).
39 Salvati and Bullinger (2013: 160–1).
40 Gardner (2007), Graham (2014) and Sotamaa (2010).
41 Dow (2013).
42 Cf. Uricchio (2005) and Vowinckel (2009).
43 Hong (2015: 42–6).
44 Ibid.
45 Ibid., 50–1.
46 Makuch (2016) and Seibert (2014).
47 Stuart (2010).
48 Hussey (2014a).
49 Cf. Gardner (2007).
50 Hussey (2014a) and Sawula (2013).
51 Meyers (2011).
52 Stuart (2010).
53 Parkin (2017).
54 Tapsell (2017).
55 Ibid.
56 Tamayo (2018).
57 Nielsen (2017).
58 Campbell (2013).
59 Hussey (2014a).
60 Nielsen (2017).
61 Ibid.
62 Ibid.
63 MacDonald (2018).
64 Ibid. and Tamayo (2018).
65 MacDonald (2018).
66 Nielsen (2017).
67 Sawula (2013).
68 Cf. Hussey (2014b).
69 MacDonald (2018).
70 Sawula (2013). For a similar analysis, see the review of *Black Flag* (from the point of view of a scholar of early modern history) in Pfister (2015) and cf. ibid. (2018).
71 Sawula (2013).
72 Hussey (2014b).
73 Harris and Nielsen (2015).
74 Ibid. See also, Hussey (2014b) and Nielsen (2017).
75 Nielsen (2017).
76 Cf. Chapman (2016).

4

The Representation of Women in
Ryse: Son of Rome

Sian Beavers

Ryse: Son of Rome was released in 2013 as a launch title for the Xbox One, and according to its developers, is a tale of 'revenge, betrayal and divine intervention'.[1] *Ryse* is of the action-adventure genre known as a hack-and-slash, using quick-time events in its sword-based combat mode. The game adopts a third person perspective, where the player takes on the character role of a legionary, Marius. The player is not freely able to roam the environment beyond specific parameters, and the player's movement through the virtual world is linear (or 'on rails') with fixed narrative emplotment. Any ludonarrative decisions made by the player do not affect the broader narrative arc or structure.[2] These linearity and movement constraints distinguish the game from other action-adventure games such as *Assassin's Creed*, where the player is able to explore the virtual world in its entirety.

Ryse is an alternative history of the events taking place in Rome and Britannia under the (now) aged Emperor Nero, and his sons, Basilius and Commodus. The game begins with a barbarian attack on Rome, led by the British warrior woman Boudica, where Marius' role at this stage is to repel the attack. The events leading up to the barbarian invasion are then outlined as a flashback narrative, and it is these flashbacks to the events taking place prior to the barbarians' invasion that form the rest of the game's narrative.

'It is sometimes said that reception sheds light on the receiving society but not the ancient text or context'.[3] With the narrative of *Ryse* firmly in the realms of alternative history, this must be truer for this game than for other historical games that adhere more closely to the historical record, as it presumably bases its representations on aspects that have some contemporary significance to the player. Given the alternative vision of ancient Rome that *Ryse* espouses, it then becomes difficult, if not contradictory, to portray characters in morally dubious ways to contemporary sensibilities and to justify it under the guise of purported historical accuracy. This chapter will discuss the representation of women in *Ryse*, and will outline how every female's representation and characterization in the game is exceedingly problematic. I will specifically address how women are portrayed in the game and adhere to certain tropes and negative stereotypes. Any discussion of the game's divergence from the historical record will consider what aspects of history the developers have drawn from, and what they omitted, suggesting potential (ludonarrative, form-specific or remediation) reasons as to why this might be the case.

As with any text, readings of media texts are interpretive, and cannot be considered as objective or as the only way a particular text can be understood. This becomes more complicated with digital games as interpretations of the content are often based on the individual choices (and outcomes of those choices) made by players. However, the player's actions in *Ryse* do not impact the narrative of the game as a whole, with cutscenes used to progress the game's narrative. These cutscenes are mandatory to progression, meaning that players are exposed to them regardless of what decisions they make in the game. It is almost exclusively within these cutscenes that the female figures in *Ryse* appear, and consequently how the women are represented in these cutscenes are specifically referred to in the following analysis. Discussions of player decisions in this regard are thus irrelevant given the mandatory nature of these cinematic cutscenes. In the absence of empirical research on player perceptions of *Ryse*, or, indeed, antiquity in digital games more broadly, what is offered in this chapter is *my* particular reading of the game, with theory and critical receptions used to illustrate the arguments herein. As stated, reception illuminates more about the receiving society than the ancient context. Applied to Ryse, this means that, although '[c]lassics in its modern manifestations unthinkingly replicates the male bias of its ancient sources',[4] the game also replicates the male bias within the contemporary context of consumption. This has been found to be the case, whereby Williams[5] has suggested that games and gender have a cyclical relationship: males are more likely to be represented in games, and, as such, males are more likely to play them. Furthermore, males are more likely to play violent video games[6] like *Ryse*; hence, on this basis (and given the following analysis) the player is consequently presumed to be male.

It appears, then, that there is a reciprocal relationship between the number of males represented in games and the number of men who play them. However, there may also be a similarly reciprocal relationship where digital games do not only reflect contemporary society but may also have the capacity to influence it. Studies have shown that games can influence the gender identities of players through the negative portrayals of women found in them:[7] '[f]or example, girls may expect that they will continue to be victims and needy and that their responsibilities include maintaining beauty and sexual appeal while boys may determine that their role is to protect and defend women and to possessive [*sic*] them even through the use of violence'.[8] Although the effects of such media upon audiences are not yet fully understood, 'it would be an error to assume that those who understand what they see in the media is not real are invulnerable to the messages being presented'.[9] As such, it is not only women that could be adversely affected by these problematic representations, but men also. Therefore, it becomes important to address these unfavourable stereotypes in games and know what they are, understand why they occur and the potential impact they may have upon the player.

These are the aims of this chapter. Through an analysis of the female characters in *Ryse: Son of Rome*, I will argue that each of them falls into at least one of three female gender tropes, as outlined by Sarkeesian,[10] and I will give my interpretations as to the reasons they may have been represented in these ways. These are the 'damsel-in-distress' trope; the objectification of women as sexual objects; and the entanglement between sexuality, female trauma and violence.

The following sections address the different ways these tropes are used in *Ryse*, what impact this has on the narrative and potentially the player-character.

Women as damsels in distress

The 'damsel-in-distress' trope has long been a familiar one when it comes to representing women in any medium, and is particularly prevalent in games. An analysis of female characters in video games carried out in 1998, found that the portrayal of women as damsels in distress was the primary way that women were depicted in games, a category second only to the absence of female characters entirely.[11] There are multiple variants of the damsel-in-distress plot device, one of which is where the trope is used in combination with explicit violence against women and 'used as a pretext for the inevitable bloody revenge quest',[12] in order to motivate a male protagonist. This is the case with *Ryse*, wherein the motivation of the male player-character, Marius, is not to rescue the female(s) as such, but to avenge the slaughter of his mother and sister at the hands of purported barbarian invaders.

The roles of Marius' mother and sister within the narrative are extremely short-lived, with their deaths taking place at the beginning of the game and functioning as the primary motivation for Marius' later actions within the narrative. We are introduced only to his mother, Septima, while she is still alive. Septima's sole interaction with Marius is to state that he looks handsome in his armour and that she will go and find his sister. Shortly after a training session with his father, the player-character hears screams occurring off-screen, after which he discovers the bloodied corpses of his mother and sister. His sister, therefore, is not seen alive within the game narrative, concurrently does not have any dialogue and, furthermore, is not even named within either gameplay or cutscenes. It is only through obtaining *Ryse*'s collectibles (which provide additional diegetic information that is non-essential, and relegated to optional information) that the player can put a name to the bloodied female corpse of Marius' sister: Honorata. However, players who do not seek or find this optional collectible would perceive Honorata as nameless; and even with the collectible she remains faceless and voiceless. Her only value in the game is not in her life, but in her death and the utility this offers to the character arc of Marius. As such, she is not afforded characterization, a face or a voice. At best, she is named almost as an afterthought.

As the first female characters on screen in *Ryse*, the portrayals of Marius' sister and mother do much to set the tone for how the representation of women functions within the game. The third-person perspective utilized in *Ryse* means there is a close player–avatar relationship that casts the player into the 'fictional role'[13] of an agent, in this case Marius, where the player effectively 'becomes them' in the context of the game. In first- and third-person (human-scale) games, the perceptual viewpoints of the player and avatar merges, unlike strategy ('God') games (such as *Total War: Rome II*), where the player has no avatar within the gameworld and controls it from a god-like perspective.[14]

This means that in the cutscene at the beginning of *Ryse*, when Marius' mother comments on how handsome Marius looks in his armour, she is implying to the player that women find a man who fights attractive. Of course, a mother expressing admiration for her son is hardly unusual, but the fact that it is his armour, the social status this implies, and the sanctioned violence it symbolizes, that makes him more attractive in her eyes has potential connotations for the player. Through Septima's statement to Marius, the player is invited to view their role as one defined by attributes of conventional masculinity: a warrior character who is physically strong with social standing. As such, the player-character is from the outset constructed as heroic, which serves to contextualize their later (generally violent) actions as moral. In this way, Septima's character functions simply to provide characterization for the male character's narrative arc.

Where Septima's statement to Marius alludes to the idea that women find violent men attractive, the irony is that she and her silent, faceless daughter will die at the hands of one shortly after. This provides the player with somewhat of a confusing message at the opening of the game, where they are invited to feel buoyed, attractive and powerful by women through the violent aspects of the game, though simultaneously see the repercussions of the violence perpetrated against women. Consequently, this is not just a question of male violence, but male violence sanctioned by some moral justification for said violence, in as much as something so bad happens to Marius (the deaths in his family) that he must supersede even his duty to the state. The lone, heroic individual becomes more important than the centralized authority, which is to be distrusted in comparison with the moral righteousness of the individual.

Hartmann and Vorderer argue that, 'violence that conflicts with one's inner moral standards triggers distressful concern',[15] partly due to the evidence stating that Non-Player Characters (NPCs) in a game are often viewed as quasi-social beings due to innate social perceptions of them as such.[16] What this means is that the deaths of Septima and Honorata are used to provide a 'moral disengagement'[17] for the player, ethically justifying Marius' later violence to NPCs, but which simultaneously reduces the female characters presence as again merely to serve the male character's narrative arc.

The damsel in distress trope in *Ryse* perpetuates the idea that women are weak, vulnerable and require protection. However, women in the game are not only portrayed as weak: they also cause weakness in other male NPCs. If we consider the characterization of Boudica, an Iceni noblewoman, and her father, Oswald, midway through the game after they have been captured by the invading Roman force, at this point in the narrative she also falls into the damsel in distress trope. (Boudica moves between different tropes throughout the game's narrative that will be discussed in due course.) Basilius (one of the game's male antagonists) threatens to have her flogged if he is not told by Oswald where Commodus, Basillius' brother, is located. Players would undoubtedly recognize the name Commodus as the antagonist of the film *Gladiator*. With the deaths of Marius' family and his narrative of a lone, avenging hero who distrusts the state as a centralized authority, the parallels with the film are numerous and explicit. This is also evidence for the idea that the Rome Hollywood has created is now the only Rome that is universally familiar,[18] where this 'Hollywood' version of Rome seen in film has become further remediated within the digital game form.

Oswald immediately gives up the location of Commodus at this threat against his daughter: he is made weak merely by his concern for her. This weakness is exemplified shortly afterwards, when he is killed by Basilius, cementing the idea presented in the game that women's vulnerability has an adverse (and, in this case, deadly) effect on men. Throughout the entirety of this exchange, which is relayed to the player via an extended cutscene, Boudica is not only constrained and helpless, but also completely devoid of any dialogue beyond a few anguished cries. Like Honorata, Boudica is relegated to a silent damsel in distress, who requires saving by a man – in this case, her father. Boudica's weakness as a woman is transferred to Oswald, in an inversion of the damsel in distress trope seen with Septima and Honorata. His death becomes Boudica's subsequent motivation for her own revenge narrative, paralleling the narrative we have seen previously with Marius. And yet, it would seem that in each case, female characters serve primarily only to develop the character of the male protagonist.

That this exchange is relayed to the player via a cutscene is also significant, as '[t]he camera gaze represents the woman as a victim, but in a way that forces the audience to confront her trauma. And, in doing so, creates a justification for her rage and subsequent vengeance.'[19] Those familiar with the historical narrative found in Tacitus regarding Boudica and her rebellion against Rome, may notice the allusion in *Ryse*'s narrative to her flogging. It must be reiterated that the object of this chapter is not to point out instances where the narrative in *Ryse* diverges from what is known from ancient sources, as *Ryse*'s narrative is firmly, and openly, in the realms of historical fiction. What is important to note, however, is that the game borrows some elements from the historical source material (such as the recognizable Boudica as a character and her rebellion against Rome) and not other elements of her story.[20] These omissions would seem to serve some kind of narrative purpose, so, consequently, it is important to consider why this is the case and how it changes the player's perspective on her role within the narrative. For this, some historical perspective is required.

We are told by Tacitus that after the death of Boudica's husband, Prasutagos, the Romans had her flogged and her daughters were raped. These crimes against noblewomen, in conjunction with the other Icenians being treated as slaves by the Romans, incited the British rebellion against Rome.[21] Although we can see some similarities between Tacitus' account and the narrative in *Ryse*, there are clear and fundamental differences. First, the changing of Boudica's role from wife and mother in Tacitus, to daughter in *Ryse* is a small change but a significant one. In Tacitus, the atrocities committed by the Romans against Boudica and her family are crimes that are first and foremost perpetrated by men against women. This means that Boudica and her family were victims of trauma in their own right, giving clear and understandable justifications for her later aggression against Rome (at least from contemporary perspectives). Though even in antiquity, classical writers reflected their concerns about the contemporary condition using the speeches of historical figures as a mouthpiece,[22] where Boudica's impassioned speech in Tacitus was used to highlight the ignobility of Rome under Nero; Boudica was servile to Rome like the people of Rome were servile to an immoral emperor.[23] In *Ryse*, changing the narrative so Boudica is the *daughter* of a man killed by the Romans relegates her to a secondary character in her own story, no more than a passive observer. This small change in *Ryse* moves the focus back to a male character, Oswald, signifying that the death of a man is more important in the narrative than the flogging of a woman. As such, there can be two interpretations of this small change in the nature of Boudica's character. First, Oswald's death is used to provide a moral justification for Boudica's revenge, consequently treating her as a character with a moral impetus for violence like Marius. Conversely, however, the fact that violence against a man was considered necessary to supplement the violence against the historical Boudica and her daughters is problematic.

Second, through having Boudica only threatened with violence and not actually having it carried out upon her, this serves to diminish some of the fiery rage that motivated the historical Boudica. Instead of fighting to avenge her own ill-treatment and the assault on her daughters, in *Ryse* Boudica's motivation, as a loving and dutiful daughter, is to avenge her father's death. Where the revenge in the narratives of male characters are used as justification for the *use* of their inherent martial abilities, in contrast, women must undergo trauma merely to *become strong* in the first place: 'In the narratives' constructions of empowerment, the women at some point are represented as having power taken away from them and are depicted . . . as victims.'[24]

Having seen that *Ryse* is not adverse to depicting violence against and/or the death of women, one must consider the developer's motives for these small changes to the narrative in comparison with the source material. As mentioned previously, this change of Boudica from wife to daughter allows parallels to be drawn between her narrative and Marius', where both are the children of murdered parents seeking vengeance for injustice. It could be argued that this was an attempt to show the injustice of the state to both citizen and non-citizen, highlighting the morality of Marius' later quest against the corrupt state. But this again means that Boudica's role of 'the other' is used merely to construct Marius' own narrative.

However, this would only explain why Boudica in *Ryse* becomes the daughter instead of the wife of Oswald, and not why the violence against her was omitted. Instead, I propose that the parts of the historical Boudica's narrative, in respect to the flogging and rapes were omitted in *Ryse* due to the 'Limits of Play'. The Limits of Play is a concept forwarded by Chapman and Linderoth, who argue that an 'intrinsic effect of ludification [of making something to be *played with*] . . . is the trivialization of the object of transformation'.[25] The Limits of Play is the idea that certain events and subjects in history (such as the Holocaust, slavery or sexual violence) are too controversial to represent in games as these would make light of sensitive historical issues. This is a particularly form-specific concept that is exclusive to games, as '[w]hat is easily allowable in a television series [or film] is considered unacceptable in a game'.[26] Chapman and Linderoth use the example of the lack of representation of the Holocaust in digital games as evidence for the Limits of Play, as one of the main reasons for this effect is that games, as an interactive form, have the ability to cast the player in a role where they can re-enact instances of cruelty or abuse.[27] Controversial historical issues such as the Holocaust, slavery or sexual violence are particularly prone to the Limits of Play, precisely because of the moral difficulties in allowing a player to 'play with' these elements or, more specifically, to re-enact them.

If this is applied to *Ryse*, we have already seen how the player is cast in the role of Marius: a Roman with heroic status and prowess in battle. If Boudica were to actually have been flogged at the point where the Roman Basilius suggests, then this would serve to make Marius complicit in this act of violence against a restrained woman, even if he was not specifically re-enacting it via the gameplay. Marius would be on the side of men who oppress and commit violence against women, a position that would be perceivably difficult for a player to countenance in good conscience. The game positions the actions taken by Basilius against the Britons as unjust actions of the state, which also reflects some of the interpretations of ancient accounts of the conflict. Clearly, the developers did not wish for the game's protagonist to have ambiguous ethical persuasions regarding violence against women (thus becoming unheroic), and again provides the player with a moral disengagement factor. It may simply have been easier to omit this part of the historical narrative and allow the violence to be committed against a man instead, removing the need to actually deal with these issues of violence against women in a meaningful or interesting way.

Having discussed how Septima, Honorata and Boudica's roles within *Ryse* aligns them with the damsel-in-distress trope, there is another female character who falls into this category. Prior to Marius' fight in the arena, he comes across a female oracle, who is wearing a collar and is chained, requiring his aid to be freed. The Oracle is also a damsel in distress who is combined with another trope surrounding the representation of women in games. This is the trope of objectifying women as sexual objects or, as Sarkeesian notes, 'women as background decoration'.[28]

Women as sexual objects

The objectification and sexualization of women is particularly prevalent in *Ryse*, combined with other tropes assigned to women. What is significant to note is that, barring Honorata and Septima (who represent Marius' honour and must remain suitably chaste, in alignment with patriarchal familial formations), every other depiction of a female character within the game has their breasts exposed in some way.

When Marius finds the female oracle, she requires his assistance in order to be freed. Relayed to us via a cutscene, we see her in the shadows, on all fours and chained from the neck. She is a supplicant, prostrated before him. Furthermore, although her body is painted, she is naked from the waist up, with her breasts exposed and only some strips of fabric covering her bottom half: she is a fetishised damsel in distress. After offering him prophetic information in exchange for her freedom, Marius cuts the rope by her collar. The presumed male player gets to feel a hero as the saviour of a vulnerable woman, but simultaneously is titillated by her nudity. The nude woman chained by the neck is a common trope of fantasy and science-fiction media (such as Princess Leia in *Star Wars*), so, here, the historical representation seems to be informed by these sources.

As this is relayed to us via a cutscene, it is unclear whether Marius would have freed her anyway, even without the promise of information that might aid him on his revenge quest. What can be seen, however, is that Marius' sword lingers a little too long next to her face before he cuts the rope and frees her, giving the action an air of a threat. Furthermore, the angle of the camera makes the sword at his hip look undisguisedly phallic next to her face. This sexualization explicitly combined with violence within the game is the topic of the next section.

The Oracle is one of many female NPCs that is sexualized within the game. Consider the unnamed goddess (again, a female character not afforded a name, though some fans refer to her as 'Summer'), who appears to Marius in cutscenes periodically throughout the game, to provide exposition and move the narrative forward. Her golden dress is open to the navel, with two small straps that barely cover her breasts, leaving most of her cleavage exposed.

This arguably unnecessary, sexualizing nudity of this character was criticized by journalists and reviewers as the content of her dialogue was relegated to a secondary function 'thanks to a distracting presence',[29] that is, her exposed breasts. Furthermore, there were remarks made about the dissonance of the representation of the goddess with her dialogue and role in the narrative, where Clubb noted, 'I think it was a bad decision to have her in those clothes [. . .]. This is supposed to be a moment of emotional gravity. Just dress the character.'[30] Another critic echoed this sentiment, saying, 'It's supposed to be an emotional scene, but damn, I'll be honest, the only thing I could focus on while the scene unfolds is how oddly the breasts are moving.'[31] Both the perceived dissonance of the visual representation alongside the dialogue designed to be emotive, as well as the criticism of peculiar physics used when representing the female form indicates the gratuitousness of the goddess' nudity. These receptions of the game add weight to the argument that the sole purpose of her nudity and hyper-sexualized representation is to titillate the perceived male player.

What this objectification and nudity implies overall is that these women are the objects of the 'male gaze', wherein female characters, according to Laura Mulvey, are positioned merely to be looked at, 'with their appearance coded for strong visual and erotic impact'.[32] The female becomes the erotic object of the male gaze, occurring because of the spectator's identification with the male protagonist. Although Mulvey was writing in reference to cinema, her arguments are equally applicable to games, especially given the prevalence of fan-made 'nude mods', such as those made for *Elder Scrolls: Skyrim* that include chain-mail bikinis for female characters.[33] It has already been outlined how the player is invited into the fictional role of the avatar through the third-person player perspective adopted in *Ryse*, but unlike a cinema spectator, the player has the option to affect the camera and which angle they would like to view the world. This means that the player is not only given the tools of the male gaze (i.e. the women's nudity) but is also potentially an active co-constructor of it within the gameworld.

Women and sex, trauma and violence

We saw in the previous section how the nudity of female characters in *Ryse* make them the object of the male gaze. However, other sexualized representations of women are evident where they are 'created to be glorified furniture' or 'minimally interactive sex objects'[34] within the gameworld. This is precisely the case with the women who feature in the Bordello, who are minor NPCs who have no dialogue within these scenes and function merely as 'background decoration'.[35] Sarkeesian specifically points to the use of the 'strip-club' trope in games, where the bordello in *Ryse* is merely the ancient world version. However, this is something commonly seen in a variety of visual media depicting ancient Rome, including TV series such as STARZ's *Spartacus*, where naked slave women are similarly used as background decoration. Although the women in the bordello are similarly the passive objects of the male gaze, the function of their representation and location has additional narrative impact.

Marius must enter the bordello in disguise as Damocles to find Basilus, in order to gain entry to the arena to face Commodus in battle. We see the bordello via a cutscene, where naked women dance and gyrate, interspersed with scenes of Marius forging the sword and armour of Damocles. From the outset, it is discernible that the naked female form goes hand in hand with violence. Throughout the scene, we also see Basilius leering at and revelling in the company of the nude women in the bordello. Of course, given the bordello context, it might appear unsurprising for there to be exposed women. However, Sarkeesian notes that having the player–character's adversary, in this case Basilius, frequent places such as these functions as a 'ham-fisted form of character development [...] defining the antagonist as "bad";[36] and it does so whilst giving the presumed male player the chance to leer at women while feeling justified being in that virtual environment.

Once Marius has found Basilus, he wishes to test him in battle before allowing him access to the arena. At this point, the physical space of the bordello building transforms into an arena where Marius must fight a range of enemies to prove his worth. The nature of the scene's beginning cutting between female nudity and Marius' forging of weapons serves to reiterate the entanglement between sex and violence in the game. The transformation of the bordello into a gladiatorial arena makes the process literal: sex and violence even occupy the same virtual, geographical space in *Ryse*.

The bordello is not the only instance where the sexualization of women is explicitly equated with violence. Although she does not specifically qualify as only 'background decoration' given her dialogue and role as antagonist, Boudica is a character who is simultaneously sexualized and violent. If we consider Boudica's outfit in *Ryse* we can see the clear parallels between hers and Keira Knightley's costume as Guinevere in *King Arthur* (2004) (Fig. 4.1).

Where Guinevere wears a metal torque, Boudica wears a taut leather neckband, though both could be considered as (intentionally?) reminiscent of collars. Both women wear arm bracers, where there appears to be somewhat of a dissonance in wearing bracers while having the more vulnerable chest area essentially exposed. The women wear thin strips of leather tight across their chest, which only barely conceal their breasts underneath. The design of these two outfits have the purpose of both revealing the breasts of the wearer as well as causing them to become more buxom. Guinevere's costume was even referred to as 'bondage bandages' by a viewer,[37] which has particular significance if the dual meaning of the word 'bondage' is considered in light of their collar-like neckwear. Bondage can mean to enslave, subjugate, oppress or exploit; but is also the (consensual) restraining of a partner in the course of sexual activity. For both Guinevere and Boudica their sexuality is inherently linked with violence. Both are exploited through their costumes, and Boudica's role within the

Fig. 4.1 Boudica in *Ryse: Son of Rome* (*l.*, 2013 © Crytek GmbH. All rights reserved) and Keira Knightley as Guinevere in *King Arthur* (*r.*, 2004 © Buena Vista Pictures Distribution. All rights reserved. Photo: Jonathan Hession).

narrative of *Ryse* is ultimately to be subjugated, unlike her filmic counterpart. Boudica's costume, therefore, provides an aesthetic shorthand for her unfolding role within the narrative of the game: to be overcome by the male protagonist.

Since *Ryse* was released in 2013 and *King Arthur* in 2004, one might conceivably assume that Keira Knightley's costume was used for inspiration for Boudica's costume. This becomes an even more reasonable assertion if we consider the critical reception of Guinevere, where some made reference to Keira as a 'Glastonbury Boudicca',[38] with others referring to her as a 'a Boudicca wannabe'.[39] What this means is that there is a complicated web of (transmediatic) reception, (re)presentation and remediation at play within these two characters. We have the character of Guinevere in *King Arthur* who is equated with and parallels the historical Boudica; with the representation of Boudica in *Ryse* remediating the aesthetic of Knightley's Guinevere. These receptions/ remediations are not unidirectional and are in fact cross-mediatic and multifaceted, happening on latitudinal as well as hierarchical directions. This points to the 'complex networks and cycles of historical exchange into which games find themselves increasingly interwoven'.[40]

Indeed, the two characters share an additional defining trait: they are both warrior women. This idea of the aggressive, fighting female could be interpreted as presenting a positive and empowering portrayal of a female on the surface, as a woman is now the perpetrator of violent acts as opposed to having these acts done to them. However, when perpetrating violence, '[t]he woman takes on male characteristics, uses male language, male weapons [and is] a warlike and destructive figure created in man's image, set apart from ordinary women and desirable only in death'.[41] In *Ryse*, Boudica adopts these male characteristics after her trauma and becomes the antagonist of the player-character. As an antagonist, her role is to eventually be overcome – subjugated – by the player character, resulting in her death. Her adoption of male characteristics functions as a moral disengagement factor for the player, meaning he does not have to feel an aversion to fighting her throughout the game, and the killing blow is not even enacted by the players themselves, but is again relayed via a cutscene, sidestepping any issues with the Limits of Play.

However, where *King Arthur* 'interprets the historical record as one of equality and shows that Guinevere leads a band of guerrillas that include both men and women'[42] in *Ryse*, Boudica as a warrior woman is the exception and not the norm. Barring Boudica, every other named character and unnamed NPC who Marius fights are universally male. Boudica is therefore unusual as a fighter in her own right, and has been made exceptional, as stated previously, precisely because of the trauma she has suffered. As Stache argues:

> For women to be allowed to use violence, they must do so in response to first becoming a victim. Violence [. . .] becomes even more problematic as a tactic when victimization is linked to subsequent empowerment. Thus, the correlation between the two seems to be that women can become strong only when they have first been weakened.[43]

Boudica's sexualizing costume actually undermines her empowerment, making her an erotic spectacle and the object of the male gaze, effectively diminishing the potentially 'positive connection between sexuality and female empowerment'.[44] Where we saw earlier in the bordello scene in *Ryse* that sex and violence occupied the same virtual space, sex and violence are embodied in the character of Boudica in the same physical space.

What we see in *Ryse* through this conflation of sex, violence and victimhood, is 'a sexualized female empowerment that masks contending messages of disempowerment, in a narrative that first makes the woman a victim of sexual, physical, and/or emotional abuse'.[45] Although Marius fights Boudica at various points throughout the game, she is never ultimately a match for him and must be defeated for the narrative to continue. She is consistently characterized as inferior to him in multiple ways: her victimhood and sexualizing costume that are linked to her gender, and also by way of her accent that denotes a lower class. Cyrino[46] uses the term 'linguistic paradigm' to describe when American audiences associate British accents with oppression through the heritage of American colonial history. In *Ryse*, where Marius has a Received Pronunciation (RP) or prestige British accent, Boudica on the other hand has a northern British, or non-prestige accent. There is a similar linguistic paradigm at play here through these different accents, as Marius' prestige accent denotes his status as someone who is an elite in society, as this accent is associated with the British upper classes.[47] Conversely, Boudica's northern accent is a non-prestige, working class accent, and 'people tend to view speakers with working-class accents as less well educated'[48] and are perceived to 'correlate with both lower status and level of sophistication'.[49] This means that there are multiple elements inherent to Boudica's characterization that highlight her lesser status in comparison with Marius, which, in turn, contributes to the systematic stereotyping of the female characters within the game as a whole.

Conclusion

This chapter has argued that the characterization of women within *Ryse* fall into three tropes: they are damsels in distress, they are sexualized objects of the male gaze, and the nature of female sexuality is entangled with violence, perpetrated by the women and unto them. Where some characters fall into only one of these tropes, others such as Boudica, move between these gendered character roles. Their roles within the game merely serve to qualify the actions of the male player-character, where this 'positioning of women as [. . .] the cause of war enables the representation of women simultaneously as fragile, in need of protection, and as a scapegoat, bearer of blame for all evil'.[50]

It was said that reception provides more insight into the receiving society than the ancient context, and this is also true within games. Although with these problematic representations of women, what are we to glean about the perceived role of women in contemporary society? Of course, *Ryse* propagates the aesthetics and tropes apparent in a wide range of games as well as other digital media, including TV and film. But where there has been a shift towards more positive portrayals of female characters in TV and film, there is still much work to be done with games to ensure that these negative representations – and any subsequent potential repercussions – are minimized. Games, as a newer interactive medium, have different formal pressures, such as the Limits of Play, than other visual media. As such, more research is needed into this form, and to highlight these concerning character portrayals, as well as an urgently-needed empirical understanding of the long-term effects of such characterizations on players. The negative stereotypes of women seen in *Ryse* specifically are part of a broader issue concerning the representation of women in digital games in general and the misogyny within gamer culture: an issue that has already had adverse consequences to the receiving society in the form of the now infamous 'Gamergate' controversy. Ultimately, through using *Ryse* as a specific example, this chapter has shown how history itself does not stand outside the values and tropes of the society in which it is constructed and received. If, as with *Ryse*, the epistemological argument (historical accuracy) for maintaining sexist characterization is removed, then historical games should instead move towards the moral imperative of offering representations deemed politically valuable in contemporary society.

Notes

1 Crytek Frankfurt (2018).
2 Chapman (2016: 128).
3 Hardwick and Stray (2008a: 3).

4 Zajko and Leonard (2006: 17).
5 Williams (2006).
6 Hartmann and Vorderer (2010: 94).
7 Dietz (1998: 426).
8 Ibid.
9 Dill et al. (2001: 126).
10 Sarkeesian (2009–18).
11 Dietz (1998: 433–5).
12 Sarkeesian (2013).
13 Linderoth (2005).
14 Jørgensen (2009).
15 Hartmann and Vorderer (2010: 97).
16 Ibid., 95.
17 Ibid., 94.
18 Coleman (2004: 57).
19 Stache (2013: 82).
20 For the importance of recognizability in the choice of Boudica, see also the chapter
     by Tristan French and Andrew Gardner in this volume.
21 Tacitus, *Annals* 14.31 (1996).
22 Lawson (2013: 111).
23 Roberts (1998: 127).
24 Stache (2013: 72).
25 Chapman and Linderoth (2015: 143).
26 Ibid., 148.
27 Ibid., 140.
28 Sarkeesian (2014a).
29 Stuart (2013).
30 Clubb, quoted after Stuart (2013).
31 Hernandez (2013).
32 Ibid.
33 Cooper (2015).
34 Sarkeesian (2014b).
35 Ibid.
36 Sarkeesian (2014c).
37 Weatherby, quoted after Blanton (2005: 102).
38 Bradshaw (2004).
39 Previews (n.d.).
40 Chapman, Foka and Westin (2016: 5).
41 Cooke (1976: 126).
42 Blanton (2005: 97).
43 Stache (2013: 82–3).
44 Ibid., 123.
45 Ibid., 112.
46 Cyrino (2005: 232).
47 Lien (2016: 23).
48 Ibid., 5.
49 Ibid., 24.
50 O'Gorman (2006: 195).

Part Two

A World at War

Martial Re-Presentations of the Ancient World

Battle Narratives from Ancient Historiography to *Total War: Rome II*

Dominic Machado

Cutscenes – short cinematic interludes between moments of continuous gameplay that provide the player with further information, introduce new missions or provide closure to a scene – have long posed significant aesthetic and ludological problems for those playing and studying video games.[1] They have been derided as the gaming equivalent of a low-budget movie due to the jerky camera angles, cheesy dialogue and bad voiceovers that they often feature.[2] Further, cutscenes are ontologically antithetical to the gaming experience. They not only take the player away from the experience of playing the game, but they frequently take control of the action out of their hands.[3] Cutscenes strip players of the agency that makes games so engrossing and enjoyable.[4]

More recently, however, scholars have begun to look at these in-game cinematics in a different light. They view cutscenes not as superfluous, but rather as playing a variety of essential roles in making meaning for the player.[5] According to these scholars, even some of the more frustrating aspects of these cutscenes, like time lags and poor cinematics, contribute meaningfully to the gaming experience.[6] Emblematic of this approach are Hancock's comments on how cutscenes enhance the game's realness: 'the cutscene is there to make a game's world real – not just by telling a story, but also by reacting to the player, by showing him the effects of his actions upon the world and thus making both the world more real and his actions more important'.[7] In short, cutscenes work to create dynamic and compelling narratives within the context of the game.

This chapter seeks to build on these new approaches by examining how cutscenes function in the historical battle mode of *Total War: Rome II*. The historical battle mode, a trademark feature of the *Total War* franchises, allows users to participate in famous battles from antiquity such as Raphia (217 BCE), Cannae (216 BCE) and Alesia (52 BCE). Each of these battles is preceded by a cutscene in which a narrator explains the historical context of the battle including the events that precede the conflict, the goals of the sides involved, and the physical location of the soldiers. While it would appear that the goal of these cutscenes is rather simple – to provide historical background about the upcoming battle to the person playing the game – in this chapter,

I will argue that these cutscenes are more than passive recapitulations of historical fact. Using the cutscene for the Battle of Teutoburg Forest (9 CE) as a case study, I will demonstrate that they are acts of reception which engage actively with narratives, both ancient and modern, about the past, reproducing, repurposing, and reimagining events from ancient history.[8] These reinterpretations of ancient history create and inspire new narratives of the past and engage in historical debates of cultural and political significance.

The Battle of Teutoburg: A long history

Before analysing this cutscene, it is necessary to discuss briefly the Battle of Teutoburg Forest. The battle, which occurred in September of 9 CE, saw a coalition of Germanic tribes launch a successful surprise attack against Roman forces under the command of Quinctilius Varus. The German attack was organized by Arminius, a Cheruscan noble who was serving as an auxiliary officer in the Roman army at the time. Although there is some question about the exact nature of the attack, there is no debating the destruction it wrought: three Roman legions were slaughtered, their standards were lost, and Varus and many of his officers died in the battle.[9] Not only was this defeat a major setback for Roman imperial ambitions in the region, but it was immediately inscribed in Roman memory as a disaster on a par with Cannae and the Caudine Forks.

However, the story of the Battle of Teutoburg Forest did not end with the battle – it has had a long and complicated afterlife. Arminius' unlikely victory captured the imagination of historians from antiquity onward. Numerous ancient historians including Velleius Paterculus, Tacitus, Florus and Cassius Dio, gave extended treatment to the battle in their writings.[10] Likewise, in modern times, many have seen the battle as a watershed moment in world history, often describing it either as a turning point for Rome's imperial ambitions or as the dawn of the barbarian resistance that would topple the Roman Empire.[11] But it is not only historians who have found the battle intriguing, as the Roman defeat has held an important place in popular imagination as well. Greek and Roman poets writing in the battle's aftermath recalled the disaster and its damaging effects on the Roman psyche.[12] From the sixteenth to the early twentieth century, various Germanic peoples came to view the story of the battle and German resistance to Roman imperial rule as essential to their history and national character.[13] More recently, the battle has garnered popular interest due to a series of archaeological finds. In 1987, archaeologists discovered the remains of a Roman battlefield at Kalkriese, a site near the town of Osnabrück.[14] The finds, which included human remains, ballistics and coins minted during the Augustan period, sparked discussion about whether the battlefield was the site of the famous battle and attracted media attention from Germany, Great Britain and the United States. The widespread popularity of the battle since antiquity is important for our purposes because it means that in engaging with the Battle of Teutoburg Forest, the developers of *Total War: Rome II* deal not only with the ancient sources that treat the battle, but also its popular reimaginings over the past two millennia.

From Suetonius to internet memes

The opening shot of the cutscene introducing the Battle of Teutoburg Forest in *Total War: Rome II*'s historical battle mode sets the stage by revealing a dark, rainy forest.[15] As the camera pans over the forest, the player hears the voice of an unnamed character shouting in anguish: 'Varus, O Quinctilius Varus, give me back my legions!'[16] The camera dives quickly into the trees where the remains of a defeated Roman army come into view. The Roman soldiers, still clad in their armour, lie in a lifeless heap. The scene fades to black before a caption reveals that the opening vignette is proleptic, describing the state of affairs three months after the battle had taken place.

The images of the opening vignette have their origins in ancient narratives about the battle. The voiceover comes from Suetonius' *Life of Augustus*. According to the 2 CE biographer, Augustus was so saddened by the disaster that he would pound his head against the door while shouting, 'Quintilius Varus, give me back my legions!' (Suet. *Aug.* 23.2: *Quintili Vare, legiones redde*). This report underscores the pain and suffering that the defeat caused Augustus. Suetonius also records that for several months Augustus did not trim his beard or cut his hair and marked the date of the battle each year with a day of mourning. The frustration and sadness of Augustus is also remarked upon by Cassius Dio who notes that the emperor rent his garments upon hearing the news and remained in mourning for a prolonged period after the disaster (Cass. Dio 56.23.1).

The image of the unburied Roman soldiers also features prominently in ancient accounts of the battle. The most vivid description comes from Tacitus. In Book 1 of the *Annales*, Tacitus relates the visit of the Roman commander, Germanicus, to the site of the battle in 15 CE (Tac. *Ann.* 1.61–62).[17] As Germanicus and his soldiers enter Varus' former campsite, they see the bones of fallen soldiers, human skulls mounted on pikes and the altars used to slaughter the captured. Survivors from the battle, now fighting in Germanicus' legions, narrate the brutal slaughter that occurred at the hands of Arminius' troops. The language that Tacitus uses to describe the reaction of Germanicus is laden with emotion: the soldiers feel pity (*permoto ad miserationem*), sadness (*maesti*), grief (*doloris*), and anger (*aucta in hostem ira*). The image is a powerful one, meant not only to induce *pathos* for the dead, but also to offer a haunting reminder of the long shadow that the battle cast in Roman imagination.[18]

Florus offers a related anecdote about the treatment of Roman soldiers after the battle. He details German abuses against Roman soldiers, claiming that the battle was the cruelest form of slaughter witnessed to date (Flor. *Ep.* 2.30.36). The Germans gouged the eyes, cuts off the hands, and sewed shut the mouths of Roman soldiers (Flor. *Ep.* 2.30.37). Most heinous of all, the Germans disinterred the body of Varus after it had been buried by his soldiers (Flor. *Ep.* 2.30.38). Unlike Tacitus, who ties the gruesome aftermath of the battle to the indelible impression it left on Roman historical memory, Florus focuses on the behaviour of the Germans. The incidents of cruelty, which betray a lack of respect for the conventions of ancient warfare, reveal the barbarous nature of the Germans. As such, the scene acts to exculpate Varus; the Roman general becomes a victim of the barbarous perfidy of Arminius and his German allies.

These powerful ancient narratives about the battle are not just reproduced by the game; they are given new meaning. For example, the image of the unburied bodies is repurposed to provide clarity for the player. The dead Roman soldiers function as a gloss to the Augustan voiceover. The image explains to the player why the nameless narrator is demanding his legions back – they have been killed in battle. Since many players will have no prior knowledge of the battle, the visual of the dead Roman soldiers informs them of the outcome of the battle (excepting the German audience, who might be more familiar with the material). For this section of players, the image of the dead soldiers is not a *lieu de mémoire* conjuring the battle's impact on Roman historical memory, but rather a point of first contact with its complex history. Beyond this didactic purpose, the unburied Roman soldiers also fulfill another game-related function: the dead soldiers signal the difficulty of the player's mission. The player will have to reverse the course of history and succeed where the Romans failed. The account of the unburied Roman soldiers, an image traditionally associated with emotion and *pathos*, is transformed into a didactic and ludological tool that structures the player's experience.

The reinterpretations of these ancient accounts, however, go beyond gameplay. Shortly after the game's release, the quote from Suetonius became the subject of an internet meme. Defined by scholars of digital media as a fixed image with an accompanying (and usually humorous) caption that achieves online notoriety, internet memes have become one of the primary modes of social interaction over the last decade.[19] Their simple format, which is, at once, malleable, comprehensible, and replicable, allows anyone with internet access to satirize and publicize shared experiences and realities with a larger audience. The memes that appropriate the quote from Suetonius took multiple forms. Some included a bust of Augustus attached to a modern body; others made the quote the subject of well-known meme templates such as 'Rage FU' and 'Y U No' (Fig. 5.1). In these memes, Augustus is not depicted as a grieving leader lamenting a serious setback with far-reaching consequences. Rather, Augustus is analogized to a petulant child or frustrated employee for the purpose of derision. Through Photoshop and the memegenerator.net site, the Battle of Teutoberg Forest, the object of much serious reflection and inquiry over the past two millennia, becomes comedic. *Rome: Total War II* allows for the creation of a new and unexpected chapter in the battle's history.

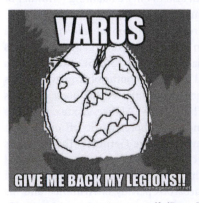 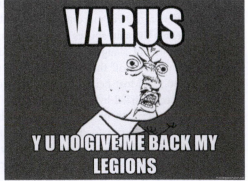

Fig. 5.1 Meme-ing Augustus (*l.*, 'Rage FU'; *r.*, 'Y U NO').

The memeification of the quote from Suetonius is indicative of how games like *Total War: Rome II* create new versions of history. The *Total War* series is massively popular – *Total War: Rome II* was Sega's top-selling video game in 2014 – and reaches an audience of millions across the globe.[20] For many of these players, the experience with the *Total War* franchise marks their first extensive engagement with the ancient world. As such, the way that game presents the past defines how players perceive antiquity. Further, their experiences with the ancient world are reinforced and shaped by the extensive online community on Facebook, Reddit and various video game forums dedicated to the *Total War* series. When players discuss strategies, complain about game features and make jokes about the series in these fora, they produce and codify insights and perspectives about the ancient world. These insights do not come from a shared experience of reading ancient texts, but from encountering the ancient world within the context and confines of these games.

Reimagining Arminius

After this opening vignette fades to black, the player is transported to the moment right before the battle begins. As the Roman army marches along a road through the forest, a caption informs them that the troops are relocating to their winter camp with the help of Arminius. At this point, the camera shifts its focus from the Roman army and Varus' missteps to the figure of Arminius. Arminius is shown riding on horseback behind the other Roman cavalrymen. Arminius does not wear the same armour and headgear as the rest of Roman soldiers. Rather, he wears a distinct costume, consisting of a wolfskin cloak and long, dark trousers (Fig. 5.2).

Fig. 5.2 Arminius' mask in *Total War: Rome II* (2013 © The Creative Assembly/SEGA. All rights reserved).

The image of the Cheruscan chieftain does not come from the ancient sources. None of our sources on the battle mention anything about Arminius' garb. Nor does it appear to be significantly influenced by the numerous statues, paintings, and movies depicting Arminius from the modern era. The Arminius of *Total War: Rome II* does not wear the winged helmet from the *Hermannsdenkmal* statue that became part and parcel of his cinematic depiction in the twentieth century (Fig. 5.3).[21] He does not have the flowing blonde hair characteristic of Arminius in eighteenth- and nineteenth-century paintings by Johannes Gehrts (Fig. 5.3) or Joseph Bergler.[22]

Fig. 5.3 Nineteenth-century depictions of Arminius ([*top*] Ernst von Bandel, *Hermannsdenkmal*, 1875 © Lippe; [*bottom*] Johannes Gehrts, *Armin verabschiedet sich von Thusnelda*, 1884 © Lippisches Landesmuseum Detmold).

Rather, the game's developers reimagine Arminius in light of modern conventions to make him recognizable to the audience of *Total War: Rome II*. Take, for instance, the trousers that Arminius wears. In addition to distinguishing him from the other Roman soldiers in the scene, the trousers signal his barbarian origins. From comics like *Asterix and Obelix* to TV series like *Barbarians*, trousers are a key part of modern depictions of barbarians from northern Europe. The wolf skin cloak functions similarly. The animal skin recalls the standard modern visual convention of a northern European barbarian.[23] Warriors from Northern Europe, usually of Germanic or Nordic descent, are frequently depicted with animal skins in comic books, movies, and card games. The animal skin reflects the distance of the barbarian from civilization, their close union with the natural world, and their beast-like strength (a trope that, itself, has ancient roots).

In addition to drawing on visual stereotypes of barbarians in portraying Arminius, the developers relied on a character type familiar to players: the berserker. Berserkers have long been a popular character in role-playing games like *Dungeons and Dragons* and *World of Warcraft* as well as historically based real-time strategy games like *Age of Mythology*. In these games, berserkers are powerful Germanic/Nordic warriors, defined by uncontrollable rage and a frenzied style of fighting, and usually adorned with an animal skin cloak. Beyond the similarities in dress, there are other explicit clues that point towards the influence of the berserker trope on Arminius. In *Total War: Rome II*, berserkers are one of the units of the only playable German faction in the game, the Suebi. Further, these units wear a wolf-skin cloak, nearly identical to Arminius' garb in the Battle of Teutoburg Forest. The 2016 Creative Assembly release, *Total War: ARENA*, a free, team-based strategy game, in which players take on the persona of a famous general, is even more direct in its association of Arminius with berserkers. One of the special characteristics that Arminius possesses in the game is 'frenzy', an attribute which the game's developers describe as the ability to inspire their troops to 'berserk rage'.[24] In depicting Arminius as a powerful German warrior with a wolf-skin cloak, the game's developers use the image of the berserker to signal the nature of the Cheruscan chieftain: savage, strong and unpredictable.

As the camera zooms in on Arminius, another distinctive aspect of his appearance is revealed. Underneath the wolf-skin cloak is a silver mask, which he puts on before riding away to meet with his fellow conspirators (Fig. 5.2). The role of the mask within the game is clear. It signals Arminius' duplicitous nature and his plan to betray the Roman army. Indeed, as Arminius dons the mask, the player hears a voice-over that reveals a conversation between Varus and one of his advisors, in which the former says, 'Arminius a traitor, I think not.' But once again, there is no precedent for the depiction: there is no ancient evidence indicating that Arminius wore a silver mask nor are there any post-classical depictions of the German leader wearing such a mask prior to the game's release. The inspiration for this aspect of Arminius' depiction seems to come from the excavations at Kalkriese: in 1990, archaeologists discovered a silver Roman cavalry mask in excellent condition at the site.[25] The mask that Arminius wears in the cutscene is identical.

However, the way the mask is figured in the scene bears little relation to the use of the object in antiquity. According to the second century CE historian, Arrian, cavalry masks were ceremonial and meant to be worn in cavalry parades and mock battles (Arr. *Tact.* 34). The masks were markers of Roman elite status and a key part of the public performance of that status.[26] The use of the mask in the cutscene runs almost exactly counter to its original purpose. As mentioned above, Arminius' donning of the mask indicates his duplicitous nature and prefigures betrayal of Rome. The game developers do not deploy this popular and relevant archaeological discovery to bolster the historicity of the scene, but rather use its modern resonances – the mask as an object of danger and duplicity – to enhance the narrative within the cutscene.[27] As such, the use of the mask in the scene underscores the variety of ways in which video games transform and repurpose the past in service to gameplay. At the same time, it also helps to illustrate the different sources that inform the version of the ancient world presented in *Total War: Rome II* – the game developers draw on and adapt recent archaeological finds, modern visual conventions, and ancient sources alike in reconstructing antiquity.[28]

The composite depiction of Arminius presented in *Total War: Rome II* has already gained cultural currency. For example, Arminius features in the show, *Barbarians Rising*, a History Channel series that attempts to chronicle different revolts against Rome from the point of view of the rebels. In the show's retelling of the Battle of Teutoburg Forest, Arminius signals his plans to defect to his fellow Germans by a change of garb. He takes off his traditional Roman battle gear and replaces it with trousers and an animal skin cloak, almost identical to the outfit that he wears in *Total War: Rome II*. Given the generalized depiction of Arminius in *Total War: Rome II*, it may seem far-fetched to suggest that his portrayal in *Barbarians Rising* is influenced by his appearance in the game. However, it is worth noting the History Channel has long used *Rome: Total War* as a visual basis for reconstructing ancient history. In 2004, the History Channel launched a series called *Decisive Battles*, in which the original *Rome: Total War* battle engine was used to simulate and reconstruct ancient battles, including the Battle of Teutoburg Forest.[29] Similarly, in *Total War: ARENA*, Arminius is depicted in nearly exactly the same way as he is in *Total War: Rome II*, only the colour of his tunic and trousers have changed. As seen above, in discussing the new-found popularity of the quote from Suetonius, *Total War: Rome II* offers an important platform for new interpretations of the ancient world and their dissemination to a broad audience.

Arminius the Liberator

After Arminius is introduced to the player, the next part of the cutscene takes place in the forest, where the Cheruscan prince addresses his supporters. He tells them that: 'Rome may have raised me. Rome may have trained me. But my loyalty is to my people.' As he delivers his speech, his German allies shout raucously in approval and prepare for battle. Here, Arminius is depicted as a freedom fighter, a man who rejects the allure of empire to serve his native land. The portrayal of Arminius as a liberator dates back to Tacitus in the early second century CE.[30] Unlike other ancient sources that cast Arminius as a turncoat, Tacitus depicts him as a man devoted to his *patria* and dedicated to *libertas*. Emblematic of Tacitus' treatment of Arminius is the short eulogy that he gives to him at the end of Book 2 of the *Annales*. In this passage, Tacitus praises him as, 'without doubt, the liberator of Germany' (*liberator haud dubie Germaniae*), and credits him for standing up to Roman power at its peak (Tac. *Ann.* 2.88.2–3). In the Tacitean discourse, total devotion of a barbarian chieftain to values that the Romans had long held so dear offer a stark contrast to the dark world of the Tiberian Principate and reveals the extent of Rome's moral decline.

In depicting Arminius as a liberator, the game's developers, however, engage with more than just the Tacitean memory of the German leader. Tacitus' heroic portrayal of Arminius as the *liberator Germaniae* has had a complicated and controversial *Nachleben*. Arminius and his successful resistance against the Roman Empire became popular in Germany from the Renaissance onwards.[31] From Heinrich von Kleist's *Hermannsschlacht* to Max Bruch's *Arminius* to the monumental *Hermannsdenkmal*, the legend of Arminius was prevalent in all forms of artistic expression in Germany during this time period. The ubiquity of Arminius in German culture was a consequence of historical circumstance. The story of a Germanic warrior rebuffing an imperial power was a fitting source of inspiration during the Napoleonic occupation of Germany in the early nineteenth century.[32] In the years after, Arminius' ability to bring together disparate German tribes served as an ideal historical model for the push towards national unification. As such, Arminius became a symbol of the innate strength and resoluteness of German character and an emblem of German nationalism.[33] This narrative did not fade from consciousness in the early twentieth century. Arminius and the Battle of Teutoburg Forest featured heavily in Nazi propaganda in the early 1930s. Hitler was hailed as a modern Arminius, destined to liberate Germany from the oppressive restrictions of the Treaty of Versailles.[34] The comparison with Arminius was one that Hitler personally accepted and encouraged: his picture appeared next to the *Hermannsdenkmal* on postcards, Kaufman's famous painting of the Cheruscan prince hung in his office, and, in his private discussions, he frequently referred to Arminius and the Battle of Teutoburg Forest as the foundation of German history.[35]

The use of Arminius by the Nazi Party had significant ramifications for the way in which the Cheruscan chieftain has been remembered after the Second World War. Arminius' popularity in Germany waned significantly in the second half of the twentieth century. In the rare circumstances in which he was invoked, those involved have either been careful and explicit in avoiding the Arminius-as-liberator trope or have openly satirized the nationalistic fervour that he formerly inspired.[36] Emblematic of this shift in attitude towards Arminius were the celebrations surrounding the 2,000th anniversary of the Battle of Teutoburg Forest in 2009.[37] The festivities, which were purposefully muted out of fear of sparking unsavoury forms of nationalism, were widely regarded as a success because the event was 'dealt with far more soberly than one might have expected'.[38] However, despite the efforts to suppress the sinister aspects of the legend, its use by the Nazis has made Arminius popular with radical conservative circles in the United States over the last decade. The *Barnes Review*, a publication whose namesake was a Holocaust denier and which touts itself as a 'journal of nationalist thought and history', dedicated an issue to the 2,000th anniversary of Teutoburg Forest and featured Arminius on the cover, hailing him as 'the man who helped free Europe from Roman domination'.[39] White nationalists have also used the internet to propagate the image of Arminius as the defender of the Aryan race and as a model for rejecting cultural, intellectual and political hegemony from outsiders (i.e. Jews and immigrants).[40] The revival of Arminius for these purposes is in some ways unsurprising. Not only do ideologies used by the Nazis inform much of the worldview of the alt-right, but, as Donna Zuckerberg has demonstrated, such groups often use antiquity to lend an intellectual lineage to their misogynistic and racist worldviews.[41]

In depicting Arminius as a freedom fighter dedicated above all to his fellow tribesman, *Total War: Rome II* thus reproduces a controversial and dangerous narrative about the Cheruscan prince. The dissemination of such a narrative is all the more problematic because, as we have seen above, the representation of the past produced by the game has a profound influence on perceptions of antiquity in modern media and internet culture. Scholars and social commentators have shown that the online gaming community is closely connected to radical conservative groups and often serves as a recruiting ground for these associations.[42] Accordingly, in casting Arminius as a freedom fighter, *Total War: Rome II* broadcasts a problematic version of events to an audience that is primed to receive and use it for harmful purposes.

Arminius the Victor?

The speech of Arminius is the last part of the cutscene before the gameplay begins. But the narrative of the German chieftain as liberator does not end here. After the gameplay ends, the player sees a second cutscene, providing a postscript to the battle. This cutscene begins with the voice-over of two soldiers talking after their escape from the battle. After thanking the gods, one of the soldiers inquires about Varus, while the other bluntly dismisses the question as unimportant. At this point, the camera cuts to a shot of Varus wandering aimlessly on horseback through a forest, where he is confronted by two German soldiers, who block his escape. As Varus' horse rears up, the camera pans to reveal Arminius right behind him. Arminius, still wearing the wolf-skin cloak and cavalry mask, grabs Varus and wrestles him to the ground, killing the Roman commander with his sword. The player is left with the image of Arminius looming over a cowering Varus.

This cutscene is remarkable in the way that it challenges the narratives that underpin the historical battle within the game. None of our ancient sources suggest that Varus was killed by Arminius. Velleius Paterculus, Cassius Dio and Florus, all record that Varus killed himself by running through a sword, just as his father and grandfather had done before him. In fact, in the narratives of Florus and Dio, Varus' suicide is an object of praise: Florus refers to his suicide as a brave deed akin to Paulus' death at the Battle of Cannae (Flor. 2.30.25), and Dio claims that it was a shrewd manoeuvre that allowed him to avoid the ignominy of being captured and tortured by Arminius (Dio. 56.21.5). While we have seen that developers of *Total War: Rome II* reinterpret and embellish ancient narratives to create a better gaming experience for the player, this is a rare instance in which the game's developers totally deviate from what the sources say about the battle.

But it is not only the ancient narratives about the battle that are destabilized in the second cutscene – it also challenges the game's internal narrative. The player's goal in playing the Teutoburg Forest scenario is to stave off the attack of Arminius and help the Roman army to arrive at the winter camp unharmed. Yet, even if the player successfully completes the scenario and helps the Roman army to reach its winter quarters, Varus, the figure with whom the player, as the commander of Roman forces, ostensibly identifies, nevertheless dies. As such, the second cutscene undercuts the player's successful completion of the battle and calls into question their agency in the scenario. In doing so, the cutscene subverts one of the defining and most appealing aspects of the historical battle mode: the player's ability to control and write their own account of history through their actions.[43]

Indeed, the desire of the developers to continue the Arminius as liberator narrative even supersedes the game's conventions. The scene in which Arminius kills Varus is the only use of a second cutscene in the historical battle mode in *Total War: Rome II* – no other historical battle receives such a coda. The game's developers have gone to great lengths – breaking with the ancient sources, the scenario's internal narrative and the game's conventions – to focus on the character of Arminius. This decision to put Arminius at the forefront of the cutscene comes into even further relief when the history of the battle in the *Total War* series is considered. The original *Rome: Total War* also featured the Battle of Teutoburg Forest among the playable historical battles. However, in the scenario from the 2004 game, Arminius features minimally. While it is mentioned briefly that he is responsible for leading Varus into an ambush, Arminius does not actually appear in the scene. There is no speech, no second cutscene in which he gets his revenge against Varus. In *Total War: Rome II*, the game developers have consciously made the choice to give Arminius the last word in the Battle of Teutoburg Forest.

Conclusion

The analysis above has shown how the cutscene for the Battle of Teutoburg Forest is grafted from a wide range of sources, fusing together ancient and modern narratives and drawing from a variety of cultural influences. In bringing together these differing narratives, the cutscene pens a new chapter in the history of the Battle of Teutoburg Forest. It reimagines Arminius in the light of modern visual conventions, casting him as a stereotypically barbarian, an echo of the berserker type commonly found in video games. The scene also invents a new ending for the battle, in which Arminius gets the ultimate revenge against Varus. At the same time, the cutscene reinvigorates old narratives about the encounter. Most prominently, it casts Arminius as a heroic liberator, recalling Tacitus' assessment of the Cheruscan chieftain and along with it his long and, at times, insidious afterlife as a German national hero. But the cutscene does not just represent an interesting and complex interpretation of a famous battle from antiquity. This short cutscene, due in large part to the popularity of the *Total War* series among online communities, has prompted further engagement with and led to new interpretations of the Battle of Teutoburg Forest. From the memeification of the Suetonian quotation to the reuse of the game's depiction of Arminius in *Barbarians Rising*, the cutscene has impacted the way that modern audiences have imagined the battle and its consequences.

On a broader scale, the above analysis reveals how video games are changing how we understand the past. Video games produce new narratives of antiquity that are designed to be accessible, legible and appealing to the modern audience. These new versions of ancient history serve as a gateway for further reinterpretation for millions, particularly within the context of online gaming communities. This reality means that it is incumbent upon classicists and ancient historians alike to think critically about video games. Video games represent a new, diverse and serious engagement with antiquity that will shape how our field of study will be perceived for years to come.

Notes

1   Egenfeldt-Nielsen, Smith and Tosca (2008: 206–8).
2   Zimmerman (2002: 120–9) criticized cutscenes and their developers as having 'cinema envy'.
3   The level of interactivity allowed in cutscenes is debated among scholars of gaming. Cf. Collins (2007: 212, 'a movie that plays, in which the player does not control any actions') vs Fritsch (2013: 13, 'intermission of gameplay in which the player usually cannot or can only slightly influence events on screen').
4   Galloway (2006: 10–12).
5   Salen and Zimmerman (2003: 406–19) provides a typology of cutscenes.
6   O'Grady (2013: 114–24).
7   Hancock (2002).
8   By reception here, I mean the act of an individual or group interpreting the past in light of their personal subjectivities. On the subject of reception, Martindale (1993) is foundational and Leonard (2009: 835–46) offers a discussion of different approaches.
9   For more on these debates about the battle, see Swan (2004: 250–70).
10 Vell. Pat. 2.117–19; Tac. *Ann.* 1.60–2; 2.88: Flor. 2.34–5; Dio 56.18–23.
11 German scholars (e.g. Wolters 2008: 125–49) have in recent times walked back from the assertion that the battle was an epoch-making event.
12 Cf. Ov. *Tr.* 4.2.31–4 and Man. *Astr.* 1.893–908. Crinagoras, a Greek poet contemporaneous with the battle, wrote two epigrams on the events (*Anthologia Graeca* 7.741, 9.291).
13 Winkler (2016: 55–79), Sommer (2016: 219–34) and Warren (2016: 235–68).
14 For publication of the findings at Kalriese, see Berger (1996), Schlüter (1999), Harnecker and Tolksdorf-Lienemann (2004), Wilbers-Rost (2007), Harnecker (2008, 2011), Wolters (2008) and Rost and Wilbers-Rost (2013).
15 The cutscene can be found at the following link: https://www.youtube.com/watch?v=JzbHl8XkRRU (accessed 29 October 2018).
16 The misspelling of Quintilius appears to be a typographical error that was not caught before production.
17 For discussion of the Tacitean scene, see Goodyear (1972: 2.94–102), and Pagan (1999: 302–20).
18 On Tacitus' portrayal of how battle influenced Roman memory, see O'Gorman (2000: 49–56) and Seidman (2014: 94–107).
19 Internet memes are defined by Davison as 'a piece of culture, typically a joke, which gains influence through online transmission'. For academic approaches to memes, see Davison (2011: 120–34), Bauckhage (2012: 42–9) and Shifman (2013a: 362–77).

20 Karmali (2014) reports that the game sold 1.13 million copies between its September 2013 release and 31 March 2014.

21 Winkler (2016: 65–79, on the *Hermannsdenkmal*, and 127–58 on its use in movies).

22 Warren (2016: 235–68) discusses the importance of Arminius in the artistic landscape of the period.

23 It should be noted that this was also the standard ancient convention as well.

24 Cf. the 2015 press release about the game, available online (accessed 6 November 2018) https://www.gamasutra.com/view/pressreleases/254483/Total_War_ARENA__Fury_of_Arminius_Update.php.

25 Rost and Wilbers-Rost (2010: 119).

26 On Roman cavalry masks, see Dixon and Southern (1992: 128–32).

27 It is worth noting that the mask, as a popular archaeological discovery, adds to the feeling that the player is entering the world of the past, regardless of its historicity. For more on this phenomenon of 'affective historicity', see Winnerling (2014: 151–70) and Rollinger (2016: 313–41).

28 The use of a mélange of source material of varying levels of reliability is indicative of the claim that video games subsume 'high' and 'low' culture in reimaging the ancient world (e.g. Lowe, 2009: 68–9).

29 Gaudiosi (2004) discusses the interaction between the two ventures.

30 Winkler (2016: 32–7).

31 Sommer (2016: 223–6) and Winkler (2016: 56–65).

32 Michelsen (1987: 115–36) and Struck (1997: 106–39).

33 The event was so ingrained in national imagination that it was occasionally satirized (cf. Heine's 1844 satirical epic poem, *Deutschland. Ein Wintermärchen*).

34 Winkler (2016: 75–91).

35 Ibid., 115–24.

36 This shift happened in a variety of media (cf. Winkler, 2016: 189–282), including academia (e.g. Timpe, 1970).

37 See also Carlà-Uhink (2017: 407–24).

38 Crossland (2009) quoting Bendikowski's reaction to the celebrations surrounding the battle.

39 Winkler (2016: 287–97).

40 The number of posts on Arminius on the prominent white nationalist/anti-Semitic site, chechar.wordpress.com, is emblematic; among recent examples is this post: https://theroperreportsite.wordpress.com/2018/05/27/arminius/ (accessed 29 October 2018).

41 Zuckerberg's (2015 and 2016) articles discuss the use of classical antiquity in the 'manosphere'.

42 Nagle (2017) discusses how online forums contribute to the American culture wars of the 2010s.

43 Chapman (2016: 231–64).

Digital Legionaries

Video Game Simulations of the Face of Battle in the Roman Republic

Jeremiah McCall

On the battlefields during the Roman Republic, soldiers fought and died in brutal clashes of wood and metal, leather and flesh. Reconstructing how these battles were fought and how actors and the elements of the physical and psychological environment engaged in a set of intertwining systems continues to interest all manner of students today. That interest understandably has extended to video game designers seeking to depict Romans in battle. In these games, players take on the roles of generals, commanding their troops in clashes of infantry and cavalry, seeking to claim victory on the battlefield against their digital foes.

Because these games, like most video games, are commercially designed to entertain players, they are often dismissed by students of ancient history and ancient battle. This is the unfortunate result of prejudices against popular visions of the past as frivolous and the general tendency among some historians to privilege the narrative and analytical text as the proper medium for translating the past to modern audiences. Certainly, progress has been made in accepting that film is a historical medium, different from text, not inferior, but video games are much younger than film – if we take *Hammurabi*, the simple text-based civilization management game of 1968 as our first historical video game, then such games have existed for about fifty years. Film is more than twice that old.[1]

Despite any misgivings, video games about ancient warfare are worth considering for several reasons. First, they are a form of popular media firmly embedded in modern society and encountered in some cases by millions of players. Accordingly, they form a considerable bridge between the past and the present, a medium by which many encounter ancient battle. Second, they offer multimodal – visual, audio and textual – models that provide a greater level of sensory input and communication than text alone, and thus have the potential for a more immersive model, capturing more of the actual sense-channels employed in battle. Third, they are interactive, enabling players to take different tacks, consider different choices, and see how those decisions produce different outcomes.

Fourth, a point not often recognized, though designed for entertainment and potentially flawed in terms of accuracy, these video games integrate formal and informal models of ancient battle. Ancient historians have developed models of battle in the Roman world since at least the nineteenth century. However strong their explanatory power, they are informal, expressed only in words.[2] They are flexible but imprecise in their relationships and difficult to test and retest, if indeed they can be tested at all. Formal models, on the other hand, use mathematics to express exact relationships between constituent elements and can be more readily tested. So, for example, where a historian might construct an informal model by simply noting, say, 'soldiers on higher ground had an advantage over their opponents', the game *Field of Glory 2* precisely, not necessarily accurately but exactly, expresses that advantage in terms of Points of Advantage, a number added to a sum of numbers and used to determine an exact range of casualties – modified by some random numbers to add a sense of contingency – that the unit on higher ground inflicts on the unit on lower ground. This is what is meant by the precision of a formal model and it allows formal models to be more easily compared, tested, and retested. Again, however, it must be noted that this precision neither means nor implies historical accuracy, only precision and, ideally, clarity in a model of the past.

Video games about Roman warfare, though they have useful and immersive informal elements of descriptive text, image, video and sound, are fundamentally mathematical models. When combined with multimodal representations and interactivity, they offer precisely interconnected, closed and fully operational multimedia systems. They are not, it must be noted, more accurate models of ancient warfare than those offered by expert historians in text. But they are more holistic in their models of ancient battle. The best informal scholarly models of ancient battle, because they are made of words and, occasionally, images, are accordingly more inexact in their models, not meaningfully interactive, and cannot function independently. It is important to be precise on this point. The research and analysis of expert historians has done much to illuminate for us the face of Roman battle. But these text descriptions of battle do not provide a fully working model that one can run, observe and hear, interact with and study. One cannot play a text model or a picture model of ancient battle, however detailed and evocative, but one can certainly play a video game model of battle. None of this is to suggest that interactive formal models of battle in video games are necessarily historically accurate, nor is it to suggest that they are categorically more accurate than historians' writings on the subject. Rather, video games offer exact (quantifiable) relations, are fully operational, notwithstanding bugs in the code, and manipulable. In short, one can play them and test them as systems. These features give them the *potential* to offer more exact and holistic ways to conceptualize and analyse the dynamics of ancient battles in the past.[3]

Furthermore, these games enable players to visualize what essentially must be imagined in operation to be analysed and understood: ancient combat. Successful history requires the ability to visualize people, places, things and interactions no longer present. Ancient battles strain that ability to imagine. Unlike fundamentally static untestable text models of battles, video games are dynamic interactive models of what was essentially a dynamic and interactive affair. They can provide a closer analogy between model and reality.[4] As such, they offer something potentially quite valuable for players, whether students of ancient battle or not: a visual and playable systems-based foil that, especially when compared to other game models, helps form questions about the realities of ancient battle. Solid video game models of battle – visual, formal and interactive – can potentially help clarify how we understand ancient battle, whether by offering sound visual models or by provoking our critique with more flawed representations.

A final thought: some have suggested that to be truly of value in understanding the past, historical video games need to be made more accurate, perhaps even be designed by trained historians.[5] Yet, video game models of ancient battles formally model and visualize dynamics already, and they *are* history, although they were not designed and coded by trained historians. They are doing the work of history, the meaningful transformation of the past into a different medium.[6] They deserve recognition as legitimate expressions of history, not as a historical technique that will be legitimate only when fully colonized by academic historians.

The remainder of this chapter examines the battle modes of two video games about Roman battle in the third and second centuries BCE: Byzantine Game's *Field of Glory 2* and Creative Assembly's *Total War: Rome II*. These games are the most recent iterations of two different approaches to ancient warfare in video games. They are also the most technologically sophisticated in the field. This chapter will consider not their point-by-point accuracy, but their ability in general to achieve some levels of accurate historical modelling. By this, I mean the extent to which a game gets the general systems and causal relationships right in *broad strokes*, that is to say, is *relatively faithful* to what we know about how such systems operated and such causal relationships functioned in the past. These are necessarily ambiguous criteria because historians necessarily will debate whether this or that understanding sufficiently fits the evidence. Nevertheless, a game with reasonably accurate models of ancient battle might not get all the details correct but would – consistent with the historical evidence – plausibly and defensibly model the systems in operation on the battlefield and offer the potential for the player to better understand how the battlefield and warriors functioned and why different sorts of occurrences happened. Such a game model could help a player not only understand and sometimes visualize the dynamics of ancient battle better, but it could inspire questions useful to historians as they similarly work to understand the ancient battlefield.

The face of battle in the Roman Republic: An outline

A basic outline of ancient battle mechanics during this period will help ground the discussion. Battles *c.* 300–100 BC, the period focused on by the games and treated more or less by Polybius, pitted Roman armies against opponents in theatres ranging from Italy and North Africa to Spain and Syria. These battles focused on more or less organized lines of close-order infantry – termed 'heavy infantry' not necessarily because of any protective armour, but because their purpose was to stand close to enemies and trade blows in hand-to-hand combat. Though armies and strategies varied from battle to battle, the outlines stayed essentially the same. Heavy infantry occupied the centre of a main battle line, standing – certainly in cases like the Hellenistic phalanx and with reasonable speculation, when it comes to Romans and others – at least several rows deep. They clashed directly with their opponents in the enemy battle line, dealing wounds and death, stirring fear, confusion and panic along the way. Light infantry – again, a designation of function, not armament – used their fleetness of foot and missile weapons like javelins to harass the heavy infantry of the battle lines. Cavalry played dual roles, attempting to attack the vulnerable flanks of their enemy's heavy infantry battle line while defending their own infantry flanks against the enemy cavalry.[7]

In the Roman mid-Republic variant of the heavy infantry army, legions of some 4,200–5,000 infantry, were divided into four classes. The *velites*, the youngest, served as light infantry. Three classes of heavy infantry, each divided into ten units called 'maniples', constituted the main battle line. Those at the front were the *hastati*, the youngest. Next came the *principes*, men in their prime. *Hastati* and *principes* were armed with *pila*, shields, short swords and small, square, bronze heart-protectors; those sufficiently wealthy wore a mail shirt for additional protection. The third line of maniples consisted of *triarii*. These veteran soldiers initially had sturdy thrusting spears and served as a final line of defence if the *hastati* and *principes* were driven back. Finally, a cavalry contingent of some 200–300 citizen troopers accompanied each Roman legion to battle. The citizen soldiers in the legions of a Roman army were regularly accompanied by an equal or greater number of Italian allied troops armed and perhaps organized in roughly the same way.[8]

Although the iron edges of weapons employed in earnest mutilated limbs and ended lives, these battles were not – as many historians have recognized since at least the nineteenth-century officer and historian Ardant du Picq – free-for-alls where the ranks of the battle lines intertwined, each soldier finding a foe in the chaos, the whole affair devolving into a monstrous brawl that produced extreme casualties.[9] Rather, the evidence suggests that Roman battles could last for hours, though only a fraction of the victorious army's soldiers died compared to the defeated, some 10 per cent versus over 50 per cent.[10] This suggests that the battles of this period, though involving a considerable amount of death-dealing, were more importantly tests of morale – defined here as the will to maintain one's position and continue fighting. Combatants who maintained sufficient morale during the tremendous stresses of battle made up units and formations that maintained their cohesion and space in the battle line. When successful in this business, cavalry could play a critical role in damaging the morale of enemy infantry.[11]

If sufficient soldiers in a front-line formation lost the will to resist, to maintain their positions against attacking foes, their formation would deform and dissolve. If sufficient formations failed to maintain their position and space against the enemy, holes in the battle line could appear that might be exploited by the enemy, whole segments of the battle line might collapse, or, most decisively, the battle line as a whole could falter, its individual soldiers fleeing for safety rather than joining with comrades to hold their positions. This kind of rout generally ended an army's effective resistance. Unless the fleeing enemies rallied, which happened occasionally through the exercise of tremendous leadership skills, there was little left for the victors to do other than pursue their opponents and cut them down indiscriminately as they fled.[12]

The common features of video game battles

Any given medium shapes its message about the past significantly. That this is true for historical narrative has been discussed for quite some time.[13] The majority of historical games – taking the definition of games that begin at a specific point in real world history and have gameplay that is directly shaped by that history – approach simulating the past in two ways.[14] Some, like the *Assassin's Creed* and *Call of Duty* series, are what Chapman calls 'realist simulations'. They focus on presenting a visually verisimilitudinous environment, the past as it is claimed to have appeared and as a world the player can navigate. Others, like the *Civilization* series, are 'conceptual simulations'. They suggest how the systems and processes of the past functioned through underlying rule sets presented to the player through more abstract symbols and graphics, not through verisimilitudinous visuals.[15] *Field of Glory 2* and *Total War: Rome II* have some realist leanings in their depictions of soldiers and terrain but rely heavily on rules and mechanics to present a conceptual-style argument about battles in the past.

Both games also, like most historical games, present the past as a series of historical problem spaces.[16] That is, they present the past in terms of:

- a primary agent with one or more roles and goals, operating within
- a physical space, a virtual world or subsection with an environment and geography that includes
- any number of elements, including other agents modelled by the AI as NPCs (non-player characters), that can afford and assist player actions, constrain player actions or both, depending on the situation; and so, the player crafts
- strategies and makes choices to take advantage of available affordances, work within or around constraints and achieve their goal.

This certainly can be a problematic way to approach the past, in that it can overemphasize agents' conscious goal-oriented behaviour, and casts those other than the primary agent as instruments. When applied specifically to the study of ancient warfare, however, the historical problem space approach of video games works quite well. For, in battle, there was a great deal of conscious goal-oriented behaviour, whether the goal was to stay alive, kill another, make one's family proud, keep the line intact, or command a great victory. The battlefield is a perfect example of a containing physical geography that had elements and agents that could assist and constrain – terrain, weather, the physical condition of agents, their morale, the presence of enemy soldiers, weapons, etc. Commanders, officers and common soldiers formed strategies and made decisions to reach their goals of the moment and long-term goals within their environment, their space.

With all this in mind, let us consider how *Field of Glory 2* and *Total War: Rome II* as conceptual simulations model the historical problem spaces of ancient Roman battle and illustrate important topics in the understanding of these battles.

The games

Originally, a digital version of a still existing commercial set of rules for tabletop miniatures battles, Byzantine Studios' *Field of Glory 2* (FoG2) has moved further from

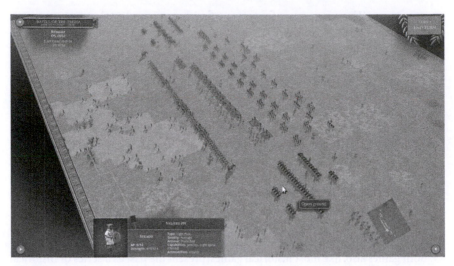

Fig. 6.1 A bird's-eye view of the Roman and Carthaginian armies at the Battle of the Trebia in *Field of Glory 2* (2017 © Slitherine. All rights reserved).

the tabletop roots of its predecessor while maintaining some core features of the original ruleset (Fig. 6.1). FoG2 is a turn-based game focused on detailed battle mechanics that the designers intend to model the historical factors of combat in the Roman world. The battlefield is rendered as a 3D topographical terrain map, divided into a grid. True to its past as a physical miniatures game, each unit is represented as a 3D model of soldiers where one individual model represents 60 combatants and there are eight models and thus 480 combatants represented in a standard heavy infantry unit. The types of units run the gamut for this period: Roman maniples, Gallic warbands, Macedonian phalanxes and so on. The unit as a whole, not the individual, is the basic element in these battles. During the player's turn, units may be manoeuvred and moved a finite number of squares. When in range, a unit can engage the enemy in melee once per turn and, potentially, missile combat, depending on the type of unit. Animations and audio of weapons and shouts punctuate these clashes, deepening a movement and battle system that is not wholly unlike a chess game. Armies battle until a significant number of one army's units rout.

Three core elements of *Total War: Rome II* (TWR2) distinguish it from FoG2. First, the battles in the game are real-time. The player can pause the game to think, survey the battlefield, make plans, and issue commands; otherwise, the game runs non-stop, units manoeuvring and clashing according to player or AI commands. Second, unlike FoG2, which uses the unit of 480 soldiers as its base, TWR2 uses the individual combatant as the base of its combat model. Third, while FoG2 is graphically appealing and stylish, TWR2 is a big-budget spectacle with hundreds of individual combatants on screen, highly detailed 3D models, digital generals delivering stirring speeches, and all manner of engaging audio-visual trappings giving it the spectacle of a blockbuster movie. Units engaged in battle continue to fight until they have driven off foes or suffered a decrease

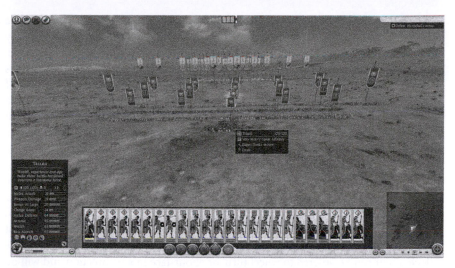

Fig. 6.2 A battlefield view in *Total War: Rome II* (2013 © The Creative Assembly/SEGA. All rights reserved).

in morale sufficient to make them rout and flee the battlefield. Victory is achieved when one side's units have all fled the battlefield perimeter (Fig. 6.2).

Three systems in these games form the core of their battle simulations: manoeuvre, combat and command. These will be considered in turn.

Manoeuvre models

The historical scenarios of FoG2, including period battles such as Cannae (216 BCE), Zama (202 BCE), Magnesia (190 BCE) and Pydna (168 BCE), start with opposing armies deployed; custom scenarios allow the player-general to manage their own deployments. From their initial positions, the player manoeuvres units to engage digital foes. FoG2's model of manoeuvre is turn-based. Orthogonal movement costs a certain number of Action Points, and diagonal movement costs 1.5 times as many points. Rugged terrain requires more points to cross than open terrain. Light units can turn in any direction once per turn while other units must pay additional points. Being in the command radius of a general unit plays an important role in movement. Any unit in command – in the command radius of a general unit – may turn 45° without using any Action Points. Units not in command must pay the Action Points to turn. On top of this, since a unit can only occupy one square and only one unit is allowed per square, the width and depth of formations cannot be changed other than by positioning multiple units of the same type adjacent to each other to form a line. This ruleset, in practice, significantly limits the ability of units to move on the battlefield and emphasizes the necessity of needing a nearby commander to effectively manoeuvre.

As with FoG2, TWR2 has historical and custom battles, such as Cannae, Zama and Pydna, with corresponding deployments. TWR2's fluid real-time manoeuvre model, however, feels very different from the turn-based FoG2. The player can pause the game at any time to issue orders, but they are not required to do so. Commands are issued by clicking on a unit and then its target, an enemy unit or a location on the battlefield. Orders are carried out in real-time: units move at a certain speed to execute commands as they are issued, hastening when ordered to run or gallop into position. A series of buttons along the bottom of the screen allow the player to reform the entire army in a variety of complex formations with the single click of a button. Units engaged will fight one another in missile combat, melee combat or both. Roman *hastati* and *principes*, for example, cast their *pila* at the enemy before closing to engage with swords. As fitting for the most mainstream and popular wargame series, the nimble speed of the units is quite pronounced. Once selected, a simple mouse-drag causes the soldiers in the unit to fan out into a shallower unit, from many ranks deep to two ranks. Another gesture draws them in, a radical change of formation width and depth that is executed quickly: although the digital soldiers trot to their new positions at the game's setting of footspeed, they have a stunning ability to find their new position quickly. The same selected unit can be ordered to wheel turn, or about-face in any direction and will do so with great ease. The manoeuvre is not instantaneous for the soldiers, but it is fast and polished at a level hardly likely to have been achieved in the ancient world for most soldiers, not even, perhaps, for the most professionally trained and drilled.[17] Where FoG2 better offers a sense of the ponderous movement of the battle line, TWR2 offers a better sense of individual soldiers engaging in a complex manoeuvre. Somewhat. Despite their speed, the jumbles of individuals fumble rather than navigate into place, and it is difficult to imagine a well-trained unit adopting such a haphazard method of manoeuvre.

These video games model manoeuvre in different ways that raise useful questions about the form and structure of units and the manoeuvrability of units in ancient battles. Most importantly, how rectilinear and orderly were unit formations in battle? FoG2 units occupy squares neatly, regardless of their cohesion, troop losses, movement or any other factor at work in the maths underneath the visuals. This has a clean look to it and emphasizes the idea that well-formed cohesive units were essential to a proper heavy infantry battle line and success in battle. Clearly, though, the model poses problems. Common sense – at times a dangerous authority but sometimes essential – dictates that soldiers could not have kept such perfect formations throughout the stresses of combat, nor indeed throughout the less stressful challenges of simply crossing terrain. TWR2 similarly begins with its heavy infantry units, and indeed most units, deployed in rectilinear formations. However, where all the soldiers in an FoG2 unit move as an organized block, neatly from square to square, units moving in TWR2 require individuals to move to their new positions. They do so with an unlikely degree of dexterity, but still the strict lines and angles are not maintained throughout the manoeuvre, instead being regained once the move is complete. Then too, units in battle tend to morph into blobs as they press against the enemy, not completely disorganized mobs, but decidedly not orderly rectangles either. These two models illustrate a scholarly debate about whether Roman maniples or other similarly orderly formations for that matter were in fact ordered into neat ranks and files or more just concentrations of soldiers around a unit standard.[18] The reality for maniples was likely closer to TWR2 than FoG2. TWR2 is almost assuredly excessive in its model, where units can morph quickly from a thin line two soldiers deep to a column two soldiers wide and everything in between. Still, TWR2 allows units to adapt to varied formations with different unit depths; indeed, FoG2 does not allow for this at all.

The ease with which units could manoeuvre is a question also raised by the two game models, and here the impressions FoG2 gives about systems and causal relationships in operation better fits our evidence. Its systems propose that complex manoeuvres were very difficult for the heavy infantry units of the battle line and mobility was limited. It also suggests units without the direct input of a commander were limited in their ability to act. This will be considered under 'Command Models' below, but for now consider that units in battle – certainly Roman ones and undoubtedly those from at least some other armies – could move and act independently; they just could not carry out streams of complicated orders from commanders. This restriction of points suggests, however, that a unit's ability to move depended on a commander, something not strictly true.

Combat models

FoG2 provides a highly detailed combat model explained in a 156-page digital manual, a signal of the importance the designers attached to modelling historical systems and details reasonably accurately.[19] Each unit has the following characteristics, visible when the player mouses over the unit. Units have a *Troop Type* and a range of types are accounted for: infantry, cavalry, ranged and so on. These types are further subdivided into classes like pikes, offensive spearmen, and defensive spearmen. Different types have different strengths and weaknesses. Pikes, for example, have a bonus to their impact and melee attacks (for definitions, see below) when fighting in open terrain, and any infantry has a bonus when defending fortifications. Each unit has a *Troop Quality*, a measure of its effectiveness in combat. Each unit also has a *Cohesion* or *Morale* level, a hidden number that is rendered to the player as one of the following descriptors: steady, disrupted, fragmented and broken/routing. *Steady* units are fully effective in combat, while *Disrupted* and *Fragmented* units suffer penalties to their attack numbers. Fragmented units also have fewer Action Points and cannot charge the enemy. *Strength* represents the number of soldiers in the unit. The standard strength is 480 soldiers. Denser infantry formations such as the Hellenistic phalanx have more soldiers and, thus, a higher Strength. Starting Strength is a baseline, and when the unit suffers a certain percentage of casualties – more than 16 per cent of its Starting Strength in a single missile attack or more than 5 per cent of its starting strength in close combat – it must take a *Cohesion Test*. Failing this test causes the unit to drop a level of cohesion: steady to disrupted; disrupted to fragmented; fragmented to routed.

Close combat and, if the unit has ranged weapons, missile combat, occur when the player (or AI opponent) orders a unit with sufficient action points to attack a nearby enemy. Missile attacks have a range of one or two squares. Close-combat attacks have two variants. Units that have not yet engaged an enemy unit can charge it, performing an *Impact Attack*. Units already engaged with an enemy will conduct a *Melee Attack*. In both cases, the game resolves the attack by calculating the strength of the unit. Here the manual is a bit confusing. It suggests, 'infantry units larger than standard cohort-sized units of 480 men fight only with 480 men, and cavalry units larger than 240 men with 240 men, the extra troops being mainly extra rear ranks'. This suggests that in FoG's calculation, all 480 men in a Roman cohort, for example, fought in the front line; actually, they were deployed at the very least in three lines of soldiers – *hastati*, *principes* and *triarii* – and likely more than that. Leaving this aside, if one unit has fewer than 480 troops (240 for cavalry), the larger unit will have a combat bonus. This may be a nod to the historical ability of larger lines of soldiers to overlap and flank smaller lines, but, if so, is a bit odd visually in that larger units and smaller units both occupy the same amount of space on the game map, one square. However that may be, relative combat strength for the engaged unit is then modified by a series of *Points of Advantage*, modifiers that range from +0 to a maximum of +200, where a unit with a 100-point advantage over an enemy would get approximately a 33 per cent bonus to its final attack number. These points of advantage are based on a number of different comparisons, including the types of troops engaged, the terrain and elevation, the unit cohesion, the quality of the troops, the presence of a general in the unit, and so on. The game code runs the calculations, includes a random number generator to add contingency to the mix, determines the number of casualties suffered by each unit in the melee and decides whether the engagement ends in a draw or one side loses the encounter. If one side loses, it takes a cohesion test; failing the test causes the unit's cohesion to drop a level.

Units engaged in close-combat remain engaged unless the commander directs them to break off – in which case, they suffer an attack from the enemy as they disengage. If they remain within the charge range of that enemy, they must take a Cohesion Test. Barring this, they will continue to fight, dealing damage and forcing cohesion checks until one unit loses sufficient cohesion for it to break and rout from the battlefield. The victorious unit will then potentially be compelled to pursue, regardless of the player-general's wishes.

Unlike FoG2's unit approach, TWR2 models the individual soldiers within the unit. These soldiers have the following variables. *Melee Attack* reflects the soldier's chances to hit an enemy, to make physical contact with a weapon. If the weapon hits, *Weapon Damage* measures the harm caused by the weapon and is divided into two categories: *Base Damage* can be blocked by enemy armour and *Armor Piercing Damage* cannot. The chances of a successful melee attack and the amount of damage increase according to the *Charge Bonus* if the individuals in the unit charge their enemy. Another set of variables define the ability of the individual to withstand physical and psychological harm. *Melee Defense*, as the name suggests, reflects the chance of the unit to be hit by an enemy weapon. *Armor*, quite reasonably, quantifies the capacity of the soldier's armour to resist missile and melee attacks (reducing the damage of both). *Health* is measured in hit points, the time-honoured gaming method to quantify a being's capacity to stay alive after repeated physical attacks. Finally, and critically to modelling human behaviour in battle, *Morale* is the individual's willingness to remain in combat under the stresses of battle. Some of these stresses are clearly noted in the game interface. Mousing over a unit engaged in battle, for example, will tell the player-general what the morale of the unit is and the primary factor affecting it: suffering casualties, being outnumbered, having exposed flanks and watching allies rout, are some of the factors that lower morale; winning a close-combat engagement, having the general nearby, being well rested and fighting from higher ground are some of the factors that can raise morale.

The combat systems of the two games differ significantly. Effectively, FoG2's system relatively transparently includes a large number of factors. Players can opt to open a dialogue window and see the actual numbers used in the calculation of every given combat. In practice, this means that, although one can certainly disagree with the values assigned to different factors, one can see those values and, if they want, run the calculations on their own with values they feel are more accurate. In other words, they can test the model using different values.

Throughout, FoG2 emphasizes Points of Advantage that are set out in the manual and thus can be clearly determined by the player, making clear and readily understandable the significance of terrain and a host of other factors on combat outcomes. FoG2's system also limits cohesion to a few states as it would have appeared to an observer and makes unit cohesion the primary factor in a unit's effectiveness. Casualties are important – injury, death and the fear of both played a crucial role in the ability of a unit to stay in formation – and, accordingly, FoG2 units must make morale tests when they have suffered a certain percentage of casualties. The success or failure of those morale checks, however, not casualties directly, determines the fate of a unit. Furthermore, those morale checks present the collapse of units as complex behaviours: somewhat predictable, but never certain. Here, FoG2 limits cohesion states to a small set that captures reasonably the general effects of low morale: steady, disrupted, fragmented and broken/routing. Disrupted and fragmented units have a reduction in their ability to inflict casualties on the enemy, fragmented units cannot charge and broken units flee unless rallied by the general.

TWR2 hides its calculations from players – though to be fair, in a real-time game where individuals combatants are modelled, the output stream would be extreme. Still, the game also lacks the detailed manual of FoG2 and does not really discuss its combat model within the digital pages. For example, what exactly is the mathematical relationship between an attacking soldier's Melee Attack and a defending soldier's Melee Defense? Simple subtraction of the latter from the former? Terrain clearly modifies attack numbers, but how and by how much? It is not clear. Given the featured variables at work, however, and drawing from developer blog posts, TWR2 seems to model unit combat in the following way.[20] In ranged combat, the game calculates whether every individual in the unit harms an individual in the enemy unit based on its *Missile Damage* number. This seems to be its chance to harm its target – there is no clearly labelled missile attack stat to match the melee attack stat. Then the damage the enemy receives is calculated, modified, presumably, by the kind of armour it wears. Melee combat is a bit more complex but similar. Here, the individuals in the unit close enough to strike an enemy soldier must be determined. If they succeed in striking their opponents, the game calculates the damage inflicted. Some of it ignores armour, as noted above, and some of it is mitigated by armour. When individuals lose all their hit points, they die. Meanwhile, as the digital soldiers fight and die, the morale of the units engaged is steadily recalculated. When the unit passes its morale threshold (presumably by dropping to 0), the unit breaks and routs. In this case, unless ordered otherwise, the victorious unit(s) will pursue their fleeing foe off the battlefield.

Both games offer playable formal models of ancient battle. They define precise relationships between types and numbers of soldiers and weapons, armours and shields, terrain, unit position, casualties and morale that point in the right directions – suggesting, for example, an inverse relationship between casualties and morale, and an inverse relationship between armour quality and harm. Going further, to date, though Sabin's *Lost Battles* system offers a tabletop ludic model of battle, there is only one published formal digital model of ancient combat of which I am aware; where this model *may* gain on the precision of its numbers, it lacks the details of these game models, the number of variables they factor.[21] Presumably, the values in these game models are derived from impressionistic guesswork rather than complex mathematical models of behaviour. This basis for the values used and the games' purpose as entertaining models certainly fosters inaccuracies. TWR2, for example, incorporates unit morale into its model (and presumably individual morale given the focus of the combat model) but tends to emphasize in practice the killing and dying of individuals as the primary determinant of a unit's success. Units do flee when their morale is sufficiently low, but not nearly often enough. Regularly, a unit will stay engaged long past receiving 50 per cent casualties, when our best guess is that units would break at perhaps half that or less. This is problematic, but a matter of the values used for morale and cohesion tests, not a flaw in the actual model that says a unit whose morale is insufficient breaks and runs.

It is difficult to judge which system better fits our evidence, particularly when FoG2 helpfully exposes most of its combat logic while TWR2 obscures a great deal, essentially 'black-boxing' the exact calculations involved in these simulated battles.[22] A more definitive judgement between the two would require running the games through a high number of interactions and assessing the mathematical outcomes. TWR2, because it is agent-based not unit-based, should theoretically be the more realistic model, attending to the details of individual soldiers and their role in the unit's cohesion. In practice though, while FoG2 does not focus on the individual in its modelling, it seems to produce reasonable outcomes in emphasizing the effect of morale and cohesion. Units more clearly lose morale and cohesion in ways that more clearly link to battlefield performance. Ultimately, units reliably break and rout when worsted over time in FoG2, with casualties generally well under 50 per cent before the breaking point. These points are in line with our best scholarly understandings of ancient battle.[23]

Command models

Successfully modelling army command is the greatest problem both games face and, indeed, the most difficult task any game on the subject faces. Even the commanders of the well-organized Roman armies of the Middle Republic had very little control over units of soldiers and how those soldiers moved and functioned when a battle was underway. A survey of Roman battles in the period from the Gallic War of 225 BCE to the late second century – the final period of the manipular system – indicates that Roman commanders had very few control points over their armies in battle. They could, sometimes, control the choice of battlefield, depending on the strategic and logistical factors pushing for the battle. The general determined how the cavalry would be divided between the wings and which legion or allied equivalent would occupy each part of the main battle line, but these were not often choices that had much effect on tactical options. Whether to keep additional reserves outside of the built-in reserves of the three-line manipular system was another decision generals made, although this decision likely depended on the stretch of reasonably level ground available for deploying a main battle line. And, of course, a general might craft a battle plan with his military council to guide sub-officers on different parts of the line as they commanded their soldiers.[24]

When battle commenced, however, the general had very little control over how units fought and manoeuvred. Consider that even half of a consular army (two legions, an equivalent or greater number of allied infantry, and several thousand cavalry) would conservatively stretch over one mile – quite out of voice range and quite likely out of effective sight of a commander.[25] Certainly, Roman commanders employed trumpets to communicate with the legions at a distance.[26] The sources suggest – common sense as well – that these trumpets were used to issue very simple orders: halt, withdraw and, most often, advance to attack. Beyond these simple whole-army commands generals had only a few means of significantly influencing their soldiers' battle. They could lead the Roman cavalry as it harried the enemy cavalry and infantry flanks. Doing so would fully occupy the general and make it impossible for him to affect any other elements of the battle. Perhaps unsurprisingly as armies grew in the second century, it became increasingly uncommon for a general to adopt this tack. More commonly, they either stayed back from the battle line and looked for places to deploy reserves or moved to different places in the battle line, offering encouragement and setting an example of courage for the soldiers in the battle line.

What they decidedly did not often do was issue commands to units during battle to execute significant tactical manoeuvres to outflank their enemies. The number of occasions when Roman armies in this period outflanked their enemies due to a significant tactical manoeuvre of infantry – defined here as infantry moving from its initial battlefield location to a distant location beyond the flanks of the enemy battle line – are very few. Scipio Africanus, a skilful commander to be sure, managed it at Ilipa (206 BCE) – but did not employ it at all at his crowning victory of Zama. Claudius Nero managed it at Metaurus (207 BCE), but the units he manoeuvred were completely unoccupied on the right of the battle line.[27]

The commander's ability to make grand tactical flanking manoeuvres and make frequent adjustments to unit orders on the fly, however, is a standard misrepresentation in most every ludic model of ancient battle – board or video game. A reasonably accurate command model would require the player to form a strategy and issue orders to the various parts of the line before the battle commenced. Then the player would mostly watch the battle unfold. They would be able to directly influence only one spot at a time according to where the player positioned their general unit, mostly in terms of raising morale or inspiring a stalwart defence or courageous charge. Or, if the player kept their general unit in the rear, they could, perhaps, dispatch messages to different parts of the battle line – though we do not have clear examples how this might work in our period. More certainly, they could issue orders for reserves to support failing parts of the line. Ultimately, however, what the player *could not do* in a more realistic ancient command model, is move all units independently at will in the battle line, ignoring the limits of hearing, and sight. Nor could they influence units close to the thick of it to move in any direction other than forward or backward – sometimes not even that, since it could be very difficult for an engaged unit to withdraw safely without becoming disorganized and routing. The problem with a game like this, of course, is that it would be a far less interactive and arguably less exciting game to many, certainly compared to a model where the general has near-complete control over each unit. Unsurprisingly, neither game does this. Commercial strategy games appeal in part because of the power fantasy they provide to players and the array of interesting choices. Limiting player control in this fashion would be a risky move for a strategy game developer hoping to have a reasonably wide audience.[28]

FoG2 does more than TWR2 to indicate the limits of the commander while still providing enough control for an enjoyable command-fantasy. One or more command units in the army can influence the units within their command range. As noted earlier, when units are within a command unit's command range, they can make one 45° turn without spending Action Points. This is the only perceivable effect of being in command, but it amounts to units manoeuvring very slowly on the battlefield if they are not properly led. This is at least an attempt to model the difficulty of command in the ancient world as units are less flexible when out of command. But it does not truly illustrate the real issue: units in ancient armies simply could not execute a commander's will, moment by moment, throughout the battle. The restrictions on communication and transportation in the ancient world guaranteed that, at best, a commander could instruct his subordinates carefully and hope they understood and could adapt when leading the units under their control. The commander might then update with new commands that took time to deliver across a battlefield. This was nothing like these game systems where a player can issue a constant stream of orders to any unit as it carries out its part of the plan. FoG2's Action Points speak to the idea that a unit would need a commander of some sort to engage in movement. The truth of that assertion would depend on the context. True, a unit would need to receive regularly – before and during battle – high command orders if it were to reliably move in ways the commander wanted. In Roman armies of the period, however, there were many sub-officers ranging from legates to tribunes, and centurions, so each legion and its constituent units could act on its own. They could not, however, follow continuous real-time orders from the general.

On top of this, the game exaggerates the player general's view of the battlefield and knowledge of conditions. The player can control the map through zooming, panning and rotating the camera, hovering over units to see their status, and issuing commands to any unit in the battle line. The only exceptions are routing units or units locked in pursuit of a fleeing foe; neither can receive commands. These two exceptions represent FoG2's effort to suggest that the general did not always have control over troops, but they are the exception. Mostly, the player general has fantastic control over their army.

TWR2 does not offer anything like FoG2's command system, understandably since units function in real time. The presence of the general unit in tactical battles does not increase manoeuvrability nor does its absence decrease it, although the proximity of the general raises the morale of nearby units and the destruction of the general can cause army morale to drop precipitously. All units can always be selected and controlled individually, except for routing units. The player has a godlike view of the battlefield and can pan, rotate and zoom on most points in the map – although the designers made sure that the player cannot zoom in on the enemy army. Any unit can be selected, even if heavily engaged in melee, and given new orders that it will always attempt to execute. TWR2 offers three concessions, however, to limited command control. First, the player cannot see all the details of the enemy units, and the camera is limited to a certain extent to a fixed distance from the nearest friendly units on the map. Second, units given orders to engage an enemy will continue to follow those orders even if it means riding to the edges of the map and leaving the battle. Third, units that rout their enemies will chase them by default unless placed in guard mode or explicitly commanded to stop. These are small concessions, however, and the control in TWR2 is, as was suggested, godlike.

Conclusion: Video games as formal, dynamic, interactive, multimodal models

The analysis in this chapter has considered at length the validity of these games as models of Roman warfare. Here, let us consider some broader implications about historical video games and their strengths and potential for modelling the past. More specifically, there is a large subgenre of games that fit the mould of FoG2 and TWR2: largely conceptualist simulations that model historical problem spaces. These sorts of historical games offer the potential to think about the past in ways that are, quite simply, not achievable by static-text and static-image models. Static text, the foundation of historical studies for well over two millennia now, has great strengths as a medium for representing the past as does static image, but they, like all media, have limits, too. These limits of text and image *should not and must not move us* to abandon text and image as means of meaningfully representing and analysing the past. At the same time, all interested in the past, every shade of historian and game player included, need to be aware that a richer understanding of the past can be gained through the employment of a variety of media to understand historical phenomena.

Accordingly, consider the limits of static text and image, when it comes to representing the dynamics, the systems of the ancient world. As noted before, ancient battle, a chaotic and brutal affair of soldiers killing and dying in earnest, a set of interlocking complex systems, is not in any way particularly analogous to a static text description, however engaging, detailed and evidence-based that text is. Imagery can, quite literally, illustrate more effectively the visual space and visual details of a battle: soldiers' positions, the use of weapons and armour, and be quite effective at suggesting emotions. But neither alone is a completely operational playable model of dynamics, of interactions between soldiers and terrain, weapons and armour.

These games are operational formal multimedia models and so provide a potential means of understanding the dynamics of ancient battle that simply cannot be achieved by static text and image. 'Potential' is an operative word here. In their detailed models of manoeuvre, combat, and command, FoG2 and TWR2 games do not provide researched and empirically quantified models of ancient battle. Nor do they refrain from simplifying and misrepresenting, especially in matters of command, in order to provide a fun and engaging play experience. Yet, both are clearly the products of educated and talented teams that cared about the history of ancient battles and attempted to make models that are consistent with ancient evidence, though, of course, models subject to the demands of their audiences. What those designers created are formal, multi-modal and interactive models of battle. They enable players to interact with exact expressions of the dynamics of combat (this unit's weaponry is 50 per cent more effective against armour than that one's; defending from a hill grants my unit +25 Points of Advantage; and so on) embedded in the game rules and code, and to visualize how these dynamics may have looked and functioned on the battlefield. As a result, they provide valuable foils for scholars and players to play with, foster their imaginations and develop critiques and supports for them. They provide the most detailed formal models extant on ancient battle and they integrate these with visualizations and interactivity. These features ensure that these games, and other games of this type, can play an important role in understanding and visualizing the operation of dynamic systems in the past.

Notes

1   See Rosenstone (2006).
2   These historians provide some of the current informal text models (or, to put it more commonly, historical accounts) of ancient warfare in the form of descriptive and analytical text and ground the discussion in this article: Culham (1989), Sabin (1996, 2000), Goldsworthy (2000), Zhmodikov (2000), McCall (2001), Quesada Sanz (2006), Koon (2011), Rubio-Campillo, Matías and Ble (2015), Anders (2015), Slavik (2018) and McCall (forthcoming).
3   See Sabin (2009: xi–xxi) for further justification of game models for understanding ancient battle.
4   McCall (2012b: 13) and Chapman (2013a: 70).
5   Clyde, Hopkins and Wilkinson (2012) and Spring (2015).
6   Dening (2006) and Chapman (2016: 22–4).
7   See n. 2 above.
8   McCall (2001).
9   Du Picq (1921: Part I). On the effects of the Roman sword: Polyb. 6.23.6–7, Liv. 31.34.4.
10 Sabin (2000: 6).
11 See n. 2.
12 Ibid.
13 McCall (2012a, 2012b) and White (1973).
14 MacCallum-Stewart and Parsler (2007: 204).
15 Chapman (2016: 59–89).
16 McCall (2012a–b, 2018b).
17 Goldsworthy (1996).
18 Quesada-Sanz (2006).

19 See: www.matrixgames.com/amazon/PDF/FOG2%20manual%20EBOOK.pdf (accessed 29 October 2018).
20 This analysis is aided by the designer comments online: Lusted (2012).
21 Sabin (2009) and Rubio-Campillo, Matías and Ble (2015).
22 Chapman (2016: 143–4).
23 See n. 2.
24 McCall (forthcoming).
25 Ibid.
26 Trumpets used to issue orders to the Roman army in our period: Polyb. 14.3; Liv. 23.16, 24.15, 24.46, 30.5, 33.9; App. Ib. 4.22, 14.89; Hann. 4.21; Plut. *Cat.* 13. Though Scipio at Zama ordered his lines of *hastati* to halt and his *principes* and *triarii* to form on the flanks of the *hastati* (Polyb. 11.22–3), it is difficult to imagine trumpets alone accomplished this. More plausibly, trumpets, and then orders dispatched to the tribunes.
27 Battle of the Metaurus: Polyb. 11.1–2; Liv. 27.48. Battle of Ilipa: Polyb. 9.21–4; Liv. 28.13–15. Battle of Zama: Polyb. 15.9–15; Liv. 30.32–5.
28 McCall (2018b: 406–10).

Part Three

Digital Epics

Role-Playing in the Ancient World

Part Three

Digital Epics

Role-Playing in the Ancient World

The Bethesda Style

The Open-World Role-Playing Game as Formulaic Epic

Roger Travis

Introduction

The digital role-playing game (hereinafter 'RPG') occupies, in its several different subgenres, a very special place in the constellation both of so-called triple-A games and in gaming culture as a whole. With its roots in the tabletop game that looms so large over modern gaming culture, *Dungeons and Dragons*, and by extension in one of the earliest digital games, the text-based *Colossal Cave* and its elaborations, the digital RPG captures the imaginations of game-players in a way that even on its face must make a classicist think of the spell cast by the Homeric bards. Who but a gamer these days can best represent Odysseus' characterization of the Phaeacians listening to Demodocus, struck to silence through immersion in the epic song?

> Lordly Alkinoos, preeminent in the sight of all peoples, truly this is a lovely thing – to listen to a bard like this one here, like the gods in the sound his voice makes. For I at least say that no occasion is more full of grace than when gladness reigns through the whole people, and the feasters throughout the hall listen to the singer, sitting in their rows, and the tables are by, full of bread and meats, and the wine-steward, drawing from the mixing bowl, carries the wine and pours into the cups: this to my mind seems to be a most lovely thing.[1]

In this chapter, I seek to add a very great deal of texture to that comparison, and especially to demonstrate that in the particular case of one style of digital RPG, that perfected by the developers of Bethesda Softworks, the element of community-affiliation implicit in Odysseus' words about Alkinoos' subjects is alive and well. Building on my previous work on what I call 'digital formulaic epic', I show that player-performance in five core Bethesda RPGs, *The Elder Scrolls III: Morrowind* (2002, hereinafter *Morrowind*), *The Elder Scrolls IV: Oblivion* (2006, hereinafter *Oblivion*), *The Elder Scrolls V: Skyrim* (2011, hereinafter *Skyrim*), *Fallout 3* (2008) and *Fallout 4* (2015), corresponds not only in a loose, evocative way with the Homeric tradition, but also very precisely with the oral formulaic composition of the *Iliad* and the *Odyssey*. The advance I make in this chapter is to demonstrate that whereas other styles of RPG shape player identity in a more personal way, the Bethesda open-world RPG ties player-performance and the magical immersion it creates to the context of affiliation and membership – and non-affiliation and non-membership – in the communities, called factions, that serve as the fulcrum of the games' narrative materials.

This chapter therefore has two tasks, one general and one specific, after laying out as briefly as possible the correspondence of RPG to oral epic through oral formulaic theory: first, to outline the particular nature of the materials Bethesda games provide for the composition of digital formulaic epic; second, to analyse the way those materials shape player-identification above all with players' own communities through their in-game identification with the fictional communities of the RPGs' narrative materials.

What is an RPG in relation to oral formulaic theory?

Generally speaking, an RPG is any game in which players perform as characters in a narrative. In the original tabletop guise of the genre, a gamemaster serves partly as narrator and partly as rule keeper, informing the players of the results of their actions. In a digital RPG, the algorithm running on the digital game platform, whether the very early text-based parser of *Colossal Cave* or a modern graphical interface in which the player can – these days, even in a virtual-reality setting – interact in some realistic-feeling fashion with the possibility-space, serves in the role of the gamemaster. Every choice the player of a digital RPG can make arises in response to the ruleset of the game as programmed by the developers.

The evolution of the tabletop RPG into the digital RPG left the latter with some very important conventions, which in the digital format became game-mechanics (a game-mechanic may be thought of as a bundle of rules that governs player-performance in a certain aspect of the game). The most important of these for my discussion in this chapter is the convention of progression in level, which in *Dungeons and Dragons* serves at once as a narrative device to allow the player's adventure-story to grow in significance and as a game-mechanic that defines many of the things a player may do within the possibility space of the adventure. Simply put, a higher-level character has more choices.

The other topic that requires some introduction if this discussion is to make sense to the general reader is oral formulaic theory. Since 1997, when Janet Murray's *Hamlet on the Holodeck* appeared,[2] critics have from time to time been exploring the analogy between oral traditional epic, as studied especially by Milman Parry[3] and Albert Lord,[4] and digital games. From a theoretical perspective, these efforts have been hampered by a failure to deploy the specific findings of oral formulaic theory in a study of games.

Milman Parry's 1928 work on the *Iliad* and the *Odyssey* opened the modern study of traditional oral epic.[5] Parry's student Albert Lord carried on this study after Parry's untimely death, with the signal aid of his study of South Slavic singers, called guslars. *The Singer of Tales*, Lord's 1960 book (second edition, Lord 1981), remains the foundational work of the field.

Parry developed the idea, confirmed by Lord in *The Singer of Tales*, that the *Iliad* and the *Odyssey* hold within them the vestiges of the system that gave them birth: bards in Dark Age Greece composing the epics as we know them, through a process of recomposition out of narrative materials available to them through their professional training as singers.

Murray observed in *Hamlet on the Holodeck* how this recompositional system stands in close analogy to the software of digital games.[6] Those programs allow their player-performers to recompose their game-stories out of the narrative materials provided by the games' developers in a potentially infinite number of different ways. In the same way the Homeric bards recomposed the stories we know as the *Iliad* and the *Odyssey* over and over, necessarily varying the story through the basic operation of the poetic system.

This comparison has value on its own, as an index of the digital games' relation to older forms of storytelling and of art, and as arrow in the quiver of those attempting to prove the value of the humanities. In this chapter, though, I build on that foundation a new, precise application of oral formulaic theory in the outline of a thick description of a certain important style of digital game.[7]

Lord defines 'theme' as a repeated element of narration or description.[8] He shows that the Homeric bards, like the South Slavic guslars, built their tales out of modular themes they had learned, through their professional training, to recombine like building-blocks. We can describe themes then as modular pieces of content that a performer can themself vary. Out of these, a singer or a game-player builds their performance. The process ensures that each performance of an oral epic or a digital RPG is a recompositional process: even the first time the performer deploys a theme they recompose it from the available performance materials.

In the same essay where he defines 'theme', Lord outlines a mode of analysis suited to such composition by theme in Homer. Scholars like Laura Slatkin have taken up that mode to great effect.[9] Composition-by-theme analysis describes the way the bard has recombined his themes in a given passage or set of passages of Homer. It describes the effect that deployment has, either within the culture of the bard or within the millennia-long reception of Homeric poetry. In this chapter I carry out that sort of analysis not of a fossilized epic tradition like the Homeric epics but of the living epic tradition of the Bethesda open-world RPG.

We might employ a composition-by-theme analysis in discussion of almost any digital game, since player-performances in these games deploy elements that inevitably recur in the games' fixed digital materials, both in their mechanics and in their narrative contents. The first ten minutes of a player's performance of *Skyrim*, for example, consist of choices among content-elements that could fairly be called 'themes' like 'conversation with a tutorial non-player-character' and 'battle'. Those themes are varied according to the exact way the player performs them, especially including dialogue choices he or she makes, for example whether to follow an imperial soldier or a Stormcloak rebel, the first non-player-characters (hereinafter, NPCs) his or her player-character (hereinafter PC) meets.

We can also describe as thematic, in Lord's sense of 'theme', the similarities in the content of digital games both within a single game and across broad ranges of games of individual genres and even of multiple genres. The taverns of *Skyrim* and the post-apocalyptic bars of *Fallout 4*, for example, are versions of a theme we could call the digital analogue of the 'assembly' theme to be found both in Homer and in South Slavic epic. Indeed, that same theme recurs not only in Bethesda games but also in the taverns and nightclubs of BioWare games and even the inns of a game like *The Lord of the Rings Online*. When we shift our consideration to the themes 'battle' and the related 'single combat', both, of course, staples of Homer and South Slavic epic, we find corresponding themes not only in the digital RPG but also in such game genres as first-person shooter and action-adventure.

Moreover, this mode of analysis corresponds interestingly to important theoretical work in the field of game studies, and in particular Ian Bogost's analysis of video games as unit operations,[10] and his development of that analysis into descriptions of video games as sites for the enactment of procedural rhetoric.[11] The work of neo-analysis done on Homeric and other traditional oral epic since Parry and Lord appears from this perspective as a form of Bogost's unit operations analysis. The recurring elements – themes and formulas – of recompositional epic manifest a sort of poetic analogue for Bogost's 'units'. The bards' techniques correspond to the procedures that in Bogost's scheme operate upon those units.

A distinctive alloy: Three hallmarks of the Bethesda style

The opening moments of *Skyrim*, to which I alluded above, serve as a very effective introduction not only to that game but also to the Bethesda style. Most importantly, the player is asked to choose to which side of the game-narrative's central conflict the PC will start out allied. Whether the player chooses to go with the Imperial Legion soldier or the Stormcloak rebel, they make their way through the same caverns and emerge in the same place, having learned the rudiments of how to function in the gameworld in such areas as combat, magic and sneaking. As the PC fights their way through, they progress in their skills, and the game notifies the player of this progression. This use-based system of mechanics is a hallmark of Bethesda's RPG's, and provides a naturalistic element to the progression experienced by the PC. At the same time, a meter clearly visible onscreen shows the PC's progression towards the next level, based on experience points gained through defeating enemies and completing assigned quests, a less naturalistic and more formulaic (indeed, thematic, in Lord's sense) source of performance materials for the player. The player can choose how exactly they wish to progress (which enemies to fight, which quests to undertake), but the result is the same at an important thematic level: the gain of experience points that results in the gain of level, which unlocks other themes in the shape of new abilities such as greater strength and more durability in combat.

Once the PC emerges into the light, the second of the two distinguishing factors of the Bethesda RPG discussed here becomes more evident: the extraordinary openness of the world, together with the breathtakingly seamless rendering of what seems to the player its minutest detail. In a Bethesda RPG, with very few exceptions, you can go anywhere visible to you, as well as places, for example under the earth, of which you have at first no knowledge; this openness is notably not the case in the BioWare RPG.

The three elements I propose as essential hallmarks of the Bethesda style show themselves to great advantage in the brief description above: *significant exploration, progression by performance* and *community affiliation*. In the remainder of this chapter, I explore their roles in the five core games of the *Elder Scrolls* and *Fallout* series in relation to composition by theme as we see it, classically, in the Homeric epics. In each of these games, the elements mix differently. *Skyrim* is the only one in which the player-performer chooses an affiliation for the PC right from the start, but in *Morrowind* for another example the PC is sent first to join a faction called the Blades and can encounter other opportunities for community-affiliation along the way. In *Oblivion*, as soon as the PC kills a non-player character (NPC) who's not hostile to them, they receive a night-time visit from the Dark Brotherhood. The post-apocalyptic landscapes of the *Fallout* games are full of factions to aid and to antagonize; the most obvious of these is the Brotherhood of Steel, central to the narratives of both *Fallout 3* and *Fallout 4*.

The exploration of the vast, open worlds of the games involves finding traces of a history in which the PC will play a very significant role, should the player-performer choose a standard narrative approach to the story – and, indeed, even if they pursue a different path they will have in all five games the ability to alter geopolitics by rising to control organizations and territory, by slaying important NPCs. Although the system for progressing in abilities (the leveling system, in the usual terminology) differs among the five games, as I detail below, the essential similarity created by the particular relation of progression to performance in both the *Elder Scrolls* and the *Fallout* levelling systems makes for a hallmark of the Bethesda style in itself. More importantly, its relation to the other two hallmarks allows the player-performer to tell a kind of story unique to the Bethesda open-world RPG.

As we look from above at this overview, before delving into the three hallmarks individually, a comparison to Homeric epic cries out for articulation. We can analogize the distinctive style embodied in the performance materials afforded to the player by these games to the distinctive style of the *Iliad* or the *Odyssey*, in relation to one another – indeed, to the distinctive styles manifested in individual books especially of the *Iliad*.[12]

Significant exploration

It is easy to see the similarities of the realistic three-dimensional worlds presented by Bethesda's adventure games, as well as many other developers' games, and discuss them in a monolithic way, perhaps invoking the much debated term *immersion* as a quasi-theoretical framework.[13] I hope to persuade the reader, however, that a thematic analysis of these worlds shows considerably more complexity – a complexity towards which Trevor Owens pointed in an article about *Fallout 3* in 2010.[14]

First, although we are accustomed to seeing such possibility-spaces in a conventionally mimetic way, as a representation of an imaginary world whose chief task is fooling the player-performer into thinking themself present there, they actually function at the same time along radically different lines. The performance materials – that is, from an oral-formulaic perspective, the themes – provided to the player-performer in a Bethesda game relate very strongly to the lore of the fantasy-world represented, in part, by the game's possibility-space. The signature theme, as it were, of this set of materials, is the importance of books in the games of the *Elder Scrolls* series, which play a role very similar to that played by the artefacts whose presence Owens analysed.

Throughout the worlds of *Morrowind*, *Oblivion* and *Skyrim*, the player-character (PC) encounters books. That is in itself notable, because very few games incorporate books as separate objects: when books do appear, it is nearly always as a row of covers of various colours to make a bookshelf look like a bookshelf. The books of *The Elder Scrolls*, however, although they are not all readable by the PC, are, nevertheless, all separately rendered. So many of them, however, are indeed readable that a player new to the series and focused upon performing a conventionally adventurous sort of narrative would be forgiven for thinking otiose the lore found in the tomes so broadly scattered.

As if to ensure that that lore not go unread, however, a few of these books, some found in notable locations and others in completely obscure ones, have a progression-effect: simply by reading one of these special books the PC gains an ability point in a relevant element of their character. The rest of the books contain a wide variety of information, written to be sure in a prose style that seems remarkably similar from one book to the next, but most of it – and here the connection to Owens' discussion of *Fallout 3* becomes obvious – concerning the history of Tamriel, the world of which Morrowind, Cyrodiil (*Oblivion*'s setting), and Skyrim make constituent parts.

The thematic materials to be found in these books, along with other themes as apparently superficial as the architectural styles used in various parts of the game's world, provide players of Bethesda's open-world RPGs with a kind of exploration-performance that on the one hand exerts a meaning-effect of its own (succinctly, *you are part of history, real and imagined*) and on the other give the more obvious distinguishing marks of the Bethesda style, *progression by performance* and *community-affiliation*, a meaningful context. As a player-performer levels-up their PC and does so within the ambit of the various communities with whom the PC affiliates themself along their long road, their adventures will, in the end, become part of the history they experience in the themes that make up the game's landscape.

We might usefully compare the significant exploration of Bethesda's game-worlds with the exploration Odysseus does both in the direct narrative portions of the *Odyssey* (exploring Phaeacia[15] and then an Ithaca rendered unfamiliar by the passage of time[16]) and in the adventures he relates in the apologue. To that obvious analogy, though, we should add such Iliadic moments as the ekphrastic lineage of Agamemnon's sceptre[17] and Nestor's wisdom about the chariot-race-course at the funeral games of Patroclus.[18] All these Homeric moments put bard and audience – and indeed the bardic occasion itself, as depicted in the passage from the *Odyssey* I quoted at the beginning of this chapter – in contact with what we might express in metaphor as the software of the Homeric system of thematic recomposition. The very simple but very telling way Circe speaks of the *Argo* as *pasi melousa* ('a care to all')[19] when telling Odysseus about the Symplegades demonstrates how the immediate story of Odysseus, recomposed on the fly from the bard's thematic materials, stands in narrative relation – as part of the very same story, when we write that story large – to older, already-told-to-death, stories. In the very same way the player-performer's discovery of the Bethesda gameworld's integral relationship to a fictional past gives the PC's actions there a self-referential weight that in turn adds a special texture to the progression the PC enacts through performance, the mechanics that make the topic of my next section.

Progression by performance

Digital RPGs have a wide variety of ways to allow the player-performer to progress their player-character towards greater prowess. The process is universally referred to as *levelling-up*, whether the game-system in question explicitly provides for character level (the vast majority do) or not.

In Bethesda RPGs, as in most such games, a player-character gains new abilities and/or improvements to existing abilities when they reach a new level. The player-performer chooses those improvements to their character with a high degree of flexibility. A magic-user, for example, might gain the capacity to do extra damage with a certain kind of spell, or instead gain more durability in battle.

In the games of the *Elders Scrolls* and *Fallout* series, Bethesda implements a set of levelling mechanics distinctive to those RPGs, which I call here *progression by performance*. As in most RPGs, the player-character gains levels by gaining experience points (XP). When the number of XP passes a certain threshold, the game notifies the player that their character has reached the next level. The way the Bethesda RPG game-systems award those XP, though, distinguishes them from all others. Although the mechanics differ between the two series, their similarities make very clear what I mean by progression-by-performance.

In *The Elder Scrolls,* whose levelling system represents the more overtly unusual of the two series, the PC earns XP by gaining skill points in the skills that comprise their abilities relevant to adventuring, through using those abilities. This mechanic may seem confusing when described that way, but, in practice, one of its hallmarks is how natural it feels to the player. For one easy-to-grasp example, if a PC sneaks around a great deal, as the player-performer uses their controller to cause their avatar to adopt the crouched bodily posture that invokes sneak mode, the PC gains skill points in Sneak, and becomes more difficult for NPCs (including animals) to detect. At the same time, the PC also gains XP, in direct relation to the gain in skill points. As in other games, when the PC's XP total rises past the threshold to level up, the player receives the level-up notification and may choose their improvements.

In the *Fallout* series the levelling system appears more conventional. Among many other things, XP are awarded for completing quests and for killing enemies, just as in nearly every RPG with the exception of *The Elder Scrolls* series. As in the *The Elder Scrolls*, however, the PC also gains XP from building, crafting, and exploring. For one very important ramification, this makes it possible to level up without killing.[20] The possibility of approaching the game in a more or less non-violent manner, though it tends to attract a good deal of attention in fan communities, does not present the most interesting feature of *Fallout's* levelling mechanics, at least from the perspective of a thematic description of the games. Rather, the availability of XP for things like crafting items and building shelters, as well as for discovering new areas, mean that a player-performer of both *Fallout* and *The Elder Scrolls* feels a crucial consistency between the two series: the PC of *Fallout* progresses in level and thus also in prowess and narrative potency *through performance*.

When considered in relation on the one hand to the significant exploration I discussed above and on the other to the essential role of community-affiliation towards which this discussion is building, the PC's progression, first *by performance*, second *in a significant game-world* and third *in relation to the communities* with whom they affiliate or disaffiliate in any of a number of ways provides the player-performer with a highly distinctive set of themes. To describe those themes in the aggregate as 'the Bethesda style' has value in and of itself, but a more important task lies ahead: because every player-performer recomposes their performance according to skills, attitudes and desires that form part of their identity and reshape that identity on the fly as the player exercises them in play, a performance in a Bethesda RPG both expresses and develops a version of the self as interconnected with an imaginary history.

Progression by perfomance has a wonderful if imprecise homeric analogue in the Iliadic aristeia, where the build-up to the final confrontation with the enemy hero serves as a sort of microcosmic progression. In the aristeia of Diomedes, for example, the bard of *Iliad* 5 'levels-up' the hero of Argos through his slaughter of Phegeus and allowing Idaeus to escape, through a memorable simile that makes the Achaean hero a winter torrent, an arrow wound, and an encounter with Athena, towards a fight with Aeneas and with his divine mother Aphrodite. By the end of *Iliad* 5, Diomedes has fought with Ares himself, and would, indeed, have slain the god of war, according to Ares' own account of the battle.

We could also compare Odysseus' stealthy return to his palace in the last books of the *Odyssey*: as he demonstrates his skill at lies and deception, he involves bard and audience in a progression by performance towards the ultimate deception embodied in stringing the bow as the climax of the contest set by Penelope. These examples from one perspective present the standard narrative mechanics by which any storyteller advances their tale, but the peculiar nature of Homeric heroism, like the peculiar nature of representing a PC in a Bethesda game, makes the experience of on-the-fly advancement in prowess meaningful in itself, as a series of moments that in a literary kind of retrospect might seem inevitably successful, while in real time the individual performance-choices that make up that steady progress are anything but obvious. The choice of whether to sneak or to stand upright, like the choice of whether Diomedes should slay a certain enemy or allow him to escape, holds in its increasingly virtuosic resolution, in which player/bard virtuosity has PC/hero virtuosity as a self-referential metaphor, a very special capacity to render player-performance meaningful. In a Bethesda RPG, where such progression is linked to significant exploration on the one hand and community-affiliation on the other, advancement through performance gives the player's time in Tamriel or post-nuclear America the feeling of historicity that marks the style I am describing.

Community-affiliation

Early on in a player's performance of their *Skyrim* narrative, if they follow more or less the course of narrative materials placed most conspicuously in their path, their PC has the opportunity to become involved in a feud between two factions of warriors who have houses in the base location for the game's early action. Again, if the player decides *not* to pursue a performance of what we might for convenience's sake call the *standard narrative* (so as to avoid confusion that might arise by using more technically connoted terms like *main quest* or *campaign*), they need not go to Whiterun at all, though huge quantities of the game's most carefully wrought content would remain closed to them. A player of *Skyrim*, and of the other four games described in this chapter, can perform a narrative that extends for an infinite stretch of time and an infinite number of incidents without completing a single quest either of the standard narrative or of any of the other related and unrelated narratives, whose materials come in the well-known-to-RPG-players form of requests made or hints given by non-player-characters that then show up in the player-performer's control-screen (usually called a journal) in the form of a bulleted to-do item. Their performance would begin to seem highly repetitive after a while, as they finished exploring the vast virtual geography of the game's possibility-space and had to return to previously visited locations to find that enemies had repopulated them, but these games' openness to free-form adventure constitutes an absolutely essential element of the Bethesda style both in and of itself and, more importantly for my purpose in the post, in relation to the standard narrative and above all to its characteristic emphasis on community-affiliation as the fulcrum for the player-character's and the player-performer's experience in the imaginary world of the game and the real world of the game-platform respectively.

The two clans centred in Whiterun, Gray-mane and Battle-born, can serve as a sort of microcosm for the function of community-affiliation in the performance of *Skyrim* and of the other four games, all of which have similar examples of 'non-joinable' factions that despite not admitting the PC to their ranks nevertheless demonstrate the importance of the joinable factions – in *Skyrim* the crucial ones are the Stormcloaks and the Imperial Legion, a divide on whose two sides the Gray-manes and the Battle-borns have settled.

Other styles of digital RPGs, of course, feature themes having to do with communities. As in literary narratives and filmed narratives, affiliation with and membership in various kinds of organizations provides a ready source of performance-materials: Harry Potter fans on every media platform understand the importance of being sorted into the proper house and Star Wars fans know the crucial choice of Jedi or Sith. Games configure the themes associated with faction in a special way, however, because of the recompositional nature of the medium: a player-performer of a game like *Skyrim* or *Fallout 3*, or any of the many other games where a central choice of faction changes the whole tenor of the performed narrative,[21] has choices analogous to a Homeric bard's characteristic favouring of Achilles in the *Iliad* or Odysseus in the *Odyssey*, at the crucial moments when the two central heroes come into contact.[22]

Whereas the divergent Iliadic and Odyssean traditions seem to have developed in a sort of adversarial companionship with one another after their initial development, a player may perform *Skyrim* in such a way as to help both the Grey-manes and the Battle-borns in a single performance, and may more importantly both liberate Skyrim (as the rebellious Stormcloaks want) and reunify Skyrim (in accordance with the Legion's wishes) with the Empire on successive playthroughs. Moreover, by comparing their performances with those of other players in the game's community, players gain a practical familiarity with the ramifications of their choices to join or to aid the various available factions.

The distinct element of the factions, both joinable and non-joinable, in the games I discuss here, lies in their prominence, their thematic relationships to the cultural effect of their games and, above all, their relationship to the two other elements of the Bethesda style I discussed previously: significant exploration and progression by performance.

Constraints of space make it impossible to discuss in detail the factions of the five games in this light. I therefore describe how the mechanics of *Skyrim* fit my model, then point towards the different but analogous mechanics in *Morrowind*, *Oblivion* and *Fallout 3* and *4*. *Skyrim*'s principal factions, as chosen by the player-performer for the PC at the start of the game, in their selection of which NPC to follow in order to escape the attacking dragon, are the Stormcloaks and the Imperial Legion. As in a fairly large number of RPGs, the struggle between these factions provides the engine of the narrative. It is important to note that, although such a struggle between factions plays a role in *Fallout 4*'s narrative materials, it does not do so in the other games under discussion here: the distinctiveness of the Bethesda style in this regard does not lie there, but rather in the subtler relationships between the faction-mechanics and other elements of the games.

Above all, the distinctive themes provided by *Skyrim*'s and the faction-mechanics of the other games arise from the attitudes displayed by NPCs, who respond to the PC based, in part, on the PC's standing with respect to their faction. The most obvious difference between attitudes lies in whether the NPC is hostile – if the NPC's faction has for some reason been set to enmity with the PC, either because of the PC's membership in an opposed faction or for any of a number of other reasons, the NPC may attack the PC on sight. If the NPC is a fellow member of a faction joined by the PC, or for any of a number of reasons the NPC's faction is friendly towards the PC, such things as conversation and trade become possible in the PC's interactions with them. Again, although the games discussed feature such mechanics more prominently than the vast majority of other RPGs, such faction mechanics figure in other developers' games with different degrees of importance. When the player-performer comes into contact with NPCs like the members of the Grey-mane and Battle-born clans, however, the distinctness to be found in games like *Skyrim* quickly appears: the ties of these proud warriors to the land the PC explores, and the lore they discover, make their conflict a potential emblem of the player-performer's thematic participation in the possibility-space of the game ('potential' because the player-performer need not make use of these narrative materials, that is, from the standpoint of the gameworld, the PC need not become involved in the clans' conflict at all).

The lands of Bethesda's RPGs, whether they lie in the fantasy realm of Tamriel or the post-nuclear wastelands of future America, are full of communities, and these communities stand in a significant relation to other communities, to the world itself and to the PC's adventures. What each faction represents within that imaginary network of relationships shifts according to what the developers have laid down in the existing narrative materials on the one hand and according to the player's ongoing performance on the other, but as a whole they make the PC in great part a creature of the NPC's they join, or aid, or refuse to join and refuse to aid. The player-character of a Bethesda game takes shape above all as an expression of sympathy and fellow-feeling, and the world as a whole – the possibility-spaces of these games – exists as a series of choices among the sympathies that provide the fundamental thematic material of every player-performance.

In the case of the Grey-manes and the Battle-borns, the player-performer may choose to ignore the Grey-mane NPC who tries to talk to the PC about her missing cousin, and the Battle-born NPC who talks to the PC about being bullied. In that case, the network of community in that performance will perhaps include having turned down these requests for assistance, though it would be possible also never to hear them at all. Indeed, a performance of *Skyrim* or any of these games, long or short, may include minimal interaction with the story of such factions.

Even in that case, however, the PC must interact with factions like the various groups of raiders, non-joinable communities of lawless enemy NPCs who exist in each of the five games. The overarching importance of what I suggest we might call *affiliation* comes through in every player-performance; performances that follow the 'standard' shape – that is, the narrative materials of the main quest – involve affiliation at such a depth that every theme that makes a part of that performance relates to the PC's affiliations in some way.

When the PC breaks into the locked closet of a bedroom in the Battle-borns' mansion in order to find the evidence that a Grey-mane is still alive and being held captive, the player-performer's deployment of a relatively frequent theme, 'breaking and entering', has a special tie to the PC's affiliation either with Imperial Legion or with Stormcloaks – or, indeed, with the PC's attempts either to remain neutral or not to get involved. The same goes for the alternative approaches to getting the same information, wherein the PC develops a relationship with the Battle-borns to the point that they give the letter containing the relevant information to the PC. Those themes, which involve either blackmailing a Battle-born with the information that he is in love with a Grey-mane, or persuading Idolaf Battle-born to tell the PC about the missing Grey-mane, have their own interactions with the rest of the player-performer's choices in recomposition: to perform the blackmail theme, the PC must pickpocket an NPC, a standard theme in *Elder Scrolls* games; persuading Idolaf involves passing a speech check by choosing a dialogue option that can succeed or fail based on the PC's speech skill and a random number. All three options involve skills the PC has developed over the course of their performance, and thus integrate into the player-performer's choices their progression by performance, their significant exploration, and their community-affiliation.

Similarly, in *Morrowind, Oblivion* and the *Fallout* games, factions like the houses of Vvardenfell, the Dark Brotherhood, and the Brotherhood of Steel, give the player-performer a nearly infinite array of recompositional choices among themes of affiliation. Each game presents the player-performer with its unique content, related essentially to the geographical region within which the PC travels: different parts of Tamriel in the *Elder Scrolls* games and different parts of post-apocalyptic America in *Fallout*. A central hallmark of the Bethesda style – perhaps *the* central hallmark – lies in the importance played by community-affiliation in the PC's adventures there. It would be possible to write at great length about each game's themes and what a player-performer might take away from them as a contextualized meaning within the various cultures in which they and Bethesda's developers take part. My discussion here seeks to demonstrate that behind the individual game's meaning-effects lies a broader continuity, which allows for the performance of a distinct sort of story wherein the PC's growing prowess at adventuring and the player-performer's growing virtuosity at recomposing the narrative tie in to the gameworld through growing community-relationships. The transformative effect of the PC's adventures on the world of the game, emblem of that prowess and that virtuosity, matter within the gameworld because of the effect they have on these communities with whom the PC affiliates themself.

In *Skyrim*, to return to our example of Grey-manes and Battle-borns, the meaning-effect of the player's performance as a whole will differ depending on the choices they make: a player can tell a story of imperial domination or nativist rebellion and can involve their PC in that story in a functionally infinite number of different ways depending on the themes they choose to incorporate into their performance. In *Fallout 4*, the communities the PC creates by building settlements can develop on their own into thriving villages whose inhabitants surprise the player-performer with their self-sufficiency. The narrative system of these games provides the modern bard with a kind of freedom unknown to the Homeric singers. That, in itself, is hardly unique to Bethesda RPGs, but the singular quality of the Bethesda style lies in a facet of the recompositional system that a Homeric bard might recognize, or at least find very congenial: just as Odysseus affiliates himself himself with the Phaeacians and against the suitors, and just as Achilles temporarily leaves the Achaean faction, at war with the Trojan faction, the PC of a Bethesda open-world RPG finds a performative identity in relation to the communities with which the player-performer chooses to affiliate them. Those communities, in turn, allow the PC and the player-performer to put their stamp on the gameworld through significant exploration and progression by performance, just as the Homeric bards did upon the layers of fossilized narrative we find in the books we call *Iliad* and *Odyssey*.

Indeed, it may help to think of those books as a collection of Let's Play videos from bardic (or perhaps rhapsodic: we still have frustratingly little evidence for the process by which the oral tradition turned into the written one) performances that took place at a very late stage of the epics' development.[23] A player's performance in a Bethesda game, were it recorded and then left to stand as the sole testament to that game, would perhaps achieve a similar status, should the software of the game itself be lost. In that (admittedly unlikely) hypothetical scenario, what a critic would notice first and foremost about the story as told on such a video would be the way the PC and the gameworld interact through community-affiliation, in relation to significant exploration and progression by performance. Our received notions of how art functions within culture perhaps make it easier to grasp the Besthesda style that way: the mechanics of play in an open-world game, with their emphasis on quasi-infinite choice on the fly, can obscure the sort of ideological effects we see so much more easily in fixed texts and images. I hope this discussion of three hallmarks of the Bethesda style of open-world RPG goes some distance towards making clear these games' essential relationship to the epic tradition, so that more detailed discussion may follow.

Notes

1 *Odyssey* 9.1–11, my translation.
2 Murray (1997).
3 Parry and Parry (1987).
4 Lord (1981).
5 Parry and Parry (1987).
6 Murray (1997: 185–94).
7 For 'thick description', see Geertz (1973) in relation to anthropology.
8 Lord (1981: 4).
9 Slatkin (2006).
10 Bogost (2006: 3–6).
11 Ibid. (2007: 44–6).
12 See, Nagy (1999: chapter 1, for the complementarity of *Iliad* and *Odyssey*).
13 For a thorough look at different ways to view immersion in games and other forms of art, see, Ryan (2001).
14 Owens (2010).
15 *Odyssey* 7.78–145.
16 Ibid., 13.185–235.
17 *Iliad* 2.100–8.
18 Ibid., 23.304–38.
19 *Odyssey* 12.69–73.
20 Hernandez (2015).
21 See, in particular, Obsidian's 2016 game *Tyranny*.
22 See Nagy (1999: chapter 3).
23 For the elusive nature of the distinction between bard and rhapsode, see, Gonzalez (2013, especially chapter 7).

Postcolonial Play in Ancient World Computer Role-Playing Games

Ross Clare

The computer role-playing game (CRPG) typically offers the player an open gameworld designed to be freely navigated, allowing her to explore dangerous new lands and converse with often fully characterized peoples living within them.[1] This play experience is usually accompanied by an epic narrative constructed through player activity within that open world.[2] Player operation takes the form of a combination of choice-driven movement, combat, speech and the completion of quests. As game and narrative develop through sustained play activity, deeper themes and subtexts arise to confront the player and potentially even impact upon the decisions she makes during play. This chapter looks at two ancient world CRPGs where players, functioning within these genre parameters, act upon the virtual antiquity facing them and so grapple with the values and meanings underpinning the games. Since these examples both involve player interaction with 'foreign' spaces, I search for moments within the games, and the play processes activating them, wherein players are confronted with issues of imperialism and colonialism and must, in turn, respond to them through the immersive, open-ended practice of computer-based role-play.

Both games analysed here present gamespaces that can be defined as 'colonial' in a broad sense, though in different ways. *Nethergate: Resurrection* (2007,[3] henceforth *NG*) allows players to choose between Roman and Celtic campaigns within a fantastical Roman Britain presented explicitly as a 'colony', a territory under the governance of imperial Rome. Players experience both cultures as they explore a large, open-plan corner of the province, and become immersed in the turmoil engendered by imperialist aggression as they either maintain or struggle against the chaos ensuing from Roman occupation. In *Titan Quest* (2006, henceforth *TQ*), players take control of a single character travelling from Greece into the East to prevent the mythical Telkines' plan to unleash the Titans from their prehistoric prison. Moving through Greece, Egypt, and a vaguely defined 'Orient', *TQ* similarly offers players the opportunity to navigate 'other' spaces as 'western' Greek. This is not an explicitly colonialist setting like in *NG*, but, nevertheless, reflects issues identified by postcolonial scholars, such as the movement of the 'West upon the East', the journey of European agents 'outwards' into foreign spaces.[4] These two games therefore require players to engage in spatial movement, to encounter Other peoples, and to perpetuate violence in, and consumption of, those lands. Both games necessarily use recognizable, even stereotypical, signifying materials made known to us through popular culture as a basis for player interpretation: fantastical beasts, armoured soldiers and worlds replete with enemies and hidden treasures await in both.

CRPGs most often utilize 'high fantasy' tropes, reflecting their indebtedness to the *Dungeons and Dragons* tabletop system, which itself took inspiration from the works of J. R. R. Tolkien.[5] Nevertheless, depending on the uses of such materials within the unique CRPG genre framework, these standardized visions of fantastical 'antiquity' may offer something more, an opportunity to build characters and adventures through personal, player-tailored responses to the gameworld, its fictional situations and the virtual constituents within. As the phrase suggests, players may role-play their characters,[6] an immersive practice situating the player 'within' the character and prompting her to think and act as them. Such deep play, wherein players choose either to follow the trajectories set by the game to act in ways appropriate to the fiction or operate subversively to serve their own motives, potentially creates opportunities for the player to engage in thoughtful play within broadly colonial spaces and themes.

I therefore seek to identify postcolonial practices in CRPG play. 'Postcolonialism', as a term referred to throughout this paper, refers to the critique of colonial histories, themes and ideologies: in Rao's words, postcolonialism is 'an ideological concept', wherein an agent (here, the player) engages in 'polemics against colonialism',[7] active confrontations of colonial pasts and the ideologies sustaining them. Repurposing of classics in, for example, former colonies to explore and confront post-imperial cultural identity demonstrates the malleability of ordinarily 'elite' subject materials as they fit into new postcolonial contexts.[8] *NG* utilizes usual representations of Romans and Celts to allow dual perspectives upon the same colonial space, granting players the opportunity to explore the consequences of imperial occupation in a fantastical, fictional first century CE Britain. *TQ*, on the other hand, offers a different form of interaction with foreign lands: a generic Greek hero travelling from West to East to save the world. Due to their settings and the journeys players undertake, both games raise issues around colonialism by requiring player movement of peoples through other cultural continuums. However, differing uses of genre affordances are seen to result in play experiences which, explicitly or otherwise, highlight those issues in very different ways through the use of familiar, popular classical materials.

'Ancient gameplay' and 'ancient CRPGs'

The 'ancient CRPG' here denotes the type of video game (computer RPG) and the setting in which it takes place. Both games here function within a typical genre apparatus, offering epic narratives structured by a quest system. Quests are obtained from non-playable characters (NPCs) who populate the gameworld, providing background information and prompting players to move into certain parts of the gameworld, retrieve special items or kill specific entities.[9] Side-quests direct the player into non-essential corners of the gameworld. All quest completion results in material rewards, and experience points spent manually by the player to improve character statistics such as 'character level, hit points, and armor ratings',[10] all of which strengthen the character and make her more able to overcome future challenges. Quests also collaborate to form an interconnecting network of storylines. Therefore, engaging with quests both improves the character functionally, and progresses the story, resulting in unity of 'both meaning and action'.[11] This means that players operating in already rich gameworlds partially control the direction of both their character's journey and the wider narrative. Playing the game and completing quests then allows interaction with values, or 'meaning', embedded deeper within.

This chapter maintains that a basic, fundamental play process is necessary to act upon the game, its narrative and thus its themes. 'Ancient gameplay' is defined as player engagement with standard, familiar reconfigurations, even stereotypes, of antiquity: these dimly familiar signifiers function as 'highly organized knowledge structures that allow them [players] to deploy the required knowledge when prompted with certain precursors (situations in the game)'.[12] Players interpret visually and cognitively, using flexible 'unofficial knowledges' of the ancient world informed by a combinatory nexus of real-world and pop-cultural access points by which consumers come to 'know' antiquity.[13] To facilitate gameplay, players refer to 'unconscious mental maps', 'patterns of knowledge' harvested from experiences with fictional works.[14] This nebulous popular-classics continuum further intersects, especially in CRPGs, with 'other' forms of popular media.[15] Ultimately, this means that players always interact with a 'pop-cultural' antiquity, one which allows easy access to more complex themes brought on by the play experience itself. Such a perspective centralizes these games' intertextual and transmedial reach across historical, popular and otherwise conventional strata. Players cognitively engage with these wide-reaching 'cultural processes',[16] here to role-play appropriately (or not) their characters, navigate open worlds and converse with virtual-world inhabitants to co-construct meanings and messages. The play process, through this standard recognition/interpretation process, allows for explicit or tacit co-creation of themes and values.

Role-playing invaders and natives in *Nethergate*

NG offers a fantastical, fictional version of Roman Britain as gameworld, and renders it through highly conventional means. As with most CRPGs, the world contains several enterable subsections – caves, mines, forests, inhabited communities – which the player encounters mostly as and when they choose. The primary game experience is structured into six main quests constituting the primary narrative, while side-quests can be obtained from all over the World Map. Both campaigns, while beginning in separate corners of the Map, follow the same 'get quest, complete quest' dynamic but in different ways and with different motivations. The Roman Britain here is set roughly within the opening years of occupation, allowing the space to operate as a kind of colony-in-progress, rather than fully fledged province. It also pays tribute to its fantasy roots by installing a third culture, a multicultural society composed of entities from Irish and

Welsh mythology. The player must interact with these fantastical natives, such as the faery 'sidhe', from both Roman and Celtic perspectives as either combatant or friend, depending on who the player operates as and how the individual virtual personalities respond to them.

Stereotypical 'Romanness' and 'Celticness' are encoded within the very statistics of both parties (see Fig. 8.1). The statistics of the Romans reflect the kinds of characteristics players might assume them to have. Their 'Roman Training' attribute improves chances to hit in combat and the strength behind that action, a trait Celts lack. Romans also have 'Tool Use' allowing them to pick locks on doors, and Celts do not. Celtic criteria prioritize less tangible dynamics, such as magic, used by Celtic players to navigate gamespaces and/or attack opponents. When executed and visualized these spells are analogous to the kinds of supposedly magical attributes of the Celts described in classical sources: 'their hands raised to heaven, pouring out terrible curses', '[Roman] bodies motionless to enemy weapons, as if their limbs were paralysed'.[17] Romans and Celts are therefore typified by different assumed characteristics: the Roman is built for combat and so is equipped with armour and sword, while the Celts rely on their 'inherent' ability to draw on intangible, abstract phenomena such as magic as opposed to the 'civilized' methods of trained hand-to-hand fighting.

Celts are represented primarily through imageries and conventional representative strategies cultivated through popular culture to both draw the player into the necessary

Fig. 8.1 Start-up screen from *Nethergate: Resurrection* (1998 © Spiderweb Software. All rights reserved).

role-playing mindset, and to identify those characters as 'native' (as they are referred to throughout). The recent TV series *Britannia* (2018), for example, juxtaposes regimented, heavily armed Roman soldiers against superstitious, nature-loving Britons, all of which (and more) characterize the two cultures in *NG*. The Celts of the imagination are, as Squire says, people 'painted with woad', who commune with druids and make 'bonfires of human beings shut up in gigantic figures of wicker-work'.[18] The Celts of the game, too, are presented in typically tribal fashion concomitant with other video game representations,[19] partially clothed, painted, and characteristically 'at one' with their natural surroundings. Players, early on in their adventure, even encounter a giant wicker figure in their village and may discuss with local authority figures the ethics of such cultural practice. Infamous images popularized by television and films like *The Wicker Man* (1973) allow players to draw on 'their background knowledge' to assist in adding 'meaning' to the representations provided.[20] The non-Roman practice of human sacrifice,[21] directly interacted with by the player, is simultaneously 'Celtic' in the popular imagination. This allows us to see, and begin playing, the Celts as they are expected to be.

The meaning of such typical characterization is further enriched when they are compared to their oppressors. The Roman campaign opens in a 'serious fortress', the game tells us, populated with soldiers who care only for the continued subjugation of the natives. This is revealed through optional conversations the player can engage in with non-playable characters who 'live' in the gameworld and is continually reinforced through automatic text boxes which appear to further impart information and descriptions to the player. The first main Roman quest, 'Arrival', begins with a passage from the *Aeneid* (6.851–4) on a textual slide, stressing the Roman priority to 'rule the people; to impose the ways of peace' on the 'proud men who will not submit'. Along with the statistical characteristics of the Romans and the visualizations used to render these sword-wielding, armoured Romans, the narrative further reinforces player belief in Roman imperial superiority, their ability and even obligation to pacify and enforce 'peace'. These two gateways into the game are designed to oppose one another, thereby offering two avenues by which to explore this colonial space.

Differences in perspective and position within the newly invaded region become evident through both play experiences, especially since the gameworld reacts differently to the player depending on which party they are operating as. Out in the wilderness both parties can encounter a monolithic stone circle, to which the Romans betray a characteristic aloofness: a text box appears informing the player from a supposed Roman point of view, 'it would be simple for the Romans to build something like this, but for the natives, it's quite important'. Such attitudes reflect the kinds of statements made by Strabo that purport the inability of non-Romans to achieve the same level of cultural superiority,[22] playing into the expectations of the Roman role-player and prompting her to belittle native monumental culture. The statement itself also demonstrates the game's willingness to characterize the Celts as native. The same stone circle functions differently for the Celts: kneeling and praying, this now sacred site bestows functional in-game spells that can be used by the Celtic player to overcome obstacles or defeat enemies in the gameworld. Not that the game implies the Celts are more culturally inclusive: encountering a shrine to Augustus elsewhere on the Map, a text box appears to the player, outlining how the Celts find the idea of venerating dead men as gods to be laughable: 'It would be humorous if those same emperors weren't the ones who subjugated your people.' Romans, on the other hand, are prompted to treat the shrine as they 'should' by dropping money into a collection box as an offering to the deified emperor. Such instances tacitly guide the player of both Romans and Celts into a rough estimate of assumed cultural identity without necessarily imposing judgements as to who is culturally or morally 'better'.

Regions within the gameworld often explicitly reflect this theme of intercultural conflict. At the Faerie Bazaar, for example, the third culture of sentient magical creatures refuses to deal with the Romans, leaving those players unable to buy equipment for adventuring and even excluding their participation in certain side-quests. In instances such as this, parts of the game are off-limits for the Romans. The Celts, on the other hand, are welcomed as heroes, receiving new side-quests and an entirely different narrative experience. The responses of these fully-characterized societal entities populating the gameworld therefore partially determine the possibilities of both parties, altering the trajectory of play depending on who they are speaking to. Celtic players may also choose to speak to nonplayable Celts, who offer highly critical assessments of the empire. One NPC warns the player of the inherent differences between combative, heavily armoured Romans and the less well-trained Celts, both expanding on the fictional paradigms that pose Roman invader against Celtic native and referring to the coded differences between Romans and Celts illustrated above. The theme of opposing cultures is therefore essential to both functional game operations and the narrative they are couched in, and here even weave in and out of one another as the player explores and interacts.

Sometimes, game situations prompt players to reflect on their position as colonizing/colonized, and the types of character they *wish* to role-play within those paradigms. Elsewhere in the gameworld, players encounter a lodge where, upon entering, they are met by an old blind man. A text box appears: 'You could sit and talk. On the other hand, you could loot the place.' The player has three options: '1 – Just Leave'; '2 – Sit and Talk'; and '3 – Steal Everything'. Here, the player juggles between what she perceives to be the correct way to operate, and the other conventions imposed by the CRPG format. This could all be a trap; stealing could result in powerful new items, but at what cost? Sitting and talking may, in itself, reward the player with items or a new side-quest. The player manoeuvres between the need to accumulate items for adventuring, a personal desire not to cheat the man, and the possibly perceived requirement to act as colonizer/Roman by forcefully and deceitfully taking without consent. The outcome of this moment depends on the player's interpretation of their character. In CRPGs, connection to the characters' 'emotional urgency' within in-game situations alters the dynamics of decision-making, conflating real-world and virtual personality.[23] It is even suggested by Laycock that players prioritize character construction over the needs of the game.[24] Where a Celtic player may choose to connect with this individual as fellow native, the Roman player must decide what kind of aggressor she wishes to be.

Elsewhere, in the Roman campaign, choice-led instances reflect more pointedly the tensions between cultures. During one adventure, the Roman player encounters a goblin shrine. 'This place offends your civilized Roman eyes,' the text says, leading to a player-initiated decision to either destroy or ignore it. Choosing to destroy the altar makes the party feel refreshed, implying the right choice has been made and that the player has role-played correctly. However, she may also choose not to 'be colonial' in her disregard for cultural difference, respecting the space and leaving it alone (an action with no negative consequences). In both examples, particularly from the perspective of the Roman, the player must consider what kind of character she wishes to construct through instances which are explicitly designed to force assessment of the ethical and moral compasses of their role-played characters.

In other parts of the gameworld, spaces are constructed specifically to confront players with the benefits of intercultural co-operation and integration. Out in the gameworld, players discover the town of Vanarium. Founded by a Roman citizen and inhabited by both Celts and Romans, the Roman residents openly expound their wish to integrate into their Celtic surroundings without entirely abandoning their own identity. Here the player picks up side-quests, trades items and even gains a new party member of the opposite culture. By intermingling with Romans and Celts, speaking with and completing quests for them, and supplementing a Roman/Celtic party with Celtic/Roman members respectively, players can now obtain new stories, equipment and experiences. It is unclear whether the developer wished to eschew the outdated concept of 'Romanization', a theory that claimed natives 'became Romans',[25] or whether this is simply reflective of contemporary perspectives on colonial spaces that might appreciate the diverse ways in which British tribes may have reacted to the Romans, which scholars claim ranged from resistance to hesitation to integration.[26] It is clear, nevertheless, that Vanarium exists to deliberately expound more up-to-date attitudes towards cultural cooperation, provoking meditation on the theme of cohabitation even within a game that relies on standard invader/invaded narrative tropes.

The final sequences of the game, while similar for both parties, are necessarily altered to mirror the two different journeys each party has undertaken. Both teams close in on an evil wizard named Sylak as he attempts to open a portal and allow the mythical creatures of Britain to leave their homeland for pastures greener. He cites explicitly that his actions are a necessary response to the operations of the Romans and the subsequent devastation they have wrought upon the land. The Roman player must close this portal and deny the flight of its new mythical citizenry: the Celtic player attempts to facilitate, ensuring their safety and disrupting the Romans' activity. Both parties necessarily fail: so long as the player keeps her party alive, Sylak always opens the portal onto 'another world beyond, lush, green, and untouched'. The magical peoples leave, and Sylak proclaims a curse upon the Empire. Final texts appear to tell the Roman player that, in future, she begins 'hearing tales of severe Roman losses', and the eventual abandonment of the area by future invaders. This contrasts with the Celtic player, who experiences through this ending the liberation of her homeland: 'Centuries later, historians are never really sure why, at the height of its power, the Empire never expanded again.' Both trajectories result in an ending, in which cultural conflict ceases and fits the narrative into the known historiographical account of the Roman Empire. While this does not reflect the kinds of characters the player has chosen to construct – sympathetic Roman colonizer or insensitive, thieving and murdering imperialist – the demonstrably differing views upon those same final sequences do reflect the multiple perspectives so central to the overall play experience.

Simply by allowing two separate perspectives, and by offering to the player of both campaigns the relatively frequent ability to respond as they choose, the game maintains the potential for reflection on ancient colonial spaces. It may be characterized as colonial because, as the examples demonstrate, events, locations and NPCs all reflect the central tension between the newly-invading imperial force, and the native(s) under threat. By offering two separate journeys within the same world and quest framework, along with subtle alterations to the gameworld and possible responses to them depending on the cultural identities of the player and the kinds of decisions they make, *NG* offers players the opportunity to actively affect this colonial space. While there is admittedly limited capability to co-construct characters and personalities, and only some capacity to act subversively, the player may at times tailor her adventures to reflect her own opinions or the assumed opinions of her characters. Of course, the play process depends on recognition first of stereotyped imagery, but that is not the end result: 'Stereotypes are simply ways of categorizing people according to a particular attribute' and relate to players' need to 'cognitively categorize'.[27] In the CRPG, this is merely a jumping-off point to facilitate role-play. Playing in-character requires 'deliberate dissociation,' the player becoming 'so completely wrapped-up in a narrative that the outside world begins to receive only secondary mental processing'.[28] This means the player may very well not 'act Roman', given the opportunity, despite the intrinsic 'Romanness' of both people and setting, instead operating in accordance with her own ideas, feelings and beliefs.[29] Otherwise, she might build a 'typical' imperialist or atypical culturally sensitive Roman.

Either way, despite being prompted initially by conventional imagery, the player may engage with an added mental dimension that enriches her play experience. Through role-playing, and so empathizing, the player of *NG* may now 'ask some questions' of herself and her real world 'concerning aspects of the Other and of Otherness, about blind spots, hidden agendas, and the stranger in ourselves'.[30] This corresponds well with the kinds of issues and terminologies used by postcolonial commentators. To think colonially, as it were, we must be 'in the persistent constitution of Other as the Self's shadow'.[31] This is impossible for a (role-)player who operates as 'Other', as native. By implicating Celts within the play process, and tying wider narrative events into known historiography, the player further denies 'a grand narrative that regulates a universal truth'.[32] This, in turn, may confront perceptions and judgements about the ancient world.[33] *NG* from start to finish demonstrates the capacity for classical places and peoples to be reformulated to suit contemporary attitudes and agendas. Players can subvert 'usual' behaviours of Romans or Celts within the coded constraints of the game, even as they depend on standard signifiers of such cultures to actually play it. Subversion of classics like this can be 'revolutionary', instrumental in readdressing power structures (ancient and modern).[34] The game therefore indicates something like a postcolonial approach that, through the affordances of the genre framework, prioritizes exploratory practice within and around fully characterized, responsive non-playable agents in an open-world setting and, through this, allows players to get playful with the 'meaning' of imperial Roman or native Celt.

While it is no perfect example of a postcolonial perspective, the centrality of thoughtful, considered play to the game may allow players to access values and messages tacitly underpinning *NG*, thereby allowing reassessment of the nature of imperialism, colonial acts, and their consequences, from the point of view of both invader and invaded. It is possible even that the Celtic player is giving voice to the voiceless, and so participating in the restoration of 'subaltern' speech. Here, the subaltern can be widely defined as non-Western (here non-Greco-Roman) 'men and women from the subordinate social groups'.[35] While operating the subaltern may implicitly support the worrying, and outdated, assertion that subaltern peoples have not the ability to represent themselves,[36] since the (likely Western) player is literally controlling them, it is far less uncomfortable than the alternative, wherein players operate only as Romans against inoperative, automatic Others. Only by experiencing both sides, conceiving of alternative approaches to characterization and role-playing from polarized perspectives can the player tease out themes of imperial encroachment, cultural disruption and differing attitudes. It is a testament to the many affordances of this unique genre framework and the malleability of antiquity as a collective of signifying materials that such opportunities can be located in *NG*.

Playing the Western hero in *Titan Quest*

TQ, on the other hand, offers a gamespace experienced through a single perspective. Unlike *NG*, players here move from West-to-East along a largely fixed trajectory, from Greece to Egypt and into the 'Orient' (as the game calls it). They fight hordes of similarly recognizable mythological creatures such as cyclopes, maenads and satyrs recently unleashed by the wizard-like Telkines, who wish to carry out the now-conventional mission of unleashing the Titans from their prison.[37] The online store page sells the game as an exploratory experience with customizable characters,[38] and while this is true to some extent, this comparatively (to *NG*) linear movement from West-to-East with an always-Greek hero offers an alternative look at the implications such spatial movements might carry. Players of *TQ* are necessarily engaging with a narrative-driven game experience towards a specific, heroic end-point, whereas *NG* presents players with a more open-world experience chiefly concerned with the (relatively) free exploration of people and places; consequently, different methods of representing Other spaces and virtual inhabitants are used, which, in turn, face the player with contrary colonial themes. Colonial encounters from postcolonial perspectives are, as Rao reports of Said, not just about the explicit violence of invasion, societal subjugation and resource appropriation, but the 'epistemic violence enacted by particular forms of knowledge tethered to imperial power'.[39] Unlike the multicultural role-playing of *NG*, the player through her heroic Greek conforms to this definition of colonial encounter, tacitly utilizing her 'knowledges' necessary for ancient gameplay to become immersed in alternative colonial resonances.

Prior to analysis, it is necessary to illustrate briefly how ancient Greece became inextricable from European colonialist ideology. Classics and classicism were traditionally the preserve of an elite, who used their knowledge of antiquity to maintain their own positions in society.[40] Such attitudes towards the classical past forged what Chakrabarty identifies as a false 'unbroken tradition' constructed by Europeans to prove their superiority and justify their movements against colonies.[41] This 'ideological construct' was directly fed by elitist intellectual connections with antiquity, and especially philhellenism.[42] Such 'fetishizing and idolizing' arguably continues today.[43] This section therefore relies on the 'conviction that the new is never a break with the past',[44] that values can surface once again via the utilization of dim resonances of antiquity and the consequent (inadvertent) recycling of such values through play. It is entirely possible to find such subtexts even when unintended by the developer: while assumptions were employed in *NG* to be negotiated and sometimes to some degree overturned, assumptions can also be *unconsciously* embedded within a game system.[45] As a result, *TQ* may be seen to possess such presumptive values. This section therefore not only looks for familiar imagery, but also the '*processes of subjectification* made possible (and plausible) through stereotypical discourse'.[46]

Both representational differences between regions and the way the player moves throughout those spaces highlights the apparent centrality of potentially colonialist values. In Athens, for example, the player encounters an oracle, speaking in verse, bracketed visually by red drapes and gold ornaments and enveloped in magical essences. Such representations play into standard images of weird oracular figures.[47] Nevertheless, player identification with her Greek character always establishes this kind of activity as normal: this, in turn, designates non-Greek areas always as *more* Other. As Lowe states, while Greece in the game is composed of 'interchangeable' monuments, Egypt and Asia 'look largely the same'.[48] The bright Greek countryside is, indeed, eventually traded in for a more monotone Egypt soon after this encounter, confronting the player with a typical 'Egyptian *mood*' and supplanting the many mythical enemy variants of Greece for waves of 'mindless' mummies,[49] giant scorpions and scarabs. Interaction with these entities is exclusively combative in nature, thus reducing the role of the player to hack-and-slash play behaviours. The lack of dynamic treatment of these typically ancient materials is further emphasized by the presentation of geographical travel as a repetitive 'A-to-B' movement. Players move from one end of a gamespace to the other, enter another space and repeat, getting stronger and more capable as they go. They may move backwards and cover old ground, but this is achieved via portals, a fantasy fiction trope by which 'a character leaves her familiar surroundings and passes through a portal into an unknown place … The portal fantasy is about entry, transition, and exploration.'[50] As the player moves from left to right, West to East, and those spaces are further intersected with portals, the game inadvertently sets up a 'boundary notion', 'testify[ing] to a willed imaginative and geographic division made between East and West'.[51] In short, the player primarily moves forwards, in a straight line, killing as she goes. Any alternative to this movement is done automatically, out of player control, further drawing illusory lines and demarcating regions. As the player progresses, the virtual worlds become both less visually appealing and simultaneously easier to traverse the further she battles away from her Greek homeland.

Where the player is required to speak to in-game constituents, she only ever does so to 'solve' the problems of Eastern peoples. Outside Memphis, the player finds the downtrodden of Egypt, self-described as 'the poor whom all disdain', who appeal to the player for help. If she chooses, she can assist by killing the monsters overrunning their 'mud huts'. This is a traditional characterization of the Egyptian peasant as 'labouring workforce'.[52] The player's seemingly inherent ability to provide a solution, and her eventual doing so, places this 'peaceful savage [...] under the protection of a master' who exercises 'dominion' and 'paternalistic assistance'.[53] It also implies that, since the player is the only one who can affect this change, that she as Greek-hero-from-the-West is the only agent possessing power.[54] This pattern is replicated throughout, wherein a rigid quest structure justifies player movement through spaces as she operates as natural 'saviour'.

Player movement into the literally named 'Orient' further positions the superior, civilized Westerner against a barbaric and alien East. The cohort of enemies in the Orient is especially ahistorical and often inapplicable to a specific culture or mythological system: the 'Tropical Spider', for example, first encountered in the Gardens of Babylon, is neither Egyptian nor Babylonian but merely generically 'exotic'. As the player battles towards China, she encounters 'Saberlions', anthropomorphized tiger-men, and even 'Neanderthals', implying the player has truly left 'the privileged center', to use Said's terminology, and has entered a place where people are literally inhuman.[55] The Orient section is no longer than Greece or Egypt, but has contained within it Babylon, Tibet, Central Asian hinterlands and China. These are necessarily played through at breakneck speed, troubling the player's sense of location and further diminishing the likelihood of these spaces to be represented as unique, distinct cultural regions. This representational strategy makes contextual sense in *TQ*'s China, which has spirits with 'specific existence[s] ... [and] distinct personalities',[56] as in Chinese folklore. Non-specific representations may even be a result of the 'disparate', unclassified nature of Chinese mythology.[57] It is unlikely, however, to be a response to the lack of codification characterizing the mythology of ancient China, and reads instead like a fleeting experience wherein the player, ever gaining power through her adventure, must 'clean' the land of Neanderthals and beast-men.[58] The result, then, is an Orient of 'half-imagined, half-known: monsters, devils, heroes; terrors',[59] encountered through continual, cyclical combative procedures and linear movements. While Greece is also populated by hordes of monsters, they are more recognizably (to a Western player, at least) concomitant with the creatures of classical myth. Homogenization of the Other, encountered almost exclusively within the contexts of player-initiated violence, engender further comparisons with colonial ideological precedents.

The final sequences, in which the player faces off against the Titan Typhon, take place on Mount Olympus, somehow accessed via a portal beneath China. First, the player meets the Yellow Emperor, an important figure in Chinese folklore, who knows all about this threat but is, apparently, unable to assist. The player is, once again, the only agent able to provide a solution, bookending an experience that consistently implies Eastern peoples are here, as Chakrabarty locates Indians and Africans in Eurocentric thought, '*not yet* civilized enough to rule themselves' or to look after themselves independently.[60] Movement into Olympus further emphasizes the stark contrast between undefined Orient and the opulent Greek mythical landscape of marble columns and golden arches. Succeeding in defeating Typhon, the player is personally thanked by Zeus: 'You have proven that men are ready to become the masters of their own fates. Your mortal world is not yet safe, but the responsibility now is yours.' The word 'men' is used regardless of the gender the player chooses to play as, perhaps implying this pseudo-imperial movement is intrinsically masculine. Zeus here admits the Greek (player) has saved the world, and as a reward agrees to leave the world in the hands of mortals. The player thus liberates the world from superstition, an activity that strongly echoes colonialist ideology – for Heit, 'a central aspect of Western identity, as distinct from other cultures, is the claim that the West has a rational worldview, understood as a Greek invention.'[61] In moving from West to East, deigning to help the peasant and clearing the lands of monsters, the player must effectively cooperate with and rehearse a peculiarly Eurocentric journey 'from myth to reason'.[62]

Conclusion

Nethergate and *Titan Quest* both demonstrate how different readings and meanings can be interpreted depending on how cultural processes, ancient materials and genre conventions are utilized. Through affordances gifted by the CRPG genre framework, players of *NG* may confront issues of imperialism and their own role within them, making decisions (within the set parameters of the game), exploring lands, conversing with peoples and, crucially, considering the consequences of their actions. Players here immerse themselves in alternative mindsets, thereby engendering alternative outlooks upon colonial spaces. This is essential for such an involving practice as role-play, where players negotiate complex moral problems from their own, and their characters', perspectives.[63] In this way it operates something like postcolonial critique, using standard representations of the province and its cultures before requiring the player to decide how she chooses to approach them. *TQ*'s comparative rigidity of both representation and play procedure instead perpetuates the notion of a Westerner assisting the helpless Other. While that Other is, indeed, a subaltern, like the Egyptian peasant in the example above, there exists no capacity for the player to explore what their position in the gameworld might be. There is no sinister agenda behind *TQ*, rather it simply takes a different approach to representing the imposition of classical/Western presences. The generic ancient materials within *TQ* are left to operate without much surrounding context for the player to navigate, which leads to potential issues: as postcolonial scholar Spivak says, 'it is when signifiers are left to look after themselves that verbal slippages happen'.[64] Future developers may benefit from Hanink's call for classical materials to be appropriated wisely and appropriately.[65] Coupled with values already attached to antiquity through years of post-antique appropriation, and the removal of freedom of movement and decision-making opportunities, *TQ* instead confronts the player with a fixed journey across geographical boundaries. Conversely, *NG* demonstrates the capacity for both genre framework and audiovisual antiquities to allow for thoughtful, free, critical play. These standardized visions of antiquity, within this genre apparatus, therefore deliberately or otherwise allow reflection on colonialism through play.

Notes

1 The female pronoun is used throughout.
2 Specifically, 'higher levels of narrative complexity' in comparison to other games, Moser and Fang (2015: 146–8).
3 *Nethergate: Resurrection* (2007) is a revamped release of *Nethergate* (1998), created with some new episodes and areas but made primarily to allow players with newer computer systems access to outdated game software.
4 Said (2003: 73 and 117, first and second quotation, respectively).
5 See Mona (2010) for an account of *D&D*'s early history. Dormans (2006) describes the basics of *D&D* play; see, Bowman (2010: 16–18) on the influence of Tolkien's work on the development of the game.
6 Bowman (2010: 180) and Hitchens and Drachen (2009: 5).
7 Rao (2015: 271).
8 E.g. use of classics in the Caribbean, saving it from 'accusations of inveterate cultural chauvinism' and so presenting 'an alternative theory of relationships between past and present', Greenwood (2005: 65, 85). Also, Hardwick (2005: 113).
9 The RPG quest-system is near universal, made especially famous by *World of Warcraft* (2004), see, Walker (2010: 307–8).
10 Laycock (2015: 258).
11 Howard (2008: xii–xiii).
12 Pillay (2002: 338).
13 The term 'unofficial knowledges' is taken from Samuel (2012: 5–6), who sees history (and antiquity) as 'learned' 'in dibs and dabs' through diverse encounters and experiences.
14 Fencott et al. (2012: 76). Upton notes a 'mental warehouse of applicable themes, characters and tropes' (2015: 220).
15 From science fiction to fantasy, film, comic books and other video games. See, Bowman (2010: 69–70). Also see, Tynes (2010: 221).
16 Hardwick (2003: 107–9).
17 Tac. *Annals* 14.30 (2008).
18 Squire (2003: 18).
19 Such as the Celts in the *Rome: Total War* expansion pack, *Barbarian Invasion* (2005).
20 Quotes from Ilieva (2013: 28).
21 Maier (2003: 50), Squire (2003: 36–8) and Henig (1984: 23).
22 E.g. Strabo, *Geography* 4.5.2 (1903): 'They have lots of milk but can't make cheese.' See, Takács (2008: 148–9) for Tacitean 'pretence'.
23 Adams (2013: 70). See, Howard (2008: 25) on 'emotional urgency'.
24 Laycock (2015: 323) claims role-players often prioritize immersion at the expense of winning.
25 Henig (1984: 41–3).
26 Mattingly (2007: 527) and Hingley (2007: 342).
27 Reference from Alhabash and Wise (2014: 1359). Costikyan (2010: 11) notes the uniqueness of 'indie' games in subverting stereotypes. Walker (2010: 308)

argues originality is far less important for RPGs. See also, Lankoski and Jarvela (2013: 24).

28 First reference from Neuenschwander (2008: 195) and the second is from Mahood and Hanus (2017: 63).

29 Adams (2013: 82–3) refers to a report, in which *D&D* players were motivated by (Western) desires to reflect, through play, individual belief in 'democracy, friendship … and ethics'.

30 Decreus (2007: 263).

31 Spivak (1988: 280).

32 Decreus (2007: 263).

33 Hardwick (2003: 10).

34 Barnard (2017: 4).

35 Chakrabarty (2000: 8).

36 Gramsci (1971: 52–5) in Rao (2015: 277), describes the 'subaltern': concerns over controlling the subaltern found in Rao (2015: 277–8) and Spivak (1988: 276–7).

37 There is no ancient precedent for the Titans' rising-up in Hesiod's account, *Theogony* 715–21 (1973), but it is, nevertheless, a trope used in film and television, e.g. Disney's *Hercules* (1997) and the *Immortals* (2011) film.

38 *Steam* 'Titan Quest' (2016).

39 Rao (2015: 272).

40 See Stray (1996: 79) on Victorian-era classical education, and Schein (2008: 80) on the nineteenth century. For classics maintaining the class system today, see Hall and Stead (2013: 1–2).

41 Chakrabarty (2000: 5). See, Stray (1996: 77–8) for classics as 'legitimating practice'.

42 Quote from Schein (2008: 81); Philhellenism and Greek philosophies and cultural achievements in Heit (2006: 725, 732). See also, Held (1997: 255).

43 Decreus (2007: 251) uses these words. For an example of twentieth-century 'idolizing', see Bolgar's twentieth-century publication for lamentation on 'our' loss of connection with 'our' 'great predecessor' (1974: 4, also 1–2, 40, 380).

44 Villarejo (2017: 104–5).

45 Garcia (2017: 233–4).

46 Bhabha (1999: 370, his emphasis).

47 See Burkert (1985: 116).

48 Lowe (2012: 81–2).

49 Huckvale (2012: 143, his emphasis). 'Mindless automata' is a phrase used by Huckvale (ibid.: 185), describing mummies as they appear in film.

50 Mendlesohn (2008: 23).

51 Said (2003: 201). This is despite popular understanding that the Greeks were 'culturally elastic', Hall (2015).

52 For the 'historical' Egyptian peasant, see, David (2007: 75).

53 Nippel (2002: 300–1).

54 The suggestion that the colonizer has all the power is implicit in Said's work, and criticized by Bhabha (1999: 274) and Rao (2015: 274).

55 Quote from Said (2003: 117). Such representations reflect cinematic tropes such as the 'deformed freaks and monsters' of Persia in the *300* (2006) film; see, Burton (2016: 321).

56 Von Glahn (2004: 258).

57 Chinese classicist Zhou Zuoren described Chinese mythology as such, Zhang (2015: 107). Western scholarship equally sees Chinese mythology as comparatively 'superficial', von Glahn (2004: 265).

58 Quote attributed to Rudyard Kipling, itself quoted in Said (2003: 226).

59 Said (2003: 102, 63, 65).

60 Chakrabarty (2000: 8, his emphasis). See also, the 'white saviour' trope used in the recent *The Great Wall* (2016) film.

61 Heit (2006: 732–3).

62 Ibid., 735. He also notes that this is re-employed in 'reconstructions of Antiquity' (ibid.: 736), implying a representational tradition.

63 Khoo (2012: 421, 425).

64 Spivak (1988: 275).

65 Hanink (2017: 277).

Playing with an Ancient Veil

Commemorative Culture and the Staging of Ancient History within the Playful Experience of the MMORPG, *The Secret World*

Nico Nolden

Behind the veil: Secret worlds of collective historical staging

With *The Secret World*, Norwegian developer FunCom has delivered an outstanding example of a historically multifaceted, rich and complex design of a gameworld: from its inception in 2012, players of that game have been able to enter a modern-day setting, in which myths and legends come to life.[1] The game belongs to the genre of Massively-Multiplayer Online Role-Playing Games (MMORPGs). Most MMORPGs are situated either in fantasy or science fiction gameworlds, though the latter scenario is nowhere near as widespread as the former. Although they often reference historical elements, virtually no scholarly study of MMORPGs from the perspective of the historian exists. Regrettably, this means that, hitherto, historians have neglected an essential source for the cultural history of digital media societies.[2] In my own previous research, I focused mainly on MMORPGs and specifically on *The Secret World* as a central empirical research subject.[3]

In this game form, players create an avatar and enter a spatial environment filled with missions they usually pursue in social groups. By solving the missions, players gain experience points ('XP') they invest in their avatar's abilities in order to push into more challenging gaming areas. MMORPGs have a long tradition dating back to the 1990s, with *World of Warcraft* being the most well-known mainstream representative of the genre. Analogue and digital predecessors appeared as early as the 1970s. In the case of *The Secret World*, this specific game touches on all periods of history, referencing academic findings as well as popular perceptions of history, and taking historical traditions of various regions of the globe into account. As agents of various secret societies, the player of *The Secret World* is tasked with investigating why history (in the shape, e.g., of historical myths) has come alive. Antiquity plays an essential role within the gaming environment's historical fabric.

My personal journey through this vast gameworld – or, more accurately, that of my avatar, Lionsheart – began in a London district, as I chose the faction of the *Templars*.

Two other factions, the *Illuminati* and the *Dragons*, would also have been available, resulting in the alternative starting areas of New York and Seoul, as well as a different ideological tone. From these headquarter cities, players set off for the playgrounds of New England, Egypt and Romania, as well as for London, Tokyo, New York and Seoul. Alongside their main quest to solve the mystery of why myths and legends have suddenly come to life, they are confronted with a broad variety of historical topics in numerous missions. Players encounter various forms of depictions of prehistory as well as early and ancient history in most regions: they visit ruins of Egyptian and Roman structures and use relics such as a priest's staff or the Roman *ancile* of Mars during missions. They encounter historical figures both divine and human, such as Akhenaten himself and his antagonist Ptahmose, a former high priest, or creatures in between, such as a once-lost and now undead Roman legion, resurrected in Egypt. Last but not least, players deal with myths and legends like the fate of Carthaginian descendants or the late Roman cult of Sol Invictus.

In a first step, this chapter will explore the various factors which inform the specific performance of antiquity within the gameworld. Neither individual elements of historical atmosphere nor the complex interplay between all components for the staging of ancient history in digital games have been investigated so far. Digital games create worlds of historical experience in various ways and to various degrees. For instance, while some gameworlds are focused on the reconstruction of specific historic artefacts, others rely especially on historical references within the narrative. *Ryse: Son of Rome* pursued the former method, *Ankh: Battle of the Gods*, for instance, the latter. Both are set in a mythological history with personified ancient pantheons. Other titles attempt meticulous macro-historical abstractions of the world, such as the grand-strategy part of *Total War: Rome II*, which models Roman politics, economy, military and society. Recently, entire world designs have emerged, which are spatially more confined, but which stage complex historical processes on a micro-historical scale. *Assassin's Creed: Origins*, for example, shows everyday life during the Roman infiltration of Ptolemaic Egypt. Of course, there is a vast continuum of mixtures within these predominant types.

In contrast to other media that can be witnessed passively, digital games assign the decisive function to the players themselves; it is only through their actions and manipulations of the game interface that a historical performance takes place at all. This chapter, therefore, is framed in terms of performance studies, assigning the main role in staging their own historical perception to the players, who use historical game assets provided to them in performing historical practices ('doing history').[4] MMORPGs go even further, as hundreds or thousands of players act and communicate with the gameworld and within the gameworld, as well as among themselves. If players of an MMORPG stage a historical setting, their communities move in a context that is relevant to commemorative culture. Hence, in a complementary second step, this chapter will explore how these communities act and communicate within and about this complex historical structure. The historical structures and processes of *The Secret World* can be of great interest to researchers working in Public History.

In this chapter, I aim to derive analytical categories from the various models of conceptualizing history within video games presented in scholarship, and to complement them with the game developers' own conceptions of history. In doing so,

I lift the veil over historical components and their systemic interactions that have so far received too little attention by utilizing what I call a Historical Knowledge System. This allows me to identify historical components of *The Secret World* and to trace them in player discourse. Studying the latter in online forums allows me to ascertain the resonance of historical elements within communities of commemorative culture among players, thus showing their relevance for cultural memory processes.

What is historical about digital games?

So far, attempts to quantify the number of digital games that refer to history have been methodologically challenging.[5] These few statistical analyses do not distinguish sufficiently between hardware platforms, such as consoles or handhelds, and their relative importance in video game history. Hence, they consider digital games to be uniform over too long periods of time, thus overstretching the significance of the data used. Genre categories are often used uncritically. Last but not least, they lack a suitable concept of the 'historical'. It is astonishing to observe that researchers rarely determine what the historical aspects – meaning the kinds of reference they regard as historical – of a digital game may actually be. I have elsewhere collected and categorized relevant terms and paraphrases for these aspects used in academic research, in an effort to distil from this a viable terminology for analysis.[6]

Some historians are already trying to approach the historical essence of games in different ways, e.g. by simply distinguishing it from non-historical scenarios, such as sports.[7] Others resort to rather vague constructs like historical 'semblance' to describe historical influence.[8] Many authors, however, do not directly address this question at all. Their investigations aim at certain aspects such as narration, game mechanics or visual impressions, by which they implicitly outline the object historically.[9]

There are ongoing attempts, however, at more solidly establishing what 'historical' means in the context of digital games. Carl Heinze proposed a model based on the characteristics of the technical system between hardware and software in which he only considers 'history' as relevant to the game itself, where it is functionally integrated into game mechanics.[10] By contrast, Martin Zusag's systems theory-based analysis model concentrates on the act of digital gaming in an interacting productive-receptive space.[11] The 'ecological' approach adapted by Adam Chapman includes players, technological artefacts and gaming experience, and phenomenologically describes a sphere in which simulation, epistemology, time, space and affordances (understood as offers for action that games intrinsically signal to the players) form the historical gaming experience.[12] With their *History-Game Relations (HGR) framework*, Vincenzo Casso and Mattia Thibault propose to combine structured investigations of game elements and their interplay with research perspectives of historical theory (such as, e.g., historism, the *Annales* tradition, or narratology).[13] In sum, then, practitioners of history have so far approached the analysis of historical aspects of digital games in a hopscotch fashion, focusing on specific aspects instead of adopting a more holistic view. Nevertheless, their work inspires further discourse and research in order to reach a more comprehensive solution.

Remarkably, game developers themselves have not been systematically screened for their conceptions of history yet, although the resulting products (i.e. the games themselves) reflect their historical imaginations. Their conceptions and notions provide a so-far unnoticed perspective that may help to unify the approaches. Among the few academic contributions to document developers' attitudes and understandings of history, the investigation of three German developers, employed by Franco-Canadian publisher Ubisoft, dominated the debate.[14] As point persons during the development process, they were involved in the production of the well-liked German game series *Anno* and *The Settlers*. The result of the investigation was disheartening as, to them, history was only a means to an end: it provided templates to construct a royalty-free universe, thus reducing costs. Developers concentrated on architecture and objects such as historical artefacts. It was not deemed necessary for historical concepts to be historically accurate, so long as they corresponded to the expectations of players (what is called *perceived history*). Conversely, German-speaking scholars seemed to be largely satisfied in having their own prejudices toward the medium and its developers confirmed.

However, the attitudes of the Ubisoft developers are by no means representative. Within the same publishing house, statements given by Patrice Désilets offer a different viewpoint. Désilets is the creator of *Assassin's Creed*, which spawned one of the most successful gaming franchises in video game history. Although he also used historical content mostly as a stage setting and therefore subordinated history to game mechanics in case of doubt, his conception of history includes historical narratives and the contemporaneous framework conditions, and was thus not limited to faithfully modelling historical artefacts and buildings.[15] He is also aware that developers always interpret history with an intersubjective distance of today's view, compiled out of fragmentary traditions from the past. Sid Meier, another long-standing leading figure in the industry, identifies the historical component rather in models that are oriented towards historical structures and processes, and reveal various alternatives for historical development to players.[16] His influential classic *Civilization* had a decisive impact on the game mechanics of other macro-historical global strategy games. A more recent phenomenon, micro-historical world designs are situated in small-scale spaces where objects, buildings and landscapes are meticulously reconstructed. Daniel Vavrà, for example, uses the resulting functionality for the role-playing game *Kingdom Come: Deliverance* and models inhabitants, flora, fauna and weather in a section of late medieval Bohemia.[17] The developers embed a network of everyday processes and stories in a larger historical narrative, seeking historically plausible solutions for game mechanics and mission design.[18]

The various approaches of scholars, as mentioned above, have so far only covered individual aspects. I suggest widening our approach by adding four elements emphasized by game developers in order to arrive at a more comprehensive understanding of the historical aspects in digital games. These historical components influence each other during gameplay and therefore form what I call a dynamic 'Historical Knowledge System': first, *object and material culture*; second, *narrative networks*; third, *macro-historical (computational) models*; and fourth, *micro-historical world designs*. The more aspects of the game are based on one or more of these categories, the more highly I estimate the degree of 'historical-ness' of a digital game. In this sense, then, this chapter investigates aspects of the (ancient) historical staging in the test case of *The Secret World*.

A historical knowledge system for ancient history

The Historical Knowledge System proves to be extraordinarily dense in *The Secret World*. Fundamental media characteristics of the MMORPG game form[19] combine with a remarkably contemporary conception of history: 'history' is represented in a number of ways and distinct perspectives, from numerous reconstructed objects to historical narratives. In addition, the game presents a well-chosen contemporary perspective:[20] the present-day view around the year 2010 bears a global-historical attitude that frames players' access to the gaming environment. This world view is further reinforced, as globalized game communities gather in the game. Structurally, the underlying globe-spanning technology of MMORPGs supports such a historical conception. Seen from the point of view of a historian, this results in one of the best realized historical experiences not only for MMORPGs, but for video games as a whole.

Among many other historical periods, the gameworld of *The Secret World* heavily and consistently references antiquity and ancient history. Because of their richness in detail, not every historical layer can be described here;[21] I have provided a complete overview of these layers of the Historical Knowledge System elsewhere in video form.[22] Still, it is worth briefly pointing out its considerable complexity for this chapter. Within the gameworld, the country of Romania is a good example of the multifaceted layers of history focused in one digital environment: Communist concrete installations can be seen towering next to an abandoned early modern village and bear witness to Soviet domination in Romania. Legends tell of the early modern country, while a Romani camp provides access to Christian and pre-Christian folklore. As the old Roman province of Dacia, imperial Roman history is also referenced. In New England, by contrast, history reaches back to the Viking landings and their encounters with native inhabitants, the Wabanaki. Scandinavian and Native American legends intertwine with local historical events from the early modern period to today, as players encounter creatures that are manifestations of New English horror literature. In Egypt, cultural tourism and terrorism in the Arab sphere collide as well as colonial exploitation and scholarly explorations of the Egyptian cultural heritage. In-game, local individuals fight for self-determination of Egypt. To prevent cultists from resurrecting Pharaoh Akhenaten, players must develop an understanding of ancient Egyptian religion and mythology.

In this vast spectrum of historical topics, four main epistemological interests for historians can be observed. There are, first, pure *historical conceptions*, visible at first glance, because they address an older time period within the components of the Historical Knowledge System. But beyond that, three other historical influences on the game are of interest: second, a *techno-cultural history of games* involving the traditions of text-adventure games or Korean network cafés (called 'PC bangs') in the gameworld.

The game also, third, deliberates on its history conception as a *Historical Knowledge System of Commemorative Culture* itself, as dialogues reoccur about the character of historical knowledge and its tradition through time. Importantly for the holistic perspective of the game, fourth, all locations continuously weave through the historical frame with *feedback loops from contemporary history*. In Egypt, for example, colonial exploitation is not limited to the past when archaeological artefacts are smuggled or wars for oil are addressed.

To document the historical aspects of the gaming experience during the research process, I have recorded my instance of play (or 'paths') as digital videos. This, in itself, poses methodological problems, discussed in greater detail elsewhere.[23] The core problem, however, is that, in documenting my play, I myself am constructing the source material which I will later investigate, thus reducing the degree of freedom inherent in gaming experiences and approximating this medium to that of film. More fundamentally, as games (particularly MMORPGs) are updated throughout their existence, the technological basis of the game does not remain unchanged. Updates of game mechanics, contents or technology occur regularly and sometimes have a deeper impact. I will therefore limit my investigation to a roughly uniform game-state between the years 2012 and 2014, that is to say the game era before the introduction of the new cultural area of Tokyo. Nevertheless, the recordings prove whether I have been able to observe what I describe. The following endnotes therefore refer to my recordings in the database while their denominations hint at topics as well as the categories above. However, it is important to remember that other players may conceivably have experiences of play that differ.

It is also important to emphasize that by choosing a contemporary player perspective in the gameworld, the online role-playing game offers a grasp on ancient history unusual for digital games. Buildings are not reconstructed to a surmised historic state but are instead in-game archaeological sites and museum exhibitions in a present form. In addition, the Imperial period architecture in the London district, for example, in itself, already reflects contemporary and Victorian imaginations of antiquity.[24] This contemporary filter overlaying other historical perspectives helps to avoid reproducing misconceptions. For example, modern views and visual impressions of ancient material culture are commonly dominated by the clean white marble look that we have learned to associate with antiquity. Archaeologists and ancient historians, on the other hand, have known the ancient world to have been a distinctly colourful place for years now, though even with mainstream media reporting, this scholarly consensus has not yet filtered down to the public at large to change collective historical perceptions.[25] Games, just as other media, have reinforced this misconception for many years.[26] Even the contemporary approach of *The Secret World* falls for this misconception occasionally, for example during time travel to a Roman settlement and an Egyptian town's ancient predecessor.[27] However, a recent example impressively shows that this may be about to change in games culture; Ubisoft's latest *Assassin's Creed* title *Odyssey* shows visuals of ancient Greece far more sophisticated than seen before.[28]

If we investigate the Historical Knowledge System in the game's different regional settings now, there are many linkages to ancient cultures. A structured approach along the categories mentioned above leads to numerous examples of ancient *object and material culture* being referenced: buildings, infrastructure, maps, vehicles, creatures and objects of everyday use. In the scorched plains of the Egyptian desert, for example, players encounter revenants of a Roman legion that worship Sol Invictus in the remains of a Roman settlement.[29] Players fight fanatic cultists, who want to awaken the Pharaoh Akhenaton from a prison in a hidden ancient temple city.[30] They literally walk on traces of the Roman Empire along Dacian streets in the Romanian setting.[31]

Individual quests lead them underneath the British capital to explore the remnants of Roman Londinium.[32] Recognizable by their respective architectural styles, the younger walls of the Egyptian settlement Al-Merayah rest on several layers of older historical remains.[33] Across all areas that cover territories that belonged to the Roman Empire, ruins and excavation sites incorporate various ancient objects like relics or everyday items like amphorae laying scattered (Fig. 9.1).

Others, such as sarcophagi or sculptures are exhibited in a museum devoted to the reign of Akhenaten.[34] Most objects are not interactive. Myths and legends resurrected as creatures, for example, are objectified, because they solely serve actions by players, commonly with no other purpose than combat. There are four major types of mythological creatures in-game: mummies, for example, comply with the established popular cultural consensus.[35] Ghouls, however, diverge from their more standard depictions; they arose because of the bloodshed caused by the Pharaoh.[36] Djinns are rooted in the original Arab concept, not necessarily vicious, but ambivalent and menacing.[37] As a fourth type, developers added their own inventions, including oily and lanky mutations.[38] Beyond fighting creatures, players can interact with more complex objects during missions. Artefacts of one kind may be manipulable to varying

Fig. 9.1 Late Roman ruins in *The Secret World* (2012 © FunCom Oslo AS. All rights reserved).

degrees depending on the specific situation. For example, in one quest, players need to obtain a Roman relic, the *ancile* of Mars, god of war. These ritual shields, attested in Roman history as being housed in the temple of Mars in Rome, are represented in-game as devices from a prehistoric sunken civilization.[39] But players also have the power to construct or repair other artefacts like the Staff of Amun, the various parts of which have to be collected across Egypt. From the player's perspective, presumably generic hieroglyphics often decorate ancient ruins (Fig. 9.2).[40] But different royal titles and names of *Akhenaten* become functional elements for a quest, as players must put his historic names in order of appearance.[41] The more important historical meaning of an object is for an in-game situation, the more historically accurate its implementation.

An especially fascinating category of ancient artefacts introduces us to *narrative networks*. In order to confine *Akhenaten*'s aggressive immortal remains, High Priest Ptahmose used the aforementioned Staff of Amun in-game to transfer the souls of his children into *ushabtis*.[42] According to ancient Egyptian belief, these small stone statuettes are able to preserve the spirit independently of the body. Ptahmose needed them to watch over the binding of *Akhenaten* to his prison through the millennia. The game credibly stages the reactions of the seven children to their father's actions, ranging from (in)comprehension and uncertainty to contempt and wrath, from age-appropriate personalities, unchanged for thousands of years.[43] Their multi-perspective expressions belong to a multitude of intertwined narratives all over the gameworld, which influence each other and branch out during a player's progress.[44]

Beyond the ancient family of eight, players are introduced to quests by a total of 100 personalities. All of them react differently to the historical environment, but their attitudes each are plausible from ethnic, social and demographic contexts. For example,

Fig. 9.2 Ancient Egyptian ruins with hieroglyphic friezes in *The Secret World* (2012 © FunCom Oslo AS. All rights reserved).

the immortal Saïd, a mummy from Egypt's Ancient Kingdom period, does not obey any of the game's factions.[45] Egypt is his ancestral domain. But as, apparently, a sense of history means less to the immortal than material wealth, he smuggles ancient artefacts to foreign countries until one of them is used in a terrorist attack. Following this, he repents and changes both his attitude and activities. Other characters, though, such as his former trading partner, the Carthaginian mercenary Tanis, or the cultist leader Daoud, warn the player about Saïd's motives – all the while following their own agenda.[46] In this way, a form of in-game Oral History emerges from dialogues among the personalities. Roger Travis' chapter in this volume shows how a player-character can become part of an oral epic in digital role-playing games with the help of an Open World and elaborate communities. Set in the present day, the gameworld of *The Secret World* allows players themselves to dive into oral traditions of history with various interpretations.

The unconventional type of 'investigation missions' forces players to deeply understand historical backgrounds with information provided in the game and complemented beyond it.[47] Their individual views are framed by the chosen faction's point of view, as these represent different historical ideologies. Thus, the moralist *Templars* divide people and creatures into moral categories of either 'bad' or 'good', while pursuing political dominance.[48] The capitalist *Illuminati* utilize the awakening mythical creatures in order to maximize profit.[49] From the Far East, the *Dragons* intend to rule the world by mastering chaos theory.[50] Interactions with representatives of these factions, as well as feedback from headquarters, shape diverging interpretations about events, persons and history.[51] A further world view is introduced by a swarm intelligence, represented in-game by bees. It shares short segments of a historical world knowledge with the player and symbolizes collective memory. These segments can be found in the form of honeycombs that are located all over the game's world and support the interwoven network of narratives.[52] As these are highly cryptic, they oblige players to develop their own interpretations, connecting historical developments, factions, events and persons, depending on how much of the fragments they find. To keep track of all the information, the game collects the fragments in an extensive database for each player, which structures information on historical topics and playgrounds in encyclopaedic fashion.[53]

At the same time, it encourages players to hunt certain creatures or to collect outfits for their avatars by promising rewards ('achievements') that can be unlocked.[54] In this way, it manages to organically connect different types of players to the historical and narrative background of gameworld and history. On one hand, the individual progress of players stores and activates knowledge in this encyclopaedia, which thus reflects the players' individual interests and persona types. On the other hand, developers regularly update the encyclopaedia and further game content as well as functionality through patches. In addition, information on the historical context and origins of seasonal events such as Christmas or Halloween are only available during these holiday periods. Those three aspects of temporal variability endow players with an experience of pastness and adds historicity to the gameworld. This individual epistemic model serves as an excellent interpretation of the process of knowledge acquisition.

Further *macro-historical (computational) models* can be found for societies, politics and economics. Particularly remarkable in the context of engaging with antiquity are in-game perceptions of science itself, characterizations of historical knowledge, and portrayals of the professions of historians and archaeologists. Heavily influenced by the aforementioned world views of factions, numerous personalities in the gameworld engage in substantial conflicts over the justifiable use and benefits of science and scholarship.[55] Historians and archaeologists themselves, as these personalities argue in-game, limit their own access to history because of their self-imposed restrictions in methodology and subject matters. In the judgement of these in-game NPCs, both professions tend to underrate oral reports from regional populations and to consider legendary and epic traditions, legends and myths, as unhelpful.[56] But, the fact that one no longer understands traditions does not mean that these traditions originally were also devoid of historical meaning, just as the absence of solid historical evidence does not necessarily indicate the absence of a civilization or any historical tradition.[57] In-game NPCs reason that professionals must master broad work fields between historical science, archaeology and ethnology, exploring unusual locations and methods, based on solid knowledge of books.[58] The cultural historical perspective of the game itself treats history in a remarkably constructivist and discursive fashion.[59]

On a *micro-historical* level, world design is also important, with landscapes, lighting, soundscapes and programmed routines converging into a coherent design with blurring boundaries between the game's environment and the everyday outside world. Topographically, the landscape of the Egyptian 'Scorched Desert' for example is dominated by sandy plains with dunes, rarely interrupted by oases, surrounded by cragged cliffs of reddish-yellow and, later, sooty-grey rock.[60] Recurring routines, such as creatures moving cyclically and periodically, and atmospheric accents set such as dust devils stage a dynamic version of a desert.[61] Together with a day-and-night-cycle, lighting moods change and influence perceptions of historical aspects.[62] Similar in effect, the gameworld dynamically combines noises, sounds and music into soundscapes, as in the case of the village of Al-Merayah.[63] Both light and sound are used as mission components, too.

Neither is it only the contemporary perspective that merges the gaming environment with the outer world. Implementing a well-thought-out model for realities, the developers rather consciously blur the game's borders. This is the case for instance when players need to investigate mission solutions outside the game itself, such as using the internet. In the aforementioned case of Akhenaten, no information present within the gameworld provides any hint as to the correct chronological order of his various historical titles and names. In order to complete the mission, players have to acquire this information independently and to arrange them in correct fashion. At the very least, they are forced to use scholarly resources or internet sources to decode the hieroglyphics. Some content is even actively set up on the actual World Wide Web by developers, such as the website of the in-game company Orochi.[64] Some game characters can be found online with their own blogs and Twitter accounts, where 'they' (that is, the developing studio) periodically upload videos or photos.[65] The lengths to which the developers go in these cases are astounding and they blur the lines between both realities, in-game and outside. This effect is further reinforced by some web content being deliberately ambivalent – occasionally, it is not at all clear if it was officially provided by developers, produced by players joining the fiction, or non-fictional and non-related to the game.

The complex interplay of all components in the Historical Knowledge System opens up fascinating new approaches for research on cultural heritage, public history and classical receptions. *Object and material culture* widen aspects of authenticity. *Narrative networks* should be integrated into narratological concepts. *Macro-historical (computational) models* refer to preliminary works on simulations. *Micro-historical world design* raises questions about what might describe a historical atmosphere, and the extent to which traditional concepts of reality are still suitable when digital and analogue systems merge.

Gaming communities and commemorative discourse about ancient history

There is another reason for scholars to focus more on MMORPGs as a distinct field of historical research: players in these games do not simply engage with the game but rather form social communities.[66] Such communities do not just gather to play – they play to come together.[67] They also continue a long tradition of analogue ('pen & paper') as well as digital predecessors ('multi-user dungeons').[68] Unwieldy as the official denomination of *Massively Multiplayer Online Role-Playing Games* indubitably is, the name itself highlights specific features of this game form: players engage online with each other and against each other in a complex spatial gaming environment which they share in large numbers (the 'massive' part). When they take action, the virtual environment reacts in real-time. Each player slips into a role and explores the gameworld from the perspective of that character. Completing quests develops the avatar's talents and skills and allows players to advance into more challenging areas. From a technological point of view, players connect to a central server by means of a software access. This so-called 'client' contains all local elements that do not need to be exchanged with the central computer. The central server, in turn, operates the gameworld at the provider level and calculates the ever-changing aspects of the game's environment. Players communicate with one another using text chat, voice-over-IP communication and in-play gestures performed by the avatars. They organize themselves into communities, typically called 'guilds' or 'clans'. Shared play consists of 'going on raids' together, solving side-quests and specific tasks and to engage with other communities. They even celebrate parties in digital pubs and nightclubs. Guilds and clans respectively do not only meet and engage inside the virtual environment however, as these acquaintances are also pursued in everyday life.

Depending on the individual nature of players, the mixture of activities may vary significantly in an MMORPG. Richard Bartle, the author of some of the most influential works on game design for virtual worlds, strongly influenced developers of later titles. His views are thus intricately interwoven with modern MMORPGs. He observed four types of players in his study of the digital predecessors of modern MMORPGs, 'multi-user dungeons' (MUDs).[69] These text-based role-playing games introduced many fundamental aspects of the later game form, gathering players to play on a central server. Bartle's typology was then later confirmed and adapted by the continuous use in game design for MMORPGs:[70] competitive *Achievers* encounter *Explorers*, communicative *Socializers* and *Imposters*. The latter player type typically attempts to break social and gameplay rules, as well as other players. These four general types are observable already as early as 1997, in Ralph Koster and Richard Garriott's classic *Ultima Online*, an online multiplayer role-playing game that was the first to earn the distinction of being 'massively' multiplayer due to its enormous number of players.[71]

In order to better understand the social dynamics of typical MMORPG players, I have previously conducted an analysis of this game form, in which I incorporated both a techno-cultural and a historical perspective pertaining not only the game form itself, but also its analogue and digital predecessors.[72] A corporate history of FunCom, the Norwegian development studio of *The Secret World*, together with a micro-level product history of the developing process, the publication and the on-going operation of the game, further helped to determine the type of players that *The Secret World* has been aiming for.[73] To summarize the results, this specific online role-playing game in essence targeted players who were disappointed by the stagnation of the game form, yearned for profound worlds with rich backstories and characters, and understood multi-perspectivity and ambiguity as being appealing rather than a burden.[74] Of the distinct player personas, three deal in a constructive way with other players and the gameworld, so that their individual perspectives also predetermine different modes of engagement with historical content.[75] This predetermination should not be taken too far, though: it would be reckless, for instance, to attribute a more intense historical gaming experience to *Explorers* simply because they may be interested most in historical content itself. For *Achievers*, an intense historical impression could also arise during challenges where they deal with mythological creatures and places, achieve success and master missions. Conceivably, *Socializers* could develop a deeper historical understanding precisely because they communicate with gamers in and about the gaming environment the most.

In MMORPGs, it is especially, though by no means exclusively, the latter player category that blends into social groups. When players both within and beyond the game's environment communicate about their individual perceptions of historical content, they create a specific historical commemorative culture within this common space which is related to other media cultures of memory. From this perspective the Historical Knowledge System represents a direct access path to the historical culture in and around *The Secret World*. The analysis of user perspectives seeks to approach historical consciousnesses of players. Observing the communication within the player's communities about the components of the Historical Knowledge System then leads to documents of a commemorative culture of the players.[76] In studying the functions individual memories fulfil in the context of cultural memory, Aleida Assmann has shown that such memories are continuously (re)established, renegotiated, mediated and adapted.[77] Both individuals and cultures as a whole construct their memories interactively through communication by language, images and ritual repetitions. Both also organize memories with external storage media and cultural practices ranging from script rolls to photographs, using a variety of cultural practices (writing form, specific styles, picture composition).[78] The outlined Historical Knowledge System of online role-playing games can thus be regarded as a technical form of collective historical memory that has been adapted to the needs and circumstances of a society in the digital network age.

Richard Bartle also described the complex hierarchical structure of social groups in multiplayer role-playing games.[79] These are, in ascending order, temporary groups, parties, clans, guilds and alliances. *Temporary groups* are ad hoc communities constituted for one game session. Loose *parties* of players play together on a regular basis. While both *clans* and *guilds* form larger social networks that also self-organize outside the gameworld, *guilds* tend to include the gameworld's background, for example in fantasy worlds, in their social behaviour. Guilds also join together to form *alliances* at the apex of online community-building. Sociopsychological considerations suggest that communication processes like those about a Historical Knowledge System occur most likely in smaller entities around a dozen players, as they concentrate most on social interaction.[80] More than 70 per cent of players in a guild declare that they regularly talk to others about topics beyond current gameplay.

In order to exchange historical conceptions in a group, MMORPGs offer several communication channels: purely internal processes (e.g. chat, mail, emotes), forms blurring the gameworld's boundaries (such as voice chat, or VoIP, in-game structures for guilds and their websites), and entirely external variants (online forums for written exchanges, *Let's Play* videos or game-streaming for audiovisual ones). The scholarly evaluation of these communication channels and their importance for the constitution of historical culture is hindered by methodical, legal and system-inherent obstacles. For instance, due to the constitutionally guaranteed right to one's own speech, one cannot simply record gameplay or communicative exchanges during the game. In the case of Germany, in order to do so, a scholar would have to request disclosure of the real name behind avatars and ask the player for consent to record them. In explaining the nature of the request and the reason for recording, however, this process would inevitably distort the outcome, as player behaviours are likely to change under direct observation. My analysis of communication processes therefore concentrated on written statements of players in the official forum of *The Secret World* in order to show discourses of commemorative culture.[81] Since the forum was already established in 2007, discussion threads extend over a period of ten years. A global search for the English terms 'lore' and 'history' resulted in 500 individual forum threads for each. Because of the semantic term analogy in German between 'Geschichte' as both history (i.e. discursive appropriations based on the sum of recordings of the human past) and storytelling, a search for the term 'Geschichte' in the German-language forum produced a large instance of fictional literary output (short stories, fan fiction) among the 309 threads found.

Players brought up significant discourses of historical elements that were identified by the investigation of the Historical Knowledge System above. Numerous discussions touch upon the depiction of ancient history. Players criticize for instance that the game adopts the demonization of Akhenaten uncritically, although his historic role could be interpreted far more positively as a reformer.[82] Others discuss ancient objects like the seal of King Salomon or the Israelite Ark of the Covenant, mentioned in the game.[83] Numerous threads collect and discuss references to other media such as documentaries, movies, websites, video portals and books (scholarly as well as literary ones). Evincing surprise about the existence of an opera on Akhenaten, they further argue his historical relevance.[84] Regarding object culture, players search for original real-world templates of in-game buildings as in the case of the Roman temple in Egypt.[85] Starting from the appearance of sexually explicit Egyptian statues, they discuss contemporary prudery and its influence on historical imaginations.[86] The components of narrative networks are considered, too. The unusual structure with its interwoven non-linear narrative style and the necessity to draw conclusions oneself from the resultant polyphony caused some irritations.[87] But most contributors compliment it as credible for an overall staging of historical uncertainty.[88] They discuss personalities and their statements, mission types, the filtering function of faction's world views, historicity emerging from updates and player's progress, the fragmentation of the background into the honeycombs and the concomitant swarm perspective in the database as aligning parts of the game's coherence.

Regarding macro-historical models, a rather intense discussion flared up on the subject of societal diversity. Advocates of as many settings as possible for the avatars to realize individual preferences collided with those who insisted on binary gender-specific preferences in particular.[89] Others discussed plausible options for accessing history in-game in contemporary MMORPGs, such as time travel.[90] Far more threads, however, concern the micro-historical world design, for example, because they wonder about the game form of *The Secret World*.[91] Many compliment how meticulously the developers connected historical details to the everyday world.[92] Many other threads deal with the boundaries between facts and fiction, whether in conspiracy theories or in technologies that could appear as magic.[93] Conversely, they discuss whether supposedly fictitious game content might be real.[94] The blurring boundaries of the gameworld also make it difficult to classify game phenomena, as in the case of an advertisement from alleged vampire hunters or rumours about a ghostly appearance in the gameworld.[95] All over the threads, players very much value how the micro-historical world design adds historical credibility to the game, by linking the gaming environment to the outside. Only a selection of examples could be given here, but as they are representative for a decade of continuous player communication about historical aspects, they enable a long-term commemorative culture.

Lifting the veil: Ancient history, commemorative culture and public history

This chapter promised to lift some veils over ancient history depicted in digital games. At the outset, it provided an overview of what the historical aspects of digital games may be understood to be, seen through several lenses of both historical scholarship and the games industry. From these elements, it derived its scientific approach. Dynamically interwoven components of *object and material culture, narrative networks, macro-historical models* and *micro-historical world designs* contoured what I have called a Historical Knowledge System. In a second section, I showed how that system works in the case of our test case, *The Secret World*. The examples of ancient history presented in the game were analysed in the context of a more general historical framing and questions of reception. In a third section, I discussed the traditions of MMORPGs as a game form and how different player personas group together in a variety of social communities therein, pointing out different forms of communication in these sociotopes. The empirical findings concentrated on the official forum of *The Secret World* as a start, the discussion threads on that forum linking the ancient historical aspects of the components from the Historical Knowledge System with discursive processes among players.

Fulfilling the initial promise, this chapter has produced at least five substantial results regarding the depiction of ancient history in digital games. First, the use of the Historical Knowledge System widened the spectrum of what should be investigated as historical conceptions and how complex the interplay of ancient historical aspects can be. The proposed structure for historical components in digital games has to be set in relation to the other models of historians, as portrayed above. However, this approach showed facets that have not yet been accounted for.

Second, instead of developers offering settings of the past directly, players access historical aspects from contemporary perspectives in *The Secret World*. Multi-perspective world-views, a global-historical integrative attitude, a post-structuralist, constructivist understanding of history and openly personal judgements of in-game personalities frame this view from the distance. These factors, which players have to take into account, prevent common misconceptions of the usual historical depictions in digital games, where historical aspects tend to serve a pseudo-authentic view on history 'as it was'. Generally speaking, game mechanics meant to access history from such a distant view seems to be a way to stage the constructed and uncertain character of history more properly.

Third, the investigation of player personas and their perspectives on history, of how they form communities and what this implies for commemorative culture, has not been able to provide an exhaustive insight into the recipients. Nevertheless, my research has shown that numerous long-term discourses about all elements of the Historical Knowledge System are present and that they are not closed loops, but rather referential to the outside – and surprisingly unagitated and well-considered for the Internet.[96] In the case of a medium whose historical staging essentially derives from the users themselves, the consequences of historical scholarship not developing an understanding of the recipients of any media type that deals with history are now painfully obvious.

Fourth, this has, nevertheless, demonstrated the importance of various channels of communication that should be investigated by historians. My survey in the official forum has already proven that players discuss every historical component that was identified with the help of the Historical Knowledge System.

Fifth, this chapter has also made very clear that historians need to improve their methodologies to cope with the scientific questions raised by digital games. To provide proper evidence, I argued in favour of videography as a method, but not without acknowledging its weaknesses. Various channels for player communication have been highlighted, some internal, some external, others of a hybrid nature. All of them offer possibilities for players to take part in discourses of commemorative culture – and they very likely do, as observations of group building and communication hint at.

Because of player numbers and the worldwide outreach, their social communication spaces must be researched as part of a Public History. MMORPGs are more than games: they are constantly changing services with dynamic, historically interested communities. Because they depend on the providers' servers, they disappear as soon as they fail to turn a profit. Hence, historians urgently need to lift as many veils as possible over the historical aspects this chapter has described for the communication sphere of *The Secret World* in and around more examples, before they will be irretrievably lost after shutdown.

Notes

1   As of 2017, the original MMORPG *The Secret World* (2012) has been relaunched as *Secret World Legends* (2017). Despite the resulting changes to game mechanics and user experience, content has been preserved by the reissued version.
2   Hausar (2013: 29).
3   Nolden (2018c: 484–767).
4   Samida, Willner and Koch (2016).
5   Schwarz (2012a: 10–14) and Heinze (2012: 109–13).
6   Nolden (2018c: 61–118). A German-language monograph based on the dissertation is being prepared. I am happy to provide the voluminous underlying data of the empirical study to other researchers.
7   Schwarz (2012a: 8–9) and Schwarz (2015: 417).
8   Kerschbaumer and Winnerling (2014a: 14).
9   Kapell and Elliott (2013a: 13–19) and Bender (2012).
10 Heinze (2012: 23–131, especially 107).
11 Zusag (2013: 93).
12 Chapman (2013a: 62–3; 2013c: 260–3; 2016: 20).
13 Casso and Thibault (2016).
14 Schüler, Schmitz and Lehmann (2012).
15 Gießler and Graf (2016: 96–7).
16 Stöcker (2005).
17 Weiss (2015).
18 The developers intended to depict an authentic piece of bohemian late Middle Ages and thus implemented an impressive concept of a local model for everyday history (Vávra, 2014). Although, personal opinions of the creators and their historical conceptions lead to severe protests. At its core, critics pointed out that Vávra positioned himself as a right-wing Czech nationalist, what has led to a biased medieval concept: viewing the events of 1403 in Bohemia in the context of the major founding myth of the Czech nation and thus depicting medieval communities consisting mostly of white Central Europeans, endangered by foreigners, the game reproduces far-right myths about homogeneous medieval populations (see, Heinemann, 2018).
19 Mortensen (2006: 400–9).
20 Nolden (2018b: 184–98).
21 Ibid. (2018c: 572–89).
22 Ibid. (2018a).

23 Ibid. (2018c: 487–501). The video titles that are subsequently quoted below represent my own personal referencing system for video material.
24 TSW_A_London_Rundgang13 Temple Court Hauptquartier 2015-07-27.
25 Bond (2017). This has very recently begun to change, as the Classical Greek world of *Assassin's Creed: Odyssey* is distinctly colourful.
26 *Caesar III* (1998), *Grand Ages: Rome* (2009), *Total War: Rome II* (2013), among others.
27 TSW_D1_QuestSabot_VW_Issue06_AllesHatSeineZeit Stufe 1d Sol Invictus329AD Übergang Nebenquest OTemporeOMores 2015-08-06; TSW_D1_QuestSabot_VW_ Issue06_AllesHatSeineZeit Stufe 2b Dokument für Replika des Ancile finden 2015-08-06; TSW_D2_OralHistory_VW_Said 4 CUTSCENE Issue06_DieStadtVorUns Zeittempel Said lebend jung 2015-08-06.
28 IGN (2018).
29 TSW_A_VerbrannteWüste_Rundgang 7 Sol Glorificus Verlassene Oase Tempel abseits 2015-07-29.
30 TSW_A_VerbrannteWüste_Rundgang16 Östliche Narbe Selbstverbrennung Tempel Tal 2015-07-29; TSW_A_StadtDesSonnengottes_Rundgang 3 Panorama Pyramide Aton Vertrocknete Quelle Agartha Durchgang 2015-08-17.
31 TSW_D2_Atmosphäre_RK_Soundscapes Licht Stimmung Eingangsbereich Sonnentempel Issue07_WennDasBeilFällt Stufe 7d Suche Orochi Agent 2015-08-28.
32 TSW_D1_QuestInvest_LO_Issue04_AlleWegeFührenNachRom Stufe 2e Ausgrabung Londinium erkunden INSTANZ 2015-07-29.
33 TSW_A_VerbrannteWüste_Rundgang 3 Ortseingang Al-Merayah 2015-07-29.
34 TSW_D1_QuestAttack_VW_EinSchattenÜberÄgypten Stufe 3a Barriere überwunden Tempel betreten 2015-08-08.
35 TSW_D1_QuestAttack_VW_DieLetzteLegion Stufe 3b Beschworene Mumie töten BERICHT 2015-08-09.
36 TSW_D1_QuestAttack_SS_EineStadtAusBlutGeboren Stufe 1a Intro Mission Ptahmose Bedrohung Aton Wächter Kinder Ägypten 2015-08-17.
37 TSW_D2_OralHistory_SS_Amir Dschinn 1 Intro Mission Mumienprobleme Gaia Menschen Hass 2015-08-19.
38 TSW_D1_QuestNeben_VW_PrimumNonNocere Stufe 2 erstatte Lisa Hui Bericht im Orochi Lager BERICHT 2015-08-12.
39 TSW_D1_QuestSabot_VW_Issue06_AllesHatSeineZeit Stufe 1a Intro Mission Said Atonisten Artefakt ÜBERGANG von Issue06_DerGefangene 2015-08-06.
40 TSW_A_VerbrannteWüste_Rundgang15 Ausgrabungsstelle 1 Oxford 2015-07-29.
41 TSW_D1_QuestInvest_VW_DasGroßeSchrecklicheGanze Stufe 4b Hieroglyphen Wahrer Name Echnaton Gebet 2015-08-11.
42 TSW_D2_OralHistory_SS_Houy 2 Issue03_DieBindung Familie Ptahmose OpferKinder Echnaton 2015-08-20.
43 TSW_A_SS_Uschebti_Aufgaben Schutz 3000 Jahre Hemitneter Thutmosis Nefertari Issue03_DieBindung CUTSCENE 2015-08-21.
44 TSW_D2_OralHistory_SS_Ptahmose 2 Intro Mission EineStadtAusBlutGeboren Bedrohung Aton Wächter Kinder Ägypten 2015-08-17.
45 TSW_D2_OralHistory_VW_Said 5 Intro Mission EinSchattenÜberÄgypten Said Echnaton Geheimbünde Rückkehr 2015-08-08.
46 TSW_D2_OralHistory_VW_Tanis 5 Intro Mission Issue05 VonKarthagoNachKairo Tanis Mumie Said Kultisten Anschläge 2015-08-03, from 3:45 min; TSW_D2_ OralHistory_VW_Abdel Daoud 4 Issue06_AllesHatSeineZeit Stufe 3a CUTSCENE Glaube Daoud Altes Reich 2015-08-06, from 0:35 min.

47 TSW_D1_QuestInvest_VW_DasGroßeSchrecklicheGanze Stufe 1b Karte und Notizen Montgomery Lager 2015-08-11; TSW_D1_QuestInvest_VW_ DasGroßeSchrecklicheGanze Stufe 2a Verschlüsselung Cäsar Notizen 2015-08-11.

48 TSW_D2_Lore_Templer Intro 2017-04-01.

49 TSW_D2_Lore_Illuminaten Intro 2017-04-01.

50 TSW_D2_Lore_SE_QuestStory Schmetterlingseffekt Stufe 2 Hoon Erklärung Wirkung Drachen Chaos Theorie 2017-04-01.

51 TSW_D2_OralHistory_LO_Richard Sonnac 1 & 2Templer Weltsicht Legenden Mythen Fraktionen 2015-07-27; TSW_B_Templer_Werte_SS_DieBefleckteOase Stufe 4 BERICHT Urteil Richten Templer Tugend 2015-08-20.

52 TSW_D2_Lore_VW_DasReich Nr 6 vollständig 2015-08-17; TSW_D2_Lore_SS_ DiePyramide Nr 5 vollständig 2015-08-25.

53 TSW_D2_Enzyklopädie_Wissen 1, 2, 3 2015-03-31.

54 TSW_D2_Enzyklopädie_Erfolge 1 u 2 2015-03-31.

55 TSW_D2_OralHistory_SC_Hayden Montag 3 Intro Mission WissenschaftKunst Eingemauerte 2015-06-26.

56 TSW_B_Wissenschaft_SW_Wikipedia Anastasia Wagen Mythen Speicher Analogie Knotenpunkt Alt Neu 2016-01-23, 0:50 - 1:25 min; TSW_B_Geschichte_SW_ Traditionen Roma Überlieferung Geschichten Oral History Milosh DieLauerndenSchrecken Erbe Tradition Geschichte 2015-10-12, 1:23- 2:00 min.

57 TSW_D1_QuestInvest_VW_DasGroßeSchrecklicheGanze Stufe 6 Erkenntnis zu Montgomery CUTSCENE Alte Zivilisationen BERICHT 2015-08-11.

58 TSW_D2_OralHistory_LO_Iain Tibet Gladstone 1 Historiker Schriftlichkeit Interpretation Secret History 2015-07-27, 1:10 - 2:28 min.

59 TSW_D2_OralHistory_LO_Iain Tibet Gladstone 2 Historiker Schriftlichkeit Interpretation Templer Secret History 2015-07-27, at 3:02 min.

60 TSW_D1_QuestSabot_VW_Issue06_DerGefangene Stufe 4c Said bei Hotel Wahid Weg dorthin 2015-08-06; TSW_A_VerbrannteWüste_Rundgang 6 Verlassene Hütten Verderbte Farm 2015-07-29.

61 TSW_A_StadtDesSonnengottes_Rundgang 2 Riss Tempel der Verschollenen Aufzeichnungen Die Verdammnis 2015-08-17; TSW_A_VerbrannteWüste_ Rundgang15 Ausgrabungsstelle 1 Oxford 2015-07-29.

62 TSW_D1_QuestNeben_VW_DasEntschärfungskommando Stufe 1 Sprengsätze in Al-Merayah entschärfen 1 2015-08-01; TSW_D2_Atmosphäre_VW_Al-MerayahSoundscapes Licht 2015-0731; TSW_A_VerbrannteWüste_Rundgang 4 Al-Merayah Teil 1 2015-07-29.

63 TSW_D2_Atmosphäre_VW_Al-Merayah Soundscapes Licht 2015-07-31; TSW_A_ VerbrannteWüste_Rundgang 8 Verbrannte Ebene Touristentempel DerSonnengott 2015-07-29.

64 FunCom 2012, TSW_D1_DiffusionGrenzen_Orochi Firmenwebseite Personal 2015-04-08.

65 Freeborn 2009 for example; TSW_D1_QuestAttack_BM_Issue05_ DieSucheNachTylerFreeborn Stufe 1a Intro Mission 2015-07-13.

66 Howard (2015).

67 Inderst (2009: 316–7).

68 Bartle (2006: 61–76) and Garriott (2017: 13–18, 27–35).

69 Bartle (1996).

70 Ibid. (2006: 128–57).

71 Ultima Online (1997), Koster (2017) and Garriott (2017: 151–92).

72 Nolden (2018c: 501–32).
73 Ibid., 533–62.
74 Ibid., 562, 734.
75 Ibid., 725–9.
76 Ibid., 737–9.
77 Assmann (2010: 27–145).
78 Ibid., 19.
79 Bartle (2006: 397–8).
80 Ducheneaut et al. (2007).
81 FunCom (2007).
82 tamino (2012).
83 Axel Denar (2010) and Yume (2011).
84 Ironblade (2013), *Akhnaten*, by Philip Glass (1983). Premiered at the Stuttgart State Theatre in 1984. Libretto by Philip Glass, Shalom Goldman, Robert Israel, Richard Riddell and Jerome Robbins.
85 Ariensky Crowley (2012).
86 Mizeraj (2012).
87 Qoun (2012).
88 Tori (2014).
89 Nethbuk (2012).
90 aero916 (2009).
91 Yogsothoth (2008).
92 z4oslo (2012).
93 T3XT (2013) and Omnires (2010).
94 Maelwydd (2012).
95 Contranoctis (2009) and Ravenhurst (2013).
96 Nolden (2018c: 764–6).

Part Four

Building an Ancient World

Re-Imagining Antiquity

Choose Your Own Counterfactual

The Melian Dialogue as Text-Based Adventure

Neville Morley

The Melian Dialogue – the archetypal triumph of might over right – seems at first glance to be the polar opposite of any sort of game, both because of its serious subject matter but above all because of the crushing inevitability of its outcome: the Melians can't win, the Athenians can't lose. My argument in this chapter is that we can, nevertheless, turn this classic episode into a game – within the genre of interactive fiction or 'choose your own adventure' – as a means of drawing out the counterfactual possibilities that are inherent in Thucydides' account and multiplied by our own distance from the past. Turning an apparently linear narrative into a series of meaningful choices, into a text that requires the reader to interact with it and confront uncertainty, opens up possibilities of reinterpretation and questioning our understanding of the dynamic of events and the constraints under which decisions are taken in a way that only games, properly handled, can achieve. Far from being mere entertainment, ancient historical games, like counterfactual analyses, are essential for historical understanding.[1]

'Parlour-games with might-have-beens'

The fundamental problem with attempts at incorporating historical games into historical research, as opposed to studying them as examples of the popular reception of the past, is often identified as the danger of anachronism: of creating confusion between the historical and the unhistorical by discussing things that did not and/or could not really happen. 'If a battle proceeds differently in a role-playing scenario than it did in actuality – which is almost inevitable – students are not learning history.'[2] The fact that a game which did not include the possibility of different outcomes would lose most, if not all, of its attractions as a game is precisely the point; we are presented with a choice between unhistorical pleasure and historical understanding. It is striking, if on reflection unsurprising, how far such critiques of games for their counterfactual nature mirror critiques of counterfactual histories – the explicit analysis of alternative possibilities in historical events and developments – for their resemblance to games. 'History is a record of what people did, not what they failed to do,' argued E. H. Carr in his still influential account of *What is History?* 'One can always play a parlour-game with the might-have-beens of history. But they have nothing [...] to do with history.'[3] History has been conventionally understood as the study of the actual, or at least an attempt at getting as close as possible to the actual through the analysis of the surviving evidence; there can be no evidence of things which did not happen, so on what basis can counterfactual accounts be evaluated, other than their qualities as fiction?[4] Of course, one can play with such ideas, but a game, especially a parlour game, is, by definition, trivial and irrelevant to true intellectual activity; a matter of mere entertainment.

It has to be admitted that many attempts at writing counterfactual histories, like many historical video games, are, indeed, superficial and often rather silly when considered from the perspective of academic historiography. Their primary purpose is, of course, entertainment, and as a result they focus on familiar figures and events, presented in traditional if not mythologized forms; their underlying understanding of historical events is thoroughly conventional, focused on military and political narratives, on short-term events rather than longer-term structures, and on the decisive roles of a small number of World-Historical Individuals.[5] But superficiality and conventionality are not intrinsic to the exercise: there is now a range of examples of counterfactual approaches in economic and social history, focusing on the historical role of longer-term structures and processes – exploring the consequences of the Black Death for medieval European economy and society, for example, or the economic impact of railroads in the United States in the nineteenth century – and of studies of individual decision-making at critical moments that emphasize the constraints under which such decisions were taken rather than presenting everything in terms of unbounded individual agency.[6] In the same way that not every video game is a crude first-player-shooter (or spear-thruster), not every counterfactual history is a simple 'What if Caesar hadn't crossed the Rubicon?'

The strongest argument in defence of counterfactual approaches, however, is that they simply cannot be avoided in *any* discussion of historical causation.[7] Any statement about why things happened as they did implies that they would have happened differently if the decisive factor had been absent, just as any statement about the consequences of a decision implies that things would have turned out differently if that decision had gone the other way.[8] It is simply a question of whether a given historical account discusses these counterfactual possibilities explicitly, so that they can be properly evaluated, or leaves them implicit, with the risk that the events then appear to have been necessary or inevitable. Any proper explanation of a historical phenomenon needs also to account for negatives – that is, why other possible outcomes did not, in fact, occur – rather than implying or assuming that a given cause or set of circumstances can only ever have one specified outcome.[9]

Explicit counterfactuals – the acknowledgement and evaluation of such possibilities, if not a fully developed counterfactual narrative – are therefore the best way for historians to avoid falling into teleology and other ahistorical errors, assuming that what did in fact happen was by definition the most likely if not the only possible outcome.[10] Counterfactual thinking emphasizes the potential openness of the past, and focus attention on questions of necessity and contingency. Historical events are always over-determined, with multiple causes; how else can we determine the significance of different conditions except by reference to the possibility of alternative outcomes?[11] We gain a proper understanding of what happened by setting it against what might have happened instead, in order to consider properly the structures and conditions that shaped historical outcomes.

A defence of counterfactual history as the legitimate if not essential study of what did not happen is also always potentially a defence of the usefulness of games in understanding historical developments. Insofar as history is seen not as the reconstruction of a fixed past and the memorization of predetermined facts about it, but as the exploration of the underlying structures and processes and the past existence of different possibilities, then there must be scope for different ways of exploring the range of possible alternative outcomes and the conditions under which they might have occurred. Just as it is not possible for a historian to escape counterfactuals and their implication entirely and still produce a credible analysis of past events, but only to decide how (and how explicitly) counterfactuals should be acknowledged and employed, so the question is not whether it is possible to engage with the past through popular culture, including games, but what kind of engagement is pursued.[12]

It is not, of course, the case that all games are equally useful, just as this is not true of all counterfactual exercises; in either case, many extant examples suffer from entertainment bias and drastic oversimplification, because they have not been designed with any thought for serious historical analysis.[13] Counterfactual histories and games alike inevitably take for granted certain underlying principles, even as they explicitly open up possibilities in other areas; they may privilege individuals over structures, or certain historical processes (exogenous technological change, for example) over others, in determining the range and nature of possible alternative outcomes and player choice. As Robison observes, one can learn to play historical simulation games quite well without requiring or acquiring much if any knowledge of real history, if one focuses on the underlying principles of the game design; one might see different social-scientific theories as playing the same role in historical counterfactuals.[14] Christian Rollinger's analysis of the city-building simulation *Caesar* reveals how the underlying simulative processes, derived from late-twentieth-century urban studies and crude Reaganomics, favour strategies that are utterly alien to historical experience; one might compare this to the persistent habit in studies of Roman cities of assuming them to be centres of trade and industry – the difference being that such assumptions are easier to identify and critique in an academic article, but baked into the fabric of the game.[15] It is vital to analyse counterfactual accounts and games alike critically, seeking to identify their underlying assumptions and explanatory models – and recognizing how far academic historians have the expertise, experience and instincts to do this for the former rather more commonly than the latter.[16] It's also worth, where possible, relying on a range of examples which can be compared and contrasted with one another, rather than relying on a single version.

Bringing together counterfactual histories and historical games offers not only a parallel defence of these traditionally marginalized or derided activities, but the possibility of mutual support. On the one hand, the more the designers of a game aim for historical verisimilitude or plausibility rather than simple entertainment value, the more attention they (and anyone seeking to analyse the game) need to pay to counterfactual questions – the range of different possibilities available to historical actors within a given context, the conditions governing key decisions and turning points and so forth – since they are seeking both to open up the range of possible outcomes beyond what actually happened, and to limit these to the more plausible (or at least to take account of their relative plausibility in constructing the game mechanics). On the other hand, and, more importantly, for historical purposes, games can offer an essential resource for exploring these counterfactual possibilities. As Jeremiah McCall has noted, one problem with conventional historical representation, video as well as text, is that it can present only one choice and one line of consequent development at a time, as a fixed sequence; even if the alternative possibilities are emphasized, there is still a bias towards the course of events that is actually shown to transpire.[17] This is true even if that course of events is actually a counterfactual alternative to what 'really happened': the majority of counterfactual histories offer only a single alternative scenario, deriving from a single decisive moment or decision, ignoring the fact that there will be more such moments subsequently, endlessly multiplying the counterfactual possibilities – indeed, this is the most significant practical criticism of existing attempts at writing counterfactual histories, as it is of attempts at predicting the future on the basis of the evidence of the past.[18]

Games, however, can generate a range of different counterfactual possibilities, which can be followed over an extended succession of choices and potential divergences rather than necessarily focusing on a single turning point – and, of course, most games are intended to be played multiple times, with the expectation of varying outcomes on each occasion.[19] Interactivity lies at the heart of the experience: games are not just to be looked at or memorized, but played, introducing an element of co-creation between game designer and player.[20] This may be a matter of decision-making within the existing parameters of the game (that is, accepting the designer's overall conception of the workings of the world and their implementation of this conception in the game design), or, more ambitiously, of 'modding' the game in order to modify that conception and its inbuilt assumptions, allowing the exploration of counterfactuals that the designer had not envizaged, and perhaps revealing the underlying biases of the basic game.[21] In either case, this offers a basis for considering the differences between the outcome(s) of the game and existing interpretations of the past, prompting players 'to articulate and explore their counterfactual imaginary', as Apperley puts it.[22] This can be useful even if the simulation mechanism is crude or anachronistic; analysing divergences between the game and any plausible historical reality offers a critical perspective both on the designers' assumptions (which are likely to mirror wider assumptions about, for example, the dynamics of empires or the nature of urbanization) and on the conditions that limited such developments in reality.[23] 'History in the Rankean sense of "wie es eigentlich gewesen ist" ["how it really was"] is subverted by an insistence on history as a multivalent process subject to many different possibilities, interpretations, and outcomes.'[24] This is still more the case when the game is designed explicitly for the purpose of exploring counterfactuals, either for pursuing the consequences of alternative lines of development or simply for opening up uncertainty and recognizing the existence of contingency and uncertainty.[25]

Thucydidean counterfactuals

Thucydides is often represented as the originator and exemplar of the conception of the historian's task as showing 'how things really were', either as an end in itself or as a basis for understanding later events and predicting future developments.[26] Different traditions of reading Thucydides' work tend to converge on this idea: nineteenth-century historicist interpretations of him as a modern critical scientific historian, emphasizing the careful evaluation of evidence in order to establish the truth of events; twentieth-century social-scientific interpretations of his real project being the identification of covering laws and the normative principles of human behaviour, so that different events reveal the inherent predictability of decisions and events (for example, the idea of the 'Thucydides Trap' that made war between Athens and Sparta inevitable); finally, literary readings, especially those that see his work in 'tragic' terms, that identify the different elements of his narrative construction that present the fate of Athens as inevitable. There are disagreements both within and between these different traditions, for example about how far coherence and predictability are attributes of historical reality as well as of Thucydides' account of it, but there is consensus that the account focused on the reconstruction of a single concrete set of events, as they occurred. Thucydides' work is seen as the epitome of history as an account of *what actually happened*, explicitly contrasted (by himself and by his readers) with the myths, misconceptions and other false notions of the past held by those who have not properly enquired into the truth of things.[27]

This Thucydides could be assumed to share the views of historians like Carr when it comes to counterfactual history, deriding it as something written for short-term entertainment rather than as a possession for ever. However, there is an alternative tradition, developed by scholars focused on understanding the literary aspects of the work, of reading Thucydides precisely in terms of his use of counterfactuals.[28] These in fact appear in his work in a variety of forms. Individuals speakers within his account regularly make counterfactual statements, predicting the possible consequences of different actions or of inaction, or pointing to how things might have turned out differently.[29] One might, of course, attribute this to Thucydides' accurate reporting of what was actually said by these speakers, rather than implying that he himself was concerned with such speculation; however, most modern readings of the speeches see them as primarily Thucydidean, aimed at least in part at raising questions and prompting reflection in the minds of his readers, given their enjoyment of the benefits of hindsight.[30] In any case, there are also counterfactual statements offered in the voice of the author, emphasizing the existence of alternative possibilities. Sometimes, these statements simply identify the role of chance and contingency in events ('If the wind had risen [...] the Plataeans would not have escaped', 2.77.5), but sometimes they explore alternate timelines in more depth, as in 8.96.4–5, considering how the entire Athenian Empire might have fallen in 411–410 BCE, if only the Peloponnesians had acted more boldly in the aftermath of the revolt of Euboia.

There is only a limited number of such explicit counterfactuals (Tordoff counts twelve), but this is enough to establish Thucydides' interest in such questions – very likely, in response to wider debates about 'what might have been' in the immediate aftermath of Athens' defeat.[31] That surely offers grounds for considering the counterfactuals offered by speakers, and those that are implicit in other parts of the account, as being likewise part of his design. For example, Thucydides famously identified the Spartans' fear of a rising Athens as the 'truest cause' of the war (however exactly that phrase is translated and interpreted, 1.23.6), but it is clear that this fear was not in itself *sufficient* to provoke war, or at least not at that specific moment; the narrative presents both the underlying dynamics of Greek historical development charted earlier in the book, and the subsequent exchanges between Corcyreans, Corinthians, Athenians and Spartans, as playing their part in the complex, multilayered causes of the outbreak of hostilities.[32] What would have happened if the Athenians had chosen not to ally with the Corcyreans – merely the postponement of an inevitable conflict that would have played out in the same way, or a quite different set of events? Similarly, the death of Pericles in the plague is clearly marked as an unexpected, unpredictable turning point, creating the 'might have been' possibility that he could have kept Athenian over-ambition in check and maintained his defensive strategy rather than embarking on ultimately disastrous overseas aggression; in this light, the entire work has been read as a reflection on the counterfactual of Pericles' survival.[33] Every battle narrative, where decisive moments and the role of chance are highlighted, and every set-piece rhetorical confrontation where the possibility of the decision going the other way is canvassed through the persuasiveness of the arguments of the speaker who in the end loses the debate, serve to prompt Thucydides' readers to acknowledge that what actually happened was not the only possibility, and not even necessarily the most likely.

This clearly offers modern readers scope for modelling the different counterfactuals that are presented explicitly and implicitly in the work, whether as a means of exploring the course of the war itself (taking Thucydides' version as a more or less reliable account of events) or as a means of examining the historian's own conception (or a combination of the two), and whether through focusing on individual decisions and turning-points or through simulations of the entire period of history. Strategy games – for example, a video game like *Hegemony Gold: Wars of Ancient Greece* or a more traditional board game like *Pericles: the Peloponnesian Wars* – can certainly play a role in such analysis. War between Athens and Sparta is taken to be inevitable, or there would be no game, but its timing, let alone its course and its outcome, are clearly left open according to the decisions of the players, the role of chance and other features of game mechanics. Athens may not attack Syracuse, for example, or it may despatch the Sicilian expedition and succeed; or, even if the end result is the same, the conditions and constraints that led the Athenians to that decision may be highlighted more clearly. But we can also use this approach to explore events in Thucydides' account where no other outcome seemed likely or even possible, to consider what would have needed to be different for it not to have occurred; that is, to explore the negative hypothesis.[34]

On the face of it, the Melian Dialogue appears to be the section of Thucydides' history least susceptible to counterfactual readings. Certainly that is the tradition of how it has been read, especially by the realist and neorealist schools of International Relations theory, taking the Athenian perspective (international anarchy and the rule of the stronger) as a straightforward description of reality or at least as a statement of

Thucydides' own view of the world.[35] Given the imbalance of power between the Athenians and the Melians, and the intransigence of both sides, an outcome where the former allowed the latter to remain neutral or the latter decided to surrender their sovereignty after all seems scarcely plausible. Further, even if a different result can be envisaged, it would be trivial in terms of the overall course of the war; this episode was by no means a decisive turning point, but rather an opportunity for Thucydides to have the Athenians display the character and attitude that will shortly lead them into the disastrous decision to attack Syracuse. In terms of the traditional understanding of counterfactual questions, as opportunities to reflect on what might have been, this seems a non-starter.

However, as with other pairs of speeches in his account, Thucydides' chosen form in the Melian Dialogue highlights counterfactual possibilities: not the fairly trivial question of what would have happened if the Athenians or the Melians had changed their stance, but rather prompting the reader to consider the conditions, if any, under which either side might have chosen to do so. Insofar as the outcome was more or less inevitable, *why* was this the case? This question is especially significant if we seek to read the passage not solely as a historical account, telling us about specific past events, but in more general political terms – both to consider it as an exercise in political analysis, but also, as I have been aiming to do as part of a wider project in public engagement, to use it as a means of engaging students with issues of power, justice and negotiation. Should we understand the dogmatic positions of each side as the product of their situation (a serious power imbalance tending to generate similar attitudes in those involved), or of their innate characters, or of their chosen values, or of external constraints on their freedom of action, or a combination of different motives? How far might there be greater scope for a different outcome if some of the contextual detail is played down, if, for example, the Athenian role is played by someone with a more modern set of assumptions and values? Developing the Melian Dialogue as a game offered me the opportunity to explore two distinct sets of issues with wider implications, which are relevant to different potential audiences: the conditions under which military and diplomatic decision-making took place in ancient Greece, emphasizing the differences between some ancient and modern attitudes, and the dynamics of power and weakness more generally.

The Melian Games

This is not, in fact, the first time that the gaming element of the Melian Dialogue has been recognized, nor is mine the first attempt at making it into a playable game. The significance of the passage for the early development of game theory (discussed by pioneers in the field like John van Neumann and Thomas Schelling) led the economist (and later Greek finance minister) Yanis Varoufakis to build a 'Prisoner's Dilemma' style game around it, in order to test theoretical predictions.[36] Each player, R and C, chooses a strategy (1–3) for the round. Fig. 10.1 shows the resulting payoffs for each of them. Rationally, it makes no sense for either player to deploy the 'cooperative' strategy (C3/R3), since even if one wishes to aim for the cooperative outcome, there is the risk

	C1	C2	C3
R1	5, 0	−1, −1	10, −1
R2	−1, −1	0, 5	−1, −2
R3	−1, 10	−2, −1	6, 6

Fig. 10.1 The first version of the 'Melian Dilemma' game in Varoufakis (1997: 89).

that the other player anticipates this and maximizes their payoff by choosing a more aggressive strategy. The experiment did, however, show a tendency for C players to choose cooperation, while R players became increasingly likely to prefer aggression. The game is structured so that R has a clear advantage overall; Varoufakis' argument is that, as in the Melian Dialogue, the weaker player will seek a cooperative argument (pleading with the Athenians for clemency) even where this is not the most logical approach.

My game is intended to engage to a much greater degree with the content of Thucydides' account, the details of the historical situation and of the arguments put forward by the two sides, rather than the underlying structure; it is still concerned with the dynamics and constraints of a situation of substantial power imbalance, and how strategies and attitudes are affected by playing one side or the other, but these are explored through a specific example rather than fully abstracted. The aim, in other words, is to prompt players to engage with Thucydides' depiction of events, while at the same time opening up (and highlighting) the counterfactual possibilities that are only implicit in his text and bringing to the foreground aspects of the historical context that he took largely or entirely for granted. While Thucydides' original readers certainly interpreted the Melian Dialogue with a degree of hindsight, in the light of the Sicilian Expedition and the eventual defeat of Athens, we moderns unavoidably encounter it also through awareness of how much has changed, especially in terms of values and humanitarian attitudes, between then and now, and how the Dialogue has been interpreted as a justification for 'realist' power untrammelled by scruples or ethics.

The idea of providing a limited degree of agency and choice within a relatively detailed depiction of an imagined, text-based world immediately brought to mind the model of the 'choose your own adventure' game. For someone of my vintage, this means the *Fighting Fantasy* books and the home computer versions of programs like *Colossal Cave Adventure*, both seeking to replicate the experience of role-playing games for a single player.[37]

For the Melian Dialogue, however, without any need to create a 'character' by generating attributes for strength, dexterity and so on, or for making use of those attributes in determining the outcomes of combat or other uncertain situations in the course of the game, a still simpler model is possible: the interactive juvenile fictions produced in the 1970s by Tracker Books and Edward Packard.[38] These offer the reader a first- or second-person narrative, normally involving a journey or an exploration, regularly interrupted by the need to choose between limited options (normally just two) by turning to different pages to continue the story from that fork in the 'decision tree'.

The Melian Dialogue represents the 'exploration' of a process of negotiation, following different lines of argument and responding to the actions of the other side rather than venturing into a maze of twisty little passages and encountering monsters, but the underlying structure, focused on the decision tree (the way that one decision determines the next step) and on the constraints on action (there are only limited options available in any such negotiation), is perfectly suited to the form of the interactive text (see Fig. 10.2). There is, again, a precedent for developing such games with a didactic purpose: Dan Davies' 2012 blogpost puts the reader in the position of 'a junior member of the One World government', tasked with producing a plan to solve the Greek debt crisis with the help of an adviser.[39] Davies' express purpose is to demonstrate the unpopular (especially in left-wing circles) case that those involved in such planning were 'conscientious international civil servants working in unimaginably difficult political constraints in an economic context that was irreparably broken before they got there'; the game successfully conveys the impression that 'the whole issue is a twisty-turny maze, which at times seems to consist of nothing but false moves', in most cases leaving players 'with a strong feeling of having been bamboozled into something they didn't really want to do'. The response of certain players was to object to both some of the constraints and some of the consequences, suggesting that the appearance of choice was an illusion as the outcomes were fixed according to Davies' theoretical preferences, but there was general agreement that the activity of playing through the sequence of decisions, even via the clumsy mechanism of scrolling up and down

---

The year is 416 BCE. It is fifteen years since the great war between Athens and Sparta, the superpowers of ancient Greece, began. The two sides rarely confront one another directly; instead, each of them tries to extend its influence in regions of strategic importance, in the hope that, when the moment comes, they will have a decisive advantage. The strength of Sparta lies in its army; Athens is above all a naval power, controlling most of the islands of the Aegean Sea in an 'alliance' that looks to most people more like an empire.

The small island of Melos in the Cyclades, halfway between Athens and Crete, was originally a Spartan colony, and so had refused to join the Athenian alliance. Officially the Melians remain neutral, but in recent years their leaders have sided openly with Sparta. Now the Athenians have sent an expedition of 38 ships and 2,000 troops to demand the island's unconditional surrender.

You are Cleomedes, son of Lycomedes, one of the commanders of this expedition; together with Tisias, son of Tisimachus, you have been ordered by the Athenian people to seize control of Melos by any means necessary.

Continue

Fig. 10.2 The opening of the Athenian version of *The Melian Game* (2018 © Neville Morley).

to different numbered sections, was useful in identifying key issues and above all constraints.

The development of a free software tool called Twine by Chris Klimas (original version 2009) has made it exceptionally straightforward to create such hypertext 'adventures', which are also easier to play than the old paper-based versions or Davies' single text.[40] You simply add 'passages' to the story map, which allows clear visualization of the developing decision tree (or, in this case, the two decision trees, one for the Athenians and one for the Melians; see Fig. 10.3); for each passage, you write text in a simple editor and mark it up to create links between different passages, which readers viewing it through a web browser (a completed story/game can be saved as an .html file) see as hyperlinks for choices, taking them down different counterfactual paths (see Fig. 10.3).[41]

With such a simple and easy-to-use tool, the greatest effort can be focused on the design of the game, both to enhance the player experience and, most importantly, to ensure that it supports the didactic aims of the project. We can distinguish between the underlying structure of the game – the decision tree, the range of player options and the implied constraints – and the textual elements. For the purposes of exploring counterfactual questions, the former are more significant; in *The Melian Dilemma*, the text is taken from an adaptation of Thucydides' original, intended to convey the essence of the arguments and rhetoric, and the thinking behind them, while being clear and accessible.[42] One possible use of the game is as a basis for discussion of the arguments

---

The Melian speaker wants to return to questions of principle. 'How can it be just as good for us to be your slaves as for you to be our masters?'

Tisias responds: 'If you surrender, you save yourselves from disaster. We benefit by saving ourselves the trouble of having to destroy you.'

'And why can't we remain neutral, friends rather than enemies, but allied to neither side?'

How do you answer?

[[Because your hatred is evidence of our power, especially in the eyes of our subjects. Don't you have any better arguments?->Gods2]]

(either: '[[Because if we fail to destroy you, others will think that we are weak. Time to decide.->Surrender]]','[[Because if we fail to destroy you, others will think that we are weak. Time to decide.->Resistance]]')

[[That's a fair point. Sparta will lose an ally, without us having to expend time and effort in besieging your city. Let's discuss this further.->Compromize2]]

Fig. 10.3 Marked-up text of *The Melian Game* within Twine (2018 © Neville Morley).

Note: The text within double square brackets shows what the player will see as their options ('Because your hatred is evidence of our power...') and the passage they will be taken to if they click on that choice. Other commands can be included within round brackets: 'either' means there is an equal chance of getting one of the two possibilities, but, of course, the player does not know that there was ever an alternative.

being presented, to evaluate the assumptions behind them and their likely effect and plausibility; within a group (e.g. of school students), either the game can be played by individuals or pairs and then discussed afterwards, or each decision can be debated within the group as a whole.[43] It is also possible, though this has yet to be tested by gathering data about how the game is played by a statistically significant number of people, that the form of the arguments might indeed be found to influence a player's decisions.

The following principles underpinned the design of the game, with the aim of balancing historical plausibility against the twin goals of considering counterfactuals and exploring the significance of those counterfactuals, including contrasts between ancient and modern assumptions.

Choices and possibilities

In its original/authentic form, the Melian Dialogue consists of a series of arguments for clemency from the Melians, and the responses from the Athenians turning them down; eventually the Athenians issue an ultimatum, and the Melians decide to fight rather than surrender. Each of these represents a potential counterfactual moment, when the Athenians could conceivably have decided to spare Melos, or the Melians could have decided to save themselves by surrendering. There are three other moments of decision, which are not so clearly marked in Thucydides: when the Athenians first arrive, and offer the Melians the chance to surrender rather than opening hostilities immediately; when the Melians request, and the Athenians agree, that the negotiation should take place in private rather than before the assembly; and the point at which the Athenians get tired of listening and bring the negotiations to a close. As should be clear from the introductory passage quoted above, there is not an option of avoiding confrontation altogether.

As in any game, a crucial principle is that 'core gameplay must offer defensible explanations of historical causes and assumptions'.[44] Players have very restricted choices – for much of the time, the Athenians simply have to decide between accepting the Melians' request, allowing them to carry on talking and insisting that they make a decision – but that reflects the situation; given the norms of ancient Greek diplomacy and the treatment of ambassadors and representatives, the option of solving the deadlock by killing or imprisoning the Melian leaders is not available. The Melians are constrained by the power of the Athenians and their own weakness; the Athenians are constrained by Greek values and – as becomes evident if certain choices are made but is already implied in the introduction – by the expectations of the Athenian assembly.

The final point to be noted with respect to the choices on offer is that the game is not wholly deterministic; at certain points, the same decision may lead to different outcomes (determined by chance), so that someone could play the game in exactly the same way several times and not always arrive at the same outcome. The prime example is that, if the Athenians do address the Melian assembly, the chances of success in persuading them to surrender improve if they are not too hasty in demanding a decision.

Outcomes

There is no specified goal, either for Athenians or Melians. Obviously, the former are not expected to leave without having reduced the Melians one way or another, but it is left open whether or not it is preferable to do this peacefully, or whether failing to persuade Melos to surrender should be considered a failure. Obviously, the ideal result for the Melians would be the preservation of their lives and freedom, but the chances of them succeeding in this are, as Thucydides' account indicates, vanishingly small; the main choice is rather between two different forms of defeat, surrendering to Athens or being slaughtered in the name of independence. Arguably, both sides are explorations of different ways to lose; the game is intended to prompt reflection on this choice, and on the constraints that set the rules of the game: the power and ruthlessness of Athens (and of its *demos*, even if a player might be more inclined to be merciful), the low probability that the gods, the Spartans or hope will prove to be reliable allies, the wider context of the war.

Strategies

Normally, players choose strategies on the basis of what seems most likely to achieve their goal. In the absence of predetermined goals, the choice of strategy is more open; indeed, the relationship between strategies and goals may be less unidirectional. It is certainly possible for a player to decide a goal for themselves and seek to achieve it as effectively as they can; but it is also possible for them to decide on a strategy and explore its consequences instead. Playing either side in a 'historically authentic' manner – the Athenians as aggressive and arrogant, the Melians as defiant and delusional – rapidly leads in most cases to the historically 'correct' result of war and destruction. Playing either side with a more modern perspective – deciding to prioritize peace and reason, for example – does not guarantee a good outcome for anyone, but it opens up a wider range of possibilities, and hence material for reflection, both as to why such options may not always be available, and as to why they may nevertheless fail.

Conclusion

As in Davies' gamified version of the Greek economic crisis – another situation where the strong confronted the weak and both sides found themselves severely constrained by external circumstances – the likely response of many players to *The Melian Dilemma* will be frustration. What sort of game offers no hope of winning, other than by becoming an imperialist Athenian? (Of course, in plenty of video games, aggressive imperialism is taken for granted as the only available strategy.) But thinking through the sources of that frustration is precisely the point: to identify the constraints (some of them self-imposed) on the original historical actors, to recognize the constraints inherent in any such situation of unequal power, and to become aware of the differences in attitudes and assumptions between ourselves and those who actually find themselves facing such decisions, ancient or modern. Ideally, the game is not to be played as an end in itself, but as a starting-point for wider discussion; and the next stage of its development will be to add contextual material, to support those who do simply stumble across it in making best use of the opportunity.

Developing historical events and processes as interactive texts demands little or no technical skill, but it requires us to clarify and model our thoughts and assumptions: to identify the significant counterfactual moments, the critical decisions and outcomes, and the structures and constraints that determine what options should be available to a player.[45] We can use this to develop games as tools to help teach students and others, introducing them to debates about causation or process; but there is also obvious potential for getting students themselves to develop Twine-based games as a form of analysis of events or structures, identifying the turning-points themselves and weighing up the different possibilities. This is not suitable for every topic or every student – there is the 'creepy treehouse' problem noted by Graham and other academics, who have attempted to incorporate digital resources into their pedagogy, namely that students may be suspicious of 'institutional' spaces and activities that mimic pre-existing digital environments and activities.[46] But there is great potential for illuminating some critical historical questions through this combination of two forms of the 'unhistorical', games and counterfactuals.

Notes

1 I am extremely grateful to Christian Rollinger, both for the invitation to contribute to this volume and for his enormously helpful editorial comments; to Seth Honnor at Kaleider (https://kaleider.com), who first suggested turning the Melian Dialogue into a game; and to Shawn Graham and Jeremiah McCall for advice in developing it.
2 Robison (2013: 578).
3 Carr (1987: 127).
4 Evans (2014).
5 Black (2008) and Brodersen (2000). For a continuing emphasis on individual agency and contingency, see, e.g., Ferguson (1997), despite its claim to defend counterfactual history as a serious intellectual exercise. In the context of classical antiquity, an obvious example is the focus on Thermopylae as crucial 'might have been' in the development of Western Civilization, and its inevitable inclusion in the new *Assassin's Creed: Odyssey* game (2018).
6 See, e.g., Fogel (1964), Hawthorn (1991) and Tetlock and Belkin (1996).
7 Hawthorn (1991) and Sunstein (2016).
8 Cf. De Landa (2000), offering a critique of 'linear' histories.
9 Tucker (2016: 335).
10 Kaye (2010) and Ben-Menahem (2016).
11 Tucker (1999).
12 Kapell and Elliott (2013a: 9) and Chapman (2016).
13 McCall (2012b: 16–17).
14 Robison (2013: 578) and Tetlock and Belkin (1996).
15 Rollinger (2015). On approaches to Roman urbanization, Morley (2011).
16 Uricchio (2005: 535) and Cicchino (2015).
17 McCall (2012b: 13).

18 Cf. Morley (2017).

19 McCall (2016: 525).

20 Kapell and Elliott (2013a: 2).

21 Cf. Graham (2014); Apperley (2013: 193–4) on modifying *Europa Universalis II* to allow the Incas the possibility of successfully resisting the Spanish invaders, which was not an option in the original game.

22 Apperley (2013: 190).

23 The obvious exceptions are FPS games with carefully constructed gameplay and narrowly defined missions, where the counterfactual possibilities are deliberately limited and essentially trivial.

24 Uricchio (2005: 328); cf. Kapell and Elliott (2013a: 7), on the way that games undermine teleology.

25 This echoes the distinction between 'inferential' and 'analytical' counterfactuals offered by Tordoff (2014: 111).

26 On interpretations of Thucydides as a model historian, see generally, Morley (2014).

27 Cf. 1.22.

28 Dover (1988), Flory (1988), Rood (1998) and Tordoff (2014).

29 Tordoff (2014: 106) gives a list of relevant passages.

30 Flory (1988: 43).

31 Tordoff (2014: 110 on explicit counterfactuals and 116–21 on counterfactual debates in Athens).

32 See generally, Jaffe (2017).

33 Will (2000).

34 Tucker (2016).

35 Morley (2018a).

36 Morley (2015).

37 On the prehistory of such games, see Barton (2008), Peterson (2014: 607–27), Winnerling (2017) and Pearson (2017). The first *Fighting Fantasy* book was Jackson and Livingstone (1982).

38 Peterson (2014: 613–6).

39 Davies (2012). See also, the extensive discussion in the comments.

40 See: https://twinery.org/.

41 See, McCall (2018a), including links to his *Path of Honors* Twine game, and Coyne (2017).

42 First published as Morley (2016).

43 See Morley (2019).

44 McCall (2014a: 233).

45 Kee (2014: 4).

46 Graham (2014).

11

Mortal Immortals

Deicide of Greek Gods in *Apotheon* and Its Role in the Greek Mythic Storyworld

Maciej Paprocki

In February 2015, *Alientrap Games* published *Apotheon*, a favourably reviewed side-scroller/platformer/hack-and-slash video game that was produced in a black-figure vase art style and set on the rich stage of ancient Greek mythology.[1] As a classicist/ ancient historian with a keen interest in Greek myth, between April 2013 and February 2015, I worked as a mythology consultant for *Alientrap Games*, ensuring that *Apotheon* stayed as true to Greek myth as possible. In this line of work, I consulted on the game narrative, co-designed the characters, and co-wrote many of the in-game dialogues. My work on *Apotheon* gave me a unique opportunity to approach game design from both a scholarly and creative perspective, as I reassessed my previously held views on the nature of myth-making. In this chapter, I discuss *Apotheon* as a creative adaptation of the Greek mythic storyworld to the video game medium, focusing on the process of rewriting Greek deities as vulnerable game opponents ('bosses', in gaming jargon) from both a scholar's and practitioner's perspective.

Even though Greek gods were commonly described as 'immortal' or 'unaging', creators of postmodern myth-inspired media (films, comics, television and gaming) often represent these deities as vulnerable to violent death.[2] In 2017, Joel Gordon published a comprehensive article on deicide of Greek gods in postmodern media, arguing that the notion goes against the spirit of the ancient Greek myth; less gods and more deified superheroes, vulnerable Greek deities of postmodern adaptations have little in common with their ancient counterparts.[3] *Contra* Gordon, I argue that the ancient Greek mythical imagination accommodated deicide, even if as an absurd (im)possibility,[4] with ancient writers either drawn to or repulsed by the notion, yet inescapably grappling with it. The narrative formula of *Apotheon* pits players in combat against the deities of the Olympus, who are made vulnerable to create space for conflict between them and the humans. Set in Hesiod's Late Iron Age, *Apotheon* pushes the limits of human and divine behaviour. Brought to extremes, Greek deities prove vulnerable and humans emerge superior as their world is destroyed and made anew. By including the polarizing element of deicide, the game reflects both postmodern and ancient anxieties about the nature of immortality, depicting gods as superheroes of old, who err and abuse their powers; their flawed idiosyncrasies and final vulnerability are what makes them believable and attractive to a modern creator.

In the initial section of this chapter, I consider the body of the Greek myth as a storyworld – a plurimedial constellation of ostensibly inconsistent and yet densely interconnected narratives about gods, monsters and heroes – and demonstrate that the characteristic polyphony and plasticity of storyworlds allows for inclusion of difficult and unpopular ideas, such as deicide. In the subsequent section, I discuss the game story and its setting in a post-apocalyptic and post-mythological milieu, where the unwritten rules of the Greek myth partially unravel to open new possibilities. Later, I examine the history of the idea of violent deicide in the Greek myth, showcasing differing approaches adopted by early Greek poets. Although gods and godlike beings could never die of old age nor illness, they apparently were not necessarily immortal and could be beholden to death or death-like states in extreme circumstances. The final section comments on the vulnerability of gods in ancient and postmodern adaptations. Creators of works set within the Greek mythic storyworld, no matter if ancient or postmodern, will need to constrain their characters' godlike powers to allow the narrative to have drama. Exploring these limitations and applying them to one's own works may lead one to ponder and reverse-engineer the unwritten rules laid down in earlier adaptations.

The Greek mythic storyworld and its plasticity

Creators of works engaging with myths and legends adopt different strategies of integrating borrowed material. Some insert appropriated elements on an ad hoc basis, a phenomenon Amanda Potter labelled as 'raiding the cultural archives'.[5] Screenwriters of *Wizards of Waverly Place* (American fantasy teen sitcom, 2007–12) had the eponymous wizard sibling trio confront diverse mythological monsters-of-the-week, including, but not limited to, elves, mummies, vampires, angels, demons, Latin American cucuys, centaurs, fairies and giants – the sole reason for their inclusion being their convenience to the plot at hand. Other creators decided to carefully blend one setting with another. In the *Percy Jackson* series, Rick Riordan melds the mythological universe of ancient Greece with the milieu of contemporary North America; Riordan's Greek gods have moved from Mount Olympus to New York City and sire children with modern mortals. Finally, some creators enter a mythical universe as is, playing by its rules and crafting narratives that will fit into its grander whole. From utilitarian raiding to respectful embellishment, all of the abovementioned strategies capitalize on certain features of myth that facilitate and, in fact, encourage adaptations: transmediality, plasticity, transformability and polyphony.

Myths are transmedial works. Parts of their stories are told in or dispersed across several different media.[6] For example, our knowledge of Greek myth comes from vase and wall paintings, mosaics, statues, inscriptions, hymns, epics, comedies, tragedies and, last but not least, mythographies. Myths are plastic works. They change from context to context, medium to medium, retelling to retelling. They are also transformative works; their adaptations build upon one another, as every retelling alludes to and yet questions previous iterations. Myths are also polyphonic. Many myths contain a constellation of variants, either well known (dominant) or obscure, with different variants of the same myth gaining more traction in different contexts.[7] Even though dominant narratives may clash if they contain mutually exclusive elements, the polyphonic nature of myth allows for the accommodation of several incongruent versions. In this context, mythical legendaria are defined by more than the sum of these features – they are best understood as 'storyworlds', or, in other words, as resilient yet flexible systems of narratives.

Sarah Iles Johnston defines storyworld as a space between stories, a unified and coherent mental universe in which numerous narratives, directly connected or not, coexist and unfold.[8] What makes storyworlds distinctive and attractive for myth scholars is their interconnectedness and self-referentiality. Narratives within a single storyworld share an imaginary setting: its history, geography, ecology and ontology. Correspondingly, characters within a storyworld, although often dissimilar, nonetheless originate in the same setting and thus behave in a fairly unified manner that reflects the authorial intent.[9] One example of a storyworld given by Johnston is Tolkien's legendarium: stories found within *The Hobbit*, *The Lord of The Rings*, *Silmarillion*, *Unfinished Tales* and other works take place on the same world (Arda) in different periods and locations, and feature an ensemble cast of characters, some of them across multiple narratives.[10] For all narratives within a storyworld, certain ontological rules tend to apply; for example, Tolkien's elves do not die of old age, but can die of sickness/exhaustion (like Fëanor's mother, Míriel) or by violent means (like the elven King Gil-galad). Self-referentiality of storyworlds reinforces these unwritten rules in 'infinitely reciprocal way[s]'.[11] Every story within a storyworld that complies with its internal rules feeds into and draws from a network of similar tales.

Self-referential and interconnected, narratives within a storyworld can also adapt to changing contexts. Storyworlds co-created by multiple authors will invariably heterogenize over time, as different authors prioritize different characters and motifs and, eventually, introduce elements that may contradict the already established continuity. Far from undermining the storyworld's integrity, polyphony can actually enhance its complexity and verisimilitude, provided the storyworld's creators ensure that novel elements do not violate its core values, or they provide a plausible explanation for circumventing the said rules.[12] In that aspect, storyworlds resemble fan-fiction; fan-created works can accommodate unorthodox ideas and narratives, as long as its canon/fanon (the set of core values the fan community has tacitly agreed upon) is respected.[13] In summation, one observes both centrifugal and centripetal forces within the storyworld. Characters and narratives diverge from one another by processes of variation and elaboration; they come together due to the myth's self-referentiality. This interaction between push and pull, expansion and contraction, results in the storyworld's plasticity as its narratives subtly shift from retelling to retelling to accommodate divergent perspectives, clashing voices and changing circumstances.[14]

Conceptualizing the body of the Greek myth as a coherent, yet flexible, storyworld offers distinct advantages to creators willing to add to it through transformative works, of which *Apotheon* is a perfect example. Every Greek myth-inspired creator that does not simply want to raid its cultural archives has to arrive at a working understanding of the storyworld's core values. According to Susana Tosca and Lisbeth Klastrup, core values of every coherent transmedial world include its *mythos* ('the central knowledge one needs to have in order to interact with or interpret events in the world successfully'), *topos* ('the setting of the world in a specific historical period and detailed geography') and *ethos* ('explicit and implicit ethics of the world and [moral] codex of behavior').[15] At the initial stage of *Apotheon*'s development, the design team and I parsed the myth-laden works of Homer, Hesiod and other authors in search of these formulae. *Apotheon*'s *mythos* encompasses knowledge of human and divine nature – the ontology of Greek myth. Its setting, or *topos*, is a fictionalized version of Mount Olympus and Greece in its archaic period. Finally, its *ethos* comprises rules governing the behaviour of and relations between gods and humans – i.e. the theology of Greek myth. In search of the mythic storyworld's coherence, we took into account that adapting Greek myth to a gaming medium would also take a great deal of flexibility. Relevantly to this paper, we wanted to rewrite Greek deities into opponents who could be fought and defeated for their powers. As I will soon demonstrate, the idea of a vulnerable immortal, or killable, deity, is not entirely foreign to the Greek mythic storyworld, but all its appearances in source material are mired in controversy.

To bring deicide into the light, I worked with Johnston and Keen's ideas on myth's flexibility, realizing that one could distinguish between *dominant narratives* and *dominant ideas*. Dominant narratives within a storyworld capture the attention of audiences, profoundly influence their worldviews, and thus establish the storyworld's core values; for Greek myth, dominant narratives are clearly reflected in the works of Homer and Hesiod. Nonetheless, even dominant narratives may contain divisive elements that ostensibly clash with their world's core values, for example deicide. Like recessive genes, controversial ideas often remain submerged but never truly disappear from the cultural code of the storyworld. They reappear from time to time in favourable circumstances, encouraged by the same narrative tension that brought them into being at their first emergence. Having analysed the source material, I found that motifs of deicide – and, more broadly speaking, divine existential anxiety – trace their origin to myths of inter-divine violence (the divine succession myth) and, arguably, to myths about the progressive degeneration of humanity (the myth of five generations of men). We wove the narrative of *Apotheon* around these two myths, shaping its core story to comment upon divine overconfidence and vulnerability.

Apotheon's story in its post-apocalyptic and post-mythological setting

The earliest fully elaborated versions of myths of divine succession and five generations of men came down to us in Hesiod's works, the former found within *Theogony* (155–82, 453–92, 617–719) and the latter in *Works and Days* (110–201). The succession myth narrates the vicious cycle of divine violence between fathers and sons. The first king of the universe, Uranos, incited the hatred of his wife, Gaia, when he refused to let their children, and his potential heirs, see the light of day. Infuriated, Gaia conspired with her youngest son, Kronos, and helped him maim and vanquish Uranos. Kronos also feared that one of his children would overthrow him, and subsequently devoured them as soon as they were born. His youngest son, Zeus, avoided the fate of his siblings and freed them from his father's gut; the children of Kronos then joined forces with other gods, and with Gaia, and managed to overcome Kronos. Zeus took a series of preventative measures to ensure no one would ever overthrow him, assimilating inferior deities into his regime, co-opting his equals and eliminating his superiors (Hes. *Theog.* 392–96, 881–85). Nevertheless, in Nancy Felson's interpretation,[16] victorious Zeus still fears potential claimants to his throne, threatening gods who dare to oppose him in the *Iliad*. In the Greek mythic storyworld, the circle of intergenerational divine violence has been stopped, but not broken – Zeus's sovereignty remains somewhat fragile to external circumstances.

In turn, the myth of five generations of men in *Works and Days* narrates the origin and history of humanity (110–201). According to Hesiod, humanity has passed through five stages of development (golden, silver, bronze, heroic and iron generations), becoming crueller and unrulier as the epochs went by. The first humans of the golden generation thrived in peace and abundance under Kronos's rule. Their successors of the silver generation lived under Zeus. Although relatively happy, they often quarrelled among themselves and refused to worship the gods, for which Zeus destroyed them. The third bronze generation, created out of ash trees, spent their days on violence and war. Brash and headstrong, they eventually perished in a flood sent by Zeus. Out of liaisons between humans and deities arose the fourth generation of demigod heroes, nobler than the previous one. Fighting among themselves, the heroic generation died out with the fall of Troy, to be replaced by the final iron generation. Toiling by night and day, the people of the iron generation will eventually perish as well, when they no longer feel shame or indignation at wrongdoing.[17] On that day, the gods will have completely forsaken humanity: 'baleful pains will be left for mortal human beings, and there will be no safeguard against evil' (Hes. *Op.* 200–1, trans. G. W. Most; see Fig. 11.1).

Fig. 11.1 Nikandreos (*l.*) encounters the Olympians' frustration in *Apotheon* (2015 © Alientrap Games Inc. All rights reserved).

Apotheon's narrative combines and develops Hesiod's succession myth and the myth of the five ages of man, beginning as the iron age ends. In the game we learn that Zeus has just decreed the final separation between deities and humanity. The Olympian gods remove their divine faculties from the earth, whereas minor gods of the countryside leave the world and travel to live on Mount Olympus until the earth is cleansed of humanity. As a result, Mount Olympus becomes a crowded divine refugee camp, whilst civilization collapses as forests and oceans become barren, springs and rivers run dry, and crops fail under the sunless sky. Jostled together and deprived of their honours and sacrifices, many gods begin to question the policies of Zeus – none more so than Hera, ever angered by Zeus' previous extramarital affairs and his domineering attitude.

The game story follows Nikandreos, a young Greek warrior from Dion in Macedonia, a historical town at the foothills of Mount Olympus. During a raider attack on his hometown, Nikandreos is plucked from the battle by Hera. The goddess, seizing her last chance to exact revenge on Zeus for his marital infidelity, decides to topple him by a mortal proxy, assume the throne in a resultant power vacuum and break the circle of father–son violence. She manipulates Nikandreos into fighting gods, ostensibly so that he may win the iconic attributes of office from the gods whom he defeats – i.e. so that he may absorb shares of power (τιμαί, *timai*, sing. τιμή, *time*) held by the gods and thus redress the balance of nature. Raised to Olympus, Nikandreos wrestles or wins the attributes of Apollo, Artemis, Demeter, Ares, Poseidon and Athena. Furthermore, the player may decide to guide him to collect the items of four remaining Olympian gods: Aphrodite's girdle, Dionysos's *kantharos* cup, Hermes' sandals, and Hephaistos's hammer. During his quest, Nikandreos learns that Zeus's edict has deeply divided the divine society, with many deities (including Helios, Thetis, Persephone, and Daphne) clandestinely opposing the divine establishment. Collecting divine shares of power, the hero grows ever godlier. At the beginning of the third act, Hera immortalizes Nikandreos and imbues him with her own τιμή so that he may become powerful enough to challenge Zeus. Her scheming uncovered, she is imprisoned by her husband. The game's narrative ends with a deicidal coup d'état: the hero challenges Zeus for his thunderbolt, defeats him in a heated battle and ascends to godhood, bringing the myth of divine succession to its conclusion (see Fig. 11.2).

The decision to set *Apotheon* at this particular stage and in this context of mythic history had much bearing on the writing process, offering unique storytelling opportunities. When I began working for *Alientrap Games* studio, the lead writer and artist Jesse McGibney proposed that, for the sake of intrigue and greater artistic freedom, *Apotheon*'s story should unfold in a hypothetical post-apocalyptic and post-mythological timeframe, long after the Trojan war. *Apotheon*'s post-apocalyptic story plays out after the end of the world as Hesiod knew it. Humanity perishes not in a nuclear holocaust or zombie apocalypse, but when gods abandon mortals, since, for ancient Greeks, gods' enduring support is what kept the world going. In turn, a post-mythological setting conveys that *Apotheon*'s story would be a sequel to surviving narratives within the Greek mythic storyworld, a story to cap all stories.[18] Crucially, the post-mythological setting gave us more leeway in terms of narrative development. The decline of the iron age, a mythical period narratively underexplored by post-Classical

Fig. 11.2 Nikandreos (*r.*) battling Zeus (*l.*) (2015 © Alientrap Games Inc. All rights reserved).

creators, presents a relatively empty canvass onto which we could paint our vision of what happened next. Nevertheless, moving into the unexplored territory also meant we had to extrapolate out of necessity how gods, as a collective and as individuals, would react to the humanity's destruction. My role as a consultant was to reverse-engineer the core values of the Greek mythic storyworld and ensure they were respected as we pushed the limits of the narrative. The process began with posing numerous questions. If Hesiod's prophecy in *Works and Days* about the end of iron age were to be fulfilled, what would its effects be for the gods who would suddenly have to leave the earth? Where would they go? What would humans do, faced with oncoming oblivion? Would not be there any gods who pity the humanity, after Prometheus' fashion? If yes, why? Would not these divine dissidents do something about the humanity's imminent destruction? Other, even more pointed questions also needed to be asked. Could you really kill (or at least permanently disable) a Greek god? If yes, how?

Set in a post-apocalyptic and post-mythological setting of Hesiod's late iron age, *Apotheon* exploits a perfect storm of events for challenging the mythic status quo and undermining the divine supremacy. The myth of divine succession questions the notion of divine infallibility: headstrong and overconfident, Greek gods can be attacked or put at odds, their arrogance used against them. Relevantly, as Zeus prepares to bring about the foretold destruction of the iron generation, he ignores the fact that he himself avoided the grim fate that met his father and grandfather and was also meant for him.[19] His pride becomes his undoing. Losing support of his fellow deities, he pushes mortals and gods to their limits: as a result, the core values of the mythic storyworld bend and unravel to allow previously unforeseen developments. Attacked and brought to extremes, Greek deities prove vulnerable: the inherent tension present in the divine rivalries flares up to the point one can revisit the controversial notion of deicide.

The startling idea of deicide and its origin within the Greek myth

As a hack-and-slash platformer set on Mount Olympus, *Apotheon* directly engages with the challenging notion of the death of Greek gods, who are widely seen as immortal and ever young. To win shares of honour from gods, the players of *Apotheon* more often than not have to pry them from their dead hands. In the main storyline, only two deities (Athena, Demeter) willingly relinquish their powers to Nikandreos in defiance of Zeus's orders, whereas five gods (Apollo, Artemis, Ares, Poseidon, Zeus) defend their powers with their lives. When slain, the bodies of Olympian gods vanish in billows of light-filled smoke, their shares of power left behind in form of small objects for Nikandreos to collect. Deicide in *Apotheon* went against the audience's preconceptions about the Greek mythic storyworld. Some players expressed their bewilderment on Steam forums and wrote posts asking for explanation.[20] Others took a more personal approach: a member of a neopagan worship circle bluntly told me that their followers found in-game deicides sacrilegious and unnecessarily gory. Finally, Vincent Tomasso and Joel Gordon have recently published articles on representations of deicide of Greek gods in postmodern media (including *Apotheon*): in their view, such narratives go against the spirit of the myth, being more closely related to postmodern depictions of imperfect and vulnerable superheroes.[21] *Contra* Gordon and Tomasso, I argue below that the ancient Greek mythic storyworld accommodated deicide, with ancient writers either drawn to or repulsed by the notion, yet inescapably grappling with it.

The key question to be pondered is whether ancient Greek deities were truly immortal. Tellingly, among the foundational archaic Greek myth-laden works, Homer's *Iliad* and Hesiod's *Theogony* provide slightly different perspectives on whether full-fledged gods can die. The formulaic compound description of a Greek deity as ἀθάνατος καὶ ἀγήραος (*athanatos kai ageraos*, 'deathless and ageless') is often taken to mean that (s)he was unconditionally immune to both death and aging; nevertheless, both *Iliad* and *Theogony* question this commonsensical interpretation. In the *Iliad*, gods can be maimed, although whether the wounds could prove fatal appears to be an open issue. A god can be harmed and shamed by a god, and at times, even by a human. Emily Vermeule stresses that Greek deities of the *Iliad* could 'be whipped [...] (Hom. *Il.* 8.12, 15.17), [...] tortured with anvils [...] (15.19), dashed out of heaven [...] and crippled, if not killed (8.13)'.[22] In Homer's worldview, hubristic mortals occasionally threaten and wound gods. The Trojan King Laomedon does not reimburse Apollo and Poseidon for their building the walls of Troy, threatening he would hold them in bondage and cut off their ears (21.441–60). In a similar vein, Greek hero Diomedes repeatedly attacks Apollo and succeeds in wounding Aphrodite and Ares (5.335–54, 431–44, 855–63). In brief, gods of the *Iliad* exhibit a degree of physical vulnerability.[23] A minor deity may be destroyed: had Hera not intervened, the river god Skamander would have been vapourized by the firestorm unleashed by Hephaistos (Hom. *Il.* 21.186–369).[24] Even major gods evidently could be harmed in very specific contexts. For example, Ares was bound and locked in a bronze jar for thirteen months by giants Otos and Ephialtes – and he explicitly would have perished there had not Hermes helped him in his predicament, 'for his grievous bonds were overpowering him' (5.388–91).[25] Would have, could have, should have: the death of gods in the *Iliad*, putative and conditional, remains an 'absurd' possibility which hovers at the edges of the text, remnant of a primeval fear of a world turned upside down.[26]

In the *Theogony*, *bona fide* gods do not fear death in the same manner they do in the *Iliad*: their bodies remain vulnerable, but not to ordinary mortal threats. The poem depicts a world in which divine immortality, agelessness and invulnerability to wounds coexist in *almost* all deities, the world in which various divine Powers split and differentiate to create the universe we know, all things dark and bright.[27] Yet, the *Theogony* also sings of a succession myth – and some gods need to be removed in order to let their successors shine. Hesiod appears to have grappled with the question that has not been sufficiently answered so far: how to depict dynastic succession if your characters do not die? Maimed, bound, but not entirely dead, Hesiod's defeated gods are stashed into Tartaros, a subterranean containment space 'for those inconveniently uppity immortals who cannot be disposed elsewhere'.[28] In the Greek mythic storyworld, gods fettered by another deity and put into Tartarus lose a vital part of their inborn powers.[29] In principle, they retain agelessness, invulnerability to wounds and immortality, but they lose their mobility and unique agency, 'power over the actions of lesser beings, and the independence to use that power as the deity sees fit'.[30] With some of their divine powers disabled, gods could be painfully harmed and kept indefinitely in that state; once again, whether the damage was beyond supernatural repair appears to be an open issue.

A conspicuous theme in the early Greek myth, divine vulnerability was most saliently showcased in myths about characters who did not know they could die – until they did. Hesiod's *Theogony* describes the monstrous brood of Phorkys and Keto, beings unaging, but apparently vulnerable to death from wounds (270–336). Their offspring included a trio of Gorgon sisters: Sthenno, Euryale and Medusa (276). Sthenno and Euryale were emphatically described as immortal, but the third sister, Medusa, for some reason was born mortal. Her vulnerability came to light only when an invading hero Perseus loped off her head: out of her neck sprang Chrysaor and Pegasus, sons fathered by Poseidon (276–83). Hesiod's idiomatic language makes one wonder whether Medusa knew about her condition before her meeting with Perseus.[31] There is no telling how long she lived without interference in her secluded realm, but the poet's wording suggests that death is something that happened to her, not an inevitable conclusion, but a chance accident that did not befall her sisters.

This curious kind of vulnerable immortality was apparently passed down to Medusa's descendants. Immortal Pegasus flew away to live forever with the Olympians, whereas his mortal brother Chrysaor married Kallirhoe, an immortal Oceanid, and sired Geryon, a three-headed cattle shepherd who lived on the western edges of the Greek world (287–94). Extant sources narrate that Heracles was required to travel to Geryon's domain in order to obtain his cattle as his tenth labour. In the sixth century BCE, Stesichorus wrote an epic poem on the herdsman, called *Geryoneis* ('The Song of Geryon'), unfortunately surviving only in fragmentary papyri. Presenting Geryon as a sympathetic character, Stesichorus comments on his undefined ontological status. The poem featured a talk between Geryon and his mother Kallirrhoe, who begged him not to confront Heracles, as they appear to have expressed some doubt as to whether Geryon would prove to be immortal.[32] The son decided to solve this uncertainty once and for all, with fatal consequences. Crucially, Geryon appears to genuinely wonder about his condition, implying that he shows no obvious signs of aging.[33] Conceptually exploring alternative paradigms of divinity, Stesichorus showcases that immortality remained a problematic status, with those of mixed parentage unsure of its possession: Geryon would have probably lived forever, had he not been killed by Heracles. Geryon's existential dilemma highlights the conceptual tension attached to the notion of divine vulnerability: early Greek poets were either drawn to (Homer, Stesichorus) or nonplussed by (Hesiod) the concept, yet they could not entirely ignore it.

The Greek myth of the five generations reveals that humanity will grow increasingly insolent, eventually altogether losing reverence for the gods. In turn, the myth of divine succession conveys that gods could harm and disable one another in specific contexts. At the intersection between these two myths we find the narrative of *Apotheon*: a mortal hero attacks gods for their powers and eventually becomes a god himself, their loss becoming his gain. This terrifying possibility also preoccupied minds of early Greek poets. Writing of intergenerational divine conflicts, poets labored to reconcile dynastic succession with divine immortality. Speaking of indeterminate beings, neither divine nor human, poets explored their unique position to underscore uncertainty in face of death, which may come late or not at all. Even for Olympian deities, deicide may not be a laughing matter: the perturbing story of Ares' imprisonment and torture suggests that, in certain circumstances, even an immortal may die.

Bearing all that (and the audience's expectations) in mind, the creators of *Apotheon* wanted to preserve a modicum of this fascinating ambiguity: the game left the final fate of the defeated gods unknown, their bodies vanishing in a puff of light-filled smoke. I like to think that they did not truly die, but were translated, faded, into an undefined state of existence, possibly descending to Tartaros. During final stages of writing, I briefly toyed with an idea of showing defeated gods in Tartaros, hung in chains from the ceiling, the voice of Hera reaffirming that their bondage would not last forever – an obvious sequel hook. However, I arrived at the conclusion that including this scene would have detracted from the game's message. All in all, players can interpret the fate of the gods however they wish. If, as Gordon argues, the audiences want to compare gods to vulnerable superheroes and read them as slain, the game story does not exclude this interpretation. Relevantly, many gods must have escaped Nikandreos' carnage: in *Apotheon*, you slay six of them, whereas Hesiod knows of over six thousand Greek deities, mostly left unnamed.[34] Untold stories of these gods unfolded in parallel to *Apotheon*'s main storyline: just as any myth, *Apotheon* does not provide you with complete closure, leaving space for new narratives to be enmeshed into its storyworld.

Conclusions

In this chapter, I discussed *Apotheon* as a creative adaptation of the Greek mythic storyworld to the video game medium, focusing on the process of rewriting Greek deities as vulnerable game opponents (bosses) from both a scholar's and practitioner's perspective. My main point was that the vulnerability of gods in ancient adaptations, a well-documented if controversial phenomenon, stemmed from unresolved tensions found within the divine character. Intersectional characters, deities of Ancient Greece thrive on contradictions. Perfectly beautiful in form and stature, they often commit foul deeds, occasionally even suffering their consequences. Living in bliss on radiant Mount Olympus, they nonetheless remain morbidly fascinated by the transitory and imperfect world of men, to the point of coupling with selected mortals and siring/ birthing demigod children. Immortal and awesomely powerful, Greek gods exhibit in equal measure raw force and raw vulnerability: myths record deities who were bound, wounded, crippled and imprisoned. This ambiguity makes them into attractive, yet challenging characters to adapt into the video game medium. Creators of transformative works set within the Greek mythic storyworld, no matter if ancient or postmodern, will need to constrain their characters' godlike powers to allow the narrative to have drama: exploring these limitations and applying them to one's own works may lead one to ponder and reverse-engineer the unwritten rules laid down in earlier adaptations. However, the palimpsest-like nature of storyworlds signifies that there is always the possibility of more than one paradigm of knowledge, more than one mythos, existing within any storyworld. The flexibility of storyworlds keeps them perpetually open to new narratives.

Notes

1 In a side-scrolling game, the player views the gameplay action from a side-view camera angle, and the onscreen characters can generally only move to the left or right. A platformer game has the player jump between suspended platforms and negotiate obstacles. Finally, hack-and-slash games focus on real-time hand-to-hand combat with weapons.

2 For example, Tomasso (2015: 147–57) discusses paradigms of deicide as found in selected television shows and films: in the analysed works, the Greek deities either fade away due to lack of cultural relevance or die in violent ways at the hands of humans, in retaliation for their cruelty.

3 Gordon (2017: 226–30).

4 Burton (2001: 46).

5 Potter (2016: 4.1).

6 Leavenworth (2011: 1).

7 Keen (2016: 3–5; and 2014).

8 Johnston (2015: 287).

9 Johnston (2015: 292–4, 299–300).

10 Ibid., 287; and Klastrup and Tosca (2004: 412–19).

11 Johnston (2015: 297).

12 Ibid., 285–6.

13 Rossdal (2015: 46–57) succinctly captures the history and nature of fan-fiction, especially in its relation to and engagement with Classical literature. For the arguments for conceptual isomorphism between Classical literature and contemporary fan-fiction, see Willis (2016), Kahane (2016). Keen (2016) questioned the isomorphic equivalence between the two, stressing that, in contrast to fan-fiction, myth does not have a

copyrighted, authorially acknowledged 'canon'. Accordingly, I prefer to use the term 'fanon', which prioritizes the creative community over the copyright holders and, in my opinion, neatly captures the dynamics of the myth-making in ancient Greece.

14 Johnston (2015: 309).

15 Klastrup and Tosca (2004: 412–13) and Leavenworth (2011: 7).

16 Felson (2011).

17 Zanker (2013: 10–12).

18 Johnston (2015: 298).

19 Felson (2011: 259).

20 See: https://steamcommunity.com/app/208750/discussions/0/611698195170776212 (accessed 28 July 2018).

21 Gordon (2017: 226–30) and Tomasso (2015: 147–57).

22 Vermeule (1979: 124).

23 See Neal (2006: 151–84). A mortal wounding a deity subverts the natural order; hence, even minor wounds bring on fits of unheroic hysteria.

24 Vermeule (1979: 126).

25 Hom. *Il.* 5.388–91: καί νύ κεν ἔνθ᾽ ἀπόλοιτο Ἄρης ἄτος πολέμοιο, [. . .] χαλεπὸς δέ ἑ δεσμὸς ἐδάμνα (trans. A. T. Murray). All acts of binding of and by gods carry potentially subversive connotations.

26 Burton (2001: 46). Tomasso (2015), however, interprets the same material in a radically different manner, arguing that the deicide was never more than a thought experiment.

27 Vernant and Zeitlin (1991: 27–49, especially 48). Characteristic for Hesiod is inclusion of all aspects of life into his theological account. Cf. Nelson (1998: 103, 'For Hesiod, each god has his (or her) share in the cosmos. That share is at once their portion, their prerogative, their particular sphere of influence, and their honor. Taken together, all the divine "honors", as all the divine "portions", comprize the cosmos itself.')

28 Burton (2001: 45).

29 Vermeule (1979: 125).

30 Burton (2001: 54–5).

31 Hes. *Theog.* 276–8: Μέδουσά τε λυγρὰ παθοῦσα. ἣ μὲν ἔην θνητή, αἳ δ᾽ ἀθάνατοι καὶ ἀγήρῳ, αἱ δύο ('Medusa, who suffered a dreadful fate. This one was mortal, but other two were immortal and ageless').

32 Page (1973: 149–50).

33 Vermeule (1979: 138, 143).

34 The vast majority of them are the 3,000 daughters and 3,000 sons of Okeanos and Tethys (Hes. *Theog.* 362–71), whose 'names are hard for a mortal to tell' (τῶν ὄνομ᾽ ἀργαλέον πάντων βροτὸν ἀνέρ᾽ ἐνισπεῖν) (370).

12

The Complexities and Nuances of Portraying History in *Age of Empires*

Alexander Flegler

Introduction

When developing or researching a historical video game, it is important to be aware of the ways in which games can tell a story. There are numerous ludological and narratological models to describe how games do this. The model introduced by Katie Salen and Eric Zimmermann seems to me to be serviceable for the subject matter of this chapter as it has previously also been used for developing several titles in the *Age of Empires* series. Due to the interactive nature of games and the play-immanent levels of meaning, this model suggests characterizing the narrative of a game using two distinct structural elements:[1]

- *Embedded narratives* are prefabricated narrative elements such as video sequences (cutscenes), descriptive texts or simply names of game objects. For example, the historical background of a game is often established via text descriptions or in cutscenes of a game. As these embedded narratives are written by the game developers, they cannot be changed by the players themselves.
- *Emergent narratives* on the other hand, are spontaneously generated by the interaction of the players with the game through its game mechanics, which can simulate historical processes. Emergent narratives can also be understood as a narrative of the game experience and be retrospectively re-presented by the players. This retrospectively turns gameplay into a construction of history in a historical game and it is unique for each gameplay session.

In the case of emergent narratives, the 'story' of any given game is thus the result of interactions between player and game mechanics and hence inherently changeable on a case-by-case basis. The narrative of a game arises from the combination of both emergent and embedded narrative components. For academic purposes, it is therefore methodologically insufficient to attempt to analyse this story exclusively on the basis of embedded narrations (i.e. descriptive texts or cutscenes). It is not just a question of which historical events are featured in a game, or which historical personalities appear and how they are presented (e.g. in cinematic cutscenes). Rather, the historical structures and processes, i.e. the underlying models of economic systems or power structures introduced to the game via game mechanics, must be brought further into focus. After all, it is precisely the resulting emergent narratives that distinguish games from linear narratives, as in film or literature.

As we shall see, different contexts of game and play have an impact on the perception of game elements and mechanics that reference history; the conception of history evoked by the games is thus context-dependent. Another pertinent factor is the possibility of players engaging creatively with the game mechanics and skirting or subverting game rules.[2]

Based on the series of real-time strategy games *Age of Empires*, specific examples will be used to explain these aspects. However, the examples have no claim to exhaustiveness or to be absolutely valid for all historical games. Rather, they should make clear that far more consideration has to be given to the analysis of games than was the case in previous investigations.

Emergent and embedded narratives in the *Age of Empires* series

Age of Empires is a strategy game series published by Microsoft and originally developed by Ensemble Studios. Since the publication of the original game in 1997, a total of thirteen titles and various expansion packs have been published, each dealing with different settings from antiquity to modern times. The series as a whole has sold more than 25 million units and remains popular today, with *Age of Empires II: HD Edition* continuously within the top 50 most popular games on the market-leading online game distribution platform Steam. Most recently, February 2018 saw the release of *Age of Empires: Definitive Edition*, an updated remaster of the original set in ancient history and produced by the developing studio Forgotten Empires. The author of this chapter was directly involved in its production as Creative Director.

In all titles of the series, the player takes control of a historical 'civilization' from an isometric, top-down view. The goal of the game is to defeat an enemy civilization by annihilating them from the map via combat or constructing a '[World] Wonder' and defending it for a certain amount of time.

Players begin with three 'villagers' on an unexplored map (Fig. 12.1). As these are moved across the map by players via mouse commands, different terrain types are revealed; sources of food, wood, stone, and gold are located, which villagers gather by hunting, fishing, foraging, farming, chopping trees, and mining. Players must gather enough resources and build enough housing to support their growing civilization. Constructing buildings allows them to train military and naval units to defend their civilization or attack enemy civilizations on land or at sea. Constructing buildings also lets players research technologies that benefit their civilization, such as increasing the resources they can gather or the strength of their military units.[3]

We will use these upgrades as an example for how the emergent and embedded narratives of a game work together. In the *Age of Empires* series, upgrades are supported and justified by the embedded narrative: they indicate technological progress and provide the player with visuals of more complex and effective weaponry. For instance,

Fig. 12.1 Start of a game session in *Age of Empires: Definitive Edition*, with a 'Town Centre', three 'Villagers' and unexplored area (2017 © Forgotten Empires/Microsoft).

wooden clubs can thus be upgraded to axes, simple bows to composite ones. If it is not possible to describe upgrades with historical terminology, an in-game increase in the experience level of military units is usually substituted. Thus, in *Age of Empires II*, the player can upgrade his 'Militia', eventually turning them into 'Champions'. But even in such cases, the visuals change with each upgrade and show the historical chronology of armaments and uniforms from migration-era Germanic warriors to late medieval swordsmen. From a game design perspective, game mechanical upgrades should, if possible, also bring about a graphical improvement that gives visual feedback to the player. The evolution of one's faction should be readable without having to look at combat statistics.

Some upgrades can only be researched if the player has already achieved certain other technological milestones. The sequence of possible upgrades may be visually arranged in a vine-like structure, a graphic design choice commonly labelled a 'technology tree'. The term 'technology' itself is used in a very loose sense in *Age of Empires* (as in most strategy games), as technologies that can be developed and unlocked by the player also include social and religious developments, such as 'Monotheism'.

Games with emergent gameplay such as *Age of Empires* rely heavily on authenticators[4] to make the history in the game recognizable as the past the audience knows – or, at least, a counterfactual variation of what the audience thinks it knows (i.e. *perceived history*). The technology tree and characteristics of units or civilizations are among the few things that place these games within a specific historical context, especially when the actual game mechanics are often interchangeable between games of the same genre. *StarCraft*, a real-time strategy game set in a science fiction scenario and depicting wars between human and alien races, is extremely similar to *Age of Empires* from the point of view of game mechanics: it is played in the same isometric perspective; units can be controlled with mouse clicks, resources have to be gathered, buildings have to be constructed in the same manner as in *Age of Empires*.

From a historical point of view, the interpretation of the technology tree is non-trivial. A historically valid justification of a technology chain by the game designers alone does not mean that the overall result is historically 'correct' or 'accurate' or, indeed, perceived as such. For instance, in *Age of Empires II*, chain mail has to be researched before plate armour can be unlocked. This could be interpreted to indicate that chain mail is a necessary pre-condition, i.e. 'no plate armour without chain mail', but could just as reasonably be seen as a sufficient condition – 'the plate armour must inevitably follow the chain mail'. Since both would be legitimate interpretations of the game mechanic, technology trees like in *Age of Empires* or the *Civilization* series can therefore be described and criticized as teleologic or deterministic – and, indeed, they have been.[5] But it would be a fallacy to conclude that this is the only possible interpretation or to even claim that the developers had a deterministic conception of history. Historically, chain mail simply had been in use for over a millennium before the appearance of plate armour in the Late Middle Ages. Both were independent developments, with plate armour ultimately proving superior, thus rendering chain mail obsolete wherever plate armour could be afforded by its wearer. Thus, the decision by game developers to have chain mail precede plate armour in the linear structure of the technology tree could just as reasonably be read as an effort by said developers to ensure that the game's chronology lines up with history.

Another pertinent example is taken from *Age of Empires III*, set during the fifteenth–nineteenth centuries. In this game, the Aztec civilization does not have access to cavalry units in the technology tree, in marked contrast to the Sioux and Iroquois peoples. The decision to deprive Aztecs of this military unit was not taken to indicate that they *could* not have acquired this 'technology' – i.e. horses and horsemanship – from the invaders, but simply that it *did not* happen. Thus, Aztecs are depicted as a horse-less (and firearm-less) society simply because the time span between initial contact with the Spanish and the downfall of the empire was too short for such innovations to take hold. The game therefore is not necessarily trying to convey that events *had* to happen that way in history, just that they *did* end up doing so. Additionally, the lack of cavalry also serves as a marker of distinction for the Aztecs, one of a number of traits that differentiate them from other civilizations and peoples in the game from gameplay perspective.

As seen in the example above, there is a selective descriptive process during the design phase of the technology trees. *Age of Empires II*, for example, has a technology tree that specifically 'narrates' the technological progress of a very specific part of the world (namely, Western Europe) but is not strictly applicable to other civilizations. Aztecs can research three-field 'crop rotation' and 'plate armour'. The process can easily slide towards the prescriptive when horses and gunpowder appear in the technology tree for Aztecs, Maya and Inca but they are prohibited from researching them. As a rule, gameplay usually takes precedence over historical accuracy during game design. In most cases, the in-game bonus of a technology is designed before its name (with a reference to history) is found. This is a fundamentally prescriptive approach.

Although the technology tree in *Age of Empires* is an interactive game mechanic, it could equally be read as a historical narration of the chronology of historical developments rather than a (deterministic) simulation of technological advancement. In a sense, there is an uncertainty principle at work when it comes to historical narration and simulation in games. Due to their interactive nature, games can either simulate gameplay-relevant structures and processes satisfactorily or accurately represent our history and its chronology, but not both at the same time, nor to the same degree. It is therefore important to consider whether a part of the game is examined within the context of a historical simulation or from a narrative point of view.

Game modes as context

Generally speaking, game modes of a single game provide another specific context in which the story of the game unfolds. The previous section of this chapter was limited to the game mode known as 'Random Map'. In this mode, players can choose the starting and winning conditions, the participating civilizations and alliances with each other, but also the map type, which is then randomly generated by the software. This is the typical game mode of single player sessions against the AI or against other human players.

The game also offers single player-only missions that are played on hand-crafted maps with preset starting conditions and unique goals. Such maps and missions are called 'scenarios' in *Age of Empires*. The game offers a dozen 'campaigns' that consists of several scenarios, which are played in sequence, and offer a continuous story. For instance, the campaign 'Ave Caesar' leads the player through scenarios such as 'Alesia' and 'Pharsalus', which tell the story of Caesar's military campaign from the Gallic Wars to the defeat of Pompey in the Roman Civil War.

Scenarios such as this, with their embedded narratives as background stories, might lead to a new interpretation of the historical periods that the games are set in, the eponymous 'ages' of *Age of Empires*. Although the gameplay itself ranges on a fluid scale from the counterfactual to the fictional, the ages themselves more or less accurately represent historical periods. This is all the more important since other authenticators for a historical classification are missing. Historical scenarios are usually confined in terms of time and geography, and the campaigns are a chronological sequence of such scenarios. Campaigns as well as their scenarios can represent different lengths of time and reflect the historical circumstances with varying accuracy.

What they all have in common is that the ages no longer represent the historical periods or epoch boundaries they are named after. To illustrate this point, let us use the campaign '*Pax Romana*' from *Age of Empires: The Rise of Rome* as an example. The campaign itself is structured in a number of missions or scenarios, the first of which is entitled 'Actium'. Its telling title and the fact that the player fights as Octavian against Mark Antony and Cleopatra in the battle notwithstanding, the scenario's starting point is, in the peculiarly arranged in-game 'ages' of the game, the 'Bronze Age'. In the following scenario, 'The Year of the Four Emperors', the player must win the internal Roman struggles during a similarly short period in 68–69 CE. They take on the role of Vespasian this time, but the scenario, nevertheless, begins in the 'Stone Age' and then has the player hold their own against rivals Otho, Galba and Vitellius before they can advance to the 'Iron Age' to erect a '[World] Wonder', which is an expensive building that will bring victory to the player who builds it and is able to defend it for a certain amount of time.

Starting 'ages' inconsistent with the history represented in a single player scenario could simply be explained away by gameplay reasons. However, in situations like this, 'ages' are not meant to be taken as representations of actual historical epochs. They can stand in for a more abstract concept of progression. They can symbolize the accumulation of the power of the player's character, increase of military means, the growth of a city or civilization.

Narratives of progress and success in different contexts

So far, we have seen that the economic, military and technological progression of the player's faction from a humble people to a higher level of civilization during a play session is a fundamental part of the emergent narrative. But players' peoples (or factions) may also progress along the eponymous 'ages', e.g. from the 'Stone Age' to the 'Iron Age' in the case of the original *Age of Empires*. Advancing to the next 'age' is a key technology in terms of game mechanics as with every 'age', further improvements, buildings or military units are unlocked. As with researching regular technologies, research – and thus crossing over into – the next 'age' is as simple as pushing a button. After a short wait, the new age is reached. Technologies, once researched, cannot be lost during a mission. This is especially true of advancements to the next 'age', a fact that seemingly supports a narrative of deterministic progress.

The idea of progress is also relatively easily identifiable in the embedded narrative. Short, explanatory in-game texts known as 'tooltips' instruct the player as to each age's technologies and exhorts them to 'advance' to the next one, a 'development' that will 'improve' the player's people (Fig. 12.2). These are clearly positive connotations, meant to encourage the player to follow this path. The reading of the underlying concept of history in light of the game mechanics as well as the embedded narratives point to the view that the *Age of Empires* games are built on a linear and simultaneously culture-optimistic conception of history. However, looking at individual games within the context of the series as a whole offers another interpretation.

Age of Empires II is set in the Middle Ages and is therefore a direct successor to *Age of Empires*. In the original game (set in antiquity), players would typically command a stately army and oversee a thriving economy at the (successful) conclusion of a campaign and gaze in satisfaction at the monumental 'Wonders' they had built such as the Colossus of Rhodes or the Pyramids of Gizah. At the start of *Age of Empires II*, however, they again have to begin with a mere handful of 'Villagers' and a 'Town Centre' in the 'Dark Age'. Thus, seen not solely within the bounds of individual games but across all titles of the series, technological (and cultural) progress achieved in one title can be (and is) at least partially lost. While a similar narrative of the rise of a people obtains in each case, it is, nevertheless, evident that a serious historical rupture has taken place and that history itself did not necessarily proceed in a linear fashion. The narrative of the rise of a people is therefore not to be equated with history itself.

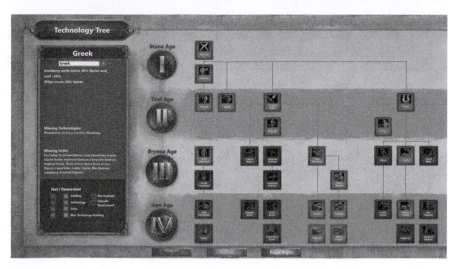

Fig. 12.2 Technology tree in *Age of Empires: Definitive Edition* – in every age, a new layer of technologies, units and buildings is unlocked (2017 © Forgotten Empires/Microsoft).

Age of Empires III, the third part of the series, covers the period from the early modern era to the age of industrialization. Here, too, the game begins with a typical 'Town Centre' and a few workers. According to one of the designers, Sandy Petersen, the creative team was aware of the historical problems with this scenario:

> The Europeans at the time didn't really fit the Age [of Empires] concept – it's ridiculous to have Napoleon's beginning nation be a town center, an explorer, and a few villagers. But this game start does make sense in the New World.[6]

Game mechanics are therefore not just schematic formulas painted over with a broad brush and a historical theme as a façade. The history referenced by the game and the emergent narrative generated by interaction with the game mechanics must be coherent (at least) to the players in order to function. Taking the events of a single play session as a context rather than the overarching narrative of the game series or a story campaign can also alter the interpretation of the game. The embedded narratives of campaigns or scenarios are often 'narrative[s] of success', such as Caesar's victories over the Gauls and Pompey, which were mentioned earlier.[7] When looking at a single play session of *Age of Empires* alone, a 'narrative of success' does in fact not have to be present.

A session of *Age of Empires* can also result in complete defeat, ending with the complete annihilation of the players' faction/civilization. The narrative of the rise of a people mentioned at the beginning thus turns out to be an ideal case of the game, which rarely reflects the reality of playing. Rather, the gameplay in *Age of Empires* turns out to be a dynamic series of ups and downs that depends on non-trivial decisions of the players and their fellow players, especially in the 'Random Map' mode. *Age of*

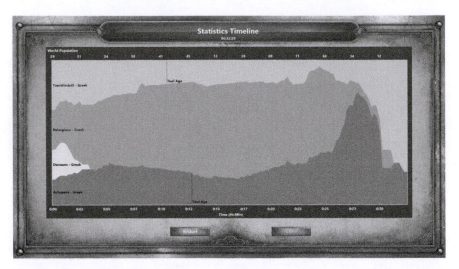

Fig. 12.3 The timeline in *Age of Empires: Definitive Edition* shows ups and downs during a session. Not every player's civilization is successful, and some are annihilated early on (2017 © Forgotten Empires/Microsoft).

Empires can also be played casually with the focus on building up cities and castles and players can spend their time creating their own worlds in the 'scenario editor'. A 'purpose of winning'[8] is not required. Progress and success narratives are therefore not necessarily inherent to *Age of Empires* but are dependant in which context the game is viewed or played at (Fig. 12.3).

Decisions and their narration

The assessment that a game can be understood as a sequence of meaningful decisions[9] has an impact on the interpretation of game mechanics such as the 'age-ing-up' mechanics of *Age of Empires*. If the researching of technologies and upgrades, including the advancement into another 'age', were always beneficial to the players, researching technologies would not logically require any choice or agency on the part of the player. Such decisions would be trivial, the development of technologies as game mechanics simply redundant.

Before researching technologies, however, players have to gauge whether and when the benefits of a technology are worth their cost, and thus make a meaningful decision: like most strategy games, the *Age of Empires* series is 'configuration critical', that is, it requires prudent regulation of multiple, interdependent values.[10] In all of the *Age of Empires* game modes, players make their decisions in the fields of economy, military and technological research. In doing so, they always have to weigh up which of these areas they intend to invest the resources they have gathered. Players who focus their efforts in researching technologies and advancing their economy ('booming') are at risk of being overwhelmed by players who instead invested resources in military and attack early on in a game session ('rushing'). Similarly, the advancement to the next 'age' is not always advantageous for the player. For example, if the advancement takes place too early, players may fall behind both economically and militarily because of the ensuing high costs, especially since the benefits of a new 'age' are only indirectly reflected in more available technologies, buildings, and troop types.

As a result, not only do 'ages' serve to accommodate a greater variety of military units in the game,[11] but also as an 'arc of suspense'[12] to provide players with new ways to play. The process of progressing to a new 'age' has be seen as a meaningful part of the game system where individual decisions can mean victory or defeat. In the context of the course of the game, advancements to the next 'age' thus do not necessarily convey a culture-optimistic conception of history, particularly if they have just caused the downfall of a people.

Freedom of play: Implicit and negotiated rules, and metagame

The game mechanics that we have hitherto considered as significant are constituted by the rules of the game. But the fact that the program code itself is digital, and therefore formal and discretizable,[13] does not mean the rules of a game cannot be altered by players. The latter can, in fact, engage creatively with the rules of the game and indeed are doing so every time they play, as implicit and negotiated rules are ubiquitous in games. The former are unwritten rules of social etiquette between players.[14]

For example, in *Age of Empires* multiplayer games, it is frowned upon to kill animals, a source of food, near the enemy base and to leave them to rot, thus depriving the opponent of a potential food income. Engaging in such tactics is called 'laming'. However, players can impose their own (sometimes the same) rules if they play against the computer. Players do this because, for example, they are looking for specific challenges, preferring a certain style of play, or because they do not want to exploit gaps in the program code ('exploits' in gaming jargon).

Furthermore, players can negotiate further rules among themselves. In the *Age of Empires* series, the so-called 'no-rush' rule enjoys great popularity. Under this agreement, players agree on trust not to attack for a set number of minutes after the game starts. The no-rush rule was so popular that it was officially included in *Age of Empires III: The Warchiefs*, *Age of Empires III: The Asian Dynasties*, and *Age of Empires II: The Forgotten* as 'treaty' mode. If one plays the game in the context of this game mode, one will find a game that is much more focused on building than fighting.

Aside from rules or game mechanics, gameplay is also largely determined by the style of play of the players, as they are basically free to decide in which way or with which strategy they want to play a game. For example, in a session of *Age of Empires*, it is quite legitimate to set oneself the goal of cutting down all forests and cultivating the entire map with fields instead of defeating the opponents.

The style of play in multiplayer game modes depend not only on the abilities or preferences of the players, but also on those of their opponents. As a result, play styles can become self-sustained – what is known as 'metagame' in gamer jargon, a term for the entirety of currently popular playing styles. The metagame is highly dynamic as new or modified styles of play are created by copying and adapting the behaviour of other players.[15]

After all, gameplay might be completely different, depending on whether the players act aggressively or passively. It even happens occasionally that different gaming communities of the same game develop a different metagame independently of each other. This is an issue, because the post-release metagame almost always deviates from the results of internal testing, as illustrated by the following example:

> While the public metagame generally evolved in a similar fashion to what happened internally, there were a few examples of it following a different path. Internally, we'd play a much more passive early game. What became the most popular strategy among all civilizations was very aggressive play.[16]

This can sometimes lead to the emergence of playing styles that were not intended by the developers. This has ramifications for academics as well, as the interpretation of a game is heavily dependent on how a game is played. One's own way to play the game is enough to be able to interpret the game by itself, but other playing styles might lead to a different, sometimes contradictory, interpretation. Therefore, a reflection of one's point of view and playing style should be the norm when analysing a game. Taking into account the metagame and various playstyles within the gaming community thus broadens the means of interpretation.

Conclusion

In summary, going beyond the underlying code or embedded narratives can be rewarding when interpreting a game. Both in-game contexts such as game modes and external contexts such as a games series as a whole provide for different frameworks in which the narrative of the game(s) unfold(s). The supposedly static story presented to the player[17] can undergo a change of meaning through the interactive nature of the play and the creativity of the players. It is therefore by no means true that in games such as the *Age of Empires* series, history inevitably appears as a 'structural process and not, or not primarily, as a consequence of human decision-making and action'.[18] It is precisely the players who are responsible for the ups and downs of the session with their decisions.

The freedom of players to deal creatively with rules and mechanics and the dynamic development of the metagame make it clear that it is difficult to speak of an 'ideology of the program code',[19] as some have done. It cannot foresee in what direction players are going to take a game once it has been released. Games simply create the framework in which individual play takes place: their possible readings are different, depending on how we approach them, in what context we look at them and, above all, how we play them. As these different stories sometimes can be contradictory, it is all the more important to lay out the context in which a game has been analysed and interpreted.

Notes

1 Salen and Zimmerman (2003: 383).
2 Schwingeler (2014).
3 Cf. *Age of Empires* (1997).
4 Winnerling (2014).
5 Kubetzky (2012: 91).
6 Petersen (2009).
7 Schwarz (2014: 50).
8 Ibid.
9 Meier (2012).
10 Pias (2004).
11 Pasternak (2012: 53).
12 Zwischenberger (2014: 264).
13 Heinze (2012: 62).
14 Salen and Zimmermann (2003: 148).
15 Phil (2013).
16 Kieffer Bryant, via Skype conversation (20 November 2013).
17 Schwarz (2014: 50).
18 Ibid.: 31.
19 Bevc (2008).

Simulating the Ancient World

Pitfalls and Opportunities of Using Game Engines for Archaeological and Historical Research[1]

Erika Holter, Una Ulrike Schäfer and Sebastian Schwesinger

Introduction

In a series of speeches to the public assembly in 349–348 BCE in which Demosthenes tried to convince the Athenians of the dangers posed by Philip of Macedon, who had just attacked their ally, the city of Olynthos, he addressed these stirring words to the public assembly, or ekklesia, of ancient Athens:[2]

> I bid you grasp these facts, men of Athens, and weigh well all the important considerations. Make up your minds; rouse your spirits; put your heart into the war, now or never. Pay your contributions cheerfully; serve in person; leave nothing to chance. You have no longer the shadow of an excuse for shirking your duty.[3]

His direct admonishment to the citizens, to make their decision wisely, reflects the importance of the public assembly within Classical Athens and of political communication between citizens.[4] In the different arenas of political life, be it in the public assembly or in the courts, the leading citizens stood before the people and spoke to them directly, as Demosthenes addresses his public as 'Men of Athens!', in order to, through their speech, convince them of the suitability of their proposed courses of action. The public assembly was the central decision-making body: the *boule*, or council, may have been able to determine the agenda of each assembly, but it was the citizens gathered in the assembly who proposed and voted on the items of the agenda at hand. The central matters of the city both foreign and domestic were debated and decided here. In the assembly in particular, the people expected the speakers to convey information relevant to the proposal at hand to them, on which basis they could then make their decision, just as Demosthenes exhorts his listeners.

The significance of the public assembly in Classical Athens is underlined by the fact that a space was set aside within the city specifically for the purpose of holding the meetings of the *ekklesia*: an entire hillside, in fact, namely the Pnyx (Fig. 13.1, *top*). This is a marked contrast to other Greek cities, both on account of the existence of a set-apart space for the assembly[5] and because of the amount of effort expended by the Athenians to configure this space. Whereas the pubic assembly originally made use of the natural slope of the hill,[6] the Athenians undertook a major renovation at the turn of the fifth century BCE. By constructing a retaining wall on the lower slope and packing it with an earth fill, they effectively reversed the direction of the hill.[7] The speaker now stood to the south, facing the assembly on the newly created artificial platform. A final major renovation dated to the third quarter of the fourth century BCE saw the Pnyx almost doubling in size, and it is the remains of this phase that can still be seen today (Fig. 13.1, *top*).[8]

Recent advances in the fields of sensory studies have shown how taking the senses into consideration expands the realm of possible interpretations of the archaeological remains.[9] Focusing on the perception of ancient spaces in this manner highlights

Fig. 13.1 (*Top*) Hill of the Pnyx today (Courtesy of the American School of Classical Studies at Athens: Agora Excavations). (*Bottom*) Model of the Pnyx Phase II in the game engine Unity3D (Courtesy of Analogue Storage Media II – Auralization of Archaeological Spaces, Humboldt-Universität zu Berlin. Created by Dirk Mariaschk and Una U. Schäfer).

questions of the suitability of the infrastructure at hand to the function of a space and the individual or collective strategies for its use.[10] In the case of the Pnyx and the public assembly, a number of questions spring to mind: how conducive was the space to the political communication that was of such central relevance? How easy or difficult was it for a citizen depending on his position in the crowd to understand a speaker?

Literary and material sources provide the foundation for approaching sensory perception in antiquity. Reconstructions and simulations in 3D of the spaces in question that are built on this foundation provide a further level on which to understand the interplays between the space and its sensory experience and how these might give an insight into the role and significance of political communication within the public assembly in Athenian democracy. For the creation of simulations, game engines, developed for the creation of video games, can be exploited for academic research. The definition of video games provided by Jeffrey Gregory as 'soft real-time interactive agent-based computer simulations',[11] illustrates how the goal of a video game is not so different from that of a simulation for research purposes. In this chapter, we would like to examine this tool and how it offers the potential to broaden historical research, even going beyond simulation. After an outline of the range of capabilities provided by game engines, we will demonstrate how these were implemented in order to create a research environment for studying the public assembly during the second building period of the Pnyx.

Game engines

A game engine is defined as a 'collection of modules of simulation code that do not directly specify the game's behaviour (game logic) or game's environment (level data)' or a 'general-purpose 3D simulation for keeping track of players, locations, and objects in complex 3D worlds'.[12] The original and main purpose of a game engine is to streamline the production of video games, so that for games where the underlying framework (physical properties of the virtual world, character animation) are the same, this infrastructure can be reused. The data necessary to create a game comes in many different media formats, such as audio files for the dialogue or sound effects, or 3D models of the characters. Game engines therefore need to facilitate the easy integration of various media and the direct importation of 3D contents from other programs in which these objects, structures and textures have been built, including 3D modelling, computer-aided design (CAD), or graphic rendering software.

Because of the differing needs of the various genres of video games, game engines were originally developed according to these specific requirements: first-person shooters (FPS) require the ability to realistically render large virtual worlds in which players can move about freely, as well as authentic movement and action of the opponents. FPS game engines therefore focused on elaborate rendering capabilities and character animation. The earliest research projects utilizing game engines used such an FPS game engine precisely for these reasons (free movement from a first-person POV in a realistically rendered virtual world), but needed to manually modify the engine in order to disable the shooter.[13] Real-time strategy (RTS) games, on the other hand, are played from a bird's-eye perspective, so that the rendering engine within the game engine that processes the in-game view can be streamlined to improve the overall performance. As game engines have continued to be developed, however, they have become increasingly all-purpose, so that a single game engine can be used to create a variety of video games in differing genres. The widespread game engines of Unity3D (by Unity Technologies, e.g. Pokémon GO), CryEngine (by Crytek, e.g. Far Cry Series) and UnrealEngine (by Epic Games, e.g. Unreal Tournament Series) represent a major step in this direction.

Among the functionalities provided by current game engines, one we would look to focus on as especially relevant for academic use is the internal physics engine. Every object (including the user's avatar) can be forced to be subject to the laws of physics (like gravity, optics, friction, dynamics, etc.), or to whichever laws the game (engine) developer determines. Game engines allow us to make use of complex mathematical models without having to write them ourselves, creating virtual worlds that simulate the physical world. However, it must not be forgotten that these codes are written with approximation and simplification in mind, not total physical accuracy. For example, phenomena such as light or sound diffraction are mostly approximated using ray-tracing algorithms. Increased use of these tools will demand a closer view of the underlying codes, as they are not yet widely studied.[14] The environment thus simulated according to physical properties can then be almost limitlessly expanded by additional scripts and simulations, integrating crowd simulations or acoustics, for instance. These environmental simulations are meant to resemble the real-world physical experience of our environment and are connected to the ability of the user to dive into a three-dimensional space from a first-person perspective (or any other desired point of view) and navigate freely within the environment independently of fixed paths (in contrast to fly-throughs, bird's-eye or top view).

A video game is by definition interactive: the player must provide input in order to advance gameplay. Game engines are therefore also designed to be dynamic, responding to player input in real time. Direct user interaction allows the exploring users to interact in and with the digital scene, for instance by moving around, orienting oneself and navigating through the environment, or by handling objects (touching, grabbing, manipulating). In addition, many games are designed to be played simultaneously by more than one player; a number of players share the virtual world, interacting with one another and with the environment. Game engines that can be used to create multiplayer games include an array of networking capabilities. Multiplayer-mode embodies the concept of social collaboration in space, that is, the possibility to meet, communicate and share experiences and knowledge in the same digital realms without the necessity of being in the same physical location.

Game engines also provide the proper infrastructure that enables the development of augmented and virtual reality applications, a feature of increasing importance. It should be noted here that VR technology is not the same thing as game engine technology. While game engines are not exclusively necessary to build VR experiences – in fact, earlier VR applications needed to be programmed individually – modern game engines significantly simplify the creation of VR applications for a larger circle of non-professionals. Provided that the necessary additional VR hardware components, such as head-mounted displays (plus sensors and controllers) or CAVE technology (with even more necessary equipment) are present, modern game engines provide an elaborate software infrastructure, which can easily be expanded by scripts and assets (software packages) in order to integrate virtual reality technology as an additional functionality.

There are advantages to using a game engine for research purposes above and beyond the technical possibilities. First, it is cost-efficient, with game engines such as Unity3D or UnrealEngine available for free if used for academic or personal use. Second, the minimal system requirements enable game engines to run on standard personal computers, negating the need for expensive equipment.[15] The combination of the intuitive design of the software architecture and its graphical user interface (GUI), editors based on the 'What You See Is What You Get' (often abbreviated as WYSIWYG) principle, as well as the ability to directly see changes and results on an internal viewer makes game engines increasingly accessible to researchers.

Game engines in current archaeological research practice

The potential of game engines for archaeological and historical research has been recognized since game engines have begun to be more widely available, and the last two decades have seen numerous explorations of the use of game engines for research and education purposes. A significant driver of game engine-based applications is the vast field of digital cultural heritage.[16] The goals of the research projects that have been specifically tied to the use of game engines include the better understanding of spatial relationships between buildings, the dynamic, visual-based dissemination of archaeological knowledge, or to better approach ancient experience: the projects of Meister and Boss for example specifically address the first two concerns, while a research project from the University of Salerno attempts the third in reconstructing funeral rites in fourth-century BCE Paestum.[17] The ease with which game engines allow the terrain and environment to be realistically modelled relatively quickly and painlessly is of great importance in this context. While the earliest projects described by Meister and Boss boasted of multiplayer capabilities that enabled school classes or researchers to visit a site together online,[18] location-independent academic collaboration in virtual research environments has for the most part remained out of reach.[19]

The ability of digital models in general and game engines in particular to incorporate alternative reconstruction hypotheses has also been considered by previous research projects.[20] However, so far, the dynamic evaluation and adaptation of the reconstructed space is limited to the creator of the virtual environment. While the interaction of the user with the elements of a scene that game engines make possible, be it with characters, objects or architecture, has been implemented, it is mostly used to provide additional information on the selected object. An interface enabling the user of the scene to become the researcher as opposed to the creator of the virtual environment as the sole researcher has thus far been lacking.

The actual applications developed in the course of these various interesting case studies are unfortunately most often known only through short, descriptive publications.[21] To a large extent, this can be traced back to a lack of appropriate publication platforms with integrated 3D/VR viewers to publish the game engine-based 3D scenes and

VR environments. Because awareness of this problem is growing, efforts are being made to find suitable solutions.[22]

Even though game engine technology and VR are increasingly applied in academic archaeological research, their inherent potential is still not truly exploited. They serve first and foremost as a means for visualization, too often simply mimicking established practices of traditional media. The issue here is that contemporary practices of archaeological data digitalization (e.g. 3D digital reconstruction, laser scanning, photogrammetry), and virtual environment creation (including animations, simulations, interaction, etc.) offer a much wider range of possibilities to achieve a useful dynamization of research environments, that is, a dynamic, interactive, user-centred research tool perfectly suited to collaborative work and knowledge exchange. It is in this sense that game engine technology might support a praxeological and sensory approach in historical research. In the following three sections, we explore three possibilities for using game engines in order to enhance the research of ancient spaces using the example of the Pnyx, although the considerations are relevant to all historical spaces that are to be analysed from the point of view of their sensory experience.

The Pnyx research environment

Let us set the scene. The Pnyx is reconstructed in its second building phase according to the suggestions of the excavators; it is populated with various 3D models, people, sounds and animations as well as user interface elements and control panels for guidance and orientation (Fig. 13.2).

When entering the virtual research environment, the users find themselves in the middle of a large crowd of people streaming towards the Pnyx, gathered from Athens and its surrounding areas to attend the assembly taking place this day in 349–348 BCE: Philip of Macedon is threatening our ally in Olynthos, and Demosthenes is set to speak today. It is possible for them to move freely with and through the crowd and around the virtual space to observe the Pnyx from a first-person perspective, with its two main stairways, the huge semicircular audience space and the speaker's platform (*bema*) centred at the rear (also see Fig. 13.1, *bottom*).

Upon their arrival on the Pnyx, Demosthenes is already speaking, urgently warning his fellow Athenians to be prepared for an oncoming war. While exploring the virtual Pnyx, the user can navigate to six listening points strategically spread across the auditorium (indicated by ears floating above the crowd). When entering such a point while wearing headphones, the user is able to listen to a binaural simulation of Demosthenes' speech. It means that his oration is made audible, or *auralized*,[23] live for this particular spot. An algorithm simulates the position of the users' two ears within this virtual architecture, including the effect that Demosthenes' voice will still be heard from the direction of the *bema* (as a fixed location) even when the users turn their heads to have a look around. The aural impression given via the headphones thereby mimics – as much as is possible using current technology – how we actually perceive sounds in everyday life. VR enables a higher degree of bodily involvement, including corporeal movements of the head, arms and hands in 360 degrees, thereby contributing

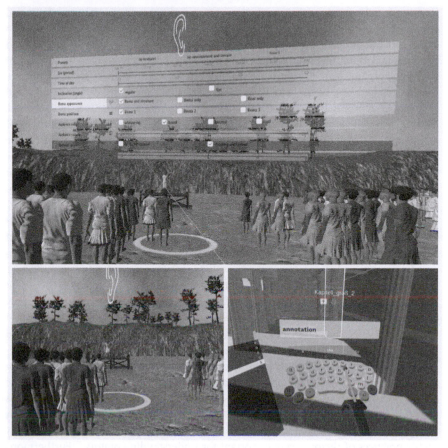

Fig. 13.2 (*Top*) Pnyx interface, (*bottom left*) listening point with floating ear, (*bottom right*) VR Annotator (Images courtesy of Analogue Storage Media II – Auralization of Archaeological Spaces, Humboldt-Universität zu Berlin. Created by Dirk Mariaschk and Una U. Schäfer).

to a more holistic and situative experience of the virtual environment. Therefore, our research environment is created for use with a head-mounted display and controllers (HTC Vive; see Fig. 13.2).

Expanding the senses

The ability to experience a VR environment from a first-person point of view in real-time with the freedom to move around lays the foundation for a spatiotemporal understanding of an architectural setting. The user in our scene is not restricted to a fixed path or schedule but can explore the scenario of a public assembly according to his or her specific interests. The user might follow the crowd up to the platform, look for a space and experience the speech, thus getting familiar with spatial procedures and details in the processes accompanying public assemblies, or gaining insight into organizational difficulties and the timing of such an event. In a more explorative and experimental mode, users can change their place and perspective, comparing different vantage spots not only in terms of visibility but also with respect to how well the speaker can be heard from them. Each mode of spatial experience can be understood as a way of appropriating a space with regards to certain research interests. Overall, moving through a space in action helps to study the cultural embeddedness of architecture in everyday procedures. Experiencing the movement of others while moving oneself makes spatial affordances and group behaviour apparent. This feature of game engines and VR is crucial for evaluating spatial functionality not only from an architectural perspective, but from the point of view of the practices in and social formation of space.

To accept that Demosthenes was potentially able to call his fellow citizens to war against Philip of Macedon we need to assume that the transmission and intelligibility of speeches during the public assembly was intended.[24] Game engines have the ability to simulate spatial audio by using specific assets (specially designed software packages), however, they are not physically accurate simulations. Our research environment therefore makes use of the aforementioned advantage of the game engine to easily apply external content, incorporating aural impressions from the professional auralization software RAVEN into our Unity 3D scene.[25] RAVEN enables the physically based simulation of the acoustic properties of architectural ensembles based on state-of-the-art room acoustical modelling techniques.[26] This allows for a subjective listening situation in which spatial, temporal and procedural cues can be taken into account. The connection of the user-centred aural with the attendant visual impression has foregrounded intersensory dependencies between sight and sound in the analysis and produced new research questions, leading us to ask, for example, in what way bodily practices of rhetoric were important for understanding orators.[27] Furthermore, subjective listening tests in this multisensory virtual environment have revealed a wide variety of intelligibility assessments depending on various factors such as familiarity with the subject, or the comprehension of content due to understanding the crucial signaling words. The latter has shifted attention towards the crowd and its behaviour as a responding agent who is an important part of a communicative setting by creating emotional peaks, forcing speakers to react, repeat or emphasize, something that the literary sources already hint at regarding participation during the assembly.[28]

Our multisensory research environment therefore enables an experimental exploration and evaluation of the sensory conditions for political communication on the Pnyx, in order to study which different forms of communication were suited to the functionality of this particular space. Were speakers able to address a large crowd, even with disruptions? How are seeing, hearing and understanding a speech related to one another? Sensory conditions of political communication, however, depend on manifold decisions made during the reconstruction of the architecture and human activity. With this in mind, we attempted to make such points of contention in archaeological research productive for further research, by utilizing game engines technology which allows us not only to visualize these uncertainties, but also to operationalize them for comparative analysis. When focusing on the sensory conditions of ancient cultures, it is necessary to stress the point that such multimodal simulations are not meant to recreate *the* historical situation but to be able to qualify abstract and static numerical analyses that compare spaces in terms of square metres of floor space or speech intelligibility indexes, and to open up new paths for questioning the past.

Adapting the environment: The interface

In the case of the second phase of the Pnyx, which is that used in this case study, there are several elements that remain contested due to the lack of clear archaeological evidence. For example, the extent of the front of the Pnyx – and, closely related to this, the total square footage of the assembly place – is not clear from the archaeological remains. The original height of the retaining wall is also unclear, leading to speculation on whether or not the earthen embankment should be reconstructed with a slope (as the excavators suggest) or flat. Is the speaker's position located below the assembled audience, as is the case in Greek theatres, or was it on the same level as the listeners?[29] Most importantly, within the context of political assembly and communication that was the fixed purpose of the Pnyx, the original location of the speaker's platform is disputed. In their reconstruction, the excavators Kourouniotes and Thompson chose to position the speaker's platform about 10 metres in front of the still visible remains of the speaker's platform from the following phase. As they admit, this was done 'arbitrarily'.[30] Since then, other locations have been suggested based on different interpretations of the remains.[31] None has found widespread acceptance. Each of these reconstruction alternatives – the slope of the hill and the location of the bema – has an influence on both the audibility and the visibility of the speaker, and understanding these as modifiable elements instead of conclusive proposals allows pragmatic considerations to enter the archaeological discussion of reconstructions. Perhaps one reconstruction is more likely because the speaker can be better heard from that position.

Beyond the architectural reconstruction, there are numerous other hypotheses and assumptions that inform the configuration of the assembly in the virtual world. Instead of considering these uncertainties an impediment that make the study of sensory conditions impossible because it makes the simulation prone to inaccuracies, game engines enable us to operationalize different hypotheses, integrating each into the scene for real-time comparison. For this purpose, an interface that the user can activate at will was implemented into the scene (see Fig. 13.2, *top*), offering a range of options to adapt the surrounding multisensory virtual environment. For example, the user is able to adapt both the reconstruction itself (by toggling between different locations of the *bema*, thereby changing the correlated acoustics as well) and the assumptions underlying the sound properties of the public assembly (e.g. by changing the volume of the speaker or the mood of the crowd). The visual appearance of the scene can be changed by removing all textures, and environmental conditions such as time of day or weather can be modified.[32] Whatever options the user chooses, they are immediately triggered in the virtual scene, allowing for the direct comparison of alternative reconstruction hypothesis or different audibility. In this way, architectural and sensory conditions regarding the proposed functionality of the Pnyx as a place for political communication can be evaluated together.

Communicating results: Collaborative research
with game engines

After exploring the VR research environment of Pnyx II – or, rather: after comparing the audiovisual properties of the six different listening spots by adapting the VR scene via the interface, testing the comprehensibility of a speaker in relation to different levels of crowd noise, or after repositioning the *bema* to compare alternative hypotheses – one of the most important processes would be to communicate all this: which impressions and insights, which problems and questions came to mind while experiencing the virtual environment?

One such possibility to communicate and share what one has observed, experienced or thought, is that of annotating inside the virtual research environment, a hitherto largely overlooked function in academic applications. For our VR scene of the Pnyx II, we took this apparent lack of communicative interaction into account by developing an application to collaboratively create, collect and exchange knowledge and experiences. Within the virtual environment, users can select any object, for example the speaker's platform, to annotate it. These annotations are always directly attached to the selected objects and are characterized by a small symbol (speech bubble), which can be found by other users who explore the scene. Moreover, the location and angle from which an annotation was originally created is visualized, helping others to deepen their understanding of the user's annotation in relation to the referenced structure, thereby adding to the transparency of the communication and research processes in VR. Thus, users can not only interactively annotate digital objects, structures and processes with their own observations within the virtual space, but are also able to comment on the reflections other researchers have left (or are currently leaving) in the same space. Annotations are only text-based at the moment, which makes them easy to create, store, edit, share and process. The addition of annotation capabilities within our VR set-up is currently limited to data entry using the controller, but future efforts will focus on the integration of speech-to-text solutions in order to free the hands up for other interactions in the virtual environment.

Especially in connection with questions of sensory experience, results based on the experience and use of the research environment can be made (relatively) easily available for other researchers to experience, so that they can experiment further and see if they come to the same conclusion. Two forms of collaboration can be utilized: the 'external' or distributing collaboration involves sharing an explored and annotated scene with colleagues and other interested parties (including public institutions and platforms), who can then explore the scene for themselves and afterwards participate in knowledge exchange and discussions. In contrast, the 'inner' or live communication allows for the simultaneous exploration, annotation, and discussion with other researchers of a given scene as well as of, for example, changes made with the interface regarding the digital reconstruction or acoustic properties of the scene. In this format, the discussants/participants can join the experience via networking and multi-user mode. So far, both approaches run into problems. For the 'external' one, existing publication practices are a hindrance, as the idea of publishing anything other than static images (in print, but also digitally) is only beginning to be accepted. As mentioned above, newer journals specializing in digital humanities offer support for embedding different digital media such as scenes created using game engines.[33] As for the 'inner' model of collaboration, a range of technical conditions and specific preparations needs to be considered for the setup of a stable network connection to enable flawless multi-user access and collaboration in virtual environments – a task which should not be underestimated, unless your research project has a trained staff composed of computer scientists and game designers, as well as plenty of money and time. Either way, the opportunity to collaborate in and with virtual environments adds an additional communicative layer to the process of validating hypothesis and questions, generating scientific insights and producing interdisciplinary discussions.

Conclusion

A dynamically designed, multi-sensory simulation, the operationalization of uncertainties, the possibility of direct user interaction and different forms of academic collaboration are the vital criteria that transform a 'simple' scene of digital reconstructions into a scientifically relevant virtual research environment able to contribute to the fundamental research work of forming questions, testing hypothesis, shifting perspectives, exchanging knowledge and experience, and eventually generating new research questions and challenges.

We have shown how the field of digital sensory archaeology might profit from developing historical scenarios in game engines with the aim of creating a research environment. The structure of game engines makes it quite easy to implement tools that enhance multimodal dynamic user experience performed on the basis of physically correct models. In this way it becomes possible to approach the sensory conditions of spatial functions and their implications for the social formation of space in ancient cultures. The link between material remains, digital reconstruction and user-centred simulation sheds light on the blind spots of textual and architectural reconstructions by foregrounding their usability in social and spatial practice. The dynamics of simulations serve an interest in the processes that filled these spatial configurations with life. By putting these historical spaces into action again we might better understand architectural changes that arose due to changing needs in terms of their intended function, their way of usage, or even changing modes of interaction and public social behaviour. Even though the recreation of historical reality remains a techno-phantasy, we can attempt to use technology in order to delineate the important factors under which a historical scenario made sense to its participants. In this way, game development in modular and preset-driven visual platforms such as Unity3D provides a powerful tool for further projects using such environments for scientific purposes. Short training periods, cheap access, growing consumer computer power, and basic integration of physical principles promise valid results within short funding cycles.

The use of game engines for archaeological research might help to bridge the gap between material and sensory oriented research of historical spaces. Nevertheless, such interdisciplinary encounters into digital sensory archaeology should critically engage with the basic simulation processes that a game engine offers. Game development is driven by different intentions than scientific research; for example, the goal of totally immersing the user within the virtual world is irreconcilable with the observation and self-observation principles of academia. In order to proceed from a virtual playground to a virtual research environment, tools that support and mimic scientific research practice in the virtual domain need to be developed. Comparative analysis via adaptation interfaces, and documentation and communication tools in virtual co-presence are just two of a range of necessary instruments in a scientist's toolbox for virtual environments. Concordantly with these technological advancements, a discussion is needed on the epistemic status of virtual simulations. This needs to include conventions for methodology, documentation, and dissemination that comply with general scientific principles such as validity, reliability, objectivity, or repeatability. Furthermore, this discussion needs to consider the researcher as user. Whereas in most natural sciences the epistemic significance of computer simulations does not directly depend on the perceptive evaluation of a researcher (take climate simulations as an example) our example has shown that the situation is different for historical research. Even more, we propose that the epistemic value of virtual simulations of the past lies precisely in individually experiencing such digital environments yourself.

This implies a perceptual complexity that needs to be clarified. Within virtual environments the sensory conditions of historical spaces are unavoidably linked to the technological conditions of virtual perception. In order to approach the former, we also need to account for the latter. We might listen very differently than historical persons, and differently in virtual environments compared to real ones as well. Drawing on empirical research in game studies, film studies and other disciplines might help virtual scholars to reflect on their own contemporary perceptual habits within the game-engine mediated sensory environments. Furthermore, research using virtual historical scenarios should adopt a cultural studies' perspective, which asks for the structures and foundations of an everyday-life experience instead of evaluating the virtual perceptions as such. Thinkers like Alfred Schutz used the phenomenological term 'lifeworld' to delineate a historically shared foundation of mundane meaning production.[34] This might be the realm in which the material conditions for sensory perception are connected with intersubjective sensory meaning. Instead of empathizing with a virtual Classical Athenian avatar, we can start to ask and experimentally approach what citizens in Classical Athens might have expected when entering the public sphere, what prospects might have guided their attention, or what ritualized social and sensory procedures structured it – all important factors for political communication to function.

Notes

1   The considerations presented here are based on the research project 'Analog Storage Media II – Auralization of Archaeological Spaces' at the Cluster of Excellence 'Image

Knowledge Gestaltung'. The interdisciplinary team, without which this research would have been impossible, is made up of Christian Kassung, Una U. Schäfer and Sebastian Schwesinger from the Department of Cultural History and Theory, and Susanne Muth, Erika Holter, Dirk Mariaschk and Jana Beutler from the Department of Classical Archaeology, both at Humboldt-Universität zu Berlin, as well as Stefan Weinzierl, Christoph Böhm and Felicitas Fiedler of the Department of Audio Communication at the Technische Universität zu Berlin. Preliminary reflections on the benefits of game engines appeared as Holter and Schäfer (2018). An earlier project, studying similar questions concerning the audio and visual conditions of political communication in public spaces of antiquity, focused on the Forum in Rome. However, in this case, individual audio and visual simulations were used. For the line of enquiry in general, see, Muth (2014); initial results can be found in Holter, Muth and Schwesinger (2018). The complete publication of the results is in progress.

2 On these speeches, called the Olynthiacs, see MacDowell (2009: 229–39).

3 Dem. 1.6, translated by J. H. Vince (Loeb Classical Library).

4 On the emergence and nature of democratic structures in Classical Athens and the importance of the public assembly within Athenian democracy, see Ober (1989: 77–9), Hansen (1991: 36–7) and Bleicken (1995: 50–4, 527–33). The public assembly especially has been studied in detail by M. H. Hansen, whose articles are collected in Hansen (1983/1989). For political communication in Classical Athens, see Ober (1989), Treu (1991), Hansen (1991), Welwei (1996), Stein-Hölkeskamp (2000) and Mann (2007).

5 Only in Agrigento is there archaeological evidence for an *ekklesiasterion* that was used solely for meetings of the public assembly. Additionally, several other *ekklesiasteria* are mentioned in inscriptions (Kenzler, 1999: 239–48).

6 On Pnyx I, see Kourouniotes and Thompson (1932: 96–113), McDonald (1943: 68–70) and Thompson (1982: 134–8).

7 On Pnyx II, see Kourouniotes and Thompson (1932: 113–38), McDonald (1943: 70–6), Forsén (1993: especially 517–20) and Stanton (1996).

8 On Pnyx III, see Kourouniotes and Thompson (1932: 139–90), McDonald (1943: 76–80), Thompson and Scranton (1943: 297–9), Thompson (1982: 141–4), Camp (1996) and Rotroff and Camp (1996).

9 Hamilakis (2014) and Betts (2017), as well as the other chapters in this volume.

10 Muth (2014) demonstrates this for the Forum in Rome.

11 Gregory (2015: 9).

12 Lewis and Jacobson (2002: 28 and 29, respectively). For an introduction to game engines, see, Lewis and Jacobson (2002); an excellent overview that informed the description here is Gregory (2015: especially 8–62).

13 Boss and Meister (2004).

14 Research into game-engine architecture is in general still in its fledgling stages: Anderson (2008).

15 These benefits are specifically emphasized by ibid. (2004).

16 See, e.g., Lepouras and Vassilakis (2003).

17 Boss and Meister (2004), Andreoli et al. (2005), Andreoli et al. (2006) and Andreoli et al. (2007). Further examples from the field of archaeology include: Anderson (2004), Ch'ng (2007), Anderson (2008), Rua and Alvito (2011), Kotarba-Morley et al. (2014) and Oikarinen (2016).

18 Boss and Meister (2004: 508). Andreoli et al. (2006: 3) have also integrated multiplayer capabilities into their educational, game-engine based archaeological environment.

19 Anderson (2004: 524), for example, anticipates the collaborative capabilities provided by game engines.

20 This is especially true of digital models in general. See, for example, Holter (2014) on the project 'digitales forum romanum' or Rua and Alvito (2011: 3299–300). How to visualize the different alternatives is an area that these research projects are still grappling with, see Schäfer (2018).

21 An exception is the Vari House project of Learning Sites Inc. (2012), which provides a functional interactive browser-based Unity3D application. However, the archaeological documentation behind the project is still lacking. The same holds true for research projects that use the creation of digital models in general as part of their methodology: a web-based publication is already a valuable step in the right direction (compare the online publication for the 'digitales forum romanum' project headed by Susanne Muth (see Muth et al., 2014) with the traditional book publication of Packer and Gorski (2015).

22 A new example is the journal *Studies in Digital Heritage*: Frischer (2017: 25) Model 1 has embedded his simulation made in the game engine Unity3D.

23 The technical term 'auralization' has been coined to describe aural impressions in virtual rooms, in analogy to its visual counterpart 'visualization': see, Kleiner, Dalenbäck and Svensson (1993).

24 Although this is considered self-evident in historical analyses of Athenian democracy (see n. 2 above for literature), studies of acoustic comprehensibility add nuance to this understanding. E.g. Johnstone (1996) suggests, based on his own preliminary acoustic analyses of the Pnyx, that it was so deficient acoustically as to call into question whether or not they even strived for comprehensibility (and following him, Fredal, 2006: 121–5).

25 Schröder and Vorländer (2011). Current technology does not allow for a real-time auralization, whereby a user can freely move around the virtual space, while the sound is simultaneously adapted in real-time. Instead, each position (and horizontal angle) of the head needs to be auralized separately, which is why only six listening positions are currently available in our research environment.

26 See Schröder (2011) for a technical description of the software RAVEN, explaining the algorithmic implementation and the features which serve as the fundamental layout to this date.

27 The preceding research project on the Forum in Rome came to a similar conclusion (see, Holter, Muth and Schwesinger, 2018) and showed the importance of integrating audio and visual simulations in a dynamic environment as provided by game engines.

28 See Tacon (2001) for an overview of the sources.

29 Level: Dinsmoor (1933: 181).

30 Kourouniotes and Thompson (1932: 121–2, quoted at 122).

31 A good overview of proposals, with his own suggestion for the *bema* location, is Forsén (1993: 519–20, and his fig. 2).

32 We realize that there are many hypothetical elements within our own reconstructed scene that have not been made adaptable (e.g. the clothing the figures wear). Whether or not the audience was standing (as in our current simulation) or seated (as a single mention in Aristoph. *Knights* 783–4 suggests), is also a profitable future addition to such an interface, as well as other elements to be integrated into the acoustic simulation (e.g. weather conditions, wind). What we wish to emphasize in this article is that game engines make these elements adjustable, and therefore part of the research process, in the first place.

33 Other options for making a game-engine-based scene available include the release of the finished scene for play (without the option of further editing), or, if the underlying game engine is installed, the sharing of the entire project (allowing for further scene editing).

34 Schutz (1967) and Schutz and Luckmann (1973/1989).

Epilogue

Quo Vadis Historical Game Studies and Classical Receptions?

Moving Two Fields Forward Together

Adam Chapman

My research specialization focusing on games as a form for historical representation and practice means that I spend a lot of my time considering the relationship between history and games. And yet, I am still frequently surprised by the complexity of this relationship and its continuing popularity. Even after decades of the industry mining the past for inspiration, game developers and their audiences continue to display an endless fascination with the various ways in which historical themes and stories can meet digital systems designed for playful activity. As I write in July 2018, this month's *EDGE* magazine (issue 321) features a number of upcoming games. I am struck, yet again, by how many of these forthcoming games are influenced by history in some way. *Metro: Exodus'* dystopian future is heavily influenced by the events and political ideologies of the twentieth century and itself results from an alternate history. *Battlefield V* is set to return to the Second World War, the series origin, after exploring the First World War in the last game. RPG *Octopath Traveller*, whilst initially seemingly non-historical, owes at the very least an aesthetic debt to the history of the Middle Ages as most (if not all) fantasy fictions do to some degree. *Fallout 76* continues the series' tradition of being influenced by and satirizing Cold War history. Finally, and most relevantly for this volume, it is announced that the next game in Disney and Square Enix's crossover *Kingdom Hearts* series will feature a level based on the former's film *Hercules*. Alongside these game previews, *EDGE* 321 also has interviews with figures or development teams from the games industry, many of whom made their names working on historical games. Nor is this unusual. Each month, new games are announced that hold some kind of distinct relation to the representation of the past. For this reason, the study of the relationship between games and history has become increasingly important.

In answer to this new challenge, the field of historical game studies has recently coalesced. This field can be broadly defined as: 'the study of games that in some way represent the past or relate to discourses about it, the potential applications of such games to different domains of activity and knowledge, and the practices, motivations and interpretations of players of these games and other stakeholders involved in their production or consumption.[1] Publications and events on the topic are becoming frequent and research networks in the field have grown rapidly.[2] Within, or in relation to, this broader field, several distinct strands of investigation have begun to appear, with scholars investigating, for example, how historical games relate to archaeology,[3] function as carriers of cultural/collective memory,[4] offer popular enfranchisement by allowing access to historical practices,[5] or offer potential in regards to education[6] and heritage.[7] As this research often argues, games are frequently startlingly unique in their engagements with the past and hold significant possibilities. And yet, they are also not as distant from other forms of historical representation as the more conservative historian might like to think.[8] It is this question of what games newly offer or newly restrict in their engagement with the past in comparison to other forms of history that is a central concern of the field of historical game studies, particularly in light of discussions within historiography and the philosophy of history in recent decades that have seen a turn towards examining how the formal means we use to talk about the past influence what we say about it and how this is received. It is therefore natural that within the field there is also an interest in how certain *kinds* of historical content is represented in games. In particular, two strands of interest have proven popular. The first is a concern with how the Middle Ages is represented in games. Whilst the second, the focus of this book, is a concern with how classical history and myth are represented in games. That investigation of these two particular types of historical content in games should reach relative prominence is probably partly due to the fact that these periods of history are (alongside the Second World War) amongst the most popular historical themes for games. However, this is probably also partly due to the fact that interest in the representation and reception of these histories has significant academic precedence in the fields of medievalism and classical receptions.

This volume can therefore be seen as the historiographical meeting of two fields (historical game studies and classical receptions), providing an opportunity to consider anew some of the core questions about the relationship between games and history. Exploring the game as a form for the representation of classical content holds potential to further our understanding of both the role and nature of classics in contemporary culture and our understanding of the broader possibilities and limitations of games as history. This investigation, therefore, has a particular utility to both fields and simultaneously requires insight from both. In 2010, Christesen and Machado argued that: 'Video games have [. . .] changed radically in the past thirty years, and classicists' attitudes must change accordingly.'[9] Whilst this rallying cry has been somewhat taken up (as the very existence of this volume proves), if anything, this call has become even more pressing as video games continue to change – not the least of which in ways that see them become an ever more popular interest increasingly woven into everyday mainstream culture. Furthermore, the specific relationship between classical history/myth and games shows no sign of abatement. In their article, Christesen and Machado note that in the five years preceding 2010, more than forty video games that drew heavily on the ancient world were released. Given the proliferation of the games industry, the growth of the indie sector and the increasing possibilities for distribution offered by online platforms, this number is likely to be much higher now. Even if we only consider mainstream releases of the past few years, many significant titles, such as *Rome: Total War II*, *Ryse: Son of Rome* and *Assassin's Creed: Origins*, are classically themed. If anything, the classics seems to be undergoing a resurgence in interest from the games industry. Again, as I write, E3 (the largest games expo) has just passed and with it a raft of announcements for games featuring classical history. *Assassin's Creed: Odyssey*, for example, as the title implies, will be set in Ancient Greece. Even the seemingly unconnected military-shooter franchise *Call of Duty* is set to get in on the action with the recent announcement that the popular 'zombies' mode of the latest game will not be set in modern urban landscapes or battlefields as previously but in Roman gladiatorial arenas. Even beyond those games that overtly deal with classical history, the influence of classical themes is apparent. In the science-fiction series *Halo*, for example, classical values and terminology becomes a signifier for the historical 'end point' (in the sense of the conventional Western Enlightenment grand narrative) of a unified, global human culture, with the 'Spartan' super soldiers defending humanity against the seemingly barbarous alien invaders.

This continuing investment in classics as a theme for games also meets an increasing interest in the games industry promoting the educational capacity of their historical games. As Lowe argues, games already make more educational claims than other media such as cinema, adding that 'most historically themed games, but classical ones in particular, choose to exploit the impressiveness and worthiness of their subject-matter: since it is something worth knowing about, engaging with it must be (or at least resemble) learning'.[10] For example, *Assassin's Creed: Origins* recently added a discovery mode (see French and Gardner's chapter), in which players can forgo the usual challenges of fighting and exploring and instead enjoy guided tours of the game's virtual version of Ptolemaic Egypt. Whilst clearly serving the economic interests of publishers and, of course, perhaps implying a reinforcement of the often epistemologically naïve but marketable claims as to authenticity frequently made by the industry, such a move is encouraging in that it speaks to the spread of the idea that history in games may be something to take seriously. This further reinforces the need for scholarly attention to be paid to these games. Both an air of caution and a sense of exciting possibility must characterize such a discourse. Simplistic claims about games and learning are all too frequent and merely placing historical knowledge inside a game and assuming learning will occur dramatically reduces the complexity of a potential pedagogical tool that even those specializing in this aspect are really only beginning to unpick. But, understanding what kind of classical content enters into these games, why this is chosen, how this relates to other historical texts (popular and 'official') and perhaps most importantly how the game form restricts this content or allows it to speak in new ways, is a task well suited to the meeting point between historical game studies and classical receptions.

Form and content

As this implies, a core issue in the meeting of classics and video games is the relationship between form and content. In the past, I have argued that it is important to adopt 'an approach that privileges understanding the video game *form* (and the varying structures this entails) and its integral role in the production and reception of historical meaning, rather than solely, or even primarily, the *content* of specific products as historical narratives'.[11] As Serrano's chapter herein indicates, the construction of *authenticity* is an important issue within historical game studies. However, a formal focus has been a necessary defence against the wider tendency to dismiss popular history on the basis of simplistic analyses using historical *accuracy* as the main criteria. Particularly as more often than not this means a blunt comparison, an 'often unconscious, ontological discrepancy whereby the notion of "accuracy" or "truth" is collapsed with and thus taken to mean, "in alignment with the narratives of book-history"'.[12] Naturally, games cannot entirely reproduce the narratives of written history, nor should they when they open up new possibilities, not necessarily better or worse but certainly different. Even where comparisons are made directly with historical sources, often little is gained by such analyses other than a small footnote in academic discourse that historical game X was considered historically inaccurate at point Y in the medium's own history. This tells us nothing of the broader formal possibilities and limitations of games as history – the necessary path to gaining any understanding of the unique meaning of this new cultural phenomenon. Furthermore, this emphasis on the consideration of form guards against simply treating games as any other historical text, when historical content cannot be considered independently of the form in which it is constituted. This last point is particularly vital given the configurative nature of history in games, i.e. the fact that history in games is not only read or viewed but also *played*. This means a medium in which historical narratives are always produced through a shared authorship between producer (developer) and audience (player) within a '*(hi)story-play-space*'.[13] To simply adopt analytical approaches from other forms of history and seek to focus on content alone is to ignore this fundamental difference.

This said, if we are to understand the representation of particular histories within games then this naturally means a refocusing on the particulars of content. But this cannot be to the exclusion of form. However, if the work performed in this volume is an indicator of wider trends, such concerns seem to be unwarranted. The chapters contained within seem to naturally strike a balance between considering classical content as a distinct thematic category of representation but also relating this to the formal structures (and external pressures) that sustain, reject and negotiate this content. This is perhaps due in part to the meeting of historical game studies and classical receptions, with the latter being a field particularly accustomed to considering not only what kind of history is preserved and reused but also the constantly changing formal means through which this has occurred. Analyses of specific games can certainly be useful but they are also intrinsically limited (particularly given the rapid movement of trends in game design), unless they seek to uncover a pattern of relations between content and its manifestation within particular video game structures. McCall's chapter achieves just this, examining the representation of Roman military history but also constantly tending to the formal elements of the two games analysed. Furthermore, McCall's piece innovates in terms of analytical approaches by its explicit concentration on the visualization of historical dynamics. Often, when content is considered in historical games, this is focused on the representation of material culture. Departing from this, McCall's chapter instead echoes movements within digital humanities/ heritage and archaeology (see, for example, Holter, Ulrike Schäfer and Schwesinger's chapter herein) by turning to questions about the representation of less tangible aspects of the past. When such things are considered in relation to games it tends to be on a grand scale (e.g. the representation of cultural dynamics in *Civilization*). However, McCall's chapter highlights the importance of considering the representation of the strategic coordinated movements and thus collective affordances of human bodies in historical space (indeed spatial collective affordances is also an important issue within Holter et al.). This is important not only because this is an avenue of investigation lying somewhere between the individual revelations of game-based re-enactment[14] and the macro-scales at which frequently analysed historical 4X or grand strategy games function, but also because this is the level at which some of the most popular historical games frequently operate. Alongside these wider implications offered by McCall's chapter, his approach is utilized effectively to reflect on how a similar facet of classical history operates quite distinctly within two different games – each formal structure having particular strengths and weaknesses in relation to this content.

Serrano also points to the importance of the relations between form and content with a chapter that begins to map how the particularities of the form of games and its historical development have, and continue to, depict the ancient world. An important part of this analysis is its inherent intertextuality, comparing the manifestation of the classics in games in comparison to the other major popular cultural form, cinema, in which the period is commonly represented. This may initially seem a departure from remaining focused on the unique characteristics of games but often Serrano's analysis points to the important differences between the two, in itself a worthy result. This indicates potentially important future avenues of investigation, useful precisely because understandings of historical cinema cannot be simply transposed. Indeed, Serrano uses these comparisons as a jumping-off point to describe a series of characteristics of classical representations within games. Significantly, the chapter does so by utilizing categories of formal division within these games. In addition to offering a viable analytical approach, this also points to the inherent complexity of video games as a form. As Linderoth argues, games generally operate through many different modes and structure many different kinds of activity, meaning that they actually constitute what he calls a 'composite form'.[15] This is important not only because it is the holistic function of these components that generally produces historical meaning but also because it implies the limitations of seeing 'games' as a singular, unified category.

Clare's chapter similarly fuses consideration of form and content by seeking to understand the game-based representation of the classical through the lens of the formal structures associated with the CRPG genre. Significantly, this chapter also takes a further step by showing how these formal elements structure classical content in order to offer meaning potentials that are ideologically and politically charged. Though again focusing specifically on only two games, the chapter has wider implications and demonstrates how the relatively open narrative structure of such games and the opportunities for player choice this implies can create space to use classical content to engage contemporary discourses concerning colonialism, even allowing players to confront these ideologies and therefore engage in a form of postcolonial play. This latter aspect, however, is far from guaranteed and is dependent on a series of developer choices. Clare's analyses show that whilst *Nethergate* indeed offers the more radical play, the second game analysed (*Titan Quest*) instead affirms the colonial ideologies frequently embedded in the algorithmic and thematic conventions of historical video games. This kind of ambiguity is something that has been discussed a great deal in relation to Sid Meier's *Civilization*, which simultaneously seems to question aspects of the teleological assumptions underpinning grand narratives that in essence seek to justify colonialism, whilst also at heart functioning through an inherently colonialist logic based precisely on these Western grand narratives.[16] Like this discussion, Clare's chapter remains focused on the political context of game-based historical representations, arguing that the form of games and the possibilities this opens up in relation to classical content can have a deep seated contemporary political significance.

Political contexts and accuracy

Clare's chapter raises an important point. Whilst formal approaches are important for the reasons discussed above, caution must also be deployed to prevent this becoming a kind of empty formalism devoid of political or ideological context. Even exploring the relationship between patterns of historical representation and formal structures, as the above chapters achieve, is itself a political exercise. For example, embedded in this approach is the assumption that popular engagements with history are valid and that the means by which an industry formed during late capitalism expresses and disseminates arguments and ideas about the past is intrinsically important to attend to. Remaining focused on the wider implications of what this means for history as a socially and culturally embedded discursive practice means considering both the potential/limitations of form and the political utility of content. This means that considerations of accuracy become once again important. Not in the simplistic terms of the power dynamics seeking to ensure that popular media align with academic writing, but in terms of considering *why* particular historical contents are chosen for representation.

Is this, for example, due to inherent formal limitations or the political context (both economic and ideological) of production? Increasingly, the cultural discourse surrounding historical games sees a kind of 'weaponized' use of 'historical accuracy'. Conservative and frequently alt-right factions within games culture often adopt this charge of inaccuracy against game developers when the latter attempt to create more diverse representations of the past by including people of colour or women in histories conventionally viewed as the exclusive domain of the white male. For example, recently, charges of historical inaccuracy were levelled by some fans as a critique against the presence of female playable characters in the upcoming WW2 FPS *Battlefield V*, despite the historical evidence that some women fought during the war. Conversely, some fans of medieval RPG *Kingdom Come: Deliverance* used this rhetorical strategy (for it is certainly that) to defend against critique of the game for its absence of people of colour, again despite significant evidence that the European Middle Ages was much more multicultural and multiethnic than it is conventionally understood to have been. Paradoxically, often these same fan communities will fall back on the notion that it does not matter that a game does not offer diverse representations, despite the evidence, because, after all, it is 'only a game'. Given that fans seem perfectly content for games to feature all manner of inaccuracies in service to gameplay (*Battlefield*, for example, allows soldiers to respawn, whilst in *Kingdom Come* players can save their game by drinking alcoholic beverages), arguing against progressive historical representations in games on the basis of 'accuracy' seems to be a rhetorical strategy that seeks to subsume ideological prejudices against diversity.

Furthermore, as work by postmodern theorists of history has indicated, constructing all histories involves subjective ethical decision making. These ethical decisions may as well be made in service to politics we wish to espouse where possible.[17] And, really, this is simply an issue of frequency. As noted, people of colour were a part of the European Middle Ages and women did fight during the Second World War, but these were admittedly rarer occurrences than concentrations of medieval white, European ethnicity or Second World War male soldiers. But, again, postmodern analysis has pointed to the fact that choices about frequency of representation are a part of the construction of all histories.[18] Historians often focus on the same event repeatedly despite its rarity or uniqueness in order to emphasize its significance or consider it from multiple perspectives. Hollywood historical films feature the same kind of events or characters over and over, representing them at a frequency with which they did not occur in the past. Even within the same film, we will often see elements occurring or repeated that were rare in reality. Yet, these films rarely meet these same critiques as the above games due to the fact that they tend to remain in the safe space of playing to established collective memory in which the same historical events are endlessly replayed by the same people.

This political utility of notions of accuracy seems as though it may be important to both the future of historical game studies and its meeting with classical receptions. For example, consider how many games represent ancient Rome as the multicultural society it in fact was? All too often, the ancient world is depicted as a myopically white past grounded in contemporary Western (particularly American) values and ideals. Inevitably, games representing the classical past will become drawn into these debates as innovative developers push against the boundaries of reductionist collective memory. Furthermore, the inherent intertextuality of games means that they will also often inherit problematic interpretations of the past from other media. The announcement trailer for *Assassin's Creed: Odyssey*, for example, displays an obvious tropic influence from the film version of Frank Miller's *300*. It remains to be seen if the game will also inherit the latter franchise's blatant orientalism. As such, whilst academic interest in games has been relatively successful in sidestepping unproductive debates about accuracy in favour of considering historical games on their own terms (rather than simply relatively irrelevant carriers of perfect immutable content), we may be forced to confront debates concerning accuracy in a different light if we are to truly examine the political work that the classical does in the world through these games.

These issues make accuracy an important concept beyond simply listing what popular games get wrong about the ancient world, instead considering the political context of patterns of representation. These contexts are important if we accept that history is never some kind of neutral, objective existent but a discourse rhetorically deployed in support of, and often responsible for forming, contemporary ideological positions. This is particularly apparent in Beavers' chapter analysing the depiction of gender in the Roman action game *Ryse*. This is particularly welcome due to the relative gap in the literature of historical game studies in terms of this topic and much needed, given that video games often have a regressive approach to the representation of gender. By showing how the game not only inadvertently reflects contemporary discourses concerning gender but also utilizes gendered identities and tropes in order to construct the historically themed world, characters and narrative offered by the game, the chapter emphasizes how history cannot be entirely separated from the cultural context in which it is constructed. Furthermore, given that many of the tropes the chapter identifies in *Ryse* serve particular ludonarratological functions and are also commonplace in other games, Beavers hints at the notion that the wider formal history of games as a medium likely holds some sway over how they approach the past.

This relationship can result in problematic depictions such as *Ryse*. However, changing formal conditions can also result in possibilities for more progressive approaches. For example, until relatively recently games with complex 3D representations tended to feature linear, relatively barren environments (well suited to the depiction of desolate battlefields and ruins and little else) due to the prohibitive cost, in both time and money, of producing these environments. However, swelling budgets and technological advancements have made the production of larger open-world environments much more commonplace in recent years. Such environments, needing interesting features to entice players into hours of travel and exploration, tend now to be filled with many settlements and characters. This has resulted in a move away from only depictions of military history and towards representations of many different types of historical places, people and practices, including representations of the fabric of everyday historical life. This is important for the representation of the ancient past for two reasons. First, this means a diversification of theme, with these games now including representations of different social and cultural aspects of life such as agriculture, religion, economics, leisure, travel, fashion, music and art (see, for example, *Assassin's Creed: Origins*). Second, this move towards open-worlds has also somewhat addressed the under-representation of women in historical games as female characters are increasingly included in order to believably populate these historical spaces. Of course, only including women when representing domestic or agricultural spheres of historical life ignores the fact that women were also affected by and part of politics, economics and warfare. Additionally, as Beavers demonstrates, the mere presence of female characters does not necessarily mean a historical game has any kind of serious or nuanced engagement with (historical or contemporary) gender identities, experiences or perspectives. As such, the ludonarratological functions of female characters must still be analysed in the manner that Beavers advocates. For example, the inclusion of female NPCs still far outweighs the presence of female playable characters, relegating women to only being subject *to* history (and one frequently depicted as determined only by men), rather than active subjects *within* history. Nonetheless, this trend towards environments with a wider historical focus is a positive one with potential to move games closer towards the broadened and inclusive perspectives on the past that social, cultural and gender history have promoted for the past few decades.

Like Beavers' chapter, Machado's piece similarly illustrates the importance of grounding our analyses in the context of the contemporary political and cultural landscape. Offering a deep analysis of two small cutscenes from within *Rome: Total War II*, the chapter demonstrates how the narrative interpretation espoused by these cutscenes (however unwittingly) taps into problematic far-right ideologies. This may be a case of the significance of this narrative not being well understood beyond Germany. However, this analysis points to the importance of identifying these problematic narratives in games, narratives that may find it more difficult to survive in other less neglected mainstream media due to critique (as Machado notes, this narrative has been eschewed by other forms of media). Furthermore, as the chapter argues, this is particularly pressing given the seemingly strong presence of alt-right ideology within contemporary games culture. Machado's approach is also laudable for its concentration on cutscenes, an important but often forgotten aspect of historical games. Though not gameplay, cutscenes are just as much a part of the inherently multimodal form of contemporary video games as their more active elements and, as Machado and others[19] note, can have an important ludological function. This attention is vindicated through Machado's analysis, which displays how even 90 seconds of cutscene from the game weaves together an alarmingly complex bricolage of historical meaning constituted from reference to both historiography and wider contemporary symbolic codes, texts and narratives. Beyond this, the chapter also displays the 'push and pull' between history and gameplay, an important feature of historical game design. Whilst it is often the violence visited upon history by games that is concentrated on, history as a thematic choice also places constraints on gameplay in return. The frequent complexity of this relationship is exemplified in the second cutscene Machado describes in which the game paradoxically both diverges from historical sources (depicting Varus as killed by Arminius) and simultaneously and unusually infringes upon player agency in service to history (making Varus' death inevitable despite player actions).

Each of these analyses remind us how contemporarily relevant popular cultural uses of the ancient past can be. Through these we gain a very real sense of the classics not as some static body of knowledge only to be preserved but as a living discourse with a role to play in our interpretation of ourselves and our contemporary world. In the combination of the past with new means of expression in an adaptive relationship to present needs, new forms of engagement with this past are opened up. The malleability of such processes can be interpreted as a curatorial nightmare to those interested in preserving a canon. But, paradoxically, these processes simultaneously demonstrate how these pasts, in this case classical history and myth, hold a contemporary utility that is part of what signifies them as something useful to preserve in the first place.

Production, consumption and people

Each of the aforementioned chapters have value in terms of understanding how we can approach history in games. However, some indicate a particularly important direction for future research. Machado's chapter is commendable not only for its consideration of the cutscene (and game level) itself and the sources that seem to inform its production, but also for its examination of the metadiscursive practices of reception beyond gameplay (in this case memes). Similarly, Nolden's chapter argues the importance of considering both player and developer activities and discussions if we are to understand the full relationship between a given game and the wider sociocultural discourses of history. So too, Serrano's chapter shows how even a brief consideration of practices such as modding, a liminal practice between both production and consumption, can offer insight into how the game form constructs (or is perceived to construct) historical authenticity. Importantly, Paprocki's chapter offers insight into an aspect of historical video game production that is rarely discussed in detail (though frequently invoked in marketing) – the role of the historical advisor.[20] Whilst *Apotheon*'s status as an indie game probably means an unusual amount of freedom for historical advisors in comparison to the AAA games industry, Paprocki's reflections on his role still offer excellent insights into the meetings between game form and historical content that must be negotiated in the production of all historical games. And, importantly, the chapter serves as an excellent example of the fact that the role of the historical advisor can extend far beyond being simply a 'fact checker' and instead include active participation in the development of the narrative world of the game. This also appears to encourage engagements with the past through more than simply material and narrative fidelity, moving, for example, towards the less tangible realm of ideas and culture in which contemporary academic history often operates – in *Apotheon*'s case, mythological uncertainty and ambiguity concerning the mortal status of deities.

These chapters raise an important point for the future of both historical game studies and classical receptions concerning video games. If all history is to some degree in service to the present, then the same must be doubly true of all studies of historiography. Alongside changes in mentalities, cultures and values, technologies of reception continually change the ways in which we construct, disseminate and receive history. This is very much apparent today, given that the last century or so has seen the greatest proliferation and diversification of forms that carry messages about the ancient past, including, of course, websites and video games. The specificities of contexts of reception that this suggests implies the need for studies of reception to move beyond considering only the material and textual and towards directly studying the actual people involved in production and reception and their discourses and practices – a luxury afforded to those of us who study contemporary receptions (in comparison to those who, for example, consider medieval receptions of the classics). Whilst the temptation to remain on safer methodological ground is admittedly significant, the advantages offered by empirical work on production/reception are significant. Historical game studies has been rather good at studying games as texts, but studies of the practices and perspectives of players or developers of historical games remain relatively rare. Classical receptions has been slightly better in this regard, with some scholars studying contemporary audiences of film/TV,[21] but still such studies remain rare. French and Gardner's chapter herein hints at the need for such studies, reminding us that history in games, and particularly a sense of authenticity, is not only constructed through images and words as in other historical media but in the gameplay actions that the text encourages or restricts. They also suggest that some gamers and critics seem to be critically engaging with the historical aspect of games, making accuracy and authenticity increasingly important components of the discursive relationship between industry and audience. We must be cautious of solidifying these broader theoretical notions without audience research. However, certainly the relationship between gameplay and authenticity is important and provides possible directions for such research. For instance, exploring if design structures such as open-worlds and avatar customizability do, indeed, make a difference to perceptions of authenticity as the author's suggest would seem to be a viable question for future empirical studies.

Luckily, the next generation of historical games scholars currently completing PhDs seem to have turned towards the kind of work that considers those that make, play and critique historical games alongside the games themselves and seem poised to publish valuable results. This empirical, ethnographic turn is particularly important to the meeting between historical game studies and classical receptions, given the high likelihood of intersubjectivity in results. Even if we dismiss the notion that reception is simultaneously an act of creation in film or literature, we cannot reject this notion in relation to the configurative game. This subjectivity makes studying the practices of players even more important. So too, as Machado's work implies, when considering a medium so inherently tied to online culture, studying metadiscursive practices such as forum discussions, memes and modding can offer useful insights. Furthermore, if, indeed, the political context of these games is important, understanding the discourses and practices of production are important in a form maturing during late capitalism. Even the vast proliferation of sources available to developers to draw from increases the complexity of understanding contemporary production. Speaking directly to those working in the industry, whilst often difficult (particularly because of legal restraints such as NDAs), can offer data valuable to unpicking these tangles. Accordingly, if we are to truly understand the role of games in the complex cycles of historical exchange that constitute collective memory of the ancient world, the move towards empirical study of stakeholders in production and reception is necessary.

(Ludo)narrative as form

Thus far, we have considered form in terms of the video game's capabilities for historical representation. But form has another important aspect within the discourses of historiography and the philosophy of history. Narrative, the primary cultural resource by which we generally explore the past beyond archaeological evidence and re-enactment (and, arguably, simple chronologies), is also an important form that constitutes historical content. Indeed, much has been written about this intrinsic relationship in the past few decades. Game studies has, in the past, had a fairly ambivalent perspective on narrative. The so-called ludology vs narratology debate in the early days of the field has frequently been somewhat overblown and many adept narrativist approaches to games now exist.[22] However, it is certainly also possible to consider games otherwise, leaving aside their narrative aspect. This is not a luxury, however, that those concerned with history in games can really afford. If history is to all intents and purposes a particular kind of narrative, then 'the idea that historical digital games are in some way working as and/or in relation to narrative is too useful a perspective to be excluded'.[23] Given the aforementioned need to simultaneously remained focused on the game form, this means that what Ryan calls a 'functional ludo-narrativism'[24] seems to be the best approach. As Kapell and Elliott eloquently put it in the introduction to their *Playing with the Past* anthology (a significant publication in historical game studies), 'for narratologists the point is about the story while for ludologists the "play's the thing". In digital games that begin from within a historical narrative, however, the thing is the play within the narrative'.[25] The function and structure of narrative in historical games can be approached from a broader formalist perspective.[26] However, yet again, focusing on the specifics of classical history allows an opportunity to consider such questions anew. Indeed, classics seems a particularly suitable lens to explore questions concerning the relationship between narrative, history and games given the discipline's inherent concentration on literary sources and storytelling and the vast knowledge that this has generated.

Flegler's chapter examining narrative in *Age of Empires* takes a broader view but points to the importance of considering the player in the construction of narrative and historical meaning – applicable, no matter the historical content considered. This configurative aspect of games (making them subject to the behaviour of their players), which has no easy parallel in other forms of history, means a frequent difficulty or at least multiplicity in terms of interpreting these texts. Indeed, this aspect goes beyond even the subjectivities, already complex, in the interpretative textual analysis of other media forms. Flegler, by examining the lack of cavalry available to the Aztec faction in *Age of Empires*, also points to another form of tension between the conventional understanding of the narrative form and purpose of history and the kind of history that games have popularized (though it certainly precedes them): the tension between providing explanations of what *did* happen in the past (and therefore inhibiting player agency) or instead providing a system in which players can make decisions that engage arguments about what *could* have happened. In the case that Flegler examines, the designers decided to prioritize what did happen, though even within the same game there are plenty of examples that use the contrary approach. Such examples not only highlight the kind of questions about the uses of and approaches to the past that games make pressing, but also the importance of gleaning insight into design decisions and the motivations behind them.

Comparatively narrowing the focus somewhat, the potential of using classical receptions to consider history and narrative in games is demonstrated by Travis' chapter. This chapter argues that the ludonarrative form in some games, particularly those that emphasize player's authorial agency (a structure also key to Clare's chapter), can echo that of the classical bardic oral epic tradition. Such arguments are important because they restrict overly sharp distinctions between games and other previous forms of history or mnemonic tool. This contextualizes the possibilities of the game form through a particular kind of historicism. Furthermore, Travis' discussion of in-game lore in these games (e.g. the books that players can read) highlights that the relationship between games and history is not only isolatable to games' reuse of particular existing historical themes but also in their very treatment of history as a practice and concept (even if this history relates only to the events of fantasy universes). Nolden's chapter on the topic of MMORPG *The Secret World* emphasizes a similar point. Even ostensibly non-historical games can be important in terms of their relationship to broader cultural discourses and patterns involving the mythologizing and construction of history and collective memory. This relationship can also be seen in the player dynamics that games can support or encourage. Webber, for example, has argued that though *EVE Online* is a science fiction-themed MMO game, the hierarchical structures, propaganda and tendency towards mythologizing their own pasts of some player factions bear a relation to wider cultural uses of history and more specifically to some patterns of behaviour found in the medieval past.[27] Webber's, Nolden's and Travis' work imply the need to move beyond considering only games with overt thematic connections to the past. Furthermore, Travis' analysis explores the particular relations between narratively charged gameplay and historical forms of storytelling through the lens of a particular studio's (Bethesda) oeuvre. Accordingly, whilst his conclusions have broader implications (and certainly other RPGs with similar ludonarrative structures would also seem to fit within this argument), this chapter also hints at the need for the consideration of production patterns and processes in order to understand the relationship between classics and video games.

Considering why certain ludonarrative design patterns reoccur is a fruitful form of investigation in this regard. For example, Linderoth, in his article 'Superheroes, Greek Gods and Sports Stars', explores why narratives of empowerment (and powerful player-characters) are overwhelmingly preferred by contemporary games.[28] He concludes that these narrative choices occur because they provide convenient diegetic explanations for the 'improved abilities'[29] mechanics – for example, think of 'levelling-up' in RPGs – that are prevalent in contemporary games (Flegler's chapter also briefly considers this issue of narrative explanations for power in *Age of Empires*). This, alongside the relatively widespread presence of classical history in collective memory, may partly explain why classical myths, epics and characters remain such a draw for games. So, too, the formal demands of games (and contemporary narrative) exert a pressure on not only the selection of this content but the way in which it manifests. Paprocki's chapter, for example, notes how the generally accepted immortality of the Greek gods must be to some degree questioned for them to function as typical video game bosses. Such tensions are not necessarily negative and can produce interesting results. In this case, as Paprocki describes, interrogating the very notion of godhood may reflect an ancient *mentalité* that perhaps was not widely, overtly held but that certainly seems readable in the sources, where it is made paradoxically present by its very suppression and fringe status.

Identifying such patterns of representation and attempting to contextualize them through reference to both the internal formal structures of games and external forces applied to them (e.g. political contexts, economic pressures, intertextual relations) is important. Classical video games, like all historical games, are a large group bound only by investment in a common (though similarly diverse) theme. In reality, this thematic category contains many different design patterns and playful activities. And yet there are identifiable trends in the ways in which the industry has approached the ancient past. Comparing the representation of this specific past to others that feature in games draws out the particular properties of this engagement. For example, the relationship between myth and history in video games seems an important topic in relation to history in games, but particularly in relation to games with classical themes.

In such games, it is common to see myth and history intertwined. That is to say that the historical societies and the mythical stories that emerged from these societies become merged into one diegetic world. This, however, is much more uncommon in relation to other historical periods represented in games. Of course, each historical society had its own *mentalité*, including some kind of mythic or spiritual cultural layer that played a role in forming, negotiating and sustaining this outlook. However, rarely does this perspective become a tangible part of the historical virtual world the player is confronted with. For example, many games deal with the European Middle Ages. However, it would be relatively unusual within such games to see, for instance, a depiction of the Christian god bestowing powers on the player-character as an explanation for their exceptionalism, or for the player-character to have the ability to call for aid from a host of angels. Whilst discussions can be had about whether religious or spiritual views in the past have always been universally held in good faith, certainly the possibility of the miraculous and the reliance (or at least the performance of reliance) on God's will for desired outcomes seem to have been an important part of medieval societies. Yet, this mythos rarely becomes actualized as a perceivable part of the diegetic world in the way it frequently does in games with classical themes. This may be partly due to the perceived 'limits of play', i.e. the fact that games seem to have a particular tendency to trigger controversy when including sensitive themes.[30] Whilst Christianity is obviously still a belief system that holds political and cultural significance in many contemporary markets, adherents to ancient religions are naturally few and far between. Thus, including these elements in a game seems less likely to cause offence (though, as the neo-pagan respondent in Paprocki's chapter offended at *Apotheon*'s deicide makes clear, this is not impossible). This may therefore simply be an issue of cultural distance. However, it is also interesting that classical mythology is such a prominent part of video games when this has arguably not been the case with cinema. Lowe, for example, notes Hollywood's relative reluctance to portray pagan gods such as the Olympian pantheon, adding that this may arise from anti-blasphemy laws.[31] As such, this might be a simple issue of timing (though notably contemporary films, such as *Troy*, still exclude overtly mythical elements), with video games reaching prominence at a time when such issues are considered much less provocative in central markets for these products. And yet, it is also possible that this is a ludonarrative (and thus formal) issue. As noted, classical myth provides diegetic explanations for game mechanics that are at least somewhat recognizable to many players. This may explain why classical themes and Asian and Viking history/mythology (the other settings in which the two are frequently intertwined) currently seem to be such popular choices for the contemporary games industry. However, this may also be a process of exoticization or othering, emphasizing the difference of historical worlds and in doing so emphasizing the attraction of escape into a virtual world quite unlike one's own.

Certainly, this weaving of myth and history within classically themed games is worthy of note and points to the paradoxical dualities of popular engagement with the ancient past. On the one hand, the mythical beasts and vindictive gods of the ancient world signify exotic difference (even if only in terms of perception or worldview), working in relation to the sense of the ancient world as alien described in Serrano's chapter. On the other hand, the classical past is an important part of the problematically reductionist grand narrative of inevitable Western progress and within this represents high ideals and the march towards *rationality*. As this implies, this pattern of representation raises a series of interesting questions. More comprehensive research is needed to begin to provide concrete answers, but this example shows the potential of considering ludonarrative patterns of representation in classical games. Furthermore, this aspect of classical history in games only becomes apparent in the context of the broader relationships between history and games and classical receptions in other media. Paprocki's chapter similarly reinforces the potential benefits of considering such relationships. His insights into the development of *Apotheon* imply that the reuse of myth in new forms not only reflects a continuation of the inherently transmedial nature of these storyworlds but may also encourage us to explore these myths from new perspectives. For example, to extend the temporal confines of the storyworld into the post-mythological for the game, Paprocki and his colleagues had to seek the very essence of the original myths (considering the *mythos*, *topos* and *ethos*) to ensure a sense of cohesion and the maintenance of an internal narrative logic between the game and the sources on which it is based. As this indicates, it is perfectly possible that history and myth may not only have utility to games, but that the act of transposition into new forms may offer new insights or ways of thinking about the past in return. Each of these issues interrogating the fusing of classical history, myth and games indicates why the meeting of classical receptions and historical game studies is such a potentially fruitful one.

Playing the past into the future

If these two fields are to continue this meeting, what challenges and possibilities is the future likely to hold for both as the video game form continues its maturation? Certainly, both fields must continue to develop approaches that account for the multiple ways in which classical content can be used by games, players and developers; the relationship and tensions between the game form and this content; and the intertextual meeting of contents generated and negotiated in different formal, economic and cultural conditions for differing purposes. Such approaches will naturally be informed by our own interests and criteria as to value as historians, historiographers and classicists – most likely involving some kind of interest in the possibility of players learning about the past through games. However, it must also prize examination of the work, good or bad, that historical games do in the 'wilds' of popular culture unprompted by academia. We must aim to understand how history is used in games in relation to gameplay, how this makes meaning about the past or (like all history) is used to make meaning about the politicized world in which we live. To understand what these games mean to those that play them and how they are used for a wide array of practices by these players. And to examine games not only as tools but as active and malleable stories that are weaved into the lives, power structures and mnemonic practices of contemporary culture in the way in which the stories of the ancient world were weaved into theirs. Ultimately, therefore, our aim should be not only to understand the possibilities and restrictions of this new form for historical representation but also to understand what these games mean as a node in the networks of cultural exchange that perhaps best answer the question 'what is history?'

One of the greatest opportunities offered by games is their capacity for popular enfranchisement. Games can offer structured, approachable popular access to historical practices, such as re-enactment or experimentation with historical narrative and counterfactual history, that were previously overwhelming, exclusive or simply unavailable.[32] In the contemporary higher education landscape, in which history and classics are increasingly beleaguered in the face of marketplace pressures, the naturally engaging nature of games and these possibilities for enfranchisement stand to become increasingly important. Like film before, games may help to garner interest in the past that is vital for the survival of our disciplines in their current form. Significant effort is expended in the public sphere to make history engaging. Games' playful possibilities to be both historical and often fun should therefore not remain undertheorized. Of course, caution is also necessary. Fun, for example, does not necessarily mean good learning. However, nor should we, in our search to defensively emphasize games as a serious historical form, underestimate their playful, irreverent and engaging aspects.

Such potential for engagement, however, must not thwart critique. It is tempting to race to include historical games in curricula to capture the attention of students. However, thoughtful and nuanced work by scholars such as McCall has shown that, whilst this holds potential, there are a number of issues that must be considered and a number of assumptions reconsidered (e.g. 'all students will enjoy games!') – not the least of which is the significant labour and logistical concerns that this involves when done properly.[33] However, there is an acute need to teach students how to effectively *critique* games. After formal education, most people will learn about history mostly through popular sources. Given their popularity, games are becoming a likely cultural tool in this regard. As aforementioned, the form of games holds significant differences in its ludological structuring of narrative and the shared authorship this implies. It therefore seems vital to teach students how to reflect effectively on the history that they will receive through games. To learn to consider the meeting of form and historical content, as well as the economic, political and cultural context of representation in the game form, in the ways that the chapters contained herein do.

The popularity of historical games means that they are a form of popular history that is here to stay. We are already arguably entering the second (or even third) decade of games significantly engaging with the past on a mass scale. As such, a historicist approach to reception will become increasingly important. This is a natural part of classical receptions and one from which historical game studies will have to learn. As historical games increasingly have their own history of use in contemporary culture, examining reception not as some abstract unchanging process but as a practice with particular historical contexts will become increasingly important. How might uses of the classics in games of the 1990s (a time of economic boom and one in which the liberal capitalist 'end of history' narrative was at its height), differ from those of the post-9/11 War on Terror geopolitics and recessions of the first decade of the twenty-first century?[34] This particular question may well prove to be an intellectual dead end. But the broader need to view history in games not as some kind of static thematic unit with a static demographic of reception but instead to historicize reception itself will inevitably come to be important. Classical receptions and medievalism here offer a wealth of methodological and theoretical precedents from which historical game studies must learn.

Alongside these changing cultural contexts of reception, certain economic and technological conditions of the games industry seem poised to affect the relationship between history and games. Holter et al.'s chapter, for example, argues the significance of game engines in terms of streamlining development. This is its own kind of enfranchisement in that it has massively increased the accessibility of games development and is partly responsible for the booming indie market. Holter et al.'s chapter focuses on the implications of this in another way, demonstrating how the relationship between games and history is far from unidirectional and historians and archaeologists stand to benefit from using game engines as tools for scholarship. However, this is also a carefully reflective analysis and the authors highlight the way that assumptions, approximations and simplifications are part of these engines, primarily designed for representation and playful activity rather than scientific modelling. As they put it, the game engines cannot 'recreate *the* historical situation'. As this implies, these technologies are not neutral. They have their own history of development and biases. Identifying these aspects, as the authors note, is therefore an important direction for future research and yet again emphasizes the ways in which form must be considered to truly understand content.

Holter et al.'s description of their project also brings us to another important development with the capacity to affect the relationship between games and history. Virtual reality, whilst still not quite the mainstream product it has long sought to be, is an increasing presence in the contemporary market. Again, here we can learn from the digital humanists, classicists and archaeologists that have already invested significant interest in how such technologies might work in relation to the visualization and dissemination of history and heritage. Such technologies have ludic implications in relation to communicating historical visual data and in terms of supporting historical practices such as re-enactment (as Holter et al.'s chapter implies, though not conceptualizing their project in these terms). However, VR technology also seems likely to introduce new means of establishing problematic yet marketable authority and reinforcing naïve epistemologies of authenticity. As this implies, and Holter et al. discuss, this renews the need to ask questions concerning how best to represent rather than sublimate uncertainty in these realistic and increasingly immersive virtual 3D spaces. The authors provide some useful suggestions in relation to their Pnyx simulation. However, such questions are also important to ask of mainstream games despite their reluctance in this regard due to the market utility of offering allegedly 'complete' and 'accurate' representations of the past. As Holter et al.'s arguments imply, the very interactivity and open-endedness of games offers some possible solutions, allowing for different interpretations to be experienced according to input from users. Similarly, the possibility of experiencing differing interpretations within the same game, even if proscribed by the developer, seems to offer possibilities. But in this aspect the industry seems wedded to the linear and cohesive narrative worlds built in cinema and much historical writing. In a sense, the counterfactual possibilities mainstream strategy games offer[35] can tap into this same capability by shifting the authorial role dramatically towards the player. But even this is somewhat restrained by the fixed internal logic, both interpretative and algorithmic, of such systems. Increasingly however, the move towards design as play in some games (which allow players to construct levels or kinds of gameplay) is becoming accepted by many players. One can see how this might offer a potential solution that allows the kind of experimental and comparative experiences offered by the Pnyx project to filter into mainstream play. This, in itself, though, has significant barriers in order to be productive – for example, the shift of methodological responsibility to players introduces a whole new raft of issues and would require significant support. Nonetheless, it is immediately apparent from this discussion how any technological change (and in the industry these are rapid and many) opens up both new possibilities and problems for the relationship between history and games, thereby implying the need for extra consideration in critical analysis.

The growth of the indie market and online digital distribution platforms also seem likely to be important market and technological trends, having already resulted in a proliferation and diversification of historical games. Games are increasingly stepping outside of the design templates established by the mainstream industry to find new historical themes, perspectives and gameplay. This growth also allows for smaller markets to be served, including those players with a particular interest in history. Increasingly, we are seeing games willing to sacrifice aspects of gameplay long held to be sacrosanct in order to offer a fuller historical experience (whatever they may determine this to be). Some of these games have run enormously successful *Kickstarter* campaigns. For example, *War of Rights*, a multiplayer FPS game set during the American Civil War and billed as a hyperrealistic and historically accurate representation of the conflict, has had over USD$800,000 pledged by interested gamers at the time of writing. The enthusiasm with which this and similar games heavily investing in their historical aspect have been received by some communities of players does seem to imply a desire to see games push the boundaries of the gameplay and history intersection. If this interest continues, it may well determine what kind of historical experiences and representations we see becoming a regular part of games.

Whatever the future holds for the relationship between games and history, it would appear that the two will remain entwined. It also seems likely that classical history and myth, alongside the Second World War and the Middle Ages, will remain a firm favourite historical setting for both industry and players. Why these settings in particular have proved so popular is probably in part due to the relative prominence of these periods in contemporary collective memory. But, it is also likely because these settings offer particular utility to the peculiarities of the game form. Investigating these relationships between form and historical content alongside the economic, cultural and political contexts of both production and reception is admittedly no small task. But it is a necessary one if we are to understand the role that the hugely popular medium of games plays in our contemporary engagements with the past. And, anyway, this is business as usual for classical receptions. But, the field, or at least those elements of it interested in games, now finds another fellow traveller in historical game studies. So, *quo vadis* historical game studies and classical receptions? The answer must be forward together with an intersubjective approach that allows historical game studies to learn from the broader implications that the deep focus on the minutiae of particular content and contexts of reception within classical receptions may reveal. And in return, for classical receptions to learn from the formal specificities of historical game studies and its broad concern with games as a mode of expression for history. If the chapters in this volume signify something about this relationship, it would appear to be that it seems poised to continue to fruitfully explore the latest way that we humans, ever the playful animals, have found to play with our past.

Notes

1 Chapman, Foka and Westin (2016: 362). See this publication for an overview of the historical game studies field.
2 E.g., see the 'Historical Game Studies Network' group on Facebook and, for those who understand German, see also, 'AKGWDS Geschichte & Digitale Spiele' (similarly, on Facebook) and the website https://gespielt.hypotheses.org/.
3 Reinhard (2018).
4 E.g. Pötzsch and Šisler (2016).
5 Chapman (2016).
6 McCall (2011).
7 Champion (2015).
8 Chapman (2013b).
9 Christesen and Machado (2010: 107).
10 Lowe (2009: 71).
11 Chapman (2012).
12 Ibid.: 42.
13 Ibid. (2016: 30–58, 119–72).
14 Ibid.: 173–230.
15 Linderoth (2015).
16 Poblocki (2002) and Apperley (2013).
17 Jenkins (2008).
18 Munslow (2007).
19 Klevjer (2002).
20 See also Rollinger (2018).
21 Potter (2013).
22 Frasca (2003).
23 Chapman (2016: 21).
24 Ryan (2006: 203).
25 Kapell and Elliott (2013a: 19).
26 Chapman (2016: 119–72).

27 Webber (2016). See also, Rollinger in this volume, particularly pp. 24–5 with n. 13–14.
28 Linderoth (2013).
29 Björk and Holopainen (2004: 174).
30 Chapman and Linderoth (2015).
31 Lowe (2009: 79 n.).
32 Chapman (2016).
33 McCall (2016).
34 Rollinger (2015) actually takes such an approach and investigates the relationship between Reagonomics and city-building games with classical themes.
35 Chapman (2016: 173–97, 230–63).

Glossary of Video Game Terms

4X games From 'eXplore, eXpand, eXploit, eXterminate'; also known as 'grand strategy games'; focused on the simulation of politico-military processes; players 'rule' nation-states, empires or civilizations and attempt world domination.

AAA games Also 'triple A'; high-budget, multiplatform games marketed to a mass audience; the video game equivalent to a 'Hollywood blockbuster'.

AI Artificial intelligence; in the context of video games, the software and algorithms that govern the responses of computer-controlled enemies to player input.

Avatar The visual depiction of the player within the gamescape.

Boss Gamer jargon term for a high-level enemy the player has to defeat.

Casual games Games that can be played without the player paying too much attention and that typically do not involve either an overarching narrative or character development (e.g. *Candy Crush*).

CRPG Computer role-playing game; a role-playing game played on a computer.

cutscene Also, 'cinematic'; cinematic sequence within a video game that serves to set up a scene or advance the narrative by emplotment.

DLC Downloadable content; additional content for video games, ranging from extras such as new graphics (e.g. clothing for avatar; 'skins') or special effects, to new units (e.g. military units in strategy games), to expansion packs providing new narrative elements or levels.

Emergent play As opposed to narrative play; describes games wherein the player is not limited to following a specific narrative but rather is at freedom to explore and interact with the game world; specific gameplay is thus a consequence of player action.

Expansion pack Additional content for video games; mostly building on the original game and providing the reader with a new story, new missions or new maps.

FPS First-person shooter, also 'shooter' or 'shoot 'em up'; video game genre mostly set in military contexts; casts the player as soldier or warrior who has to fight their way through 'maps'.

Game engine Software controlling both graphics and rules of the game itself.

Gamescape The visual representation of a video game's universe.

Gating A process used by game designers to (temporarily) limit players and player characters to a certain narrative or geographic sections of the gamescape; can consist of either an in-game structure (i.e. a 'physical' gate) or a limitation in player abilities (difficulty levels).

Hack-and-slash Arguably a subgenre of action-adventure games; mostly focused on close-up fighting; often set in medieval or fantasy realms, hence the name.

HUD Heads-up display; a method of providing information to the player by displaying it on screen.

Let's play A genre of YouTube videos; players record their gameplay of video games
for others to watch, sometimes while providing a running commentary; frequently
used as playing aids by players who encounter difficulties in the game.

level-up A term used to describe the process of achieving progress within a game;
mostly refers to avatars in RPGs or MMORPGs; progression ('levelling-up')
through this level scale provides the player with additional abilities.

MMO/MMORPG Massively multiplayer online game/Massively multiplayer online
role-playing game; the latter is a role-playing game that allows interaction and play
with thousands or tens of thousands of human players simultaneously present in
the gamescape.

mod/modding The process of modifying a published game by changing its internal
components from graphical elements to the game's programming code; modding
is a form of player–game interaction that has grown in popularity and is
particularly commonplace in historical video games, where mods can reflect
different approaches to 'playing' history.

Nonlinear gameplay A type of gameplay, wherein player decision determines the
outcome of events, in contrast to narrative-focused gameplay.

NPC Non-player character; a character within a game that is controlled by the game's
AI; in contrast to a 'PC', a character or avatar within a game that is controlled by a
human player.

open world See 'sandbox game'.

Quest A term used mostly in RPGs/MMORPGs to describe a specific mission within
the game.

Quick time event In action/action-adventure games, a sequence within a fight that is
a mixture between playing and watching a cutscene; typically, the player's control
possibilities are limited to pushing a number of buttons on the gamepad in an
indicated sequence, in order to produce a cinematic event.

Rage quit The act of angrily quitting a game out of frustration; frequently
accompanied by screaming, hurling drinks and/or snacks, and the occasional
smashing of keyboards and/or computer mice; 'ragequit' has also become a
cultural meme.

RPG Role-playing game; in contrast to action-adventures, with which RPGs are
closely related, role-playing games focus on character development and allows
players to completely immerse themselves in a gameworld.

RTS Real-time strategy; simulations of military conflict, typically as tactical battles; in
contrast to round-based strategy, RTS sees events play out live.

Sandbox game Also 'open world game'; a genre of action/action-adventure games
whose gamescape is not limited to depicting those geographical areas relevant to
the prime narrative; instead, it provides players with a developed and populated
world that they are at complete liberty to explore.

Serious games A relatively new genre of games that attempts to combine
entertainment and 'serious' engagement or didactic benefits; often found in the
context of historical video games.

Skill tree Akin to 'tech tree'; a mostly linear process of attaining additional
capabilities in RPGs by 'levelling-up', wherein skills mostly build on each other.

Skin The visual appearance of an avatar or an NPC.

Tech tree Also 'technology tree'; a visual representation of cultural, industrial and economic progress, mostly used in the context of strategy games; individual 'technologies' (which can encompass a wide variety of elements) build on each other and thus have to be 'researched' or 'achieved' in a linear fashion.

XP Experience points; used to measure progress in 'levelling-up'.

Bibliography

Aarseth, E. (1997) *Cybertext: Perspectives on Ergodic Literature*, Baltimore, MD: Johns Hopkins University Press.

Aarseth, E. (2001) 'Computer Game Studies, Year One', *Game Studies*, 1 (1). Available at: http://gamestudies.org/0101/editorial.html (accessed 23 June 2018).

Aarseth, E. (2012) '*Ad Ludum!* The study of games from the Colosseum to the computer', in T. S. Thorsen (ed.), *Greek and Roman Games in the Computer Age*, 11–23, Trondheim: Akademika Publishing.

Adams, A. (2013) 'Needs met through role-playing games: A fantasy theme analysis of Dungeons & Dragons', *Kaleidoscope*, 12: 69–86.

Adams, E. (2010) *Fundamentals of Game Design: 2nd Edition*, Berkeley, CA: New Riders.

aero916 (2009) 'anyone else feel this way? Thread', *The Secret World, English Forum*, 21.09.2009. Available at: http://bit.ly/2FdXMpO (accessed 25 January 2018).

Age of Empires (1997) *Age of Empires User Manual*. Available at: http://ftp.ubi.com/emea/kol/manuels/UK/Age_Of_Empire_Collector/Age_Of_Empire1/Manual_AOE1.pdf (accessed 25 October 2018).

Agnew, V. (2007) 'History's affective turn: Historical reenactment and its work in the present', *Rethinking History: The Journal of Theory and Practice*, 11 (3): 299–312.

Aguado Cantabrana, O. (forthcoming) 'Screening the face of Roman battle: Violence from the eye of the soldier in film', in *Imagines V. The Fear and the Fury: Ancient Violence in Modern Imagination*, London: Bloomsbury.

Aguado-Cantrabana, O. and Etxeberria Gallestegi, E. (2016) '*Veni, lusi, vinci*: el "rostro de la batalla" en Roma y la Edad Media a través de los videojuegos', in J. M. Jiménez, I. Mugueta and G. F. Rodriguez (eds), *Historia y videojuegos*, 105–22, Murcia: Centro de Estudios Medievales de la Universidad de Murcia-Ed.

Ahl, D. H. (1973) *101 BASIC Computer Games*, New York: Workman Publishing. Available at: https://annarchive.com/files/Basic_Computer_Games_Microcomputer_Edition.pdf (accessed 6 November 2018).

Alhabash, S. and Wise, K. (2014) 'Playing their game: Changing stereotypes of Palestinians and Israelis through videogame play', *New Media & Society*, 17 (8): 1358–76.

Anders, A. (2015) 'The "Face of Roman Skirmishing"', *Historia*, 64: 263–300.

Anderson, M. (2004) 'Computer games and archaeological reconstruction: The low-cost VR', in K. Fischer-Ausserer, W. Börner, M. Goriany and L. Karlhuber Vöckl (eds), *Enter the Past: The E-Way into the Four Dimensions of Cultural Heritage: CAA 2003, Proceedings of the 31st Annual Conference on Computer Applications and Quantitative Methods in Archaeology*, 521–24, Oxford: Archaeopress.

Anderson, M. (2008) 'Putting the "reality" in virtual reality: New advances through game engine technology', in A. Posluschny, K. Lambers and I. Herzog (eds), *Layers of Perception: Proceedings of the 35th International Conference on Computer Applications and Quantitative Methods in Archaeology (CAA), Berlin, Germany, April 2–6, 2007*, 144, Bonn: Rudolf Habelt.

André, L.-N. (2016) *Game of Rome: Ou l'Antiquité vidéoludique*, Paris: Éditions Passage.

André, L.-N. and Lécole-Solnychkine, S. (2008) 'La réference à l'antique dans les jeux vidéo: Paysages et structures mythologiques', in H. Ter Minassian and S. Rufat (eds), *Construire les jeux vidéo comme objet de recherche*, 88–102, Paris: Éditions Questions Théoriques, diffusion Vrin.

André, L.-N. and Lécole-Solnychkine, S. (2013) 'L'Antiquité vidéoludique, une résurrection virtuelle?', *Nouvelle Revue d'Esthétique*, 11: 87–98.

Andreoli, R., De Chiara, R., Erra, U. and Scarano, V. (2005) 'Interactive 3D environments by using videogame engines', in *Ninth International Conference on Information Visualisation (IV'05)*, 515–20. Doi: 10.1109/IV.2005.64.

Andreoli, R., De Chiara, R., Erra, U., Iannaccone, A., La Greca, F. and Scarano, V. (2006) 'Some real experiences in developing virtual environments', in *Tenth International Conference on Information Visualisation (IV'06)*, 545–52. Doi: 10.1109/IV.2006.98.

Andreoli, R., De Chiara, R., Erra, U., Scarano, V., Pontrandolfo, A., Rizzo, M. L. and Santoriello, A. (2007) 'An interactive 3D reconstruction of a funeral in Andriuolo's Necropolis in Paestum', in A. Figueiredo and G. Leite Velho (eds), *The World is in Your Eyes: CAA2005, Computer Applications and Quantitative Methods in Archaeology. Proceedings of the 33rd Conference, Tomar, March 2005*, 51–4, Tomar: CAA Portugal.

Anon. (1987) 'Review of Annals of Rome, 1987 PSS. Programmed by A. D. Boyse and J. G. Langdale-Brown', *ZZAP!64* (10 December). Available at: http://www.gamebase64. com/oldsite/gameofweek/33/gotw_annalsofrome.htm (accessed 6 November 2018).

Antunes, M. (2013) 'Building blocks of sandbox and open world games: Eve, GTA and Minecraft', *Gaming Development* (2 January). Available at: https://gamedevelopment. tutsplus.com/articles/building-blocks-of-sandbox-and-open-world-games-eve-gta-minecraft--gamedev-3016 (accessed 25 July 2018).

Apperley, T. (2013) 'Modding the historians' code: Historical verisimilitude and the counterfactual imagination', in M. W. Kapell and A. B. R. Elliott (eds), *Playing with the Past: Digital Games and the Simulation of History*, 185–98, London: Bloomsbury.

Arbeitskreis (2016) 'Manifest: Updated version 1.1 – für geschichtswissenschaftliches Arbeiten mit Digitalen Spielen!', *Arbeitskreis Geschichtswissenschaft und Digitale Spiele* (20 September). Available at: https://gespielt.hypotheses.org/manifest_v1-1 (accessed 4 May 2019).

Ariensky Crowley (2012) 'Help us find the Ultor temple. Thread', *The Secret World, English Forum*, 10.09.2012. Available at: http://bit.ly/2DD76Xg (accessed 24 January 2018).

Aristopoulos, M. (2017) 'A portfolio of recombinant compositions for the videogame *Apotheon*', PhD thesis, City, University of London.

Assmann, A. (2010) *Erinnerungsräume. Formen und Wandlungen des kulturellen Gedächtnisses*, München: C. H. Beck.

Ayers, E. L. (1999) *The Pasts and Futures of Digital History*, Charlottesville, VA: University of Virginia. Available at: http://www.vcdh.virginia.edu/Pastsfutures.html (accessed 16 June 2018).

Axel Denar (2010) 'The Seal of Solomon and Pentacle of the Moon: Thread', *The Secret World, English Forum*, 20.02.2010. Available at: http://bit.ly/2F70yx3 (accessed 23 January 2018).

Bakogianni, A. (2016) 'What is so "classical" about Classical Reception?', *Codex. Revista de Estudo Clássicos*, 4 (1): 96–113.

Barnard, J. (2017) *Empire of Ruin: Black Classicism and American Imperial Culture*, Oxford: Oxford University Press.

Bartle, R. A. (1996) '"Hearts, Clubs, Diamonds, Spades": Players who suit MUDs'. Available at: http://bit.ly/2hizlh3 (accessed 8 August 2018).

Bartle, R. A. (2006) *Designing Virtual Worlds* [=Repr. 2004], Berkeley, CA: New Riders.

Barton, M. (2008) *Dungeons and Desktops: The History of Computer Role-Playing Games*, Wellesley, MA: Taylor & Francis.

Bauckhage, C. (2012) 'Insights into internet memes', in *Proceedings of the Fifth International Conference on Weblogs and Social Media*, Barcelona, 42–9, Menlo Park, CA: AAAI Press.

Beavers, S. (2017) Game-Based Learning, Institute of Educational Technology, Open University. Available at: https://iet.open.ac.uk/people/sian.beavers#biography (accessed 26 November 2018).

Beigel, T. (2013) 'With your shield or on it: The gender of heroism in Zack Snuder's *300* and Rudolph Maté's *The 300 Spartans*', in A.-B. Renger and J. Solomon (eds), *Ancient Worlds in Film and Television: Gender and Politics*, 65–78, Leiden and Boston, MA: Brill.

Bembeneck, E. J. (2013) 'Phantasm of Rome: Video games and cultural identity', in M. W. Kapell and A. B. R. Elliott (eds), *Playing with the Past: Digital Games and the Simulation of History*, 77–90, London: Bloomsbury.

Ben-Menahem, Y. (2016) 'If counterfactuals were excluded from historical reasoning . . .', *Journal of the Philosophy of History*, 10 (3): 370–81.

Bender, S. (2012) *Virtuelles Erinnern. Kriege des 20. Jahrhunderts in Computerspielen*, Bielefeld: transcript Verlag.

Berger, F. (1996) *Kalkriese 1. Die römischen Fundmünzen*, Mainz: Verlag Philipp von Zabern.

Berti, I. and García Morcillo, M. (2008) 'Introduction: Does Greece – and the cinema – need another Alexander?', in I. Berti and M. García Morcillo (eds), *Hellas on Screen: Cinematic Receptions of Ancient History, Literature and Myth*, 9–20, Stuttgart: Franz Steiner Verlag.

Betts, E. (2017) 'Afterword: Towards a methodology for Roman sensory studies', in E. Betts (ed.), *Senses of Empire: Multisensory Approaches to Roman Culture*, 193–9, London: Routledge.

Bevc, T. (2008) 'Gesellschaft und Geschichte in Computerspielen', *Einsichten und Perspektiven* 01/2008. Available at: http://www.blz.bayern.de/publikation/einsichten-und-perspektiven-12008.html (accessed 7 October 2018).

Bhabha, H. (1999) 'The other question: The stereotype and colonial discourse', in J. Evans and S. Hall (eds), *Visual Culture: A Reader*, 370–8, London: Sage.

Björk, S. and Holopainen, J. (2004) *Patterns in Game Design*, Boston, MA: Charles River Media.

Black, J. (2008) *What If? Counterfactualism and the Problem of History*, London: Social Affairs Unit.

Blakely, S. (2018) 'Sailing with the gods: Serious games in an ancient sea', *thersites*, 7: 107–53.

Blanshard, A. and Shahabudin, K. (2011) 'Greek history on screen: The 300 Spartans', in A. Blanshard and K. Shahabudin (eds), *Classics on Screen: Ancient Greece and Rome on Film*, 100–24, Bristol: Bristol Classical Press.

Blanton, V. (2005) '"Don't worry, I won't let them rape you"', *Arthuriana*, 15 (3): 91–111.

Bleicken, J. (1995) *Die athenische Demokratie*, Paderborn: Schöningh.

Bogost, I. (2006) *Unit Operations: An Approach to Videogame Criticism*, Cambridge, MA: MIT Press.

Bogost, I. (2007) *Persuasive Games: The Expressive Power of Videogames*, Cambridge, MA: MIT Press.

Bolgar, R. (1974) *The Classical Heritage and Its Beneficiaries*, Cambridge: Cambridge University Press.

Bolter, J. D. and Grusin, R. (1999) *Remediation: Understanding New Media*, Cambridge, MA, and London: MIT Press.

Bond, S. (2017) 'Whitewashing ancient statues: Whiteness, racism and the color in the ancient world', *Forbes* (27 April). Available at: http://bit.ly/2MTJPl1 (accessed 18 August 2018).

Boss, M. and Meister, M. (2004) 'On using state of the art computer game engines to visualize archeological structures in teaching and research', in K. Fischer-Ausserer, W. Börner, M. Goriany and L. Karlhuber-Vöckl (eds), *Enter the Past: The E-Way into the Four Dimensions of Cultural Heritage, CAA 2003, Proceedings of the 31st Annual Conference on Computer Applications and Quantitative Methods in Archaeology. Vienna, Austria, April 2003*, 505–9, Oxford: Archaeopress.

Bowman, S. (2010) *The Functions of Role-Playing Games: How Participants Create Community, Solve Problems and Explore Identity*, Jefferson, NC: McFarland.

Bradshaw, P. (2004) 'King Arthur', *The Guardian* (30 July). Available at: http://www.guardian.co.uk/arts/fridayreview/story/0,12102,1271611,00.html (accessed 27 June 2018).

Brian Sutton-Smith Library and Archives of Play (2016) 'Finding aid to the *Sumerian Game* Collection, 1962–1967, 2015'. Available at: http://www.museumofplay.org/sites/default/files/uploads/Finding%20Aid%20to%20the%20Sumerian%20Game%20collection_012916_0.pdf (accessed 6 November 2018).

Brodersen, K. (ed.) (2000) *Virtuelle Antike: Wendepunkte in der Alten Geschichte*, Darmstadt: Wissenschaftliche Buchgesellschaft.

Brown, F. (2013) 'Placing authenticity over accuracy in *Total War: Rome II*', *PCgamesN* (23 August). Available at: https://www.pcgamesn.com/totalwar/placing-authenticity-over-accuracy-total-war-rome-ii (accessed 28 May 2018).

Burkert, W. (1985) *Greek Religion: Archaic and Classical*, trans. J. Raffan, London: Blackwell.

Burnett, I. R. (2015) 'The text adventure: Relic of gaming history, or timeless medium?', *The Artifice* (12 November). Available at: https://the-artifice.com/text-adventure-gaming-history/ (accessed 15 October 2018).

Burton, D. (2001) 'The death of gods in Greek succession myths', in F. Budelmann and P. Michelakis (eds), *Homer, Tragedy and Beyond: Essays in Honour of P.E. Easterling*, 43–56, London: Society for the Promotion of Hellenic Studies.

Burton, P. (2016) 'Eugenics, infant exposure, and the enemy within: A pessimistic reading of Zack Snyder's *300*', *International Journal of the Classical Tradition*, 24 (3): 308–30.

Camp, J. M. (1996) 'The Form of Pnyx III', in B. Forsén and G. Stanton (eds), *The Pnyx in the History of Athens*, 41–6, Helsinki: Foundation of the Finnish Institute at Athen.

Campbell, C. (2013) 'Truth and fantasy in *Assassin's Creed 4: Black Flag*', *Polygon* (22 July). Available at: https://www.polygon.com/2013/7/22/4543968/truth-and-fantasy-in-assassins-creed-4-black-flag (accessed 26 July 2018).

Carlà-Uhink, F. (2017) '(Alte) Geschichte in der Werbung: Berichte aus einem Heidelberger Seminar', *thersites*, 6: 367–457.

Carr, E. H. (1987) *What is History?*, 2nd edn, London: Penguin.

Casso, V. I. and Thibault, M. (2016) 'The HGR framework: A semiotic approach to the representation of history in digital games', *gamevironments*, 5: 156–204.

Ch'ng, E. (2007) 'Using games engines for archaeological visualisation: Recreating lost worlds', in *Proceedings of CGames '07 (11th International Conference on Computer Games: AI, Animation, Mobile, Educational & Serious Games)*, 26–30, La Rochelle, France.

Chakrabarty, D. (2000) *Provincializing Europe: Postcolonial Thought and Historical Difference*, Princeton, NJ: Princeton University Press.

Champion, E. (2015) *Critical Gaming: Interactive History and Virtual Heritage*, London: Ashgate Publishing.

Chaniotis, A. (2008) 'Making Alexander fit for the twenty-first century: Oliver Stone's Alexander', in I. Berti and M. García Morcillo (eds), *Hellas on Screen: Cinematic Receptions of Ancient History, Literature and Myth*, 185–202, Stuttgart: Franz Steiner Verlag.

Chapman, A. (2012) 'Privileging form over content: Analysing historical videogames', *Journal of Digital Humanities*, 1: 42.

Chapman, A. (2013a) 'Affording history: *Civilization* and the ecological approach', in M. W. Kapell and A. B. R. Elliott (eds), *Playing with the Past: Digital Games and the Simulation of History*, 61–74, London: Bloomsbury.

Chapman, A. (2013b) 'Is Sid Meier's *Civilization* history?', *Rethinking History*, 17 (3): 312–32.

Chapman, A. (2013c) 'The great game of history: An analytical approach to and analysis of the videogame as a historical form', PhD thesis, University of Hull.

Chapman, A. (2014) 'The history beyond the frame: Off-screen space in the historical first-person shooter', in T. Winnerling and F. Kerschbaumer (eds), *Early Modernity and Videogames*, 38–51, Newcastle upon Tyne: Cambridge Scholars Publishing.

Chapman, A. (2016) *Digital Games as History: How Videogames Represent the Past and Offer Access to Historical Practice*, New York and London: Routledge.

Chapman, A. and Linderoth, J. (2015) 'Exploring the limits of play: A case study of representations of Nazism in games', in T. E. Mortensen, J. Linderoth and A. M. L. Brown (eds), *The Dark Side of Game Play: Controversial Issues in Playful Environments*, 137–53, London: Routledge.

Chapman, A., Foka, A. and Westin, J. (2016) 'Introduction: What is Historical Game Studies?', *Rethinking History*, 21 (3): 358–71. Doi:10.1080/13642529.2016.1256638.

Christesen, P. and Machado, D. (2010) 'Video games and classical antiquity', *Classical World* 104, 107–9.

Cicchino, M. I. (2015) 'Using game-based learning to foster critical thinking in student discourse', *Interdisciplinary Journal of Problem-Based Learning*, 9 (2): 57–74.

Clyde, J., Hopkins, H. and Wilkinson, G. (2012) 'Beyond the "historical" simulation: Using theories of history to inform scholarly game design', *Loading . . . The Journal of the Canadian Game Studies Association*, 6: 3–16. Available at: http://journals.sfu.ca/loading/index.php/loading/article/view/105/122 (accessed 15 September 2018).

Coert, J. (2018) 'Der digitale *furor Teutonicus*. Zur Rezeption von Germanenbildern im Videospiel am Beispiel von *Total War: Rome II*', *thersites*, 7: 58–106.

Cohen, S. (1984) *Zap! The Rise and Fall of Atari*, New York: McGraw-Hill.

Coleman, K. C. (2004) 'The pedant goes to Hollywood: The role of the academic consultant', in M. A. Winkler (ed.), *Gladiator: Film and History*, 45–52, Oxford: Blackwell.

Collins, K. (2007) 'In the loop: Creativity and constraint in 8-bit video game audio', *Twentieth-Century Music*, 4: 209–27.

Contranoctis (2009) 'Fvza: Thread', *The Secret World, English Forum*, 23.11.2009. Available at: http://bit.ly/2EbCbyN (accessed 26 January 2018).

Cooke, P. (1976) 'Exploitation films and feminism', *Screen*, 17 (2): 122–7. Doi:10.1093/screen/17.2.122.

Cooper, V. (2015) '"Better Females": Exploring the dissonance between medievalist tropes of gender and modern ideals in fantasy RPGs', in *The Middle Ages in the Modern World*, University of Lincoln, presentation, 30 June.

Copplestone, T. J. (2017) 'But that's not accurate: The differing perceptions of accuracy in cultural-heritage videogames between creators, consumers and critics', *Rethinking History*, 21 (3): 415–38.

Costikyan, G., (2010) 'Games, storytelling, and breaking the string', in P. Harrigan and N. Wardrip-Fruin (eds), *Second Person: Role-Playing and Story in Games and Playable Media*, 5–13, Cambridge, MA: MIT Press.

Coyne, L. (2017) 'Destory history', *Epoiesen*. Doi: 10.22215/epoiesen/2017.4.

Crecente, B. (2018) 'Teachers still more effective at educating than "*Assassin's Creed*"', *Variety* (28 June). Available at: https://variety.com/2018/gaming/news/assassins-creed-origins-discovery-tour-effectiveness-1202861325/ (accessed 4 May 2019).

Crossland, D. (2009) 'Germany recalls myth that created the nation', *Spiegel Online* (28 August). Available at: http://www.spiegel.de/international/germany/battle-of-the-teutoburg-forest-germany-recalls-myth-that-created-the-nation-a-644913.html (accessed 13 June 2018).

Crytek Frankfurt (2018) '*Ryse®: Son of Rome* – Overview', *Crytek.Com*. Available at: http://www.crytek.com/games/ryse/overview (accessed 18 July 2018).

Cyrino, M. S. (2005) *Big Screen Rome*, Oxford: Blackwell Publishing.

Culham, P. (1989) 'Chance, command, and chaos in ancient military engagements', *World Futures*, 27: 191–205.

David, R. (2007) 'Ancient Egypt', in J. Hinnels (ed.), *A Handbook of Ancient Religions*, 46–104, Cambridge: Cambridge University Press.

Davies, D. (2012) 'So, what would your plan for Greece be?', *Crooked Timber* (16 February). Available at: http://crookedtimber.org/2012/02/16/so-what-would-your-plan-for-greece-be/ (accessed 8 August 2018).

Davison, P. (2011) 'The language of internet memes', in M. Mandiberg (ed.), *The Social Media Reader*, 120–34, New York: New York University Press.

De Groot, J. (2008) *Consuming History: Historians and Heritage in Contemporary Popular Culture*, London: Taylor & Francis.

De Landa, M. (2000) *A Thousand Years of Linear History*, New York: Zone Books.

Decreus, F. (2007) '"The same kind of smile?" About the "use and abuse" of theory in constructing the classical tradition', in L. Hardwick and C. Gillespie (eds), *Classics in Post-Colonial Worlds*, 245–64, Oxford: Oxford University Press.

Dening, G. (2006) 'Performing cross-culturally', *Australasian Journal of American Studies*, 25: 1–11.

Diak, N. (2017) *The New Peplum: Essays on Sword and Sandal Films and Television Programs Since the 1990s*, Jefferson, NC: McFarland.

Dietz, T. (1998) 'An examination of violence and gender role portrayals in video games: Implications for gender socialization and aggressive behavior', *Sex Roles*, 38: 425–42. Doi: 10.1023/a:1018709905920.

Dill, K. E., Gentile, D. A., Richter, W. A. and Dill, J. C. (2001) 'Violence, sex, race, and age in popular video games: A content analysis', in E. Cole and J. Henderson Daniel (eds), *Featuring Females: Feminist Analyses of Media*, 115–30, Washington, DC: APA Books.

Dinsmoor, W. B. (1933) Review of K. Kourouniotes and H. A. Thompson (1932), 'The Pnyx in Athens', *American Journal of Archaeology*, 37: 180–2.

Dixon, K. R. and Southern, P. (1992) *The Roman Cavalry*, London: Routledge.

Djaouti, D., Alvarez, J., Jessel, J.-P. and Rampnoux, O. (2011) 'Origins of serious games', in M. Ma, A. Oikonomou and L. C. Jain (eds), *Serious Games and Edutainment Applications*, 25–44, London and New York: Springer.

Donovan, T. (2010) *Replay: The History of Video Games*, Hove: Yellow Ant Media.

Dor, S. (2018) 'Strategy in games or strategy games: Dictionary and encyclopaedic definitions for game studies', *Game Studies*, 18 (1). Available at: http://gamestudies. org/1801/articles/simon_dor (accessed 6 November 2018).

Dormans, J. (2006) 'On the role of the die: A brief ludologic study of pen-and-paper roleplaying games and their rules', *Game Studies*, 6 (1). Available at: http://gamestudies. org/0601/articles/dormans (accessed 1 July 2019).

Dover, K. J. (1988) 'Thucydides' historical judgement: Athens and Sicily', *Greek and the Greeks: Collected Papers, Vol. II*, 74–82, Oxford: Oxford University Press.

Dow, D. N. (2013) 'Historical veneers: Anachronism, simulation, and art history in *Assassin's Creed II*', in M. W. Kapell and A. B. R. Elliott (eds), *Playing with the Past: Digital Games and the Simulation of History*, 215–31, London: Bloomsbury.

Drain, B. (2013). 'EVE Online hits 500,000 subscribers, heads into second decade', *Engadget* (28 February). Available at: https://www.engadget.com/2013/02/28/eve-online-hits-500-000-subscribers-heads-into-second-decade/ (accessed 6 November 2018).

Du Picq, A. (1921) *Battle Studies: Ancient and Modern Battle*, New York: Macmillan.

Ducheneaut, N., Yee, N., Nickell, E. and Moore, R. J. (2007) 'The life and death of online gaming communities: A look at guilds in *World of Warcraft*', *Proceedings of ACM CHI 2007 Conference on Human Factors in Computing Systems*, 2007: 839–48. Available at: http://bit.ly/2vhXuZr (accessed 8 August 2018).

Durham Centre for Classical Reception, Durham University. Available at: https://www.dur. ac.uk/classical.tradition/ (accessed 6 November 2018).

Egenfeldt-Nielsen, S., Smith, J. H. and Pajares Tosca, S. (2008) *Understanding Video Games: The Essential Introduction*, New York and London: Routledge.

Elliott, A. B. R. (2017) 'Simulations and simulacra: History in video games', *Práticas da História,* 5: 11–41.

English, W. K., Engelbart, D. C. and Huddart, B. (1965) *Computer-Aided Display Control*, Menlo Park, CA: Stanford Research Institute.

Evans, R. J. (2014) *Altered Pasts: Counterfactuals in History*, New York: University Press of New England.

Felson, N. (2011) 'Children of Zeus in the *Homeric Hymns*: Generational succession', in A. Faulkner (ed.), *The Homeric Hymns: Interpretative Essays*, 257–83, Oxford: Oxford University Press.

Fencott, C., Clay, J., Lockyer, M. and Massey, P. (2012) *Game Invaders: The Theory and Understanding of Computer Games*, Hoboken, NJ: Wiley-IEEE Press.

Ferguson, N. (ed.) (1997) *Virtual History: Alternatives and Counterfactuals*, London: Penguin.

Field of Glory 2 (2017) *Game Manual*. Available at: http://www.matrixgames.com/ amazon/PDF/FOG2%20manual%20EBOOK.pdf (accessed 15 September 2018).

Fiscal Times (2013) 'The 10 bestselling video games of 2013', *The Fiscal Times* (13 December). Available at: http://www.thefiscaltimes.com/Media/Slideshow/2013/12/13/10-Bestselling-Video-Games-2013?page=2 (accessed 25 July 2018).

Fischer, D. (1970) *Historian's Fallacies: Toward a Logic of Historical Thought*, New York and London: Harper & Row.

Flory, S. (1988) 'Thucydides' hypotheses about the Peloponnesian War', *Transactions of the American Philological Association,* 118: 43–56.

Fogel, R. (1964) *Railroads and American Economic Growth: Essays in Econometric History*, Baltimore, MD: Johns Hopkins Press.

Fogu, C. (2009) 'Digitalizing historical consciousness', *History and Theory*, 47: 103–21.

Ford, D. (2016) '"eXplore, eXpand, eXploit, eXterminate": Affective writing of postcolonial history and education in Civilization V', *Games Studies*, 16 (2). Available at: http://gamestudies.org/1602/articles/ford (accessed 1 July 2019).

Forsén, B. (1993) 'The Sanctuary of Zeus Hypsistos and the Assembly Place on the Pnyx', *Hesperia*, 62: 507–21.

Frasca, G. (2003) 'Ludologists love stories, too: Notes from a debate that never took place', in M. Copier and J. Raessens (eds), *Level-Up: Digital Games Research Conference*, n.p., Utrecht: Utrecht University.

Fredal, J. (2006) *Rhetorical Action in Ancient Athens: Persuasive Artistry from Solon to Demosthenes*, Carbondale, IL: Southern Illinois University Press.

Freeborn, T. (2009) 'Monsters of Maine: An investigation into the cryptozoological and occult events occuring on Solomon Island'. Available at: http://monstersofmaine. blogspot.com/ (accessed 8 August 2018).

French, T. (2016) 'Playing through the past: An analysis of video games as a method of public engagement with archaeology', MA thesis, University College London.

Friedman, T. (1999) '*Civilization* and its discontents: Simulation, subjectivity and space', in G. M. Smith (ed.), *On a Silver Platter: CD-ROMs and the Promises of a New Technology*, 132–50, New York and London: New York University Press.

Frischer, B. (2017) 'New light on the relationship between the Montecitorio Obelisk and Ara Pacis of Augustus', *Studies in Digital Heritage*, 1: 18–119. Doi:10.14434/sdh. v1i1.23331.

Fritsch, M. (2013) 'History of video game music', in P. Moorman (ed.), *Music and Game: Perspectives on a Popular Alliance*, 11–40, Wiesbaden: Springer.

FunCom (2007) 'The Secret World [Official Forums]'. Available at: http://forums. thesecretworld.com (accessed 10 August 2018).

FunCom (2012) *Orochi*, official website. Available at: www.orochi-group.com (accessed 8 August 2018).

Furtwängler, F. (2012) 'God of War and the mythology of games', in T. S. Thorsen (ed.), *Greek and Roman Games in the Computer Age*, 27–51, Trondheim: Akademika Publishing.

Gainsford, P. (2019) Kiwi Hellenist, blog (31 January). Available at: https://kiwihellenist. blogspot.com/2019/01/sea-shanties-assassins-creed-odyssey.html (accessed 4 May 2019).

Galloway, A. (2006) *Gaming: Essays on Algorithmic Culture*, Minneapolis, MN: University of Minnesota Press.

Garcia, A. (2017) 'Privilege, power, and *Dungeons & Dragons*: How systems shape racial and gender identities in tabletop role-playing games', *Mind, Culture & Activity*, 24 (3): 232–46.

García Martín, R. and Cadiñanos, B. (2015) 'Kratos como paradigma del *casus belli* en los videojuegos', in I. Martínez de Salazar Muñoz and D. Alonso Urbano (eds), *Videojuegos: Diseño y sociología*, 343–54, Madrid: ESNE Editorial.

García Morcillo, M. (2015) 'The East in the West: The rise and fall of ancient Carthage in modern imagery and in film', in M. García Morcillo, P. Hanesworth and O. Lapeña Machena (eds), *Imagining Ancient Cities in Film: From Babylon to Cinecittà*, 135–62, London: Routledge.

Gardner, A. (2007) 'The past as playground: The ancient world in video game representation', in T. Clack and M. Brittain (eds), *Archaeology and the Media*, 255–72, London: UCL Press.

Gardner, A. (2012) 'Strategy games and engagement strategies', in C. Bonacchi (ed.), *Archaeology and Digital Communication: Towards Strategies of Public Engagement*, 38–49, London: Archetype Publications.

Garriott, R. (2017) *Explore/Create: Gamer Adventurer Pioneer – My Life in Pursuit of New Frontiers, Hidden Worlds, and the Creative Spark*, with the assistance of D. Fisher, New York: William Morrow.

Gaudiosi, L. (2004) 'Rome: First a game, now on TV', *Wired* (17 May). Available at: https://www.wired.com/2004/05/rome-first-a-game-now-on-tv/?currentPage=all (accessed 13 June 2018).

Geertz, C. (1973) *The Interpretation of Cultures: Selected Essays*, New York: Basic Books.

Ghita, C. and Andrikopoulos, G. (2009) '*Total War* and *Total Realism*: A battle for antiquity in computer game history', in D. Lowe and K. Shahabudin (eds), *Classics for All: Reworking Antiquity in Mass Culture*, 109–26, Newcastle upon Tyne: Cambridge Scholars Publishing.

Ghys, T. (2012) 'Technology trees: Freedom and determinism in historical strategy games', *Game Studies*, 12 (1). Available at: http://www.gamestudies.org/1201/articles/tuur_ghys (accessed 6 November 2018).

Giere, D. (2019) *Computerspiele – Medienbildung – historisches Lernen. Zu Repräsentation und Rezeption von Geschichte in digitalen Spielen*, Schwalbach am Taunus: Wochenschau Verlag.

Gießler, D. and Graf, M. (2016) 'Das spielbare Gestern: Geschichte in Spielen, Teil 1', *Gamestar*, 8: 90–7.

Goldstein, J. (2005) 'Violent video games', in J. Raessens and J. Goldstein (eds), *Handbook of Computer Game Studies*, 341–57, Cambridge, MA: MIT Press.

Goldsworthy, A. (1996) *The Roman Army at War 100 BC–AD 200*, Oxford: Clarendon Press.

Goldsworthy, A. (2000) *Roman Warfare*, London: Cassell.

Gonzalez, J. (2013) *The Epic Rhapsode and His Craft: Homeric Performance in a Diachronic Perspective*, Washington, DC: Center for Hellenic Studies.

Goodyear, F. R. D. (1972) *The Annals of Tacitus, Books 1–6*, Edited with a Commentary by F. R. D. Goodyear, *Vol. 1: Annals 1. 1–54*, Cambridge Classical Texts and Commentaries, 15, Cambridge: Cambridge at the University Press.

Gordon, J. (2017) 'When Superman smote Zeus: Analysing violent deicide in popular culture', *Classical Receptions Journal*, 9 (2): 211–36.

Graham, S. (2014) 'Rolling your own: On modding commercial games for educational goals', in K. Kee (ed.), *Pastplay: Teaching and Learning History with Technology*, 214–54, Ann Arbor, MI: University of Michigan Press.

Graham, S. (2017a) 'Romans Must Die', Recorded conference presentation, Shawn Graham. YouTube channel, available at: https://www.youtube.com/watch?v=eCe5QEnoioI (accessed 6 November 2018).

Graham, S. (2017b) 'On games that play themselves: Agent-based models, archaeogaming, and the useful deaths of digital Romans', in A. A. A. Mol, C. E. Ariese-Vandemeulebroucke, K. H. J. Boom and A. Politopoulos (eds), *The Interactive Past: Archaeology, Heritage & Video Games*, 123–32, London: Sidestone Press.

Gramsci, A. (1971) *Selection from the Prison Notebooks*, trans. Q. Hoare and G. N. Nowell Smith, London: Lawrence and Wishart.

Greenwood, E. (2005) '"We speak Latin in Trinidad": Uses of classics in Caribbean literature', in B. Goff (ed.), *Classics & Colonialism*, 65–91, London: Duckworth.

Gregory, J. (2015) *Game Engine Architecture*, 2nd edn, Boca Raton, FL: CRC Press.

Grosch, W. (2002) *Computerspiele im Geschichtsunterricht*, Schwalbach am Taunus: Wochenschau Verlag.

Hagia Sophia (n.d.) (Bissera Pentcheva). Available at: https://hagiasophia.stanford.edu (accessed 4 May 2019).

Hall, E. (2015) 'Classics for the people: Why we should all learn from the ancient Greeks', *The Guardian* (20 June). Available at: https://www.theguardian.com/books/2015/jun/20/classics-for-the-people-ancient-greeks (accessed 11 April 2018).

Hall, E. and Stead, H. (2013) 'Is the study of the Greek and Latin classics Elitist?', *Classics and Class*. Available at: http://www.classicsandclass.info/wp-content/uploads/2014/03/cw_005.pdf (accessed 11 April 2018).

Hamilakis, Y. (2014) *Archaeology and the Senses: Human Experience, Memory and Affect*, Cambridge: Cambridge University Press.

Hancock, H. (2002) 'Better game design through cutscenes', *Gamasutra* (2 April). Available at: https://www.gamasutra.com/view/feature/131410/better_game_design_through_.php (accessed: 13 June 2018).

Hanink, J. (2017) *The Classical Debt: Greek Antqiuity in an Era of Austerity*, Cambridge: Belknap Press of Harvard University Press.

Hansen, M. H. (1983/1989) *The Athenian Ecclesia*, 2 vols, Copenhagen: Museum Tusculum Press.

Hansen, M. H. (1991) *The Athenian Democracy in the Age of Demosthenes: Structure, Principles, Ideology*, Oxford: Blackwell.

Harari, Y. N. (2007) 'The concept of "decisive battles" in world history', *Journal of World History*, 18 (3): 251–66.

Hardwick, L. (2003) *Reception Studies*, Oxford: Oxford University Press.

Hardwick, L. (2005) 'Refiguring classical texts: Aspects of the postcolonial condition', in B. Goff (ed.), *Classics & Colonialism*, 107–17, London: Duckworth.

Hardwick, L. and Stray, C. (2008a) 'Introduction: Making connections', in L. Hardwick and C. Stray (eds), *A Companion to Classical Reception*, 1–10, Malden, MA, and London: Blackwell.

Hardwick, L. and Stray, C. (eds) (2008b) *A Companion to Classical Reception*, Malden, MA, and London: Blackwell.

Harnecker, J. (2008) *Kalkriese 4. Katalog der römischen Funde vom Oberesch. Die Schnitte 1–22*, Mainz: Verlag Philipp von Zabern.

Harnecker, J. (2011) *Kalkriese 5. Katalog der römischen Funde vom Oberesch. Die Schnitte 23–39*, Mainz: Verlag Philipp von Zabern.

Harnecker, J. and Tolksdorf-Lienemann, E. (2004) *Kalkriese 2. Sondierungen in der Kalkrieser-Niewedder Senke. Archäologie und Bodenkunde*, Mainz: Verlag Philipp von Zabern.

Harris, A. and Nielsen, H. (2015) 'Reductive, superficial, beautiful – A historian's view of *Assassin's Creed: Syndicate*', *The Guardian* (9 December). Available at: https://www.theguardian.com/technology/2015/dec/09/assassins-creed-syndicate-historian-ubisoft (accessed 25 July 2018).

Hartmann, T. and Vorderer, P. (2010) 'It's okay to shoot a character: Moral disengagement in violent video games', *Journal of Communication*, 60: 94–119. Doi:10.1111/j.1460-2466.2009.01459.x.

Hatlen, J. F. (2012) 'Students of *Rome: Total War*', in T. S. Thorsen (ed.), *Greek and Roman Games in the Computer Age*, 175–98, Trondheim: Akademika Publishing.

Hausar, G. (2013) 'Gespielte Geschichte: Die Bedeutung von "Lore" im Massive Multiplayer Spiel Eve Online', *Historische Sozialkunde*, 4: 29–35.

Hawthorn, G. (1991) *Plausible Worlds: Possibility and Understanding in History and the Social Sciences*, Cambridge: Cambridge University Press.

Heinemann, J. (2018) 'Das "authentischste" Historienspiel aller Zeiten?! Die gewaltige Schräglage von "Kingdom Come: Deliverance"', Let's Play History Blog (13 January). Available at: http://bit.ly/2P4ORMw (accessed 28 September 2018).

Heinze, C. (2012) *Mittelalter – Computer – Spiele. Zur Darstellung und Modellierung von Geschichte im populären Computerspiel*, Bielefeld: transcript Verlag.

Heit, H. (2006) 'Western identity, Barbarians and the inheritance of Greek universalism', *European Legacy*, 10 (7): 725–39.

Held, D. (1997) 'Shaping Eurocentrism: The uses of Greek antiquity', in J. Coleman and C. Walz (eds), *Greeks and Barbarians*, 255–72, Bethesda, MD: CDL Press.

Henig, M. (1984) *Religion in Roman Britain*, London: Batsford.

Herman, L. (1994) *Phoenix: The Fall and Rise of Videogames*, Springfield, NJ: Rolenta Press.

Hernandez, P. (2013) 'That's not how breasts work, Ryse', *Kotaku* (2 December). Available at: https://kotaku.com/thats-not-how-breasts-work-ryse-1474988961 (accessed 22 June 2018).

Hernandez, P. (2015) 'Guy beats *Fallout 4* without killing anyone, nearly breaks the game', *Kotaku* (28 December). Available at: https://kotaku.com/guy-beats-fallout-4-without-killing-anyone-nearly-brea-1749882569 (accessed 22 June 2018).

Hesiod (1973) *Theogony*, trans. D. Wender, London: Penguin.

Hingley, R. (2007) 'Rural settlement in Northern Britain', in M. Todd (ed.), *A Companion to Roman Britain*, 327–48, London: Blackwell.

Hingley, R. and Unwin, C. (2006) *Boudica: Iron Age Warrior Queen*, London: Hambledon & London.

Hitchens, M. and Drachen, A. (2009) 'The many faces of role-playing games', *International Journal of Role-Playing*, 1: 3–21.

Hoggins, T. (2013) '*Ryse: Son of Rome* – Review', *The Telegraph* (4 December). Available at: http://www.telegraph.co.uk/technology/video-games/video-game-reviews/10492053/Ryse-Son-of-Rome-review.html (accessed 25 July 2018).

Holter, E. (2014) 'Vom Arbeiten mit digitalen Rekonstruktionen', in S. Muth, J. Bartz, E. Holter and N. Dietrich (eds), *digitales forum romanum*. Available at: http://www.digitales-forum-romanum.de/projekt/vom-arbeiten-mit-digitalen-rekonstruktionen (accessed 15 March 2018).

Holter, E. and Schäfer, U. U. (2018) 'Research in motion: VR as an archaeological tool', in C. Busch, C. Kassung and J. Sieck (eds), *Kultur und Informatik – Hybrid Systems*, 87–98, Glückstadt: vwh.

Holter, E., Muth, S. and Schwesinger, S. (2018) 'Sounding out public spaces in antiquity: Acoustic simulations of public speeches and assemblies in late Republican Rome', in S. Butler and S. Nooter (eds), *Sound and the Ancient Senses*, 44–60, London: Routledge.

Holtorf, C. (2005) *From Stonehenge to Las Vegas: Archaeology as Popular Culture*, Walnut Creek, CA: AltaMira Press.

Holub, R. C. (1984) *Reception Theory: A Critical Introduction*, London and York: Methuen.

Hong, S. (2015) 'When life mattered: The politics of the real in video games' reappropriation of history, myth, and ritual', *Games and Culture*, 10 (1): 35–56.

Hooper, G. (2018) 'Sounding the story: Music in video games', in D. Williams and N. Lee (eds), *Emotion in Video Game Soundtracking*, 115–42, Cham: Springer Nature.

Howard, J. (2008) *Quests: Design, Theory, and History in Games and Narratives*, Wellesley, MA: AK Peters.

Howard, J. (2015) 'The oral history of MMOs', *Play the Past* (3 September). Available at: http://bit.ly/2mwINlA (accessed 8 August 2018).

Howells, S. A. (2002) 'Watching a game, playing a movie: When media collide', in G. King and T. Krzywinska (eds), *Screenplay Cinema/Videogames/Interfaces*, 110–21, London: Wallflower.

Huckvale, D. (2012) *Ancient Egypt in the Popular Imagination: Building a Fantasy in Film, Literature, Music and Art*, Jefferson, NC: McFarland.

Huizinga, J. (1955) *Homo Ludens: A Study of the Play-Element in Culture*, Boston, MA: Beacon Press.

Hussey, D. R. (2014a) 'Assassin's Creed Week Part 4 – Grand Narratives', *Play the Past* (20 February). Available at: http://www.playthepast.org/?p=4503 (accessed 25 July 2018).

Hussey, D. R. (2014b) 'Assassin's Creed Week Part 1 – Introduction', *Play the Past* (17 February). Available at: http://www.playthepast.org/?p=4395 (accessed 25 July 2018).

IGN (2018) 'Assassin's Creed: Odyssey: How Ubisoft rebuilt Athens', Channel *IGN* (15 August). YouTube channel, available at: https://youtu.be/VooYYEeFKEo (accessed 18 August 2018).

Ilieva, A. (2013) 'Cultural languages of role-playing', *International Journal of Role-Playing*, 4: 26–38.

Inderst, R. T. (2009) *Vergemeinschaftung in MMORPGs*, Boizenburg: Hülsbusch.

Ironblade (2013) 'Akhenaten, the Opera! Thread', *The Secret World, English Forum*, 02.02.2013. Available at: http://bit.ly/2E5vsXn (accessed 24 January 2018).

Ivey, R. (2000) 'Pompei: The Legend of Vesuvius', Walkthrough for *justadventure.com*. Available at: https://web.archive.org/web/20020617061520/http:/www.justadventure. com/reviews/Pompei/Pompei2.shtm (accessed 6 November 2018).

Jackson, S. and Livingstone, I. (1982) *The Warlock of Firetop Mountain*, London: Puffin.

Jaffe, S. N. (2017) *Thucydides on the Outbreak of War: Character and Contest*, Oxford: Oxford University Press.

Jancovich, M. (2014) 'There's nothing so wrong with a Hollywood script that a bunch of giant CGI scorpions can't solve: Politics, computer-generated images and camp in the critical reception of the post-*Gladiator* historical epics', in A. B. R. Elliott (ed.), *The Return of the Epic Film: Genre, Aesthetics and History in the Twenty-First Century*, 57–73, Edinburgh: Edinburgh University Press.

Jauss, H. R. (1982) *Ästhetische Erfahrung und literarische Hermeneutik*, Frankfurt am Main: Suhrkamp.

Jauss, H. R. (1994) 'Literaturgeschichte als Provokation der Literaturwissenschaft', in R. Warning (ed.), *Rezeptionsästhetik. 4. Auflage*, 126–62, München: C.H. Beck.

Jenkin, A. (2015) 'Meet the historical experts: Laurent Turcot on "Assassins [*sic*] Creed Unity"', *History Matters* (16 April). Available at: http://www.historymatters.group.shef. ac.uk/meet-historical-experts-laurent-turcot-assassins-creed-unity/ (accessed 6 November 2018).

Jenkins, D. (2013) 'Ryse: Son of Rome review: Are you not entertained?', *Metro Online* (21 November). Available at: https://metro.co.uk/2013/11/21/ryse-son-of-rome-review-are-you-not-entertained-4195516/ (accessed 25 July 2018).

Jenkins, H. (2002) 'Game design as narrative architecture', in N. Wardrip-Fruin and P. Harrigan (eds), *First Person: New Media as Story, Performance, and Game*, 118–30, Cambridge, MA: MIT Press.

Jenkins, K. (2008) '"Nobody does it better": Radical history and Hayden White', *Rethinking History*, 12 (1): 59–74.

Johnston, S. I. (2015) 'The Greek mythic story world', *Arethusa*, 48 (3): 283–311.

Johnstone, C. L. (1996) 'Greek oratorical settings and the problem of the Pnyx: Rethinking the Athenian political process', in C. L. Johnstone (ed.), *Theory, Text, Context: Issues in Greek Rhetoric and Oratory*, 97–127, Albany, NY: State University of New York Press.

Jørgensen, K. (2009) '"I'm overburdened!" An empirical study of the player, the avatar, and the gameworld', *Breaking New Ground: Innovation in Games, Play, Practice and Theory: Proceedings of the 2009 DIGRA Conference*. Available at: http://www.digra.org/dl/display_html?chid=09287.20429.pdf (accessed 18 September 2018).

Junkelmann, M. (2004) *Hollywoods Traum von Rome. 'Gladiator' und die Tradition des Monumentalfilms*, Mainz: Verlag Philipp von Zabern.

Juul, J. (2004) 'Introduction to Game Time', in N. Wardrip-Fruin and P. Harrigan (eds), *First Person: New Media as Story, Performance, and Game*, 131–42, Cambridge, MA: MIT Press.

Kahane, A. (2016) 'Fan fiction, early Greece, and the historicity of canon', *Transformative Works and Cultures*, 21. Doi: 10.3983/twc.2016.0681.

Kamen, M. (2014) '*Assassin's Creed* historian on merging the past with fiction', *Wired* (23 October). Available at: https://www.wired.co.uk/article/assassins-creed-unity-interview-maxime-durand (accessed 6 November 2018).

Kapell, M. W. and Elliott, A. B. R. (2013a) 'Introduction: To build a past that will "stand the test of time" – Discovering historical facts, assembling historical narratives', in M. W. Kapell and A. B. R. Elliott (eds), *Playing with the Past: Digital Games and the Simulation of History*, 1–29, London: Bloomsbury.

Kapell, M. W. and Elliott, A. B. R. (eds) (2013b) *Playing with the Past: Digital Games and the Simulation of History*, London: Bloomsbury.

Karmali, L. (2014) 'Sega Financials reveal *Total War: Rome 2* as best-seller', *IGN* (9 May). Available at: http://www.ign.com/articles/2014/05/09/sega-financials-reveal-total-war-rome-2-as-best-seller (accessed 13 June 2018).

Kaye, S. T. (2010) 'Challenging certainty: The utility and history of counterfactualism', *History and Theory*, 49 (1): 38–57.

Kee, K. B. (2014) 'Introduction', in K. B. Kee (ed.), *Pastplay: Teaching and Learning History with Technology*, 1–20, Ann Arbor, MI: University of Michigan Press.

Keen, T. (2014) 'What is myth?', *Tony Keen's Personal Blog*, Open University (13 October). Available at: https://learn1.open.ac.uk/mod/oublog/viewpost.php?post=151603 (accessed 30 May 2018).

Keen, T. (2016) 'Are fan fiction and mythology really the same?', *Transformative Works and Cultures*, 21. Doi: 10.3983/twc.2016.0689.

Kennedy, H. W. (2002) 'Lara Croft: Feminist icon or cyberbimbo? On the limits of textual analysis', *Game Studies*, 2 (2). Available at: http://www.gamestudies.org/0202/kennedy/ (accessed 6 November 2018).

Kent, S. L. (2001) *The Ultimate History of Video Games: From Pong to Pokémon and Beyond – The Story Behind the Craze that Touched Our Lives and Changed the World*, New York: Three Rivers Press.

Kenzler, U. (1999) *Studien zur Entwicklung und Struktur der griechischen Agora in archaischer und klassischer Zeit*, Frankfurt am Main: Lang.

Kerschbaumer, F. and Winnerling, T. (2014a) 'Postmoderne Visionen des Vor-Modernen: Des 19. Jahrhunderts geisterhaftes Echo', in F. Kerschbaumer and T. Winnerling, (eds), *Frühe Neuzeit im Videospiel: Geschichtswissenschaftliche Perspektiven*, 11–24, Bielefeld: transcript Verlag.

Kerschbaumer, F. and Winnerling, T. (eds) (2014b) *Early Modernity and Videogames*, Newcastle upon Tyne: Cambridge Scholars Publishing.

Kerschbaumer, F. and Winnerling, T. (eds) (2014c) *Frühe Neuzeit im Videospiel: Geschichtswissenschaftliche Perspektiven*, Bielefeld: transcript Verlag.

Khoo, A. (2012) 'Video games as moral educators?', *Asia Pacific Journal of Education*, 32: 416–29.

King, G. and Krzywinska, T. (2002) 'Cinema/videogames/interaces', in G. King and T. Krzywinska (eds), *Screenplay Cinema/Videogames/Interfaces*, 1–32, London: Wallflower.

Klastrup, L. and Tosca, S. (2004) 'Transmedial worlds: Rethinking cyberworld design', *2004 International Conference on Cyberworlds*, 409–16, Tokyo: IEEE.

Kleiner, M., Dalenbäck, B.-I. and Svensson, P. (1993) 'Auralization: An overview', *Journal of the Audio Engineering Society*, 41 (11): 861–75.

Klevjer, R. (2002) 'In defense of cutscenes', in F. Mäyrä (ed.), *Computer Games and Digital Cultures Conference Proceedings*, 191–202, Tampere: Tampere University Press. Available at: http://www.digra.org/wpcontent/uploads/digital-library/05164.50328.pdf (accessed 15 September 2018).

Koon, S. (2011) 'Phalanx and Legion: The "face" of Punic War battle', in D. Hoyos (ed.), *A Companion to the Punic Wars*, 77–94, Malden, MA: Wiley.

Koster, R. (2017) 'UltimaOnline's influence [=Answering Questions for UO's 20th Anniversary]', *RaphKoster's Website* (28 September). Available at: http://bit.ly/2xTORL3 (accessed 8 August 2018).

Köstlbauer, J. (2013) 'The strange attraction of simulation: Realism, authenticity, virtuality', in M. W. Kapell and A. B. R. Elliott (eds), *Playing with the Past: Digital Games and the Simulation of History*, 169–83, New York: Bloomsbury.

Kotarba-Morley, A., Sarsfield, J., Hastings, J., Bradshaw, J. and Fiske, P. N. (2014) 'Building blocks of the lost past: Game engines and inaccessible archaeological sites', in G. Earl, T. Sly, A. Chrysanthi, P. Murrieta-Flores, C. Papadopoulos, I. Romanowska and D. Wheatley (eds), *Archaeology in the Digital Era, Volume II: e-Papers from the 40th Conference on Computer Applications and Quantitative Methods in Archaeology*, 949–60, Amsterdam: Amsterdam University Press.

Kourouniotes, K. and Thompson, H. A. (1932) 'The Pnyx in Athens', *Hesperia*, 1: 90–217.

Kubetzky, T. (2012) 'Computerspiele als Vermittlungsinstanzen von Geschichte? Geschichtsbilder in Aufbausimulationsspielen am Beispiel von *Civilization III*', in A. Schwarz (ed.), *Wollten Sie auch immer schon einmal pestverseuchte Kühe auf Ihre Gegner werfen? Eine fachwissenschaftliche Annäherung an Geschichte im Computerspiel*, 75–106, Münster: LIT Verlag.

Lankoski, P. and Jarvela, S. (2013) 'An embodied cognition approach for understanding role-playing', *International Journal of Role-Playing*, 3: 18–32.

Lauwers, J., Dhont, M. and Huybrecht, X. (2013) '"This is Sparta!": Discourse, gender, and the Orient in Zack Snyder's *300*', in A.-B. Renger and J. Solomon (eds), *Ancient Worlds in Film and Television: Gender and Politics*, 79–94, Leiden and Boston: Brill.

Lawson, S. (2013) 'Nationalism and biographical transformation: The case of Boudicca', *Humanities Research*, 19, (1): 101–19.

Laycock, J. (2015) *Dangerous Games: What the Moral Panic over Role-Playing Games Says about Play, Religion, and Imagined Worlds*, Berkeley, CA: University of California Press.

Learning Sites Inc. (2012) 'Vari House Unity virtual world'. Available at: http://www.learningsites.com/Vari02/Vari02_Unity/Vari02_Unity-WebPlayer_edited.html (accessed 22 October 2018).

Leavenworth, M. L. (2011) 'Transmedial texts and serialized narratives', *Transformative Works and Cultures*, 8. Doi: 10.3983/twc.2011.0361.

Lebow, R. N. (2010) *Forbidden Fruit: Counterfactuals in International Relations*, Princeton, NJ: Princeton University Press.

Leonard, M. (2009) 'Reception', in B. Graziosi, P. Vasunia and G. Boy-Stones (eds), *The Oxford Handbook of Hellenic Studies*, 835–46, Oxford: Oxford University Press.

Lepouras, G. and Vassilakis, C. (2003) 'Virtual museums for all: Employing game technology for edutainment', *Virtual Reality*, 8: 96–106. Doi: 10.1007/s10055-004-0141-1.

Lesser, H. G. (1984) 'The Return of Heracles', *Softline*, 4 (January–February): 50. Available at: http://www.cgwmuseum.org/galleries/issues/softline_3.3.pdf (accessed 6 November 2018).

Lewis, M. and Jacobson, J. (2002) 'Game engines in scientific research – Introduction', *Communications of the ACM*, 45: 27–31. Doi: 10.1145/502269.502288.

Lien, Y. A. (2016) '*Game of Thrones*: A game of accents? A sociolinguistic study of the representation of accents in HBO's television series', MA thesis, Norwegian University of Science and Technology.

Lillo Redonet, F. (2008) 'Sparta and ancient Greece in *The 300 Spartans*', in I. Berti and M. García Morcillo (eds), *Hellas on Screen: Cinematic Receptions of Ancient History, Literature and Myth*, 117–30, Stuttgart: Franz Steiner Verlag.

Linderoth, J. (2005) 'Animated game pieces: Avatars as roles, tools and props', paper presented at the Aesthetics of Play Conference, University of Bergen. Available at: www.aestheticsofplay.org/papers/linderoth2.htm (accessed 6 November 2018)

Linderoth, J. (2013) 'Superheroes, Greek gods and sport stars: Ecological empowerment as a ludo-narratological construct', in K. Mitgutsch, S. Huber, J. Wimmer, M.-G. Wagner and H. Rosenstingl (eds), *Context Matters! Proceedings of the Vienna Games Conference 2013*, 17–30, Vienna: New Academic Press.

Linderoth, J. (2015) 'Creating stories for a composite form: Video game design as Frame Orchestration', *Journal of Gaming & Virtual Worlds*, 7 (3): 279–98.

Loo, B. F. W. (2009) 'Decisive battle, victory and the revolution in military affairs', *Journal of Strategic Studies*, 32 (2): 189–211.

Lord, A. (1981) *The Singer of Tales*, Cambridge, MA: Harvard University Press.

Lowe, D. (2009) 'Playing with antiquity: Videogame receptions of the classical world', in D. Lowe and K. Shahabudin (eds), *Classics for All: Reworking Antiquity in Mass Culture*, 64–90, Newcastle upon Tyne: Cambridge Scholars Publishing.

Lowe, D. (2012) 'Always already ancient: Ruins in the virtual world', in T. S. Thorsen (ed.), *Greek and Roman Games in the Computer Age*, 53–90, Trondheim: Akademika Publishing.

Lowenthal, D. (1968) *The Heritage Crusade and the Spoils of History*, Cambridge: Cambridge University Press.

Lowenthal, D. (2015) *The Past Is a Foreign Country – Revisited*, Cambridge: Cambridge University Press.

Lusted, J. (2012) 'Exclusive content and Dev Chart for Total War Center', Total War Center. Available at: https://web.archive.org/web/20180527111621/http://www.twcenter.net/forums/showthread.php?548136-Exclusive-Content-and-Dev-chat-for-Total-War-Center&p=12805863&viewfull=1 (accessed 15 September 2018).

MacCallum-Stewart, E. (2014) '"Take that, bitches!" Refiguring Lara Croft in feminist game narratives', *Game Studies*, 14 (2). Available at: http://gamestudies.org/1402/articles/maccallumstewart (accessed 6 November 2018).

MacCallum-Stewart, E. and Parsler, J. (2007) 'Controversies: Historicizing the computer game', in *Situated Play, Proceedings of the DiGRA 2007 Conference*. Available at: http://www.digra.org/wp-content/uploads/digital-library/07312.51468.pdf. (accessed 15 September 18).

MacDowell, D. M. (2009) *Demosthenes the Orator*, Oxford: Oxford University Press.

MacDonald, K. (2018) '"We give access to a lost world": *Assassin's Creed* new life as a virtual museum', *The Guardian* (27 March). Available at: https://www.theguardian.com/games/2018/mar/27/assassins-creeds-origins-discovery-tour-virtual-museum-ancient-egypt-ubisoft (accessed 25 July 2018).

Maelwydd (2012) 'What if everything IS real? Thread', *The Secret World, English Forum*, 03.08.2012. Available at: http://bit.ly/2ncvUMe (accessed 26 January 2018).

Magnet, S. (2006) 'Playing at colonization: Interpreting imaginary landscapes in the video game *Tropico*', *Journal of Communication Inquiry*, 30 (2): 142–62.

Mahood, C. and Hanus, M. (2017) 'Role-playing video games and emotion: How transportation into the narrative mediates the relationship between immoral actions and feelings of guilt', *Psychology of Popular Media Culture*, 6 (1): 61–73.

Maiberg, E. (2014) '*Ryse: Son of Rome*', review, *PC Gamer* (9 October). Available at: https://www.pcgamer.com/ryse-son-of-rome-review/ (accessed 25 July 2018).

Maier, B. (2003) *The Celts: A History from the Earliest Times to the Present*, trans. Kevin Windle, Edinburgh: Edinburgh University Press.

Makuch, E. (2016) '*Assassin's Creed* franchise reaches 100 million copies sold', *Gamespot* (13 September). Available at: https://www.gamespot.com/articles/assassins-creed-franchise-reaches-100-million-copi/1100-6443544/ (accessed 25 July 2018).

Mann, C. (2007) *Die Demagogen und das Volk: Zur politischen Kommunikation im Athen des 5. Jahrhunderts v. Chr.*, Berlin: Akademie Verlag.

Manuelian, P. der (2018) 'History respawned: Harvard Egyptologist on *Assassin's Creed: Origins*', *History Respawned* (17 February). YouTube channel, available at: https://www.youtube.com/watch?v=ANQL5z_JEpQ (accessed 6 Novemebr 2018).

Martindale, C. (1993) *Redeeming the Text*, Cambridge: Cambridge University Press.

Martindale, C. (2006) 'Introduction: Thinking through reception', in C. Martindale and R. F. Thomas (eds), *Classics and the Uses of Reception*, 1–13, Malden, MA, and Oxford: Wiley-Blackwell.

Mattingly, D. (2007) *An Imperial Possession: Britain in the Roman Empire, 54 BC–AD 409*, London: Penguin.

Mäyrä, F. (2008) *An Introduction to Game Studies: Games in Culture*, Los Angeles, CA: Sage Publications.

McCall, J. (2001) *The Cavalry of the Roman Republic: Cavalry Combat and Elite Reputations in the Middle and Late Republic*, London: Routledge.

McCall, J. (2011) *Gaming the Past: Using Video Games to Teach Secondary History*, Abingdon: Routledge.

McCall, J. (2012a) 'Historical simulations as problem spaces: Criticism and classroom use', *Journal of Digital Humanities*, 1 (2). Available at: http://journalofdigitalhumanities.org/1-2/historical-simulations-as-problem-spaces-by-jeremiah-mccall (accessed 15 September 2018).

McCall, J. (2012b) 'Navigating the problem space: The medium of simulation games and the study of history', *History Teacher*, 46: 9–28.

McCall, J. (2014a) 'Simulation games and the study of the past: Classroom guidelines', in K. Kee (ed.), *Pastplay: Teaching and Learning History with Technology*, 228–56, Ann Arbor, MI: University of Michigan Press.

McCall, J. (2014b) *Swords and Cinema: Hollywood vs. The Reality of Ancient Warfare*, Barnsley: Pen & Sword.

McCall, J. (2016) 'Teaching history with digital historical games: An introduction to the field and best practices', *Simulation & Gaming*, 47: 517–42.

McCall, J. (2018a) 'Path of Honors: Towards a model for interactive history texts with Twine', *Epoiesen*. Doi: 10.22215/epoiesen/2017.16.

McCall, J. (2018b) 'Video games as participatory public history', in D. Dean (ed.), *A Companion to Public History*, 405–16, Malden, MA: Wiley.

McCall, J. (forthcoming) 'The Manipular Army system and command decisions in the second century BCE', in J. Armstrong and M. Fronda (eds), *Romans at War: Soldiers, Citizens, and Society in the Roman Republic*, London: Routledge.

McDonald, W. A. (1943) *The Political Meeting Places of the Greeks*, Baltimore, MD: Johns Hopkins Press.

McGonigal, J. (2012) *Reality is Broken: Why Games Make Us Better and How They Can Change the World*, London: Vintage.

Meier, S. (2012) 'Interesting Decisions', GDC Vault. Video available at: http://gdcvault.com/play/1015756/Interesting (accessed 7 October 2018).

Mendlesohn, F. (2008) *Rhetorics of Fantasy*, Middletown, CT: Wesleyan University Press.

Messner, S. (2018) 'EVE Online had its biggest battle ever last week and now an even bigger one is happening', *PC Gamer* (2 August). Available at: https://www.pcgamer.com/the-biggest-battle-in-eve-onlines-entire-history-ishappening-right-now-and-you-can-watch (accessed 6 November 2018).

Meyers, K. (2011) 'Lessons from *Assassin's Creed* for constructing educational games', *Play the Past* (25 October). Available at: http://www.playthepast.org/?p=2077 (accessed 25 July 2018).

Michelakis, P. and Wyke, M. (2013) *The Ancient World in Silent Cinema*, Cambridge: Cambridge University Press.

Michelsen, P. (1987) '"Wehe, mein Vaterland, dir!": Heinrichs von Kleist "Die Hermannsschlacht"', in H. J. Kreutzer (ed.), *Kleist-Jahrbuch*, 115–36, Berlin: Erich Schmidt Verlag.

Mizeraj (2012) 'Art department's jokes: Thread', *The Secret World, English Forum*, 13. 07.2012. Available at: http://bit.ly/2n8MGuD (accessed 24 January 2018).

Mona, E. (2010) 'From the basement to the basic set: The early years of *Dungeons & Dragons*', in P. Harrigan and N. Wardrip-Fruin (eds), *Second Person: Role-Playing and Story in Games and Playable Media*, 25–30, Cambridge: MIT Press.

Moncreiff, B. (1965) '"The Sumerian Game": Teaching economics with a computerized P.I. Program', *Programed Instruction*, 4 (5): 10–11.

Moore, B. (2014) 'Inside the epic online space battle that cost gamers $300,000', *Wired* (2 August). Available at: https://www.wired.com/2014/02/eve-online-battle-of-b-r (accessed 6 November 2018).

Moore, G. E. (1965) 'Cramming more components onto integrated circuits', *Proceedings of the IEEE*, 86 (1): 82–4.

Moore, G.E. (1975) 'Progress in digital integrated electronics', IEEE Text Speech. Available at: http://www.eng.auburn.edu/~agrawvd/COURSE/E7770_Spr07/READ/Gordon_Moore_1975_Speech.pdf (accessed 6 November 2018).

Morley, N. (2011) 'Cities and economic development in the Roman Empire', in A. Bowman and A. Wilson (eds), *Settlement, Urbanization and Population*, 143–60, Oxford: Oxford University Press.

Morley, N. (2014) *Thucydides and the Idea of History*, London: I.B. Tauris.

Morley, N. (2015) 'The Melian Dilemma: Varoufakis, Thucydides and game theory', *The Sphinx Blog* (27 March). Available at: https://thesphinxblog.com/2015/03/27/the-melian-dilemma-varoufakis-thucydides-and-game-theory/ (accessed 10 October 2018).

Morley, N. (2016) 'Return to Melos: Facing the reality of how things are, in order to understand it better', *Disclaimer* (9 April). Available at: http://www.disclaimermag.com/other-stuff/return-to-melos-facing-the-reality-of-how-things-are-in-order-to-understand-it-better-3520 (accessed 13 August 2018).

Morley, N. (2017) 'Counterfactualism and anticipation', in R. Poli (ed.), *Handbook of Anticipation: Theoretical and Applied Aspects of the Use of Future in Decision Making*, Berlin: Springer Verlag. Doi: 10.1007/978-3-319-31737-3.

Morley, N. (2018a) 'Thucydides: Origins of realism?', in M. Hollingsworth and R. Schuett (eds), *The Edinburgh Companion to Political Realism*, 111–23, Edinburgh: Edinburgh University Press.

Morley, N. (2018b) *Classics: Why it Matters*, Cambridge: Polity.

Morley, N. (2019) 'The Melian Dilemma: Remaking Thucydides', *Epoiesen* (4 February). Doi: 10.22215/epoiesen/2019.2.

Mortensen, T. E. (2006) 'WoW is the New MUD: Social gaming from text to video', *Games and Culture*, 1 (4): 397–413. Available at: http://bit.ly/2vAjDGh (accessed 8 August 2018).

Moser, C. and Fang, X. (2015) 'Narrative structure and player experience in role-playing games', *International Journal of Human-Computer Interaction*, 31 (2): 146–56.

Mulvey, L. (1975) 'Visual pleasure and narrative cinema', *Screen*, 16 (3): 6–18. Doi: 10.1017/CBO9781107415324.004.

Munslow, A. (2007) *Narrative and History*, Basingstoke: Palgrave Macmillan.

Murnanes, K. (2018) 'Ubisoft puts people before profits with the "Discovery Tour" for "*Assassin's Creed: Origins*"', *Forbes* (23 February). Available at: https://www.forbes.com/sites/kevinmurnane/2018/02/23/ubisoft-puts-people-before-profits-with-the-discovery-tour-for-assassins-creed-origins/#4474340d67f6 (accessed 6 November 2018).

Murray, J. H. (1997) *Hamlet on the Holodeck: The Future of Narrative in Cyberspace*, New York: Simon and Schuster.

Muth, S. (2014) 'Historische Dimensionen des gebauten Raums: Das Forum Romanum als Fallbeispiel', in O. Dally, T. Hölscher, S. Muth and R. Schneider (eds), *Medien der Geschichte: Antikes Griechenland und Rom*, 285–329, Berlin: De Gruyter.

Muth, S., Bartz, J., Holter, E. and Dietrich, N. (eds) (2014) *digitales forum romanum*. Available at: www.digitales-forum-romanum.de (accessed 15 March 2018).

Nagle, A. (2017) *Kill All Normies: Online Culture Wars from 4Chan and Tumblr to Trump and The Alt-Right*, Alresford: Zero Books.

Nagy, G. (1999) *The Best of the Achaeans: Concepts of the Hero in Archaic Greek Poetry*, revd edn, Baltimore, MD: Johns Hopkins University Press.

Neal, T. (2006) *The Wounded Hero: Non-Fatal Injury in Homer's Iliad*, Bern: Lang.

Nelson, S. A. (1998) *God and the Land: The Metaphysics of Farming in Hesiod and Virgil*, Oxford: Oxford University Press.

Nethbuk (2012) 'Clothing options & gender: Thread', *The Secret World, English Forum*, 05.05.2012. Available at: http://bit.ly/2FdFncA (accessed 25 January 2018).

Neuenschwander, B. (2008) 'Playing by the rules: Instruction and acculturation in role-playing games', *E-Learning*, 5 (2): 189–98.

NEWZOO (2017) *Global Games Market Report*. Available at: https://newzoo.com/insights/trend-reports/newzoo-global-games-market-report-2017-light-version (accessed 6 November 2018).

NEWZOO (2018) *Global Games Market Report*. Available at: https://newzoo.com/insights/trend-reports/newzoo-global-games-market-report-2018-light-version (accessed 6 November 2018).

Nichols, D. (2014) 'History behind the game: *Ryse: Son of Rome*', *Venture Beat* (8 February). Available at: http://venturebeat.com/community/2014/02/08/history-behind-the-game-ryse-son-of-rome/ (accessed 25 July 2018).

Nielsen, H. (2017) '*Assassin's Creed: Origins*: How Ubisoft painstakingly recreated ancient Egypt', *The Guardian* (5 October). Available online: https://www.theguardian.com/technology/2017/oct/05/assassins-creed-origins-recreated-ancient-egypt-ubisoft (accessed 6 November 2018).

Nippel, W. (2002) 'The construction of the "other"', in T. Harrison (ed.), *Greeks and Barbarians*, 278–310, Edinburgh: Edinburgh University Press.

Nolden, N. (2018a) 'DissTSW2 – Erinnerungskulturelle Wissenssysteme – 2 Das historische Wissenssystem', *TheBlitzechse* (19 August). YouTube channel, available at: https://youtube/jh3ex3WZG5s (accessed 19 August 2018).

Nolden, N. (2018b) 'Keimzellen verborgener Welten. Globalisierungsprozesse beim MMORPG The Secret World als globalhistorische Zugriffswege', in J. Köstlbauer, E. Pfister, T. Winnerling and F. Zimmermann (eds), *Weltmaschine Computerspiel. Digitale Spiele als globalgeschichtliches Phänomen*, 181–201, Vienna: mandelbaum.

Nolden, N. (2018c) 'Erinnerungskulturelle Wissenssysteme in Computerspielen. Historische Inszenierungen digitaler Spielwelten in Massively-Multiplayer Netzwerken', PhD thesis, University of Hamburg.

O'Gorman, E. (2000) *Irony and Misreading in the* Annals *of Tacitus*, Cambridge: Cambridge University Press.

O'Gorman, E. (2006) 'A woman's history of warfare', in V. Zajko and M. Leonard (eds), *Laughing with Medusa: Classical Myth and Feminist Thought*, 189–207, Oxford: Oxford University Press.

O'Grady, D. (2013) 'Movies in the gameworld: Revisiting the video game cutscene and its temporal implications', in J. C. Thompson and M. A. Ouelette (eds), *The Game Culture Reader*, 103–24, New Castle: Cambridge Scholars.

Ober, J. (1989) *Mass and Elite in Democratic Athens: Rhetoric, Ideology, and the Power of the People*, Princeton, NJ: Princeton University Press.

Oikarinen, T. (2016) 'Utilisation of a game engine for archaeological visualization', in S. Campana, R. Scopigno, G. Carpentiero and M. Cirillo (eds), *Keep the Revolution Going: CAA 2015, Proceedings of the 43rd Annual Conference on Computer Applications and Quantitative Methods in Archaeology*, 27–34, Oxford: Archaeopress.

Omnires (2010) 'Magic vs. technology: Thread', *The Secret World, English Forum*, 01.08.2010. Available at: http://bit.ly/2n9GlzU (accessed 25 January 2018).

Owens, T. (2010) 'The presence of the past in *Fallout 3*', *Play the Past* (13 December). Available at: http://www.playthepast.org/?p=459 (accessed 7 June 2018).

Packer, J. E. and Gorski, G. J. (2015) *The Roman Forum: A Reconstruction and Architectural Guide*, Cambridge: Cambridge University Press.

Pagan, V. E. (1999) 'Beyond Teutoburg: Transgression and transformation in Tacitus *Annales* 1.61–62', *Classical Philology*, 94 (3): 302–20.

Page, D. (1973) 'Stesichorus: The Geryoneïs', *Journal of Hellenic Studies*, 93: 138–54.

Parkin, J. (2017) '*Assassin's Creed: Origins* guide: Crafting', *Polygon* (27 December). Available at: https://www.polygon.com/assassins-creed-origins-guide/2017/12/27/16551058/crafting-hidden-blade-quiver-stabilizer-glove-bracer-breastplate-tool-pouch (accessed 25 July 2018).

Parry, M. and Parry, P. (1987) *The Making of Homeric Verse: The Collected Papers of Milman Parry*, Oxford: Oxford University Press.

Pasternak, J. (2012) '500.000 Jahre an einem Tag. Möglichkeiten und Grenzen der Darstellung von Geschichte in epochenübergreifenden Echtzeitstrategiespielen', in A. Schwarz (ed.), *Wollten Sie auch immer schon einmal pestverseuchte Kühe auf Ihre Gegner werfen? Eine fachwissenschaftliche Annäherung an Geschichte im Computerspiel*, 35–74, Münster: LIT Verlag.

Paul, J. (2010) 'Oliver Stone's *Alexander* and the cinematic epic tradition', in P. Cartledge and F. Rose Greenland (eds), *Responses to Oliver Stone's* Alexander: *Film, History, and Cultural Studies*, 15–35, Madison, WI: University of Wisconsin Press.

Paul, J. (2013) *Film and the Classical Epic Tradition*, Oxford: Oxford University Press.

Pearson, J. (2017) 'The first text adventure game ever is finally open source', *Motherboard* (29 May). Available at: https://motherboard.vice.com/en_us/article/ywmyn5/the-first-text-adventure-game-ever-is-finally-open-source (accessed 15 October 2018).

Petersen, S. (2009) 'Ask Sandy XIII', HeavenGames 2009. Available at: http://aoe3.heavengames.com/cgi-bin/forums/display.cgi?action=ct&f=1,37630,1200,all (accessed 7 October 2018).

Peterson, J. (2014) *Playing at the World: A History of Simulating Wars, People and Fantastic Adventures from Chess to Role-Playing Games*, San Diego, CA: Unreason Press.

Petrovic, I. (2008) 'Plutarch's and Stone's *Alexander*', in I. Berti and M. García Morcillo (eds), *Hellas on Screen: Cinematic Receptions of Ancient History, Literature and Myth*, 163–84, Stuttgart: Franz Steiner Verlag.

Pfister, E. (2015) 'Der Pirat als Demokrat: *Assassin's Creed IV: Black Flag* – eine Rezension', *Frühneuzeit-Info*, 26: 289–90.

Pfister, E. (2018) '"In a world without gold, we might have been heroes!" Cultural imaginations of piracy in video games', *Forum for Inter-American Research*, 11 (2): 30–43.

Phil, N. (2013) 'On memes and the meta-game', *Making Games*, 4: 52–5.

Pias, C. (2004) *Computerspiele*, Universität Duisburg-Essen. Available at: https://www.uni-due.de/~bj0063/texte/k+u.pdf (accessed 7 October 2018).

Pierce, J. B. (2013) 'Oliver Stone's unmanning of Alexander the Great in *Alexander* (2004)', in M. Cyrino (ed.), *Screening Love and Sex in the Ancient World*, 127–42, New York: Palgrave Macmillan.

Pillay, H. (2002) 'An investigation of cognitive processes engaged in by recreational computer game players', *Journal of Research on Technology in Education*, 34 (3): 336–50.

Plunkett, L. (2019) '*Assassin's Creed Odyssey's* sea shanties are actual Greek poems', Kontaku (31 January). Available at: https://kotaku.com/assassins-creed-odysseys-sea-shanties-are-actual-greek-1832218435 (accessed 4 May 2019).

Poblocki, K. (2002) 'Becoming-state: The bio-cultural imperialism of Sid Meier's *Civilization*', *Focaal*, 39: 163–77.

Pöhlmann, M. and Walter, D. (1998) 'Guderian furs Kinderzimmer? Historische Konfliktsimulationen im Computerspiel', *Zeitschrift für Geschichtswissenschaft*, 46 (12): 1087–1108.

Pomeroy, A. J. (2008) 'Alexander the Hero', in A. J. Pomeroy (ed.), *'Then it was Destroyed by the Volcano': The Ancient World in Film and on Television*, 95–111, London: Duckworth.

Poole, S. (2000) *Trigger Happy: Videogames and the Entertainment Revolution*, New York: Arcade Publishing.

Porter, J. (2018) '*Assassin's Creed* has a new mission: Working in the classroom', *New York Times* (16 May). Available at: https://www.nytimes.com/2018/05/16/arts/assassins-creed-origins-education.html (accessed 4 May 2019).

Potter, A. (2013) 'Viewer reception of classical myth in *Xena: Warrior Princess* and *Charmed*', PhD thesis, Open University, Milton Keynes. Doi:10.1017/ CBO9781107415324.004.

Potter, A. (2016) 'Classical monsters in New *Doctor Who* fan fiction', *Transformative Works and Cultures*, 21. Doi: 10.3983/twc.2016.0676.

Potter, A. (2018) 'Feminist heroines for our times: Screening the Amazon Warrior in *Wonder Woman* (1975–1979), *Xena: Warrior Princess* (1995–2001) and *Wonder Woman* (2017)', *thersites*, 7: 30–57.

Pötzsch, H. and Šisler, V. (2016) 'Playing cultural memory: Framing history in *Call of Duty: Black Ops* and *Czechoslovakia 38–89*: Assassination', *Games and Culture*. Doi: 10.1177/1555412016638603.

Prensky, M. (2001) 'Digital natives, digital immigrants', *On the Horizon*, 9 (5): 1–6.

Previews, Presley (n.d.) 'King Arthur', *ABCActionNews.com*. Available at: http:// abcactionnews.com/entertainment/moviereviews/kingarthur.shtml (accessed 6 November 2018).

Qoun (2012) 'Storyproblem: Thread', *The Secret World, Deutsches Forum*, 11.07.2012. Available at: http://bit.ly/2n8LLuj (accessed 26 January 2018).

Quesada Sanz, F. (2006) 'Not so different: Individual fighting techniques and small unit tactics of Roman and Iberian armies within the framework of warfare in the Hellenistic age', *Pallas*, 70: 245–63.

Rao, R. (2015) 'Postcolonialism', in M. Freeden, L. Tower Sargent and M. Stears (eds), *The Oxford Handbook of Political Ideologies*, 271–89, Oxford: Oxford University Press.

Raupach, T. (2014) 'Towards an analysis of strategies of authenticity production in World War II first-person shooter games', in F. Kerschbaumer and T. Winnerling (eds), *Early Modernity and Videogames*, 123–38, Newcastle upon Tyne: Cambridge Scholars Publishing.

Rauscher, A. (2011) *Spielerische Fiktionen. Transmediale Genrekonzepte in Videospielen*, Marburg: Schüren.

Ravenhurst (2013) 'Bloody Mary and the mirror in the attic in Franklin Mansion: Thread', *The Secret World, English Forum*, 15.01.2013. Available at: http://bit.ly/2nd1nxV (accessed 26 January 2018).

Reichert, R. (2008) 'Government-Games und Gouverntainment. Das Globalstrategiespiel *Civilization* von Sid Meier', in R. Nohr and S. Wiemer (eds), *Strategie spielen. Medialität, Geschichte und Politik des Strategiespiels*, 189–212, Münster: LIT Verlag.

Reinhard, A. (n.d.) 'Consulting for Ubisoft on *Assassin's Creed: Odyssey*', *Archaeogaming*. Available at: https://archaeogaming.com/2019/04/19/consulting-for-ubisoft-on- assassins-creed-odyssey/ (accessed 4 May 2019).

Reinhard, A. (2018) *Archaeogaming: An Introduction to Archaeology in and of Video Games*. New York: Berghahn Books.

Rejack, B. (2007) 'Toward a virtual reenactment of history: Video games and the recreation of the past', *Rethinking History*, 11 (3): 411–25.

Richards, J. (2008) *Hollywood's Ancient Worlds*, London and New York: Continuum.

Richards, J. (2015) 'Sir Ridley Scott and the rebirth of the historical epic', in A. B. R. Elliott (ed.), *The Return of the Epic Film: Genre, Aesthetics and History in the Twenty-First Century*, 19–35, Edinburgh: Edinburgh University Press.

Roberts, M. (1998) 'The revolt of Boudicca (Tacitus, *Annals* 14.29–39) and the Assertion of *Libertas* in Neronian Rome', *American Journal of Philology*, 109: 118–32.

Robison, W. B. (2013) 'Stimulation, not simulation: An alternate approach to history teaching games', *History Teacher*, 46 (4): 57788.

Rollinger, C. (2014) 'Roma victrix? Konstruktion, Simulation und Rezeption antiker Inhalte im Computerspiel', *Der Altsprachliche Unterricht*, 2 (3): 8892.

Rollinger, C. (2015) 'Brot, Spiele . . . und Latrinen? Zur Darstellung römischer Stadträume im Computerspiel', *thersites*, 1 (= C. Walde and C. Stoffel [eds], *Caesar's Salad: Antikerezeption im 20. und 21. Jahrhundert*): 1–45.

Rollinger, C. (2016) 'Phantasmagorien des Krieges. Authentizitätsstrategien, affektive Historizität und der antike Krieg im modernen Computerspiel', *thersites*, 4 (= A. Ambühl [ed], *War of the Senses – The Senses in War: Interactions and Tensions between Representations of War*): 313–41.

Rollinger, C. (2018) 'Battling the gods: An interview with the creators of "Apotheon" (2015): Jesse McGibney (Creative Directors), Maciej Paprocki (Classical Scholar), Marios Aristopoulos (Composer)', *thersites*, 7: 11–29.

Rood, T. (1998) *Thucydides: Narrative and Explanation*, Oxford: Oxford University Press.

Rosenstone, R. A. (1995) 'The historical film as real history', *FilmHistoria*, 5 (1): 5–23.

Rosenstone, R. A. (1998) *Visions of the Past: The Challenge of Film to Our Idea of History*, Cambridge, MA: Harvard University Press.

Rosenstone, R. A. (2006) *History on Film/Film on History*, Boston, MA: Addison-Wesley Longman.

Rossdal, M. (2015) 'All of the Greek and Roman classics: Antikerezeption in *Fanfiction*', *thersites*, 1: 46–74.

Rost, A. and Wilbers-Rost, S. (2010) 'Weapons at the Battlefield of Kalkriese', *Gladius*, 30: 117–36.

Rost, A. and Wilbers-Rost, S. (2013) *Kalkriese 6: Verteilung der Kleinfunde auf der Oberesch in Kalkriese. Kartierung und Interpretation der Römischen Militaria unter Einbeziehung der Befunde*, Mainz: Verlag Philipp von Zabern.

Rotroff, S. I. and Camp, J. M. (1996) 'The date of the third period of the Pnyx', *Hesperia*, 65: 263–94.

Royster, F. T. (2003) *Becoming Cleopatra: The Shifting Image of an Icon*, New York and Basingstoke: Palgrave Macmillan.

Rua, H. and Alvito, P. (2011) 'Living the past: 3D models, virtual reality and game engines as tools for supporting archaeology and the reconstruction of cultural heritage – The case study of the Roman villa of Casal de Freiria', *Journal of Archaeological Science*, 38: 3296–308.

Rubio-Campillo, X., Matías, P. and Ble, E. (2015) 'Centurions in the Roman Legion: Computer simulation and complex systems', *Journal of Interdisciplinary History*, 46: 245–63.

Ruggill, J. E. and McAllister, K. S. (2013) 'Against the use of computer games in the classroom: The wickedness of ludic pedagogies', in J. C. Thompson and M. A. Ouellette (eds), *The Game Culture Reader*, 86–102, Newcastle upon Tyne: Cambridge Scholars.

Rughiniș, R. and Matei, Ș. (2015) 'Play to remember: The rhetoric of time in memorial video games', in M. Kurosu (ed.), *Human–Computer Interaction: Interaction Technologies: HCI 2015*, 628–39, Berlin: Springer Nature.

Ryan, M. L. (2001) *Narrative as Virtual Reality*, Baltimore, MD: Johns Hopkins University Press.

Ryan, M. L. (2006) *Avatars of Story*, Minneapolis, MN: University of Minnesota Press.

Sabin, P. (1996) 'The mechanics of battle in the Second Punic War', in T. Cornell, B. Rankov and P. Sabin (eds), *Bulletin of the Institute of Classical Studies*, Supplement No. 67, *The Second Punic War: A Reappraisal*, 59–79, London: University of London.

Sabin, P. (2000) 'The face of Roman battle', *Journal of Roman Studies*, 90, 1–17.

Sabin, P. (2009) *Lost Battles: Reconstructing the Great Clashes of the Ancient World*, London: Continuum.

Said, E. (2003) *Orientalism*. London: Penguin.

Salen, K. and Zimmerman, E. (2003) *Rules of Play*, Cambridge, MA: MIT Press.

Salvati, A. and Bullinger, J. M. (2013) 'Selective authenticity and the playable past', in M. W. Kapell and A. B. R. Elliott (eds), *Playing with the Past: Digital Games and the Simulation of History*, 153–67, London: Bloomsbury.

Samida, S., Willner, S. and Koch, G. (2016) 'Doing history – Geschichte als Praxis: Programmatische Annäherungen', in S. Willner, G. Koch and S. Samida (eds), *Doing History: Performative Praktiken in der Geschichtskultur*, 1–25, Münster: Waxmann.

Samothracian Networks (n.d.). Available at: https://scholarblogs.emory.edu/samothraciannetworks/the-game/ (accessed 4 May 2019).

Samuel, R. (2012) *Theatres of Memory: Past and Present in Contemporary Culture*, London: Verso.

Sapieha, C. (2017) 'How Ubisoft Montreal used historians to make ancient Egypt authentic in *Assassin's Creed: Origins*', *Financial Post* (27 October). Available at: https://business.financialpost.com/technology/gaming/how-ubisoft-montreal-used-historians-to-make-ancient-egypt-authentic-in-assassins-creed-origins (accessed 6 November 2018).

Sarkar, S. (2014) 'Blizzard reaches 100M lifetime *World of Warcraft* accounts', *Polygon* (28 January). Available at: https://www.polygon.com/2014/1/28/5354856/world-of-warcraft-100m-accounts-lifetime (accessed 6 November 2018).

Sarkeesian, A. (2009–18) 'Tropes vs women in video games', *Feminist Frequency*. Available at: https://feministfrequency.com/series/tropes-vs-women-in-video-games/ (accessed 28 June 2018).

Sarkeesian, A. (2013) 'Damsel in Distress: Part 1 – Tropes vs Women in Video Games', *Feminist Frequency* (7 March. Available at: https://feministfrequency.com/video/damsel-in-distress-part-1/ (accessed 28 June 2018).

Sarkeesian, A. (2014a) 'Damsel in Distress: Part 2 – Tropes vs Women in Video Games', *Feminist Frequency* (28 May). Available at: https://feministfrequency.com/video/damsel-in-distress-part-2-tropes-vs-women/ (accessed 28 June 2018).

Sarkeesian, A. (2014b) 'Women as Background Decoration: Part 1 – Tropes vs Women in Video Games', *Feminist Frequency* (16 June). Available at: https://feministfrequency.com/video/women-as-background-decoration-tropes-vs-women/ (accessed 28 June 2018).

Sarkeesian, A. (2014c) 'Women as Background Decoration: Part 2 – Tropes vs Women in Video Games', *Feminist Frequency* (25 August). Available at: https://feministfrequency.com/video/women-as-background-decoration-part-2/ (accessed 28 June 2018).

Sawula, C. (2013) '*Assassin's Creed: Black Flag* and historical interpretation', *Play the Past* (3 September). Available at: http://www.playthepast.org/?p=3965 (accessed 25 July 2018).

Schäfer, U. U. (2018) 'Uncertainty visualization and digital 3D modeling in archaeology: A brief introduction', *Digital Art History*, 3: 87–106.

Schein, S. (2008) '"Our debt to Greece and Rome": Canon, class and ideology', in L. Hardwick and C. Stray (eds), *A Companion to Classical Reception*, 75–85, Oxford: Blackwell.

Schlüter, W. (1999) 'The Battle of the Teutoburg Forest: Archaeological research at Kalkriese near Osnabrück', in J. D. Creighton and R. J. A. Wilson (eds), *Roman Germany: Studies in Cultural Interaction*, 125–59, Portsmouth, RI: Journal of Roman Archaeology.

Schröder, D. (2011) 'Physically based real-time auralization of interactive virtual environements', PhD thesis, Rheinisch-Westfälische Technische Hochschule Aachen.

Schröder D. and Vorländer, M. (2011) 'RAVEN: A real-time framework for the auralization of interactive virtual environments', *Proceedings of Forum Acousticum*, 2011: 1541–6.

Schüler, B., Schmitz, Chr. and Lehmann, K. (2012) 'Geschichte als Marke. Historische Inhalte in Computerspielen aus der Sicht der Softwarebranche', in A. Schwarz (ed), *Wollten Sie auch immer schon einmal pestverseuchte Kühe auf Ihre Gegner werfen? Eine fachwissenschaftliche Annäherung an Geschichte im Computerspiel*, 245–62, Münster: LIT Verlag.

Schut, K. (2007) 'Strategic simulations and our past: The bias of computer games in the presentation of history', *Games and Culture*, 2 (3): 213–35.

Schutz, A. (1967) *Phenomenology of the Social World*, Evanston, IL: Northwestern University Press.

Schutz, A. and Luckmann, T. (1973/1989) *Structures of the Life-World*, 2 vols, Evanston, IL: Northwestern University Press.

Schwarz, A. (2012a) 'Computerspiele: Ein Thema für die Geschichtswissenschaft?', in A. Schwarz (ed), *Wollten Sie auch immer schon einmal pestverseuchte Kühe auf Ihre Gegner werfen? Eine fachwissenschaftliche Annäherung an Geschichte im Computerspiel*, 7–33, Münster: LIT Verlag.

Schwarz, A. (ed) (2012b) *Wollten Sie auch immer schon einmal pestverseuchte Kühe auf Ihre Gegner werfen? Eine fachwissenschaftliche Annäherung an Geschichte im Computerspiel*, Münster: LIT Verlag.

Schwarz, A. (2014) 'Narration und Narrativ. Geschichte erzählen in Videospielen', in F. Kerschbaumer and T. Winnerling (eds), *Frühe Neuzeit im Videospiel: Geschichtswissenschaftliche Perspektiven*, 27–54, Bielefeld: transcript Verlag.

Schwarz, A. (2015) 'Game studies und Geschichtswissenschaft', in K. Sachs-Hombach and J.-N. Thon (eds), *Game Studies: Aktuelle Ansätze der Computerspielforschung*, 398–447, Köln: Herbert von Halem.

Schwarz, A. (2016) 'Rezension zu: Chapman, Adam: Digital games as history: How videogames represent the past and offer access to historical practice, London 2016', *H-Soz-u-Kult* (16 January). Available at: http://www.hsozkult.de/publicationreview/id/rezbuecher-26231 (accessed 26 November 2018).

Schwingeler, S. (2008) *Die Raummaschine. Raum und Perspektive im Computerspiel*, Boizenburg: Werner Hülsbusch.

Schwingeler, S. (2014) *Kunstwerk Computerspiel – Digitale Spiele als künstlerisches Material*, Bielefeld: transcript Verlag.

Seibert, D. J. (2014) '*Assassin's Creed* franchise sales exceed 73 million', *IGN* (21 April). Available at: http://uk.ign.com/articles/2014/04/21/assassins-creed-franchise-sales-exceed-73-million (accessed 25 July 2018).

Seidman, J. (2014) 'Remembering the Teutoburg Forest: *Monumenta* in Annals 1.61', *Ramus*, 43: 94–114.

Serrano Lozano, D. (forthcoming) '*Si vis ludum para bellum*: Violence and war as predominant language of Antiquity in video games', in *Imagines V. The Fear and the Fury: Ancient Violence in Modern Imagination*, London: Bloomsbury.

Seymour, M. (2015) 'The Babylon of D. W. Griffith's *Intolerance* in Modern Imagery and in film', in M. García Morcillo, P. Hanesworth and O. Lapeña Machena (eds), *Imagining Ancient Cities in Film: From Babylon to Cinecittà*, 18–34, London: Routledge.

Shahabudin, K. (2010) 'The appearance of history: Robert Rossen's *Alexander the Great*', in P. Cartledge and F. Rose Greenland (eds), *Responses to Oliver Stone's* Alexander: *Film, History, and Cultural Studies*, 92–118, Madison, WI: University of Wisconsin Press.

Shifman, L. (2013a) 'Memes in a digital world: Reconciling with a conceptual troublemaker', *Journal of Computer-Mediated Communication*, 18: 362–77.

Shifman, L. (2013b) *Memes in Digital Culture*, Boston, MA: MIT Press.

Siclier, J. (1962) 'L'âge du péplum', *Cahiers du cinéma*, 22 (131): 26–38.

Slatkin, L. (2006) *The Power of Thetis and Selected Essays*, 2nd edn, Cambridge, MA: Harvard University Press.

Slavik, J. F. (2018) '*Pilum* and *Telum*: The Roman infantryman's style of combat in the Middle Republic', *Classical Journal*, 113: 151–71.

Smith, K. (2013) 'Video game myth busters – Did the "Crash" of 1983/84 affect arcades?', blog entry, *The Golden Age Arcade Historian* (22 December). Available at: http://allincolorforaquarter.blogspot.com/2013/12/video-game-myth-buster-did-crash-of.html (accessed 6 November 2018).

Solomon, J. (2001) *The Ancient World in the Cinema*, New Haven, CT, and London: Yale University Press.

Sommer, M. (2016) 'Hermann the German: Nineteenth-century monuments and histories', in T. Fögen and R. Warren (eds), *Graeco-Roman Antiquity and the Idea of Nationalism in the 19th Century: Case Studies*, 219–34, Berlin: De Gruyter.

Sotamaa, O. (2010) 'When the game is not enough: Motivations and practices among computer game modding culture', *Games and Culture*, 5 (3): 239–55.

Spierings, H. C. J. M. (2007) 'Rewriting *Xena: Warrior Princess*: Resistance to representations of gender, ethnicity, class and sexuality in fanfiction', PhD thesis, Utrecht University.

Spivak, G. (1988) 'Can the subaltern speak?', in C. Nelson and L. Grossberg (eds), *Marxism and the Interpretation of Culture*, 271–313, Urbana, IL: University of Illinois Press.

Spring, D. (2015) 'Gaming history: Computer and video games as historical scholarship', *Rethinking History*, 19: 207–21.

Squire, C. (2003) *Celtic Myth and Legend*, New York: Dover.

Squire, K. D. (2004) 'Replaying history: Learning world history through playing *Civilization III*', PhD thesis, Indiana University Bloomington.

Squire, K. D. (2013) 'Video game-based learning: An emerging paradigma for instruction', *Performance Improvement Quarterly*, 26 (1): 101–30. Doi: 10.1002./piq.21139.

St. Andre, K. (1984) 'Return of Heracles', *Computer Gaming World*, 4 (6): 36. Available at: http://www.cgwmuseum.org/galleries/issues/cgw_4.6.pdf (accessed 6 November 2018).

Stache, L. (2013) 'The rhetorical construction of female empowerment: The avenging-woman narrative in popular television and film', PhD thesis, University of Wisconsin-Milwaukee.

Stanton, G. R. (1996) 'The shape and size of the Athenian Assembly place in its second phase', in B. Forsén and G. Stanton (eds), *The Pnyx in the History of Athens*, 7–21, Helsinki: Foundation of the Finnish Institute at Athen.

statista (2018) *Film Industry – Statistics and Facts*. Available at: https://www.statista.com/topics/964/film (accessed 6 November 2018).

Steam 'Titan Quest' (2016) (Online store description). Available at: https://store.steampowered.com/app/475150/Titan_Quest_Anniversary_Edition (accessed 1 November 2018).

Stein-Hölkeskamp, E. (2000) 'Perikles, Kleon und Alkibiades als Redner: Eine zentrale Rolle der athenischen Demokratie im Wandel', in C. Neumeister and W. Raeck (eds), *Rede und Redner: Bewertung und Darstellung in den antiken Kulturen*, 79–93, Möhnesee: Bibliopolis.

Stöcker, Chr. (2005) '"Wenn Ghandi Ihnen mit Krieg droht": Interview mit Spieledesigner Sid Meier', *Spiegel Online* (15 December). Available at: http://bit.ly/29aIlm8 (accessed 7 August 2018).

Stray, C. (1996) 'Culture and discipline: Classics and society in Victorian England', *International Journal of the Classical Tradition*, 3: 77–85.

Struck, W. (1997) *Konfigurationen der Vergangenheit: Deutsche Geschichtsdramen im Zeitalter der Restauration*, Tübingen: Niemeyer.

Stuart, K. (2010) '*Assassin's Creed* and the appropriation of history', *The Guardian* (19 November). Available at: https://www.theguardian.com/technology/gamesblog/2010/nov/19/assassin-s-creed-brotherhood-history (accessed 25 July 2018).

Stuart, K. (2013) 'Ryse and the problem of breasts in video games', *The Guardian* (6 December). Available at: https://www.theguardian.com/technology/gamesblog/2013/dec/06/ryse-breasts-video-games-physics (accessed 14 June 2018).

Sunstein, C. R. (2016) 'Historical explanations always involve counterfactual history', *Journal of the Philosophy of History*, 10 (3): 433–40.

Swan, P. M. (2004) *The Augustan Succession: An Historical Commentary on Cassius Dio, Books 55–56 (9 B.C.–14 A.D.)*, Oxford: Oxford University Press.

T3XT (2013) 'What conspiracies do you believe in? Thread', *The Secret World, English Forum*, 22.12.2013. Available at: http://bit.ly/2nc54D9 (accessed 25 January 2018).

Tacon, J. (2001) 'Ecclesiastic "Thorubos": Interventions, interruptions, and popular involvement in the Athenian Assembly', *Greece & Rome*, 48: 173–92.

Takács, S. (2008) *The Construction of Authority in Ancient Rome and Byzantium: The Rhetoric of Empire*, Cambridge: Cambridge University Press.

Tamayo, P. (2018) 'Discovery mode turns *Assassin's Creed: Origins* into a museum', *Kotaku* (20 February). Available at: www.kotaku.co.uk/2018/02/20/discovery-mode-turns-assassins-creed-origins -into-a-museum (accessed 25 July 2018).

tamino (2012) 'Aton Kult in Ägypten: Thread', *The Secret World, Deutsches Forum*, 28.07.2012. Available at: http://bit.ly/2rvknvT (accessed 25 January 2018).

Tapsell, C. (2017) '*Assassin's Creed: Origins* crafting materials – Resources, animal goods, and their locations', *Euro Gamer* (21 November). Available at: www.eurogamer.net/articles/2017-11-21-assassins-creed-origins-crafting-materials-resources-animal-goods-locations-4849 (accessed 25 July 2018).

Tetlock, P. E. and Belkin, A. (1996) 'Counterfactual thought experiments in world politics: Logical, methodological, and psychological perspectives', in P. E. Tetlock and A. Belkin (eds), *Counterfactual Thought Experiments in World Politics: Logical, Methodological, and Psychological Perspectives*, 3–38, Princeton, NJ: Princeton University Press.

Thompson, H. A. (1982) 'The Pnyx in models', *Hesperia Suppl.*, 19: 133–47.

Thompson, H. A. and Scranton, R. L. (1943) 'Stoas and city walls on the Pnyx', *Hesperia*, 12: 269–383.

Thorsen, T. S. (ed.) (2012) *Greek and Roman Games in the Computer Age*, Trondheim: Akademika Publishing.

Timpe, D. (1970) *Arminius-Studien*, Heidelberg: Carl Winter Universitätsverlag.

Tomasso, V. (2015) 'The twilight of Olympus: Deicide and the end of the Greek gods', in M. S. Cyrino and M. E. Safran (eds), *Classical Myth on Screen*, 147–57, New York: Palgrave Macmillan.

Tordoff, R. (2014) 'Counterfactual history and Thucydides', in V. Wohl (ed.), *Probabilities, Hypotheticals and Counterfactuals in Ancient Greek Thought*, 101–21, Cambridge: Cambridge University Press.

Tori (2014) 'Is there a repository of histories? Thread', *The Secret World, English Forum*, 04.09.2014. Available at: http://bit.ly/2DF9xbC (accessed 24 January 2018).

Torino Abstracts (2016) *The Fear and the Fury: Ancient Violence in Modern Imagination*, Imagines Conference, Universitá degli Studi di Torino, 29 September–1 October. Available at: http://www.imagines-project.org/torino-2016/torino-abstracts/ (accessed 6 November 2018).

Treu, K. (1991) 'Rede als Kommunikation: Der Attische Redner und sein Publikum', *Philologus*, 135: 124–30.

Tucker, A. (1999) 'Historiographical counterfactuals and historical contingency', *History and Theory*, 38 (2): 264–76.

Tucker, A. (2016) 'Historiographic counterfactuals and the philosophy of historiography', *Journal of the Philosophy of History*, 10 (3): 333–48.

Tynes, J. (2010) 'Prismatic play: Games as windows on the real world', in P. Harrigan and N. Wardrip-Fruin (eds), *Second Person: Role-Playing and Story in Games and Playable Media*, 221–8, Cambridge, MA: MIT Press.

Upton, B. (2015) *The Aesthetic of Play*, Cambridge, MA: MIT Press.

Universität Stuttgart (n.d.) Historisches Institut, Peter Scholz. Available at: https://www.hi. uni-stuttgart.de/ag/forschung/rom (accessed 4 May 2019).

Uricchio, W. (2005) 'Simulation, history, and computer games', in J. Raessens and J. Goldstein (eds), *Handbook of Computer Game Studies*, 327–38, Cambridge, MA: MIT Press.

Varoufakis, Y. (1997) 'Moral rhetoric in the face of strategic weakness: Experimental clues for an ancient puzzle', *Erkenntnis*, 46 (1): 87–110.

Varoufakis, Y. (2014) 'War spikes in the Eve Online universe: A political economist's account', blog entry, *Yanis Varoufakis* (30 January). Available at: https://www. yanisvaroufakis.eu/2014/01/30/war-spikes-in-the-eve-online-universe-a-political-economists-account (accessed 6 November 2018).

Vávra, D. (2014) 'AAA as an Indie: *Kingdom Come: Deliverance*', *Making Games Magazin*, 3: 12–17.

Vermeule, E. (1979) *Aspects of Death in Early Greek Art and Poetry*, Berkeley, CA: University of California Press.

Vernant, J. P. and Zeitlin, F. I. (1991) *Mortals and Immortals: Collected Essays*, Princeton, NJ: Princeton University Press.

VGChartz (2018) '*Ryse: Son of Rome* sales summary', VGC. Available at: http://www. vgchartz.com/game/73070/ryse/ (accessed 25 July 2018).

Villarejo, A. (2017) 'Critiquing the media: Stuart Hall on television', *Soundings: A Journal of Politics and Culture*, 67: 103–13.

von Glahn, R. (2004) *The Sinister Way: The Divine and the Demonic in Chinese Religious Culture*, Berkeley, CA: University of California Press.

Vowinckel, A. (2009) 'Past futures: From re-enactment to the simulation of history in computer games', *Historical Social Research*, 34 (2): 322–32.

Vrtačič, E. (2014) 'The grand narratives of video games: Sid Meier's *Civilization*', *Teorija in praksa*, 51 (1): 91–105.

Waldrop, M. M. (2016) 'More than Moore', *Nature*, 530: 144–7. Doi: 10.1038/530144a.

Walker, J. (2010) 'A network of quests in *World of Warcraft*', in P. Harrigan and N. Wardrip-Fruin (eds), *Second Person: Role-Playing and Story in Games and Playable Media*, 307–10, Cambridge, MA: MIT Press.

Walters, M. (2018) Tweet on Twitter (23 November). Available at: https://twitter.com/ MarkWalters_/Status/1065936760759304192 (accessed 4 May 2019).

Walton, M. (2013) '*Ryse: Son of Rome* review', *Gamespot* (21 November). Available at: https://www.gamespot.com/reviews/ryse-son-of-rome-review/1900-6415571/ (accessed 25 July 2018).

Warren, R. (2016) 'Arminius in Bohemia: Two uses of Tacitus in Czech art', in T. Fögen and R. Warren (eds), *Graeco-Roman Antiquity and the Idea of Nationalism in the 19th Century: Case Studies*, 235–68, Berlin: De Gruyter.

Watrall, E. (2002) 'Digital pharaoh: Archaeology, public education and interactive entertainment', *Public Archaeology*, 2 (3): 163–9.

Webber, N. (2016) 'Public history, game communities and historical knowledge', paper presented at the Playing with History: Games, Antiquity and History Workshop, *DiGRA and FDG Joint International Conference*, Dundee, August 1–6.

Webster, A. (2018) '*Assassin's Creed: Origins*' new educational mode is a violence-free tour through ancient Egypt', *The Verge* (20 February). Available at: https://www.theverge. com/2018/2/20/17033024/assassins-creed-origins-discovery-tour-educational-mode-release (accessed 4 May 2019).

Weiss, S. (2015) '*Kingdom Come: Deliverance* – Interview Special: Teil 1 – Von Ketzern, Sex und Entwicklersorgen', *PC Games* (14 April). Available at: http://bit.ly/29Yv1xW (accessed 7 August 2018).

Welwei, K. W. (1996) 'Politische Kommunikation im klassischen Athen', in G. Binder and K. Ehlich (eds), *Kommunikation in politischen und kultischen Gemeinschaften*, 25–50, Trier: WVT.

Wesener, S. (2007) 'Geschichte in Bildschirmspielen. Bildschirmspiele mit historischem Inhalt', in T. Bevc (ed.), *Computerspiele und Politik: Zur Konstruktion von Politik und Gesellschaft in Computerspielen*, 141–64, Berlin: LIT Verlag.

White, H. (1973) *Metahistory: The Historical Imagination in Nineteenth-Century Europe*, Baltimore, MD: Johns Hopkins University.

Wieber, A. (2008) 'Celluloid Alexander(s): A hero from the past as role model for the present?', in I. Berti and M. García Morcillo (eds), *Hellas on Screen: Cinematic Receptions of Ancient History, Literature and Myth*, 147–62, Stuttgart: Franz Steiner Verlag.

Wilbers-Rost, S. (2007) *Kalkriese 3 – Interdisziplinäre Untersuchungen auf dem Oberesch in Kalkriese: Archäologische Befunde und naturwissenschaftliche Begleituntersuchungen*, Mainz: Verlag Philipp von Zabern.

Will, W. (2000) 'Perikles: eine Konjektural-Biographie des Thukydides', in K. Brodersen (ed.), *Virtuelle Antike: Wendepunkte der alten Geschichte*, 27–36, Darmstadt: Wissenschaftliche Buchgesellschaft.

Williams, D. (2006) 'A brief social history of game play', in J. Bryant and P. Vordere (eds), *Playing Video Games: Motives, Responses, and Consequences*, 197–212, Mahwah, NJ: Erlbaum.

Willis, I. (2016) 'The classical canon and/as transformative work', *Transformative Works and Cultures*, 21. Doi: 10.3983/twc.2016.0807.

Wing, R. L. (1966) 'Two computer-based economic games for sixth graders', *American Behavioral Scientist*, 10 (3): 31–5.

Wing, R. L. (1967) *The Production and Evaluation of Three Computer-Based Economics Games for the Sixth Grade: Final Report*, Yorktown Heights, NY: US Department of Health, Education, and Welfare.

Winkler, M. (2004) '*Gladiator* and the traditions of historical cinema', in M. Winkler (ed), *Gladiator: Film and History*, 16–30, Oxford: Blackwell.

Winkler, M. (2009) *The Roman Salute: Cinema, History, Ideology*, Columbus, OH: Ohio State University Press.

Winkler, M. (2016) *Arminius the Liberator: Myth and Ideology*, Oxford: Oxford University Press.

Winnerling, T. (2014) 'The eternal recurrence of all bits: How historicizing video game series transform factual history into affective historicity', *Eludamos*, 8 (1): 151–70. Available at: http://www.eludamos.org/index.php/eludamos/article/view/vol8no1-10 (accessed 13 June 2018).

Winnerling, T. (2017) 'Jäger des verlorenen Spiels – IBM: The Sumerian Game', *Spiel-Kultur-Wissenschaften* (8 January). Available at: http://spielkult.hypotheses.org/1547 (accessed 10 October 2018).

Winnerling, T. (2018) 'Projekt Sumerian Game: Digitale Rekonstruktion eines Spiels als Simulation eines Modells', blog entry, *Arbeitskreis Geschichtswissenschaft und Digitale Spiele* (9 January). Available at: https://gespielt.hypotheses.org/1796 (accessed 6 November 2018).

Wolf, P. (1996) 'Der Traum von der Zeitreise. Spielerische Simulation von Vergangenheit mit Hilfe des Computers', *Geschichte in Wissenschaft und Unterricht*, 47: 535–47.

Wolf, P. (1998) 'Historismus auf dem Bildschirm? Überlegungen zu Computerspielen mit historischer Thematik', in Bergbau- und Industriemuseum Ostbayern und Haus der Bayerischen Geschichte Augsburg (eds), *EDV-Tage Theuern 1997. Tagungsbericht*, 68–74, Kümmersbruck: Bergbau- und Industriemuseum Ostbayern.

Wolf, M. J. P. (2001) *The Medium of the Video Game*, Austin, TX: University of Texas Press.

Wolf, M. J. P. (ed.) (2012) *Encyclopedia of Video Games: The Culture, Technology, and Art of Gaming, Volume I*, Santa Barbara, CA: Greenwood.

Wolters, R. (2008) *Die Schlacht im Teutoburger Wald: Arminius, Varus und das römische Germanien*, München: C. H. Beck.

Woolf, G. (2011) *Tales of the Barbarians: Ethnography and Empire in the Roman West*, Chichester: Wiley-Blackwell.

Wottge, M. (2011) 'Der Einsatz von Computerspielen im Geschichtsunterricht am Beispiel von "Caesar III"', *Geschichte in Wissenschaft und Unterricht*, 62: 469–77.

Wyke, M. (1997) *Projecting the Past: Ancient Rome, Cinema and History*, London: Routledge.

Yogsothoth (2008) 'Mmoarsng? Thread', *The Secret World, English Forum*, 16.08.2008. Available at: http://bit.ly/2DIb0Oq (accessed 25 January 2018).

Yume (2011) 'Ark of the Covenant being moved – because of a leaky roof: Thread', *The Secret World, English Forum*, 07.12.2011. Available at: http://bit.ly/2DChCxK (accessed 23 January 2018).

z4oslo (2012) 'I gotta give it to you Funcom, you did your homework: Thread', *The Secret World, English Forum*, 17.07.2012. Available at: http://bit.ly/2DHhWLR (accessed 25 January 2018).

Zajko, V. and Leonard, M. (2006) 'Introduction', in V. Zajko and M. Leonard (eds), *Laughing with Medusa: Classical Myth and Feminist Thought*, 1–20, Oxford: Oxford University Press.

Zanker, A. T. (2013) 'Decline and parainesis in Hesiod's race of iron', *Rheinisches Museum für Philologie*, 156 (1): 1–19.

Zhang, W., (2015) 'Zhou Zuoren and the uses of ancient Greek mythology in modern China', *International Journal of the Classical Tradition*, 22 (1): 100–15.

Zhmodikov, A. (2000) 'Roman Republican heavy infantrymen in battle (IV–II centuries B.C.)', *Historia*, 49: 67–78.

Zimmerman, E. (2002) 'Do independent games exist?', in L. King and C. Bain (eds), *Game On*, 120–9, London: Barbican.

Zuckerberg, D. (2015) 'Bang Rome: Ovid and the original sin of pickup artistry', *Eidolon* (21 December). Available at: https://eidolon.pub/bang-rome-2214f4a3d5c5 (accessed 13 June 2018).

Zuckerberg, D. (2016) 'How to be a good classicist under a bad emperor', *Eidolon* (21 November). Available at: https://eidolon.pub/how-to-be-a-good-classicist-under-a-bad-emperor-6b848df6e54a (accessed 13 June 2018).

Zusag, M. (2013) 'Digitale Spiele in der Geschichtswissenschaft: Betrachtungen zum Quellenwert und zu den methodischen Grundlagen ihrer wissenschaftlichen Analyse', MA thesis, University of Vienna.

Zwischenberger, A. (2014) 'Epochengrenzen in Videospielen. *Age of Empires III* und *Europa Universalis III*', in F. Kerschbaumer and T. Winnerling (eds), *Frühe Neuzeit im Videospiel: Geschichtswissenschaftliche Perspektiven*, 257–68, Bielefeld: transcript Verlag.

Mediography

300 (2006) Zack Synder (dir.). Film. Warner Bros.

Alexander (2004) Oliver Stone (dir.). Film. Warner Bros.

Alexander the Great (1956) Robert Rossen (dir.). Film. United Artists.

Atari: Game Over (2014) Zak Penn (dir.). Film. Netflix.

Black Sails (2014–17) Created by Jonathan Steinberg and Robert Levine. TV. STARZ.

Britannia (2018–) Created by Jez Butterworth, Tom Butterworth and James Richardson. TV. Sky and Amazon Prime.

Cabiria (1914) Giovanni Pastrone (dir.). Film. Italia Film.

Gladiator (2000) Ridley Scott (dir.). Film. DreamWorks Pictures and Universal Pictures.

Hercules (1997) John Musker and Ron Clements (dir.). Film. Walt Disney Studios.

Immortals (2011) Tarsem Singh (dir.). Film. Relativity Media.

Jason and the Argonauts (1963) Don Chaffey (dir.). Film. Columbia Pictures.

King Arthur (2004) Antoine Fuqua (dir.). Film. Buena Vista Pictures.

Saving Private Ryan (1998) Stephen Spielberg (dir.). Film. Paramount Pictures.

Spartacus (2010–13) Created by Stephen S. DeKnight. TV. STARZ.

Star Wars Episode VI: Return of the Jedi (1983) Richard Marquand (dir.). Film. Lucasfilm Ltd.

The 300 Spartans (1962) Rudolph Maté (dir.). Film. 20th Century Fox.

The Eagle (2011) Kevin Macdonald (dir.). Film. Universal Pictures.

The Great Wall (2016) Zhang Yimou (dir.). Film. Universal Pictures.

The Wicker Man (1973) Robin Hardy (dir.) Film. British Lion Films.

Xena: Warrior Princess (1995–2001) Created by John Schulian and Robert Tapert. TV. MCA TV/Universal Television Enterprises/Studios USA.

Ludography

Games are cited according to the following template:

Title (*Year*), *developer(s)/publisher(s), platform.*

Title refers to the international title under which the game was released, independent of
   local translations. Game modifications ('mods') are labelled as such. Their entries
   include the title of the original games in square brackets. As mods are produced by
   large groups of volunteers, no developer or publisher is given.
Year refers only to the year of first release. Later updates ('patches') or modifications are
   not listed. Where several years are listed, these refer to releases across different
   platforms. In the case of game series, the years given indicate the release of the first and
   latest entry in the series.
Developer refers to the developing studio that created the software. *Publisher* refers to the
   corporate entity that releases and markets games. Occasionally, developing and
   publishing studios may be identical; in that case, the studio is named only once. For
   very early games, the names of individual programmers are given instead of developing
   or publishing studios.
Platform refers to both hardware and software environments on which the game is
   available. These include the Sony PlayStation (PS1–4), Microsoft XBOX (Xbox, XBOX
   360, XBOX One), Nintendo (Nintendo Entertainment System, Game Boy, Game Boy
   Colour, Nintendo DS, Nintendo 3DS) and Sega (Sega Saturn, Sega Genesis) gaming
   consoles, as well as mobile gaming platforms (Android and iOS systems) and personal
   computers (PC). For convenience, games are listed as 'PC' even in the case of operating
   systems (MacOS, Linux) or hardware that do not traditionally fall under the PC
   heading (this includes now obsolete hardware platforms such as ZX Spectrum,
   Amstrad CPC, Commodore 64, Atari ST, Atari 8-bit, NEC PC-9801, FM Towns,
   PDP-8, PDP-10 and Amiga). 'Multiplatform' indicates that this title was released across
   a large variety of older and modern platforms, including PC, consoles, handheld and
   mobile platforms.

Games set in antiquity

0 A.D.: Empires Ascendant (2017) Wildfire Games, PC.
Age of Empires (1997–2018) [Game Series] Ensemble Studios, Forgotten Empires/
   Microsoft, PC.
Age of Gladiators (2016) Creative Storm Entertainment, PC.
Age of Mythology (2002) Ensemble Studios/Microsoft Game Studios, PC.
Ancient Mediterranean Civilization (2012) [*Civilization V* mod].
Ankh (2005) Deck13 and VIS Interactive/BHV Software, Xider Games, Daedalic
   Entertainment, PC/Nintendo DS.

Ankh: Battle of the Gods (2008) Deck13/BHV Software, PC.

Ankh: Heart of Osiris (2006) Deck13 Interactive/Xider, PC.

Annals of Rome (1986) Level 9 Computing/Personal Software Services, PC.

Apotheon (2015) Alientrap Inc/Alientrap Inc, PC/PS4.

Assassin's Creed (2007–present) [Game Series] Ubisoft/Ubisoft, multiplatform.

Ben-Hur (2016) Krome Studios/Float Hybrid Entertainment, Xbox.

Caesar (1992–2006) [Game Series] Impressions Games and Tilted Mill Entertainment/
    Sierra On-Line and Vivendi Universal Games, PC.

Centurion: Defender of Rome (1990) Bits of Magic/Electronic Arts, PC/Sega Genesis.

Chariot Wars (2015) OM Entertainment, PC.

Circus Maximus: Chariot Wars (2002) Kodiak Interactive/Encore & THQ), PS2/Xbox.

Civilization (1991) Microprose/Microprose, PC.

Civilization V (2010) Firaxis Games/2K and Aspyr Games, PC.

Cleopatra: Queen of the Nile (2000) BreakAway Games/Sierra Entertainment, PC.

Cohort: Fighting for Rome (1991) Impressions Games/Merit Software, PC.

Colosseum: Road to Freedom (2005) Ertain/Koei, PS2.

Disney's Hercules (1997) Disney Interactive/Disney, PC/PS.

Egypt: 1156 B.C.: Tomb of the Pharaoh (1997/99) Cryo Interactive Entertainment/Cryo
    Interactive Entertainment and Canal+ Multimedia and Réunion des Musées Nationaux
    and DreamCatcher Games, PC/PS.

Egypt 2: The Heliopolis Prophecy (2000) Cryo Interactive/ DreamCatcher Initiative, PC/PS.

Egypt 3: The Egyptian Prophecy (2004) Kheops Studio/The Adventure Company, PC.

Field of Glory II: Rise of Rome (2017) Byzantine Games/Slitherine Ltd., PC.

Gladiator Begins (2010) GOSHOW/Acquire and Aksys Games and Zen United, PSP.

God of War (2005–18) [Game Series], SCE Santa Monica Studio/Sony Computer
    Entertainment and Sony Interactive Entertainment, PS1–4.

Grand Ages: Rome (2009) Haemimont Games/Kalypso Media, PC.

Hammurabi (1973) Doug Gyment, PC.

Hegemony Gold: Wars of Ancient Greece (2011) Longbow Games/Longbow Games, PC.

Herc's Adventures (1997) Big Ape Production/LucasArts, PS/Sega Saturn.

Hercules: Slayer of the Damned (1988) Cygnus Software/Gremlin Graphics, PC.

Imperator: Rome (2019) Paradox Development Studio/Paradox Interactive, PC.

Imperium (2002–19) [Game Series] Haemimont Games/FX Interactive, PC.

Kid Icarus (1986) Nintendo R&D1 and Project Sora/Nintendo, NES/Game Boy/Nintendo
    3DS.

Legionnaire (1982) Chris Crawford/Avalon Hill, PC.

Legions of Death (1987) MC Lothlorien Ltd., PC.

Mount and Blade: Warband (2010–14) TaleWorlds Entertainment/Paradox Interactive and
    Ravenscourt, multiplatform.

Myth: History in the Making (1989) System 3, PC.

Mytheon (2011) Petroglyph Game/True Games, PC.

Nethergate (1998) Spiderweb Software, PC.

Nethergate: Resurrection (2007) Spiderweb Software, PC.

Octopath Traveler (2018) Square Enix and Acquire/Nintendo and Square Enix, Nintendo
    Switch.

Pandora's Palace (1984) Konami/Interlogic, Arcade cabinet.

Pericles: The Peloponnesian Wars (2017) Mark Herman/GMT Games, boardgame.

Pharao (1999) Impressions Games/Sierra Entertainment, PC.

Pompeii: The Legend of Vesuvius (2000) Axel Tribe/Cryo Interactive, PC.

Poseidon: Master of Atlantis Expansion Pack (2001) Impressions Games/Vivendi Universal Interactive Publishing, PC.

Praetorians (2003) Pyro Studios/Eidos Interactive, PC.

QVADRIGA (2014) Turnopia/Slithering, PC.

Roma Universalis (2015) [Europa Universalis mod], PC.

Roma Victor (2006) RedBedlam/RedBedlam, PC.

Rome: Pathway to Power (1992) Firstlight/Millennium Interactive and Maxis, PC.

Rome Rise of an Empire (2015) [Mount and Blade: Warband mod], PC.

Rome: Total Realism (2005–10) [Rome: Total War mod], PC.

Rome: Total War (2004) The Creative Assembly/Activision, PC.

Rome: Total War: Barbarian Invasion (2005) The Creative Assembly/SEGA, PC.

Ryse: Son of Rome (2013) Crytek, PC/Xbox.

Spartacus Legends (2013) Kung Fu Factory/Ubisoft, PS/Xbox.

The Battle of Olympus (1988) Infinity and Radical Entertainment/Imagineer and Brøderbund and Nintendo, NES/Game Boy.

The Melian Dilemma (2019) N. Morley, web-based, PC (http://philome.la/NevilleMorley/the-melian-dilemma).

The Return of Heracles (1983) Stuart Smith/Quality Software, PC.

Titan Quest (2006) Iron Lore Entertainment/THQ, PC.

Total War: Rome II (2013) The Creative Assembly/SEGA, PC.

Xena: Warrior Princess (1999) Universal Studios Digital Arts and Titus Interactive Studio/Electronic Arts and Titus Interactive, PS/Game Boy Color.

Warrior of Rome (*Caesar no Yabou*) (1991) Micronet, Sega Mega Drive/Genesis.

Zeus: Master of Olympus (2000) Impressions Games/Sierra Studios, PC.

Other games

Alone in the Dark (1992–2015) [Game Series], Infogrames and Darkworks and Eden Games and Pure FPS/Infogrames and Atari SA, multiplatform.

Battlefield I (2016) EA DICE/Electronic Arts, PS/Xbox/PC.

Battlefield V (2018) EA DICE/Electronic Arts, PS/Xbox/PC.

Bayonetta (2009) PlatinumGames/Capcom, PS/Xbox/PC.

Brothers in Arms (2005–8) [Game Series], Gearbox Software/Ubisoft, multiplatform.

Call of Duty: Ghosts (2013) Infinity Ward/Activision, PS/Xbox/PC.

Colossal Cave Adventure (1976) Crowther, Will (dev.)/unpublished, PC.

Counter-Strike (2000) Valve L.L.C./Sierra Studios and Valve Corporation, PC.

Devil May Cry (2001) Capcom/Capcom, PS.

Diablo (1996–2012) [Game Series], Blizzard North/Blizzard Entertainment, PC.

Dune II: The Battle for Arrakis (1992) Westwood Studios/Virgin Interactive, PC.

Eastern Front 1941 (1981) Chris Crawford/Atari Program Exchange and Atari Inc., PC.

Europa Universalis (2000–2013) [Game Series], Paradox Interactive, PC.

Fallout 3 (2008) Bethesda Game Studios/Bethesda Softworks, multiplatform.

Fallout 4 (2015) Bethesda Game Studios/Bethesda Softworks, multiplatform.

Fallout 76 (2018) Bethesda Game Studios/Bethesda Softworks, multiplatform.

Far Cry (2006–18) Crytek and Ubisoft Montreal/Ubisoft, multiplatform.

Football Manager 2017 (2016) Sports Interactive/Sega, PC.

Grand Theft Auto III (2001) DMA Design/Rockstar Games, multiplatform.

Grand Theft Auto V (2013) Rockstar Games/Rockstar Games, multiplatform.

Half Life 2 (2004) Valve Corporation/Valve Corporation and Vivendi Universal and Sierra
 Entertainment and Electronic Arts, PC.
Halo (2001–present) [Game series], Bungie, 343 Industries, Ensemble Studios/Microsoft
 Studios, Xbox/Windows.
Horizon Zero Dawn (2017) Guerilla Games/Sony, PS4.
IL-2 Sturmovik (2001) 1C:Maddox Games/Ubisoft, PC.
Kingdom Come: Deliverance (2018) Warhorse Studios/Warhorse Studios, multiplatform.
Kingdom Hearts (2002–17) Square Enix/Square Enix and Disney, multiplatform.
Mario Kart (1992–2014) [Game Series], Nintendo EAD Software Development
 Department No. 1/Nintendo, multiplatform.
Medal of Honor (1999) Dreamworks Interactive/Electronic Arts, PS.
Metal Gear Solid 2: Sons of Liberty (2001) Konami Computer/Entertainment/Konami,
 PS1–4.
Metro: Exodus (2019) 4A Games/Deep Silver, multiplatform.
Out of the Park Baseball 18 (2016) Out of the Park Developments/Out of the Park
 Developments, PC.
Populous: The Beginning (1998) Bullfrog Productions/Electronic Arts, PC/PS.
Pro Cycling Manager 2017 (2016) Cyanide Studio/Focus Home Interactive, PC.
Red Dead Redemption (2010–18) [Game Series], Rockstar San Diego/Rockstar Games,
 PS3–4/Xbox 360 and Xbox One.
Secret World Legends (2017) FunCom/FunCom, PC.
Serious Sam (2001–17) [Game Series], Croteam/Take 2, PC.
SimCity (1989–2014) [Game Series], Maxis/Maxis and Electronic Arts, PC.
Starcraft II (2010) Activision/Blizzard Entertainment, PC.
Super Mario (1985–) [Game Series], Nintendo Research and Development/Nintendo,
 multiplatform.
The Elder Scrolls III: Morrowind (2002) Bethesda Game Studios/Bethesda Softworks,
 multiplatform.
The Elder Scrolls IV: Oblivion (2006) Bethesda Game Studios/Bethesda Softworks and 2K,
 multiplatform.
The Elder Scrolls V: Skyrim (2011) Bethesda Game Studios/Bethesda Softworks,
 multiplatform.
The Legend of Zelda: Breath of the Wild (2017) Nintendo/Nintendo, Nintendo Switch.
The Lord of the Rings Online (2007) Turbine/Turbine, Inc., PC.
The Secret World (2012–17) FunCom/FunCom and Electronic Arts, PC.
The Witcher 3: Wild Hunt (2015) CD Projekt RED/Namco Bandai Games and Warner
 Bros. Interactive and Spike Chunsoft, multiplatform.
Theme Park (1994) Bullfrog Productions/Electronic Arts, PC.
Tomb Raider (1996–2018) [Game series], Core Design, Crystal Dynamics, Eidos Montreal/
 Eidos Interactive, Square Enix, multiplatform.
Tyranny (2016) Obsidian Entertainment/Paradox Interactive, PC.
Ultima Online (1997) Origin Systems/Electronic Arts, PC.
Uncharted: Drake's Fortune (2007) Naughty Dog/Sony Computer Entertainment, PS3/PS4.
Wild Blood (2012) Gameloft, Android/iOS (mobile gaming).
Wolfenstein 3D (1992) id Software/Apogee Software, PC.
World of Warcraft (2004) Blizzard Entertainment/Vivendi (2004–8) and Activision
 (2008–), PC.
Zelda (1986–2017) [Game Series], Nintendo R&D4 and Nintendo Entertainment Planning
 & Development/Nintendo, multiplatform.

Index

300 (Frank Miller graphic novel) 239
300 (movie) 10, 55

accuracy 6–8, 57, 69–9, 108–9, 160–4, 224,
    236, 238–41, 249
affective historicity 6, 54–5
affordances 111, 142, 148–9, 152, 159, 224,
    237
Alexandria 38–9, 71, 73
archaeogaming xvii, 9–11, 31, 63–4
archaeology 72–4
authenticity 5–8, 40, 52, 54–8, 63–9, 75,
    167, 235–6, 242–3
    see also affective historicity
    see also realism 5–8, 69–74
avatar 157, 167, 220, 243

blogs 9–10
Boudica 82–3, 85–8

Cold War 20–1
Colosseum 30, 54, 67
commemorative culture 158, 167–70
community affiliation 132–8
counterfactual history 179–85, 248
cultural memory 167–70
cutscenes (cinematics) 16, 53, 67, 78–81,
    83–7, 93–104, 205

didactics 7–8
    Discovery Mode 56
Dungeons and Dragons 99, 127, 128, 142

Egypt 74, 141, 149–51, 158, 161–6
Egyptian culture 161

First World War 25, 233
freedom of play 213–14

game designers
    Ahl, D.H. 29–30

Dillenberger, P. 19
Heinemann, B. 19
Rawitsch, D. 19
Turek, J. 31
game designers (studios)
    Alientrap Games 193
    Atari 1–2
    Bethesda 127, 130–1
    Creative Assembly 99, 109,
    Ensemble Studios 206
    Forgotten Empires 206
    MECC 19
    Paradox 33
    Ubisoft 39, 69–74, 160, 162
game engine 219–21
    in archaeological research 221–2
game studies 2–3
    see Historical game studies/research
gamescape 20
genres 22–6
    4X 6, 32–5, 40, 48, 50, 58, 237
    AAA 242
    according to S. Poole, 22–3
    according to M. Wolf, 23
    action-adventure 22–6, 35–8, 77,
    city-building/economic simulations
        29–31, 40, 48, 50
    first-person shooter 22–7, 37, 47, 49,
        219
    God-games 22–3, 49–51
    human-scale games 49–52
    MMORPGs 15–16, 23–5: 48–50, 157ff.,
        245
    process-oriented 22–5, 30
    real-time 20, 24, 32–5, 48, 57, 99,
        112–18, 120, 167, 206
    RPGs 22–5, 127–40, 141–56, 157–78
    sandbox 38–9
    strategy game 31–4
    turn-based 31–2, 48, 112–18, 120
graphic user interface 21

hardware 2, 19–22, 222
    coin-ops/arcade games 20–1
    computer mouse 21–2
    gamepad/controller 1, 21–2
    microcomputers 29
    Nintendo, NES 2, Switch 72
    PC 1–2, 21, 29, 221
    Playstation 2, 28, 72
    Xbox 2, 64, 67, 77
    see also technological-cultural history
history
    concepts of history 158–61
    historical-ness 161
    history as process 50–2, 55, 205–6
    pastness 3
    see also counterfactual history, affective
        historicity, teleology
historical game studies/research 1–10, 15,
    234–52
(hi)story-play-space xvii, 236–7
historiography
    in-game historical traditions 165
    in EVE Online 23 with n.14, 245
    oral history (in-game) 165
Homer/Homeric tradition 128–30

iconicity 53–4
immersion 23, 52, 64, 67, 73, 128, 131

King Arthur (film) 66, 85–7

levelling-up/XPs 28, 37, 133–4
    achievements/rewards 165
Limits of Play 82–3
ludic 47–50, 55–7, 249
ludology vs narratology debate 243–4

metagame 213–14
methodology
    ecological approach (A. Chapman)
        159
    empirical research (lack thereof)
        15–16
    Historical Knowledge System 162–5,
        168–71
    instances of play, 162
        paths 162
        recordings 162
modelling 113–21, 205–10

modifications (mods) 68
    *Civilization V Ancient Mediterranean
        Civilizations* 56
    Roma Universalis 55
    Rome: Rise of an Empire 56
    Rome: Total Realism 55
MUDs (multi-user dungeons) 167, 227
myth/mythology 37, 52, 56, 65, 69, 146–9,
    151, 157–8

narrative
    diegetic perspective 22, 25, 79, 245–6
    embedded 205
    emergent 205–6, 210–11
    emplotment 15, 77
    epic tradition 129, 138, 166, 244
        see also Homer/Homeric tradition
    ludonarrative 49–50, 55–8, 77–8,
        240–1, 243–7
    narratology 159, 243
NPC (non-player character) 10, 136–7,
    146, 148, 166, 240

object and material culture 51–2, 160–7
oral formulaic theory 128–30

pen & paper 167
    MUDs
    see also Dungeons and Dragons
players
    online communities 13, 15, 95–7,
        102–4, 127–8, 132–8
    player types 167–8

realism 5–8, 69–74
reception studies 3–4, 5–8, 10, 15
    Rezeptionsästhetik 3–4
researchers
    Adams, E. 35–7
    Assmann, A. 168
    Bartle, R. 167–9
    Blakely, S. 8
    Bulliger, J.M. 68
    Chapman, A. 2–3
    Egenfeldt-Nielsen, S. 25, 30, 25
    Elliott, A. 5, 244
    Foka, A. 2–3
    Gainsford, P. 10
    Graham, S. 31, 191

Holub, R. 3
Huizinga, J. 3
Jauss, H.R. 3
Junkelmann, M. 49
Kapell, M. 5, 244
Lord, A. 128
Lowe, D. 3, 5
Lowenthal, D. 5
Magnet, S. 20
Martindale, C. 3–4
Murray, J.H. 128–9
Muth, S. 8
Owens, T. 131
Parry, M. 128
Poole, S. 5, 22
Reinhard, A. xvii, 9, 31
Rosenstone, R. 6, 49
Salvati, A. 68
Schut, K. 33
Schütz, A. 33
Schwarz, A. 8, 26
Smith, J.H. 25, 30, 25
Tosca, S.P. 25, 30, 25
Uricchio, W. 2, 50
Walters, M. 10
Westin, J. 2–3
Winnerling, T. 6, 29, 55,
Wolf, M. 23

Second World War 5, 23, 25–6, 32, 68, 101,
    233
simulations
    conceptual simulation 25, 111, 121,
    economic simulations 29–31, 40, 48, 50
    realist simulation 25, 111,
slavery 30

technological-cultural history 20–2
    term 161f.
technological progress 208, 247
    narratives of 210–12
tech(nology) tree 7, 207–9, 211
teleology 7, 180, 208
twine 188–91
Twitter 9–10

video games
    as agent-based modelling 31
    as ergodic texts 16 with n.54

and films 53–8
and gender 14–15, 77–106, 170, 240–1
market/sales 2–3, 22
as pop culture 47–62, 95–7, 242–3
as re-enactment 39, 52, 57, 63, 69, 82,
    237, 243, 248–50
video games (titles)
    1156 B.C.: Tomb of the Pharao 57
    Age of Gladiators 1–2 28, 49
    Alone in the Dark 37
    Ankh 57
    Annals of Rome 32–3, 52
    Anno 25, 160
    Assassin's Creed
        Odyssey 10, 26, 38, 70, 235, 239
        Origins 26, 38, 39, 56, 67, 70–3, 158,
            235
    Asteroids 1
    The Battle of Olympus 35–7
    Battle of the Gods 57
    Battlefield 1 25
    Brothers in Arms 25
    Builders of Egypt 31
    Call of Duty 25
    Cathode-Ray Amusement Device 16 n.3
    Caesar 24, 52
    Circus Maximus 27, 49
    Civilization 52
    Cleopatra 31
    Cohort: Fighting for Rome 52
    Colossal Cave Adventure 20, 35, 127–8,
        186
    Colosseum: Road to Freedom 28, 49
    Computer Bismarck 32
    Counterstrike 26
    Diablo 23
    Donkey Kong 21
    Dune II 32
    Eastern Front 32
    The Egyptian Prophecy 57
    The Elder Scrolls 23, 52
    Europa Universalis 33
    EVE Online 24, 245
    Far Cry 52, 71, 220,
    Fields of Glory 2 111–18, 120–1
    God of War 52
    Grand Ages: Rome 31
    Grand Theft Auto 26, 48, 65,
    Half-life 2 23

Hammurabi 29–30
Heart of Osiris 57
The Heliopolis Prophecy 57
Il-2 Sturmovik 26
Imperator: Rome 33
Kid Icarus 37
Kingdom Come: Deliverance 25, 41
    n.19, 160, 238–9
Legionnaire 32–3
Mario Bros. 21, 23, 26
Mario Kart 27
Medal of Honour 25
Missile Command 20–1
Mytheon 52
Numantia 27, 32
The Oregon Trail 1, 19, 20, 29
Pac-Man 1
Pandora's Palace 37, 52
Panzer General 32
Pharao 31
Pompeii: The Legend of Vesuvius 57
Pong 1, 4, 20
Poseidon 31, 52
QVADRIGA 28
Red Dead Redemption 38
The Return of Heracles 35–7

Roma Victor 25
Rome: Pathway to Power 57
Rome: Total War 48, 52
Ryse: Son of Rome 64–9, 77–88, 158,
    235, 240
The Secret World 157–78, 245
The Settlers 160
SimCity 24, 30–1
Space Invaders 1
The Sumer Game 29
The Sumerian Game 29
Tennis for Two 1
Theme Park 24
Tomb Raider 37–8
Total War 7, 24–6, 52
Total War II: Rome 16, 33–5, 79,
    93–104, 109, 111–22, 158, 235,
    241
The Witcher 23, 52
Wolfenstein 25
World of Warcraft 23
Zelda 26, 72
Zeus 52
violence 56–8
virtual reality 221–7
visual representation 54–6